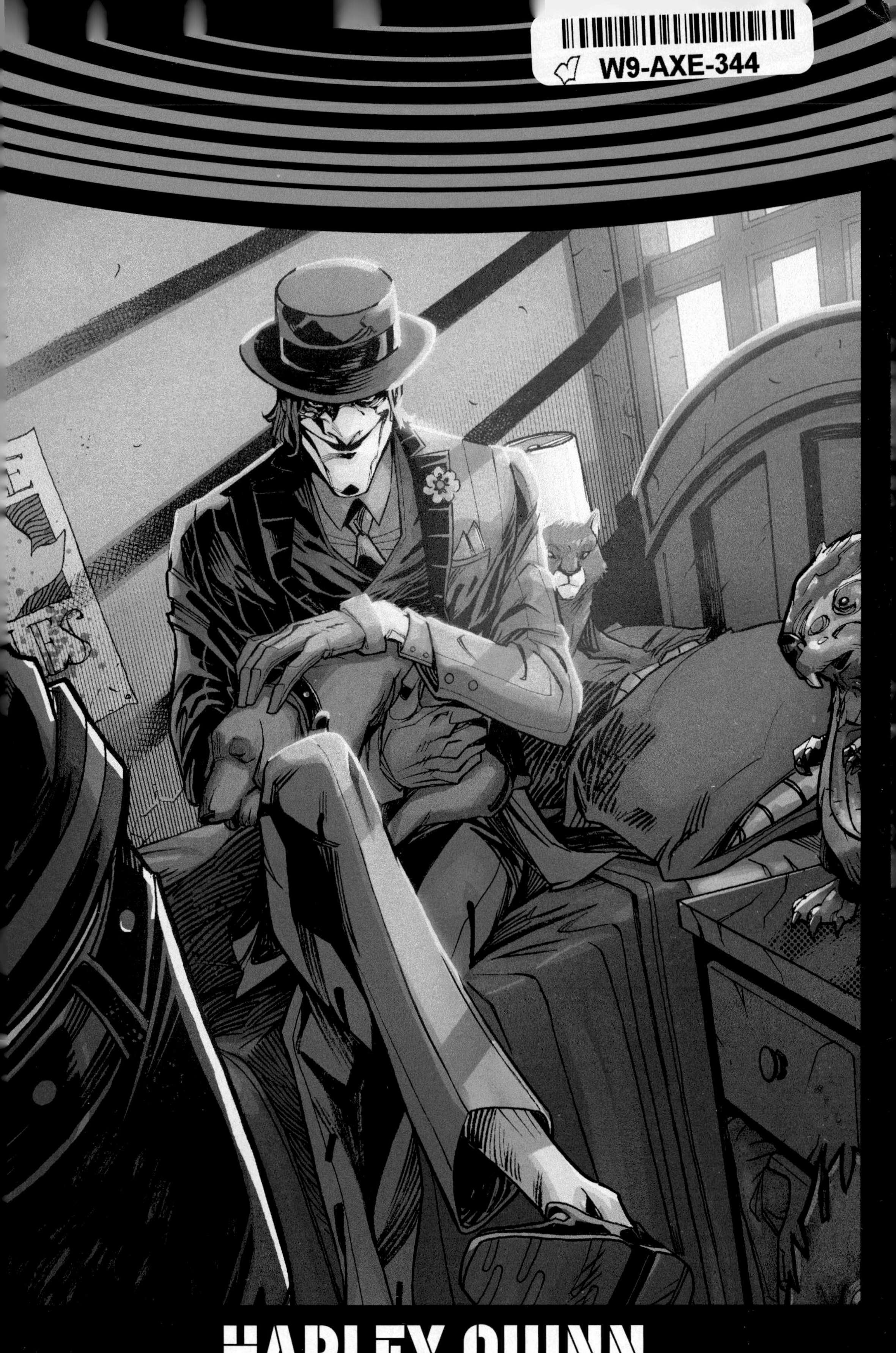

HARLEY QUINN

VOL. 2 JOKER LOVES HARLEY

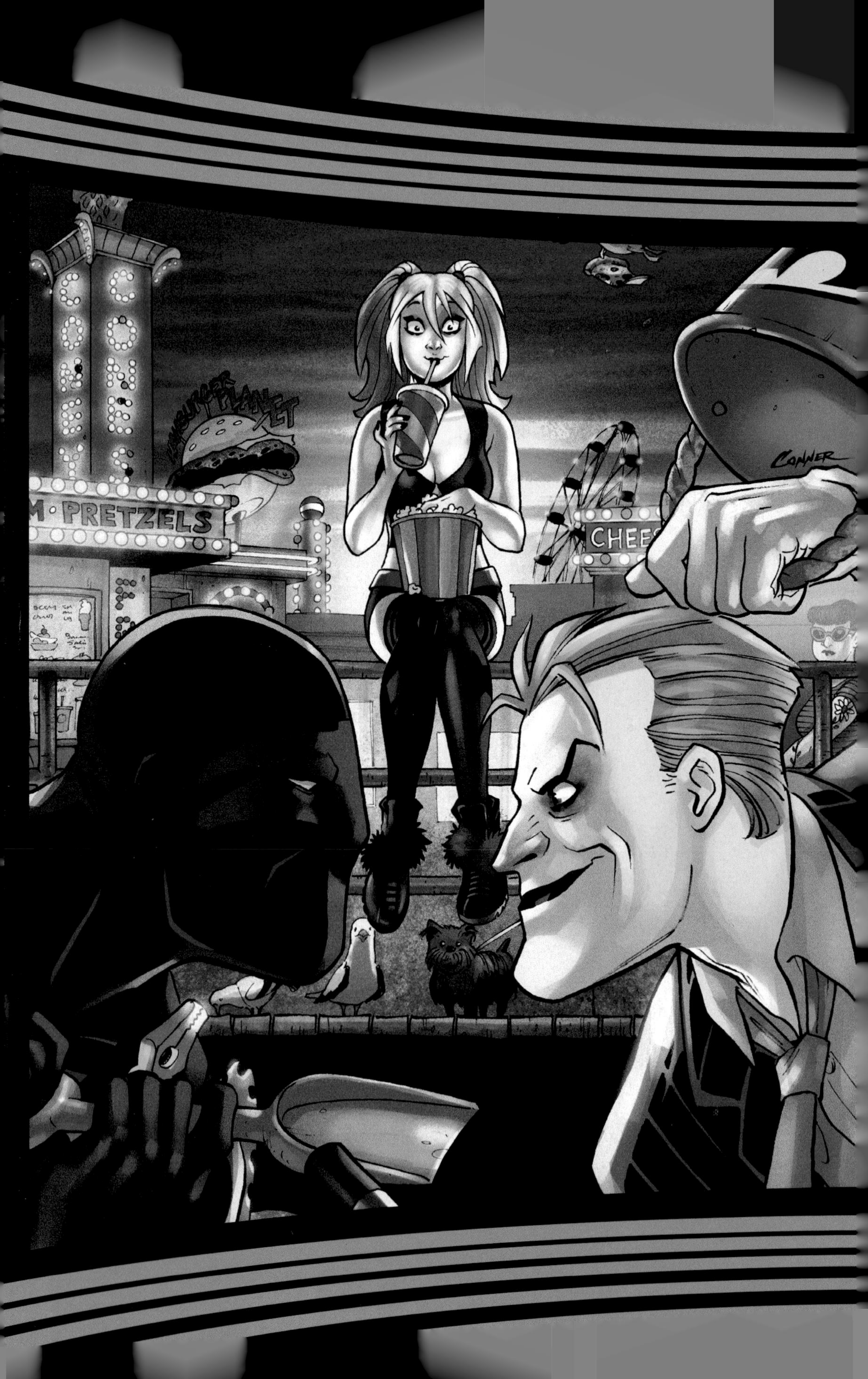
CONEYS
PRETZELS
CONNER

HARLEY QUINN
VOL.2 JOKER LOVES HARLEY

JIMMY PALMIOTTI
AMANDA CONNER
writers

JOHN TIMMS
CHAD HARDIN * BRANDON PETERSON * MORITAT
BRET BLEVINS * JOSEPH MICHAEL LINSNER
MICHAEL KALUTA * INAKI MIRANDA * ANDREW ROBINSON
artists

HI-FI
ALEX SINCLAIR * ANDREW ROBINSON
colorists

DAVE SHARPE
letterer

AMANDA CONNER and **ALEX SINCLAIR**
collection cover artists

HARLEY QUINN created by **PAUL DINI** and **BRUCE TIMM**

CHRIS CONROY Editor - Original Series ◆ **DAVE WIELGOSZ** Assistant Editor - Original Series
JEB WOODARD Group Editor - Collected Editions ◆ **ROBIN WILDMAN** Editor - Collected Edition
STEVE COOK Design Director - Books ◆ **MONIQUE GRUSPE** Publication Design

BOB HARRAS Senior VP - Editor-in-Chief, DC Comics

DIANE NELSON President ◆ **DAN DiDIO** Publisher ◆ **JIM LEE** Publisher ◆ **GEOFF JOHNS** President & Chief Creative Officer
AMIT DESAI Executive VP - Business & Marketing Strategy, Direct to Consumer & Global Franchise Management ◆ **SAM ADES** Senior VP - Direct to Consumer
BOBBIE CHASE VP - Talent Development ◆ **MARK CHIARELLO** Senior VP - Art, Design & Collected Editions
JOHN CUNNINGHAM Senior VP - Sales & Trade Marketing ◆ **ANNE DePIES** Senior VP - Business Strategy, Finance & Administration
DON FALLETTI VP - Manufacturing Operations ◆ **LAWRENCE GANEM** VP - Editorial Administration & Talent Relations
ALISON GILL Senior VP - Manufacturing & Operations ◆ **HANK KANALZ** Senior VP - Editorial Strategy & Administration
JAY KOGAN VP - Legal Affairs ◆ **THOMAS LOFTUS** VP - Business Affairs
JACK MAHAN VP - Business Affairs ◆ **NICK J. NAPOLITANO** VP - Manufacturing Administration
EDDIE SCANNELL VP - Consumer Marketing ◆ **COURTNEY SIMMONS** Senior VP - Publicity & Communications
JIM (SKI) SOKOLOWSKI VP - Comic Book Specialty Sales & Trade Marketing ◆ **NANCY SPEARS** VP - Mass, Book, Digital Sales & Trade Marketing

HARLEY QUINN VOL.2: JOKER LOVES HARLEY

Published by DC Comics. Compilation and all new material Copyright © 2017 DC Comics. All Rights Reserved.
Originally published in single magazine form in HARLEY QUINN 8-13. Copyright © 2016, 2017 DC Comics.
All Rights Reserved. All characters, their distinctive likenesses and related elements featured in this publication are trademarks of DC Comics.
The stories, characters and incidents featured in this publication are entirely fictional.
DC Comics does not read or accept unsolicited submissions of ideas, stories or artwork.

DC Comics, 2900 West Alameda Ave., Burbank, CA 91505.
Printed by LSC Communications, Salem, VA, USA. 5/19/17. First Printing
ISBN: 978-1-4012-7095-7

Library of Congress Cataloging-in-Publication Data is available.

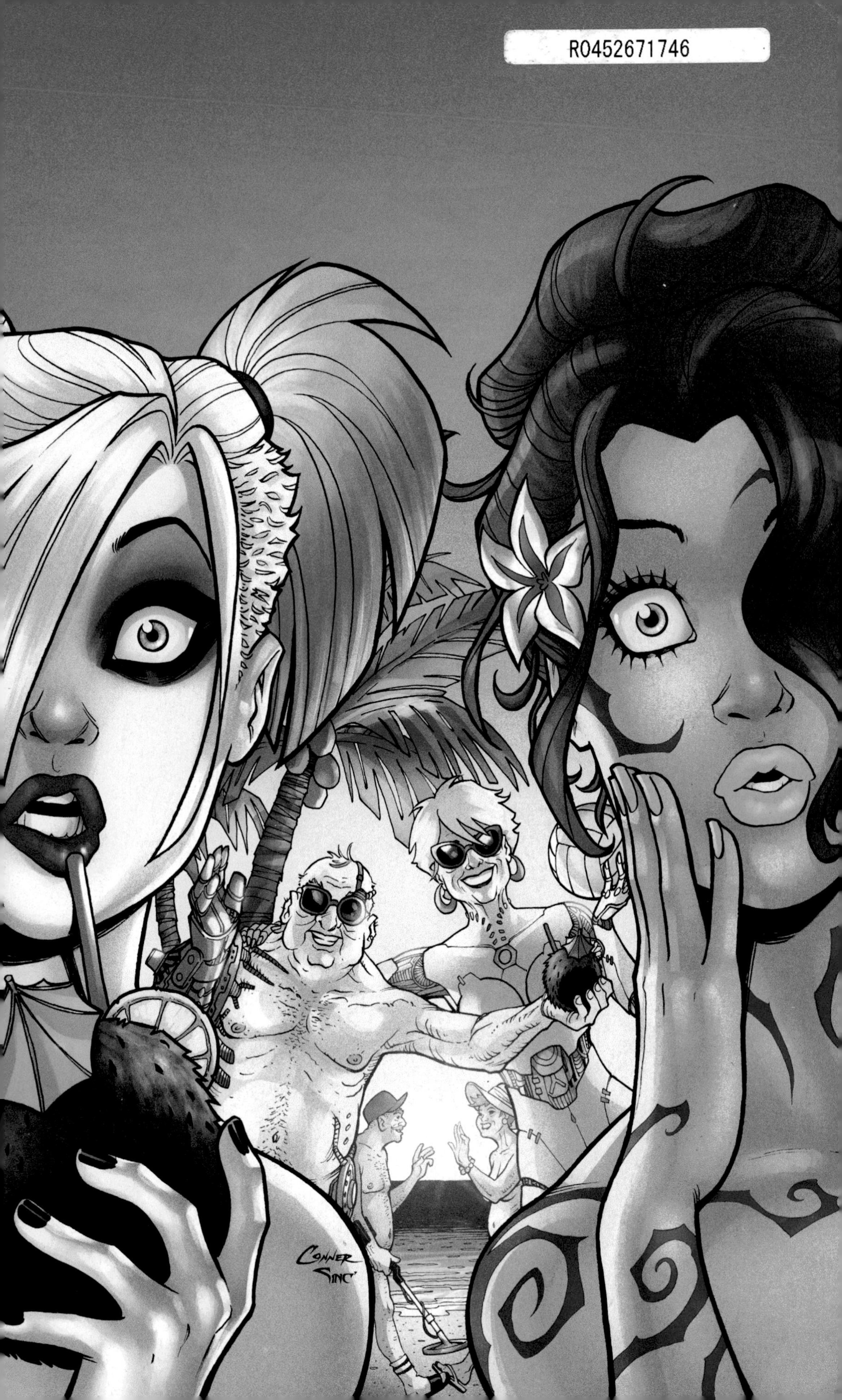
CONNER
SINC'

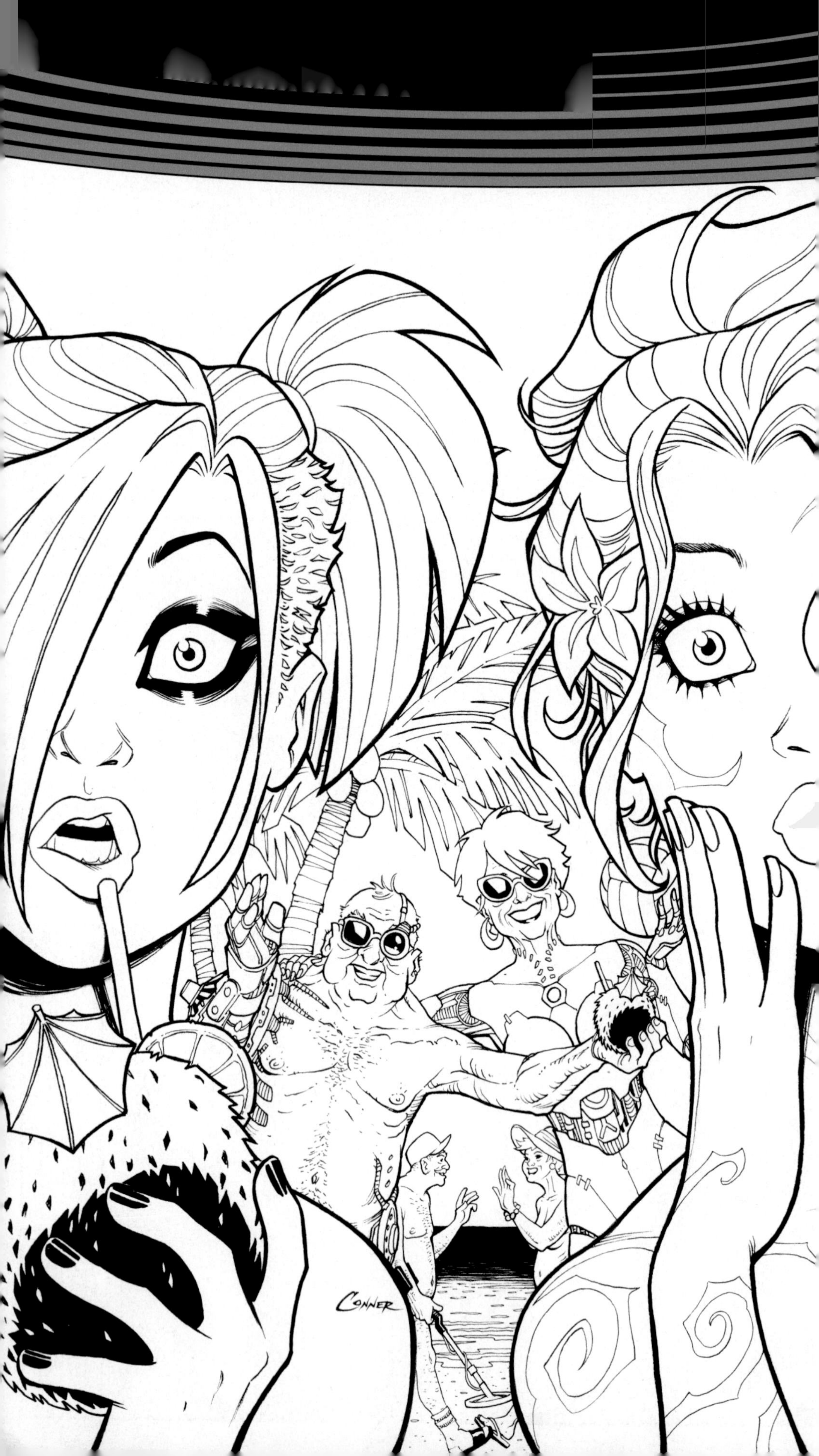
CONNER

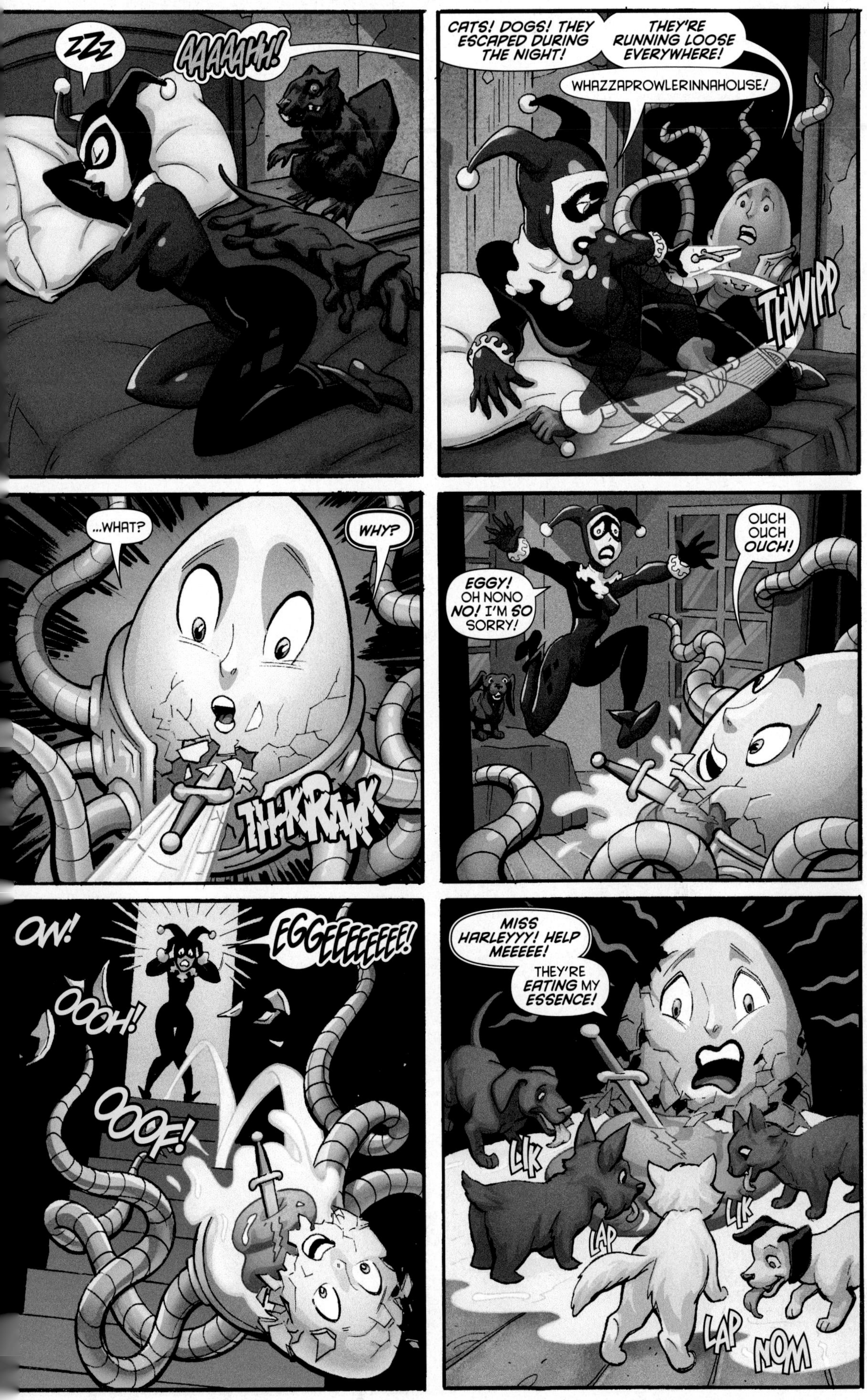

ZZZ
AAAAAHH!
CATS! DOGS! THEY ESCAPED DURING THE NIGHT!
THEY'RE RUNNING LOOSE EVERYWHERE!
WHAZZAPROWLERINNAHOUSE!
THWIPP
...WHAT?
WHY?
THKRAKK
EGGY! OH NONO NO! I'M SO SORRY!
OUCH OUCH OUCH!
OW!
EGGEEEEEEEE!
OOOH!
OOOF!
MISS HARLEYYY! HELP MEEEEE!
THEY'RE EATING MY ESSENCE!
LIK
LIK
LAP
LAP
NOM

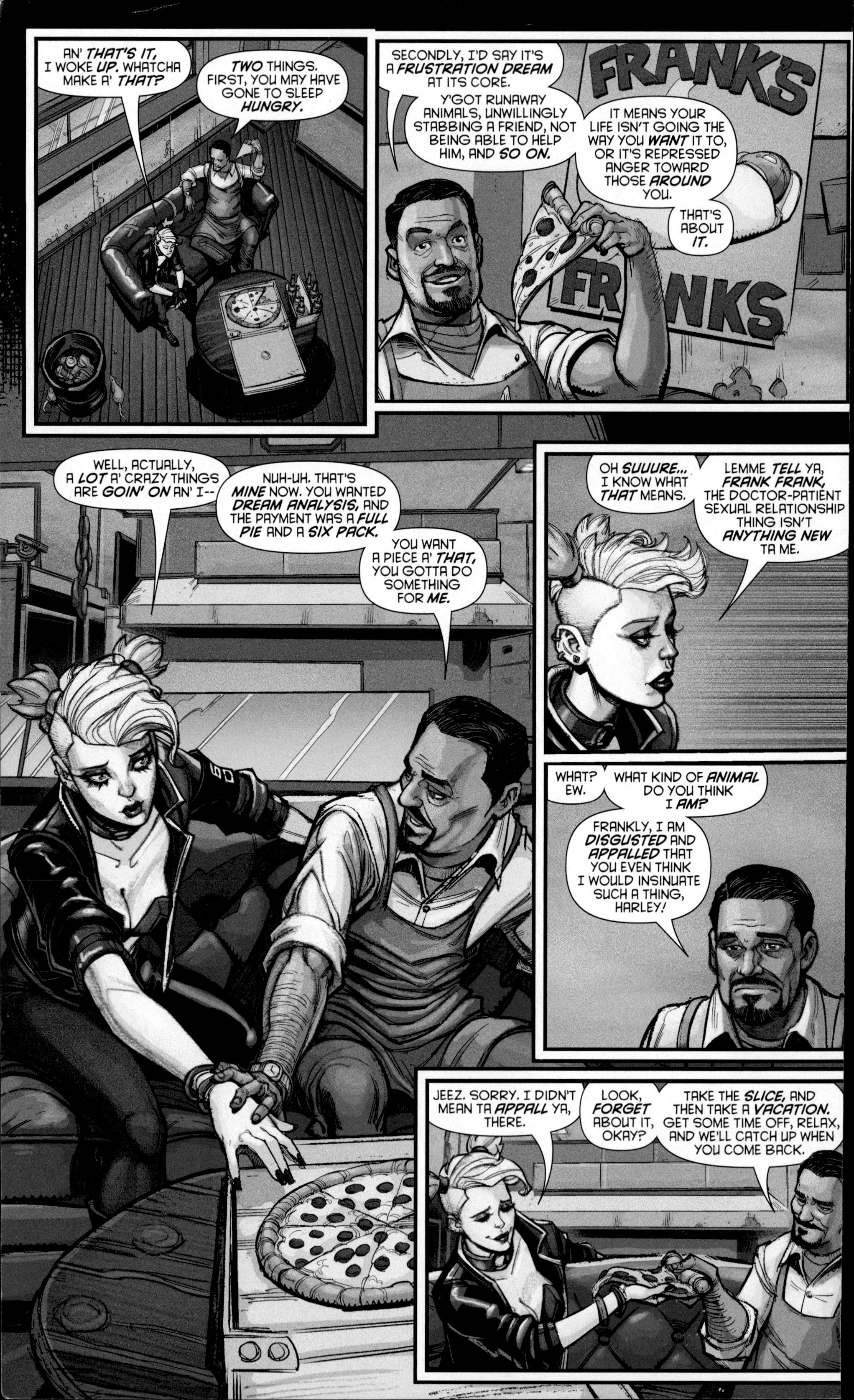
AN' THAT'S IT, I WOKE UP. WHATCHA MAKE A' THAT?
TWO THINGS. FIRST, YOU MAY HAVE GONE TO SLEEP HUNGRY.
SECONDLY, I'D SAY IT'S A FRUSTRATION DREAM AT ITS CORE.
Y'GOT RUNAWAY ANIMALS, UNWILLINGLY STABBING A FRIEND, NOT BEING ABLE TO HELP HIM, AND SO ON.
IT MEANS YOUR LIFE ISN'T GOING THE WAY YOU WANT IT TO, OR IT'S REPRESSED ANGER TOWARD THOSE AROUND YOU.
THAT'S ABOUT IT.
FRANK'S
FR NKS
WELL, ACTUALLY, A LOT A' CRAZY THINGS ARE GOIN' ON AN' I--
NUH-UH. THAT'S MINE NOW. YOU WANTED DREAM ANALYSIS, AND THE PAYMENT WAS A FULL PIE AND A SIX PACK.
YOU WANT A PIECE A' THAT, YOU GOTTA DO SOMETHING FOR ME.
OH SUUURE... I KNOW WHAT THAT MEANS.
LEMME TELL YA, FRANK FRANK, THE DOCTOR-PATIENT SEXUAL RELATIONSHIP THING ISN'T ANYTHING NEW TA ME.
WHAT? EW.
WHAT KIND OF ANIMAL DO YOU THINK I AM?
FRANKLY, I AM DISGUSTED AND APPALLED THAT YOU EVEN THINK I WOULD INSINUATE SUCH A THING, HARLEY!
JEEZ. SORRY. I DIDN'T MEAN TA APPALL YA, THERE.
LOOK, FORGET ABOUT IT, OKAY?
TAKE THE SLICE, AND THEN TAKE A VACATION. GET SOME TIME OFF, RELAX, AND WE'LL CATCH UP WHEN YOU COME BACK.

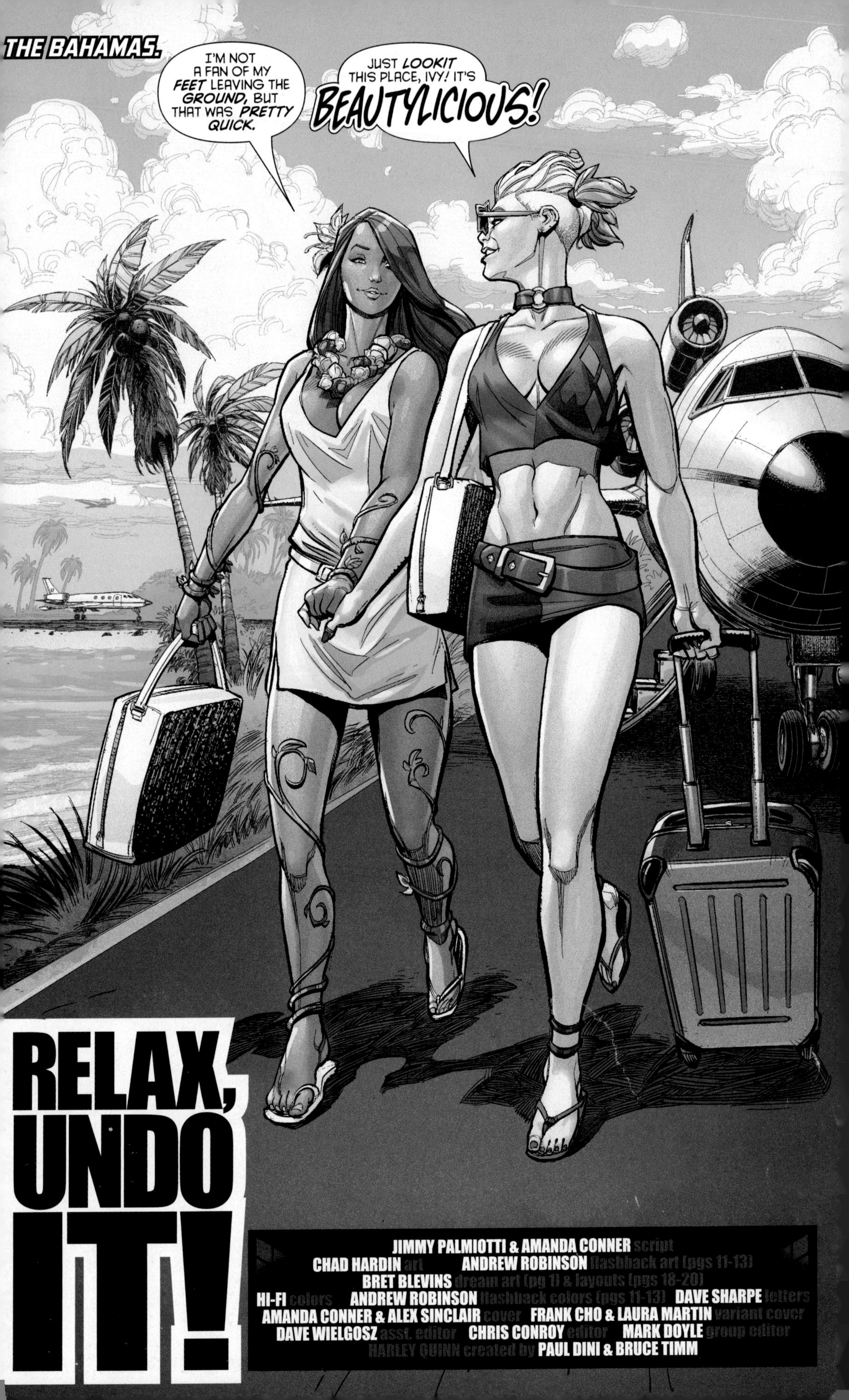
THE BAHAMAS.
I'M NOT A FAN OF MY FEET LEAVING THE GROUND, BUT THAT WAS PRETTY QUICK.
JUST LOOKIT THIS PLACE, IVY! IT'S BEAUTYLICIOUS!
RELAX, UNDO IT!
JIMMY PALMIOTTI & AMANDA CONNER script
CHAD HARDIN art ANDREW ROBINSON flashback art (pgs 11-13)
BRET BLEVINS dream art (pg 1) & layouts (pgs 18-20)
HI-FI colors ANDREW ROBINSON flashback colors (pgs 11-13) DAVE SHARPE letters
AMANDA CONNER & ALEX SINCLAIR cover FRANK CHO & LAURA MARTIN variant cover
DAVE WIELGOSZ asst. editor CHRIS CONROY editor MARK DOYLE group editor
HARLEY QUINN created by PAUL DINI & BRUCE TIMM

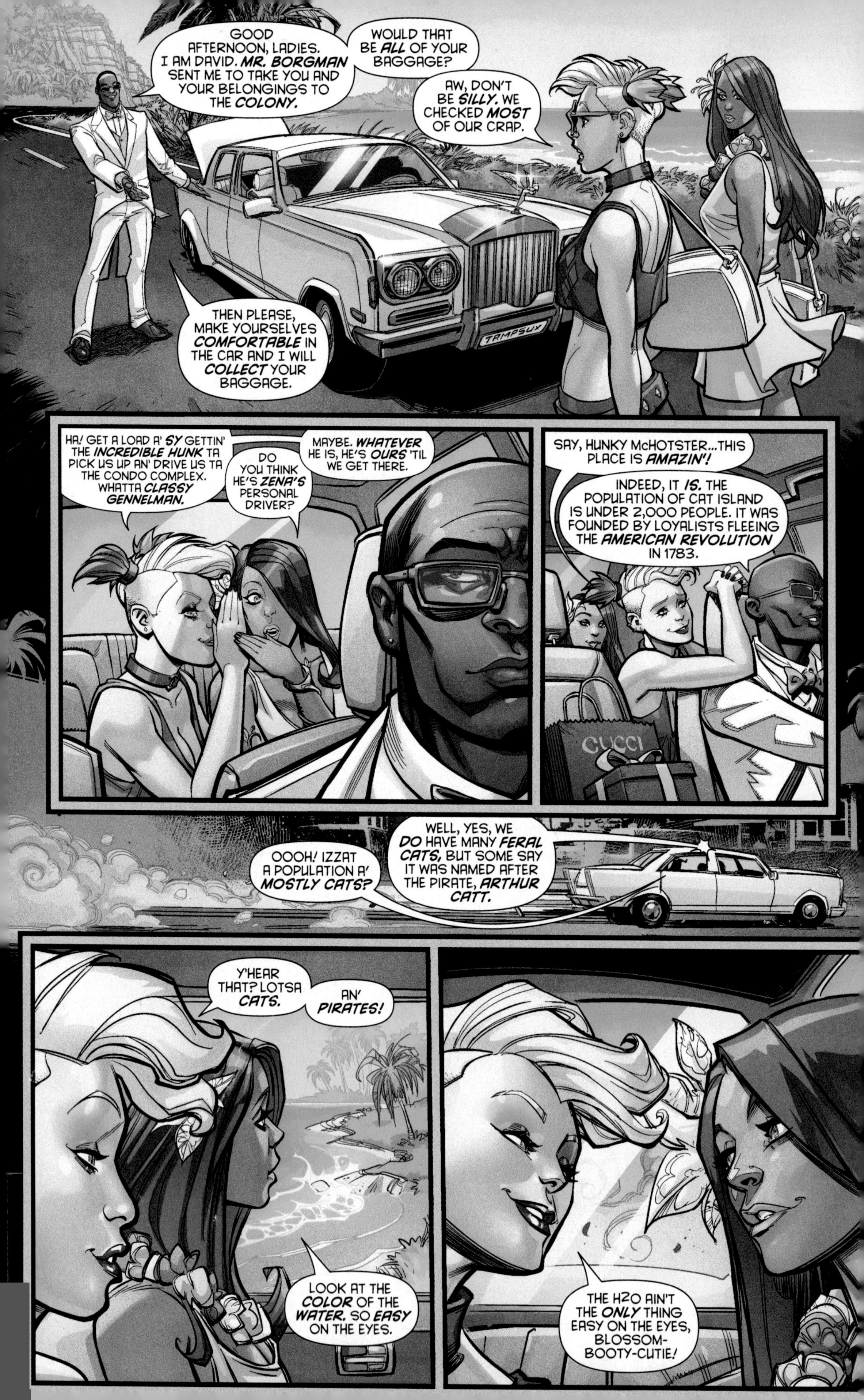
GOOD AFTERNOON, LADIES. I AM DAVID. MR. BORGMAN SENT ME TO TAKE YOU AND YOUR BELONGINGS TO THE COLONY.
WOULD THAT BE ALL OF YOUR BAGGAGE?
AW, DON'T BE SILLY. WE CHECKED MOST OF OUR CRAP.
TRMPSUX
THEN PLEASE, MAKE YOURSELVES COMFORTABLE IN THE CAR AND I WILL COLLECT YOUR BAGGAGE.
HA! GET A LOAD A' SY GETTIN' THE INCREDIBLE HUNK TA PICK US UP AN' DRIVE US TA THE CONDO COMPLEX. WHATTA CLASSY GENNELMAN.
DO YOU THINK HE'S ZENA'S PERSONAL DRIVER?
MAYBE. WHATEVER HE IS, HE'S OURS 'TIL WE GET THERE.
SAY, HUNKY McHOTSTER...THIS PLACE IS AMAZIN'!
INDEED, IT IS. THE POPULATION OF CAT ISLAND IS UNDER 2,000 PEOPLE. IT WAS FOUNDED BY LOYALISTS FLEEING THE AMERICAN REVOLUTION IN 1783.
GUCCI
OOOH! IZZAT A POPULATION A' MOSTLY CATS?
WELL, YES, WE DO HAVE MANY FERAL CATS, BUT SOME SAY IT WAS NAMED AFTER THE PIRATE, ARTHUR CATT.
Y'HEAR THAT? LOTSA CATS.
AN' PIRATES!
LOOK AT THE COLOR OF THE WATER. SO EASY ON THE EYES.
THE H2O AIN'T THE ONLY THING EASY ON THE EYES, BLOSSOM-BOOTY-CUTIE!

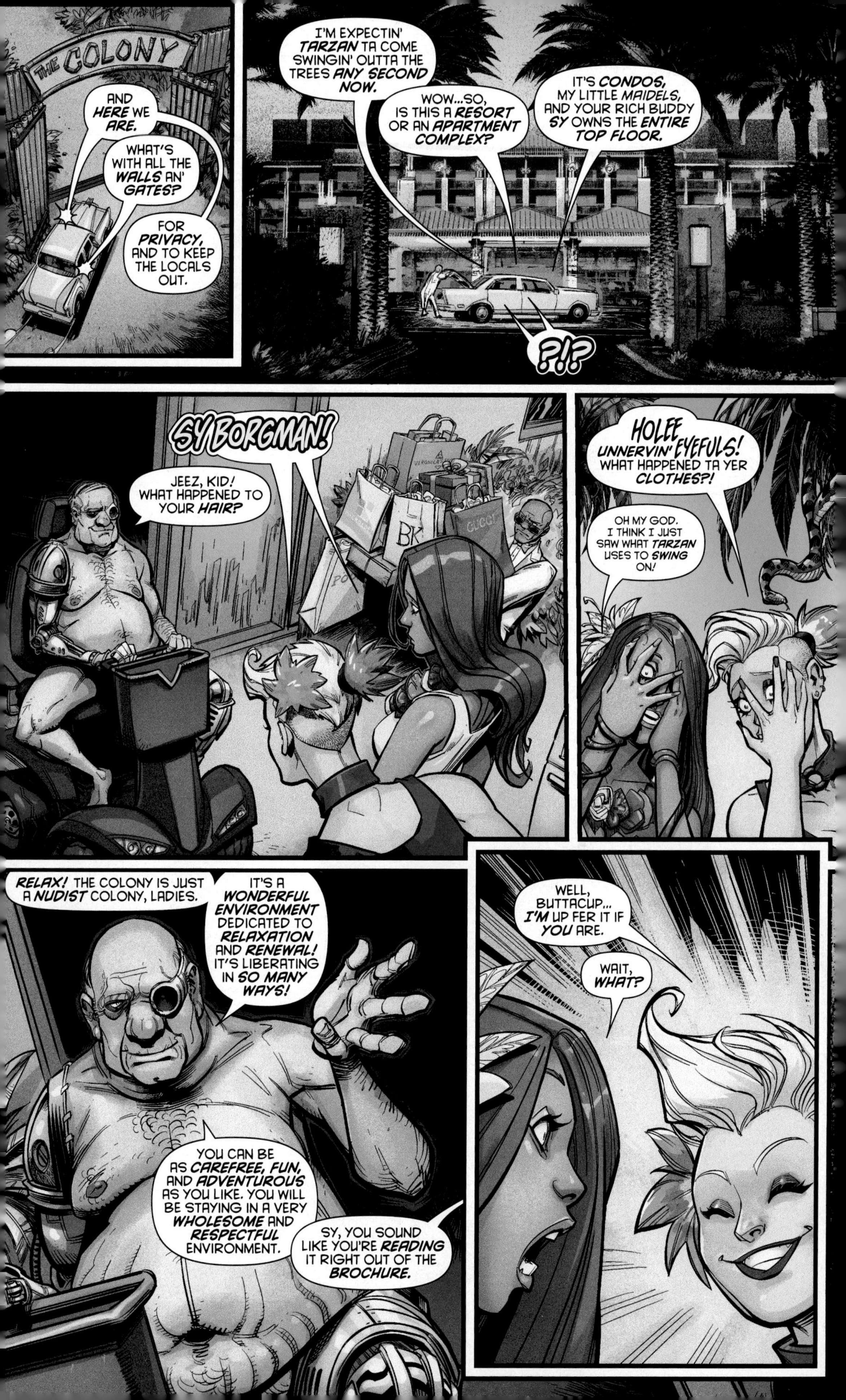

THE COLONY
AND HERE WE ARE.
WHAT'S WITH ALL THE WALLS AN' GATES?
FOR PRIVACY, AND TO KEEP THE LOCALS OUT.
I'M EXPECTIN' TARZAN TA COME SWINGIN' OUTTA THE TREES ANY SECOND NOW.
WOW...SO, IS THIS A RESORT OR AN APARTMENT COMPLEX?
IT'S CONDOS, MY LITTLE MAIDELS, AND YOUR RICH BUDDY SY OWNS THE ENTIRE TOP FLOOR.
?!?
SY BORGMAN!
JEEZ, KID! WHAT HAPPENED TO YOUR HAIR?
BK
GUCCI
HOLEE UNNERVIN' EYEFULS! WHAT HAPPENED TA YER CLOTHES?!
OH MY GOD. I THINK I JUST SAW WHAT TARZAN USES TO SWING ON!
RELAX! THE COLONY IS JUST A NUDIST COLONY, LADIES.
IT'S A WONDERFUL ENVIRONMENT DEDICATED TO RELAXATION AND RENEWAL! IT'S LIBERATING IN SO MANY WAYS!
YOU CAN BE AS CAREFREE, FUN, AND ADVENTUROUS AS YOU LIKE. YOU WILL BE STAYING IN A VERY WHOLESOME AND RESPECTFUL ENVIRONMENT.
SY, YOU SOUND LIKE YOU'RE READING IT RIGHT OUT OF THE BROCHURE.
WELL, BUTTACUP... I'M UP FER IT IF YOU ARE.
WAIT, WHAT?

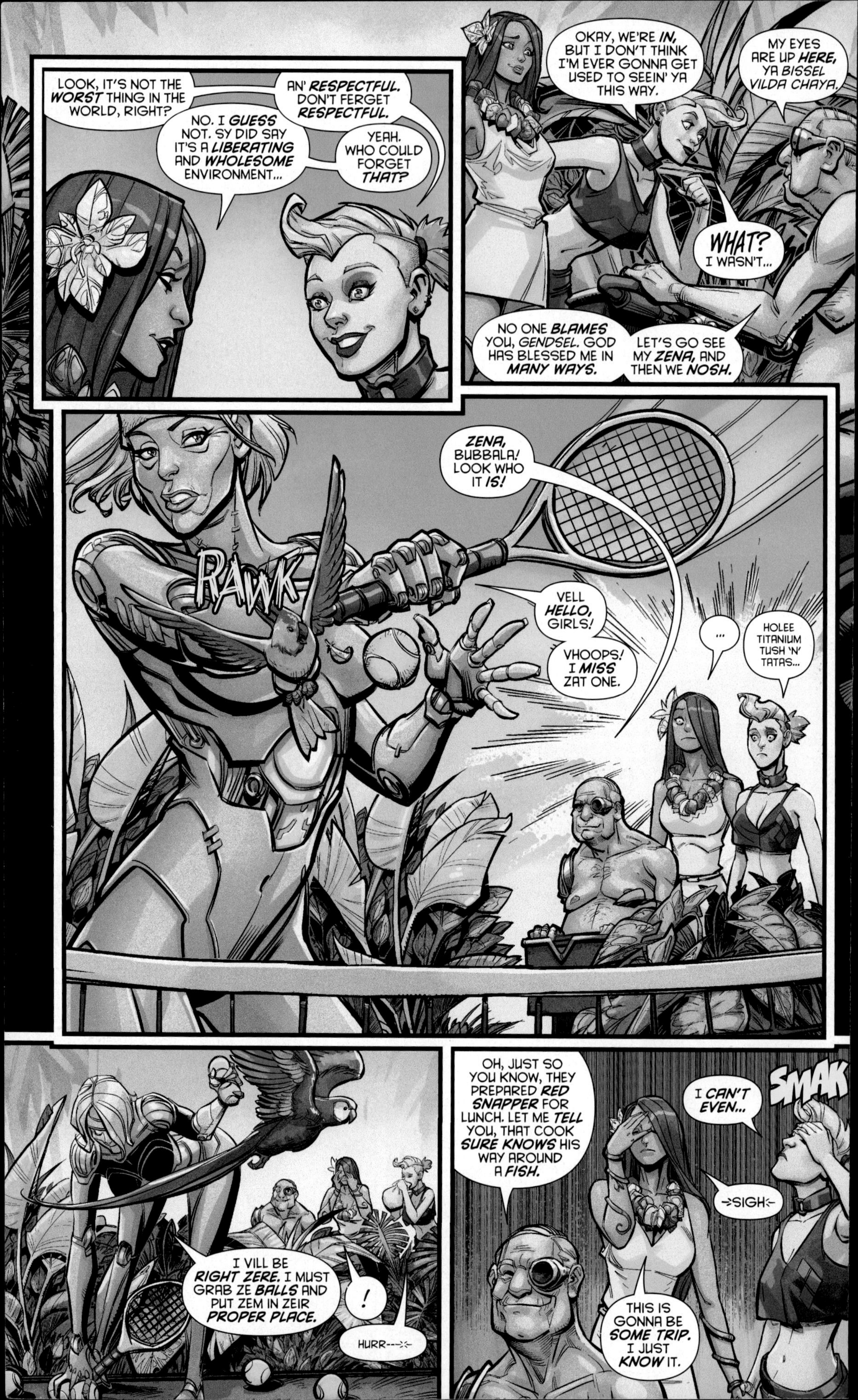
LOOK, IT'S NOT THE WORST THING IN THE WORLD, RIGHT?
AN' RESPECTFUL. DON'T FERGET RESPECTFUL.
NO. I GUESS NOT. SY DID SAY IT'S A LIBERATING AND WHOLESOME ENVIRONMENT...
YEAH. WHO COULD FORGET THAT?
OKAY, WE'RE IN, BUT I DON'T THINK I'M EVER GONNA GET USED TO SEEIN' YA THIS WAY.
MY EYES ARE UP HERE, YA BISSEL VILDA CHAYA.
WHAT? I WASN'T...
NO ONE BLAMES YOU, GENDSEL. GOD HAS BLESSED ME IN MANY WAYS.
LET'S GO SEE MY ZENA, AND THEN WE NOSH.
ZENA, BUBBALA! LOOK WHO IT IS!
RAWK
VELL HELLO, GIRLS!
VHOOPS! I MISS ZAT ONE.
...
HOLEE TITANIUM TUSH 'N' TATAS...
I VILL BE RIGHT ZERE. I MUST GRAB ZE BALLS AND PUT ZEM IN ZEIR PROPER PLACE.
!
HURR---
OH, JUST SO YOU KNOW, THEY PREPARED RED SNAPPER FOR LUNCH. LET ME TELL YOU, THAT COOK SURE KNOWS HIS WAY AROUND A FISH.
I CAN'T EVEN...
SMAK
SIGH
THIS IS GONNA BE SOME TRIP. I JUST KNOW IT.

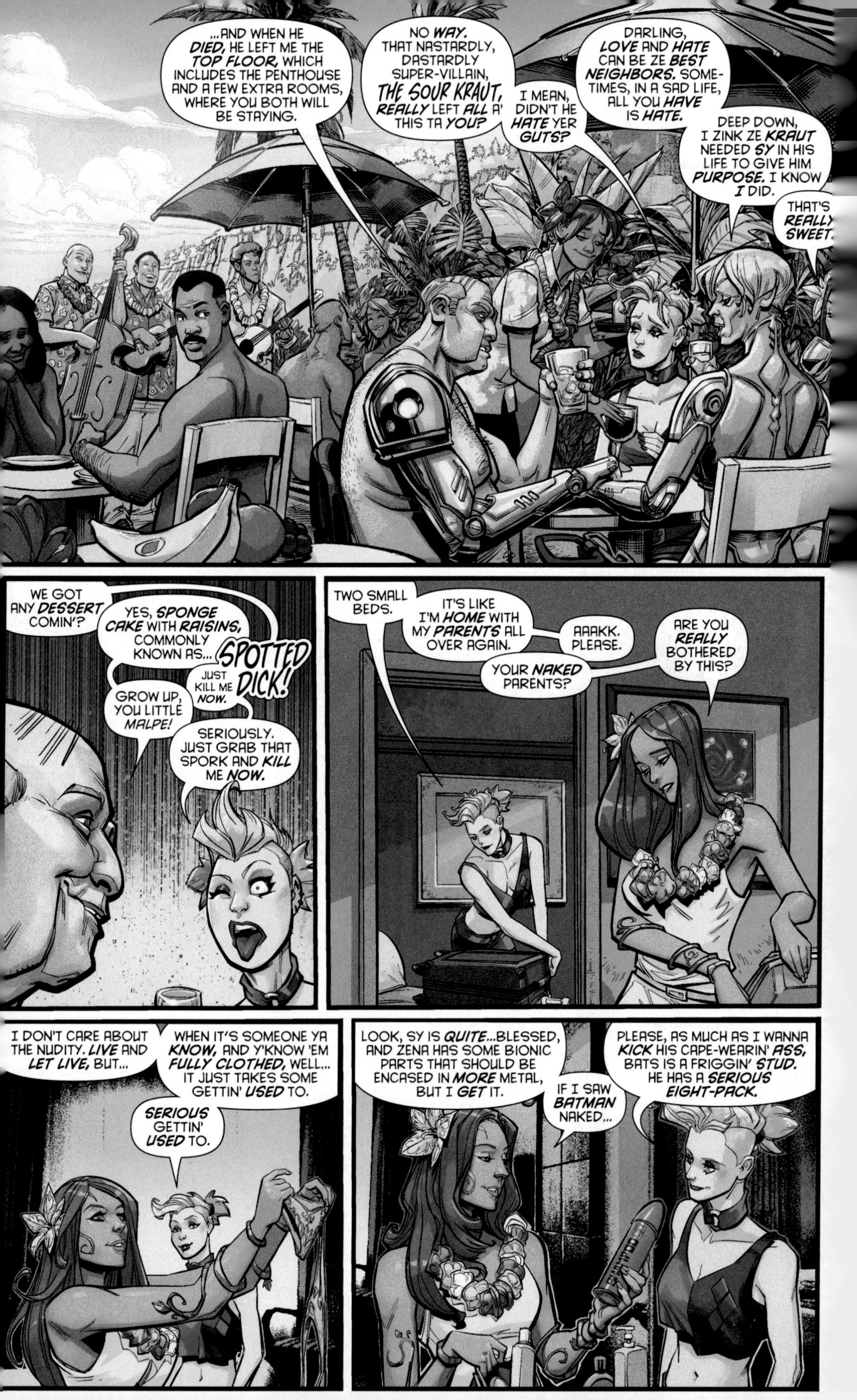
...AND WHEN HE DIED, HE LEFT ME THE TOP FLOOR, WHICH INCLUDES THE PENTHOUSE AND A FEW EXTRA ROOMS, WHERE YOU BOTH WILL BE STAYING.
NO WAY. THAT NASTARDLY, DASTARDLY SUPER-VILLAIN, THE SOUR KRAUT, REALLY LEFT ALL A' THIS TA YOU?
I MEAN, DIDN'T HE HATE YER GUTS?
DARLING, LOVE AND HATE CAN BE ZE BEST NEIGHBORS. SOMETIMES, IN A SAD LIFE, ALL YOU HAVE IS HATE.
DEEP DOWN, I ZINK ZE KRAUT NEEDED SY IN HIS LIFE TO GIVE HIM PURPOSE. I KNOW I DID.
THAT'S REALLY SWEET.
WE GOT ANY DESSERT COMIN'?
YES, SPONGE CAKE WITH RAISINS, COMMONLY KNOWN AS...
SPOTTED DICK!
JUST KILL ME NOW.
GROW UP, YOU LITTLE MALPE!
SERIOUSLY. JUST GRAB THAT SPORK AND KILL ME NOW.
TWO SMALL BEDS.
IT'S LIKE I'M HOME WITH MY PARENTS ALL OVER AGAIN.
AAAKK. PLEASE.
YOUR NAKED PARENTS?
ARE YOU REALLY BOTHERED BY THIS?
I DON'T CARE ABOUT THE NUDITY. LIVE AND LET LIVE, BUT...
WHEN IT'S SOMEONE YA KNOW, AND Y'KNOW 'EM FULLY CLOTHED, WELL... IT JUST TAKES SOME GETTIN' USED TO.
SERIOUS GETTIN' USED TO.
LOOK, SY IS QUITE...BLESSED, AND ZENA HAS SOME BIONIC PARTS THAT SHOULD BE ENCASED IN MORE METAL, BUT I GET IT.
IF I SAW BATMAN NAKED...
PLEASE, AS MUCH AS I WANNA KICK HIS CAPE-WEARIN' ASS, BATS IS A FRIGGIN' STUD. HE HAS A SERIOUS EIGHT-PACK.

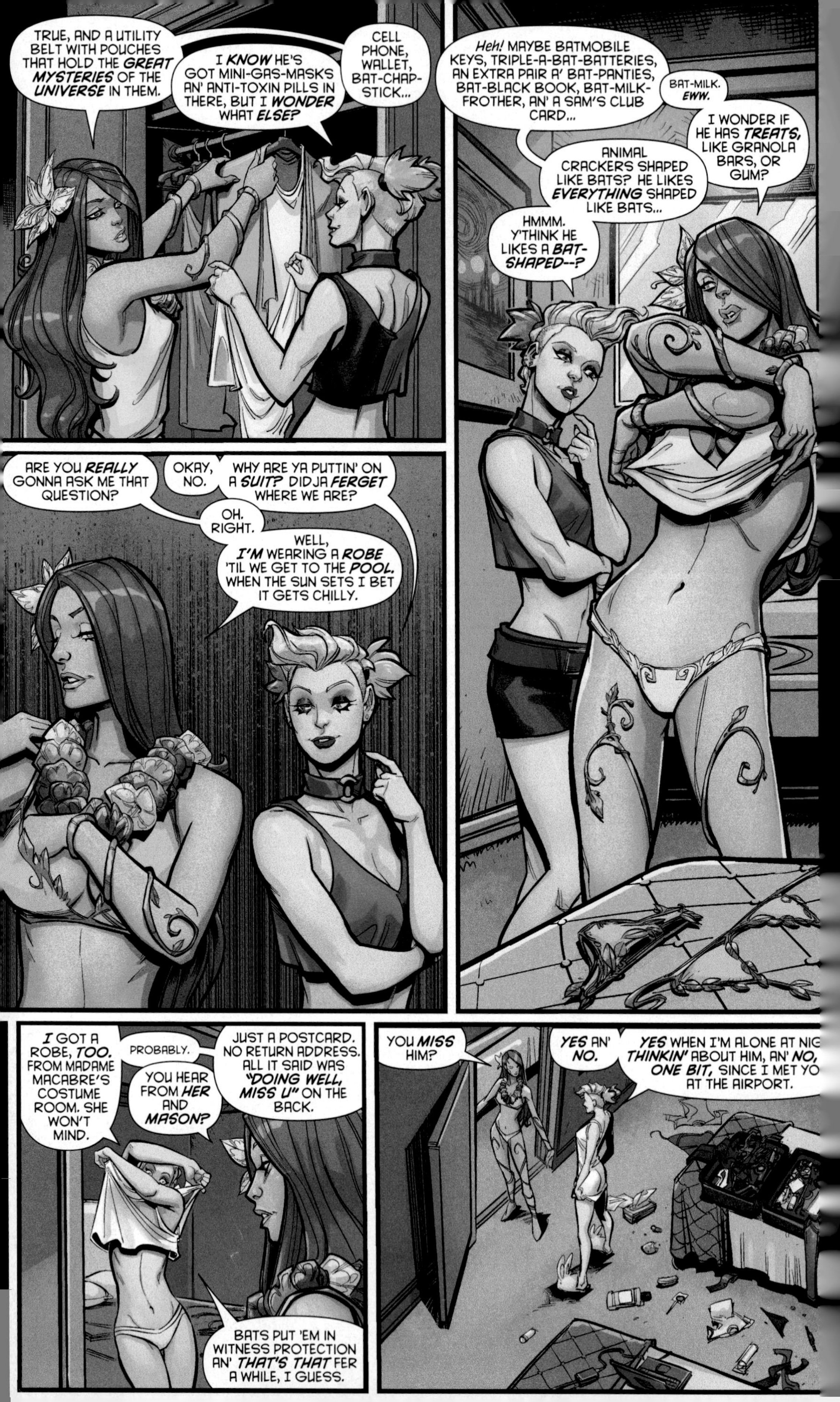

TRUE, AND A UTILITY BELT WITH POUCHES THAT HOLD THE GREAT MYSTERIES OF THE UNIVERSE IN THEM.
CELL PHONE, WALLET, BAT-CHAPSTICK...
I KNOW HE'S GOT MINI-GAS-MASKS AN' ANTI-TOXIN PILLS IN THERE, BUT I WONDER WHAT ELSE?
Heh! MAYBE BATMOBILE KEYS, TRIPLE-A-BAT-BATTERIES, AN EXTRA PAIR A' BAT-PANTIES, BAT-BLACK BOOK, BAT-MILK-FROTHER, AN' A SAM'S CLUB CARD...
BAT-MILK. EWW.
I WONDER IF HE HAS TREATS, LIKE GRANOLA BARS, OR GUM?
ANIMAL CRACKERS SHAPED LIKE BATS? HE LIKES EVERYTHING SHAPED LIKE BATS...
HMMM. Y'THINK HE LIKES A BAT-SHAPED--?
ARE YOU REALLY GONNA ASK ME THAT QUESTION?
OKAY, NO.
WHY ARE YA PUTTIN' ON A SUIT? DIDJA FERGET WHERE WE ARE?
OH. RIGHT.
WELL, I'M WEARING A ROBE 'TIL WE GET TO THE POOL. WHEN THE SUN SETS I BET IT GETS CHILLY.
I GOT A ROBE, TOO. FROM MADAME MACABRE'S COSTUME ROOM. SHE WON'T MIND.
PROBABLY.
YOU HEAR FROM HER AND MASON?
JUST A POSTCARD. NO RETURN ADDRESS. ALL IT SAID WAS "DOING WELL, MISS U" ON THE BACK.
BATS PUT 'EM IN WITNESS PROTECTION AN' THAT'S THAT FER A WHILE, I GUESS.
YOU MISS HIM?
YES AN' NO.
YES WHEN I'M ALONE AT NIG
THINKIN' ABOUT HIM, AN' NO,
ONE BIT, SINCE I MET YO
AT THE AIRPORT.

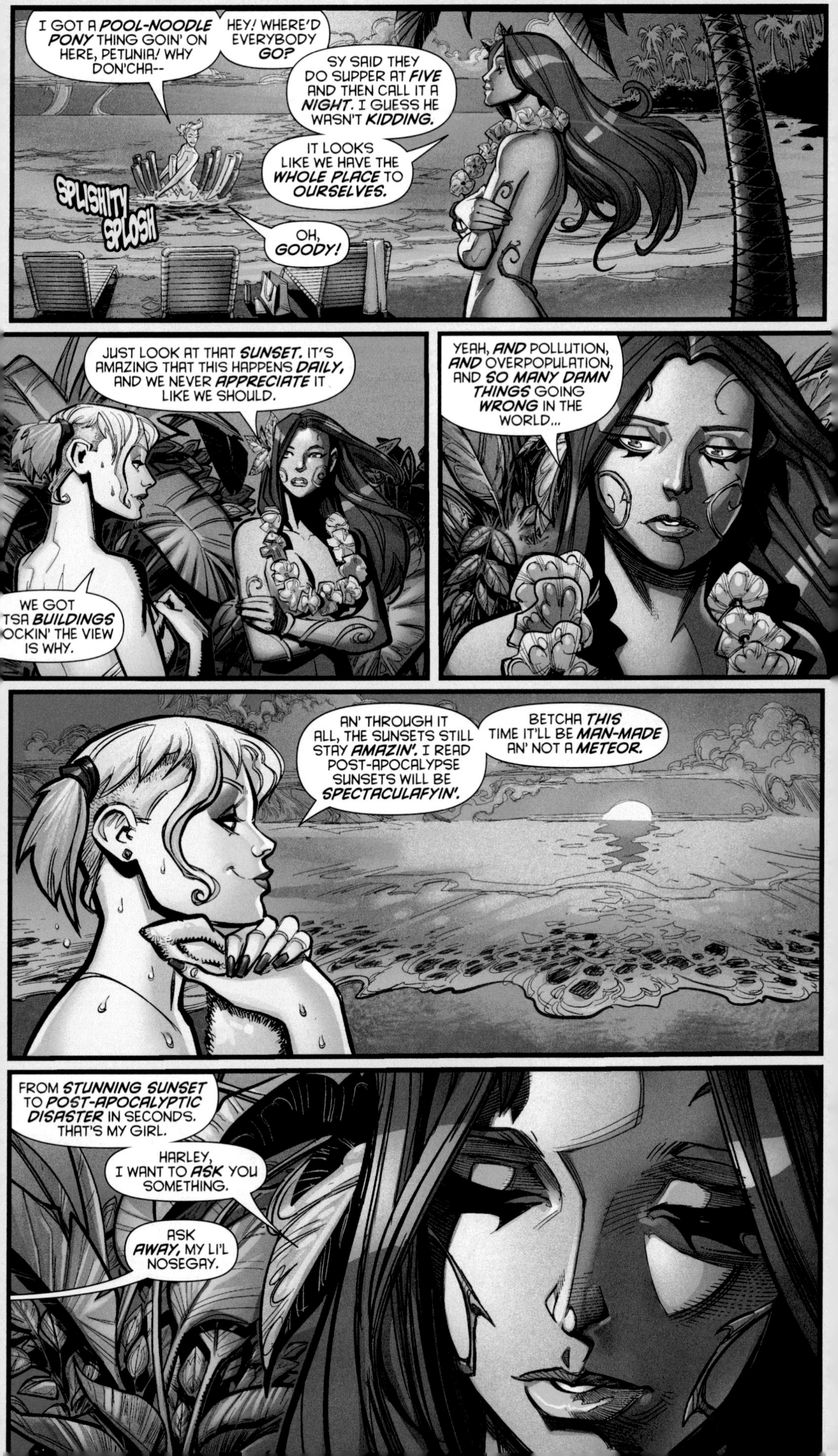

I GOT A POOL-NOODLE PONY THING GOIN' ON HERE, PETUNIA! WHY DON'CHA--
HEY! WHERE'D EVERYBODY GO?
SY SAID THEY DO SUPPER AT FIVE AND THEN CALL IT A NIGHT. I GUESS HE WASN'T KIDDING.
IT LOOKS LIKE WE HAVE THE WHOLE PLACE TO OURSELVES.
SPLISHITY SPLOSH
OH, GOODY!
JUST LOOK AT THAT SUNSET. IT'S AMAZING THAT THIS HAPPENS DAILY, AND WE NEVER APPRECIATE IT LIKE WE SHOULD.
WE GOT TSA BUILDINGS OCKIN' THE VIEW IS WHY.
YEAH, AND POLLUTION, AND OVERPOPULATION, AND SO MANY DAMN THINGS GOING WRONG IN THE WORLD...
AN' THROUGH IT ALL, THE SUNSETS STILL STAY AMAZIN'. I READ POST-APOCALYPSE SUNSETS WILL BE SPECTACULAFYIN'.
BETCHA THIS TIME IT'LL BE MAN-MADE AN' NOT A METEOR.
FROM STUNNING SUNSET TO POST-APOCALYPTIC DISASTER IN SECONDS. THAT'S MY GIRL.
HARLEY, I WANT TO ASK YOU SOMETHING.
ASK AWAY, MY LI'L NOSEGAY.

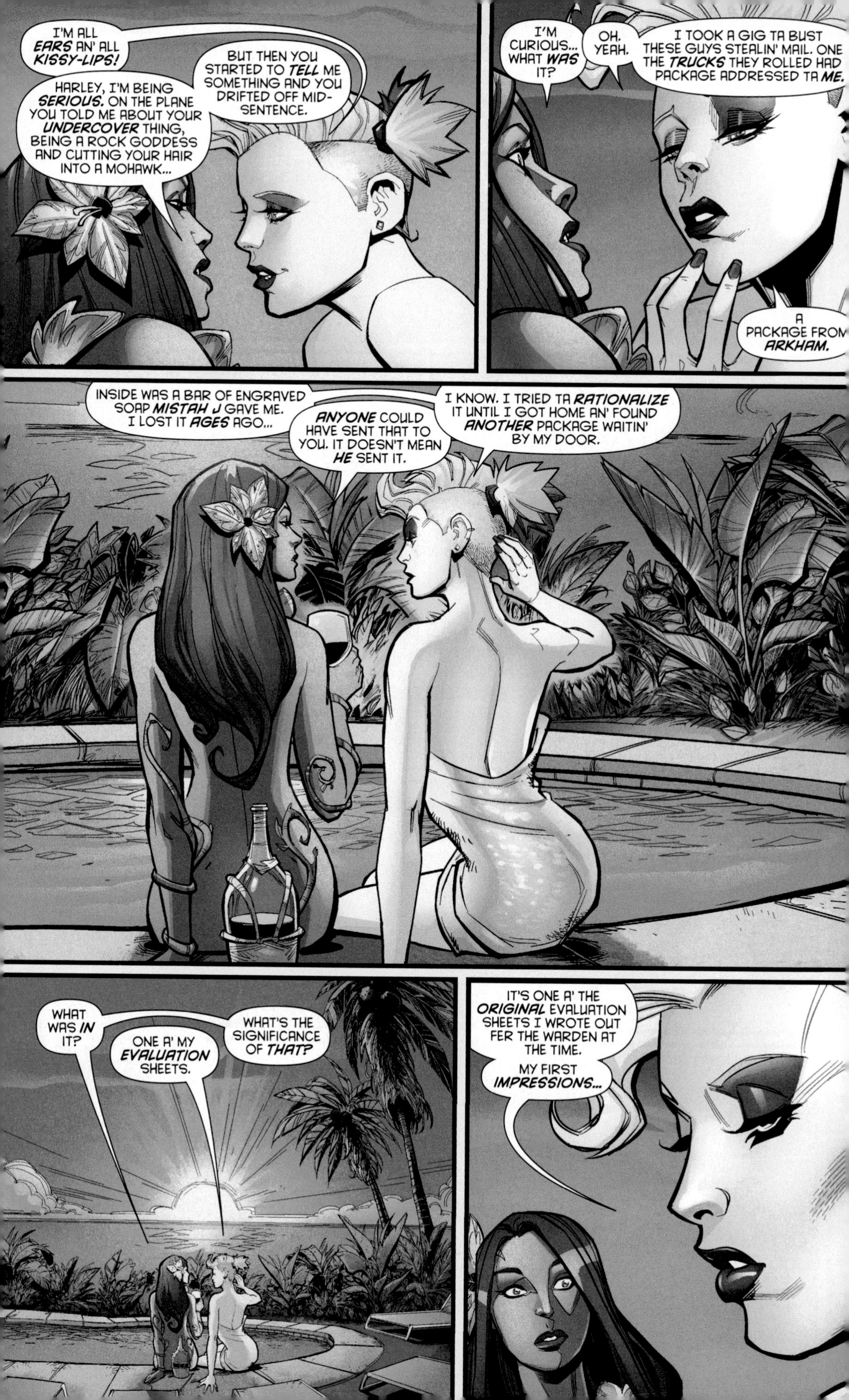
I'M ALL EARS AN' ALL KISSY-LIPS!
HARLEY, I'M BEING SERIOUS. ON THE PLANE YOU TOLD ME ABOUT YOUR UNDERCOVER THING, BEING A ROCK GODDESS AND CUTTING YOUR HAIR INTO A MOHAWK...
BUT THEN YOU STARTED TO TELL ME SOMETHING AND YOU DRIFTED OFF MID-SENTENCE.
I'M CURIOUS... WHAT WAS IT?
OH. YEAH.
I TOOK A GIG TA BUST THESE GUYS STEALIN' MAIL. ONE THE TRUCKS THEY ROLLED HAD PACKAGE ADDRESSED TA ME.
A PACKAGE FROM ARKHAM.
INSIDE WAS A BAR OF ENGRAVED SOAP MISTAH J GAVE ME. I LOST IT AGES AGO...
ANYONE COULD HAVE SENT THAT TO YOU. IT DOESN'T MEAN HE SENT IT.
I KNOW. I TRIED TA RATIONALIZE IT UNTIL I GOT HOME AN' FOUND ANOTHER PACKAGE WAITIN' BY MY DOOR.
WHAT WAS IN IT?
ONE A' MY EVALUATION SHEETS.
WHAT'S THE SIGNIFICANCE OF THAT?
IT'S ONE A' THE ORIGINAL EVALUATION SHEETS I WROTE OUT FER THE WARDEN AT THE TIME.
MY FIRST IMPRESSIONS...

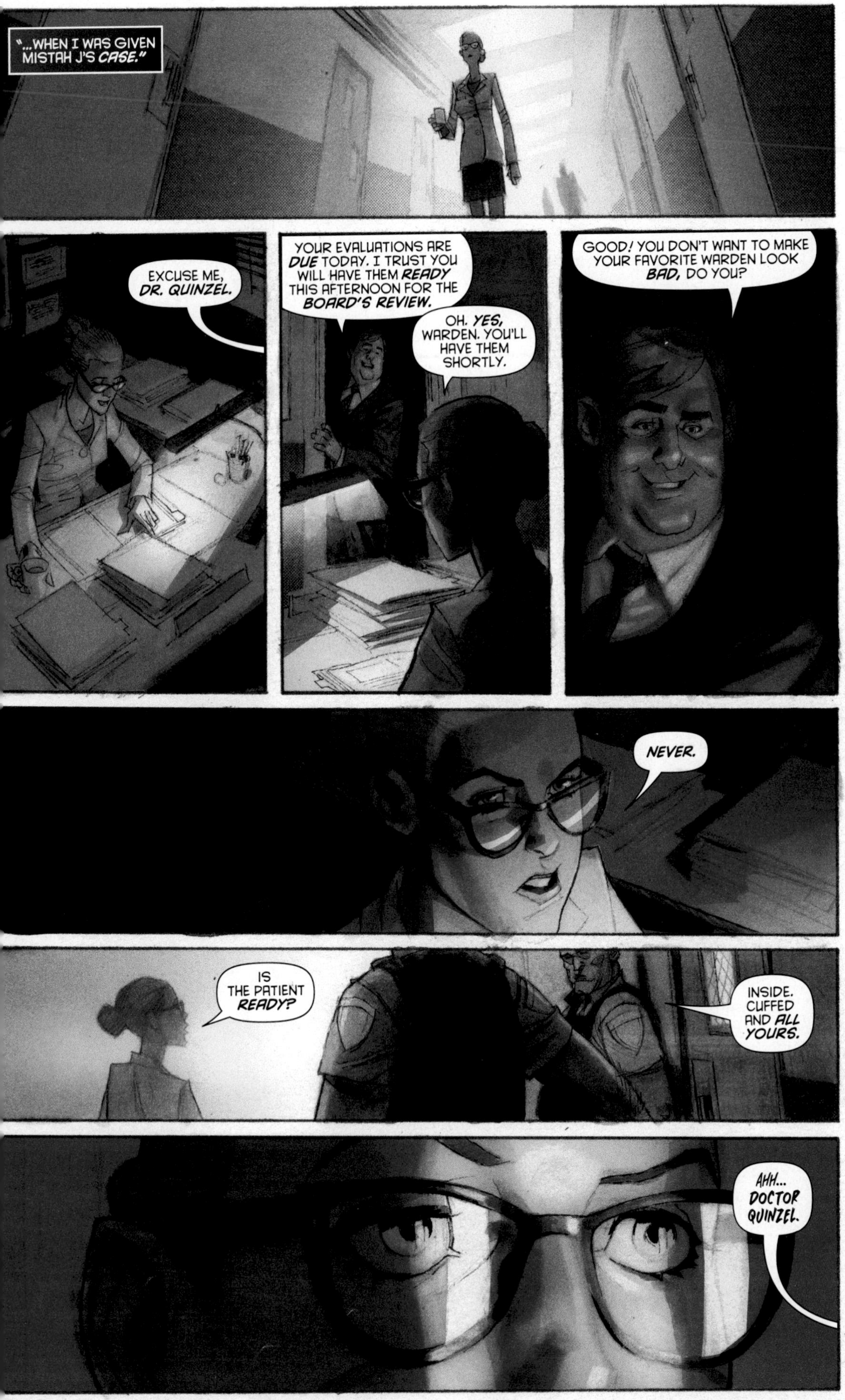

"...WHEN I WAS GIVEN MISTAH J'S CASE."
EXCUSE ME, DR. QUINZEL.
YOUR EVALUATIONS ARE DUE TODAY. I TRUST YOU WILL HAVE THEM READY THIS AFTERNOON FOR THE BOARD'S REVIEW.
OH. YES, WARDEN. YOU'LL HAVE THEM SHORTLY.
GOOD! YOU DON'T WANT TO MAKE YOUR FAVORITE WARDEN LOOK BAD, DO YOU?
NEVER.
IS THE PATIENT READY?
INSIDE. CUFFED AND ALL YOURS.
AHH... DOCTOR QUINZEL.

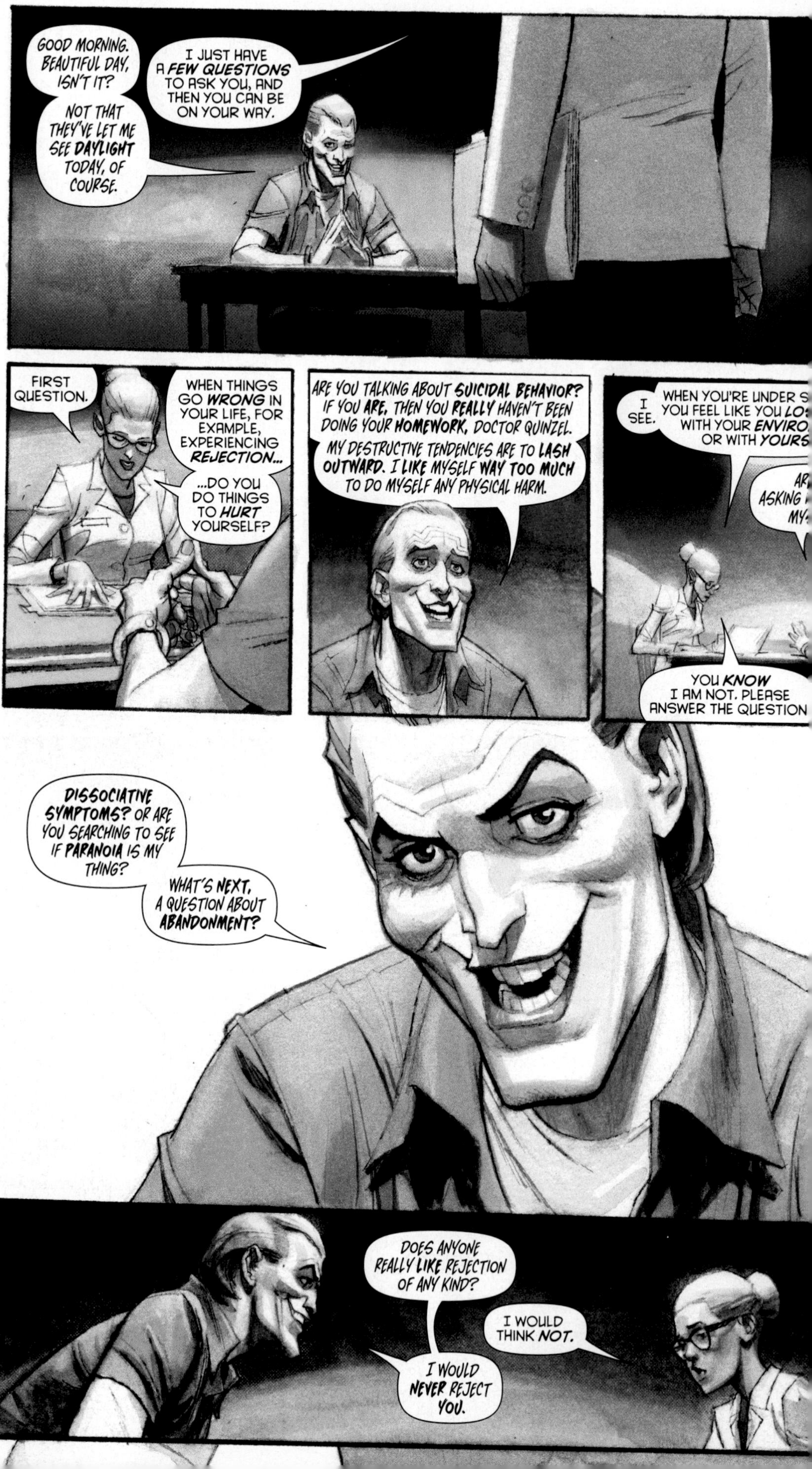
GOOD MORNING. BEAUTIFUL DAY, ISN'T IT?
NOT THAT THEY'VE LET ME SEE DAYLIGHT TODAY, OF COURSE.
I JUST HAVE A FEW QUESTIONS TO ASK YOU, AND THEN YOU CAN BE ON YOUR WAY.
FIRST QUESTION.
WHEN THINGS GO WRONG IN YOUR LIFE, FOR EXAMPLE, EXPERIENCING REJECTION...
...DO YOU DO THINGS TO HURT YOURSELF?
ARE YOU TALKING ABOUT SUICIDAL BEHAVIOR? IF YOU ARE, THEN YOU REALLY HAVEN'T BEEN DOING YOUR HOMEWORK, DOCTOR QUINZEL.
MY DESTRUCTIVE TENDENCIES ARE TO LASH OUTWARD. I LIKE MYSELF WAY TOO MUCH TO DO MYSELF ANY PHYSICAL HARM.
I SEE.
YOU KNOW I AM NOT. PLEASE ANSWER THE QUESTION
DISSOCIATIVE SYMPTOMS? OR ARE YOU SEARCHING TO SEE IF PARANOIA IS MY THING?
WHAT'S NEXT, A QUESTION ABOUT ABANDONMENT?
DOES ANYONE REALLY LIKE REJECTION OF ANY KIND?
I WOULD THINK NOT.
I WOULD NEVER REJECT YOU.

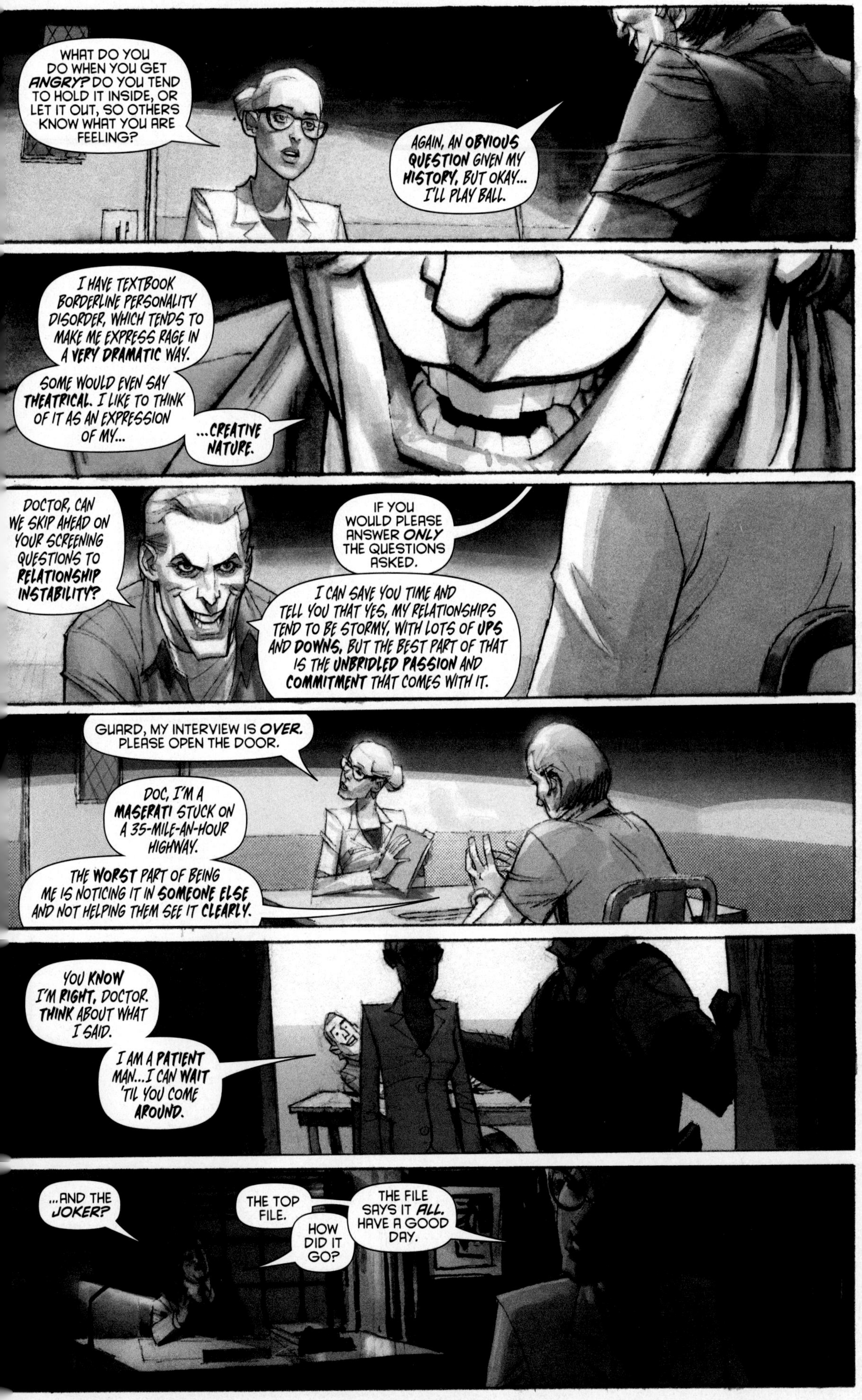

WHAT DO YOU DO WHEN YOU GET ANGRY? DO YOU TEND TO HOLD IT INSIDE, OR LET IT OUT, SO OTHERS KNOW WHAT YOU ARE FEELING?
AGAIN, AN OBVIOUS QUESTION GIVEN MY HISTORY, BUT OKAY... I'LL PLAY BALL.
I HAVE TEXTBOOK BORDERLINE PERSONALITY DISORDER, WHICH TENDS TO MAKE ME EXPRESS RAGE IN A VERY DRAMATIC WAY.
SOME WOULD EVEN SAY THEATRICAL. I LIKE TO THINK OF IT AS AN EXPRESSION OF MY...
...CREATIVE NATURE.
DOCTOR, CAN WE SKIP AHEAD ON YOUR SCREENING QUESTIONS TO RELATIONSHIP INSTABILITY?
IF YOU WOULD PLEASE ANSWER ONLY THE QUESTIONS ASKED.
I CAN SAVE YOU TIME AND TELL YOU THAT YES, MY RELATIONSHIPS TEND TO BE STORMY, WITH LOTS OF UPS AND DOWNS, BUT THE BEST PART OF THAT IS THE UNBRIDLED PASSION AND COMMITMENT THAT COMES WITH IT.
GUARD, MY INTERVIEW IS OVER. PLEASE OPEN THE DOOR.
DOC, I'M A MASERATI STUCK ON A 35-MILE-AN-HOUR HIGHWAY.
THE WORST PART OF BEING ME IS NOTICING IT IN SOMEONE ELSE AND NOT HELPING THEM SEE IT CLEARLY.
YOU KNOW I'M RIGHT, DOCTOR. THINK ABOUT WHAT I SAID.
I AM A PATIENT MAN...I CAN WAIT 'TIL YOU COME AROUND.
...AND THE JOKER?
THE TOP FILE.
HOW DID IT GO?
THE FILE SAYS IT ALL. HAVE A GOOD DAY.

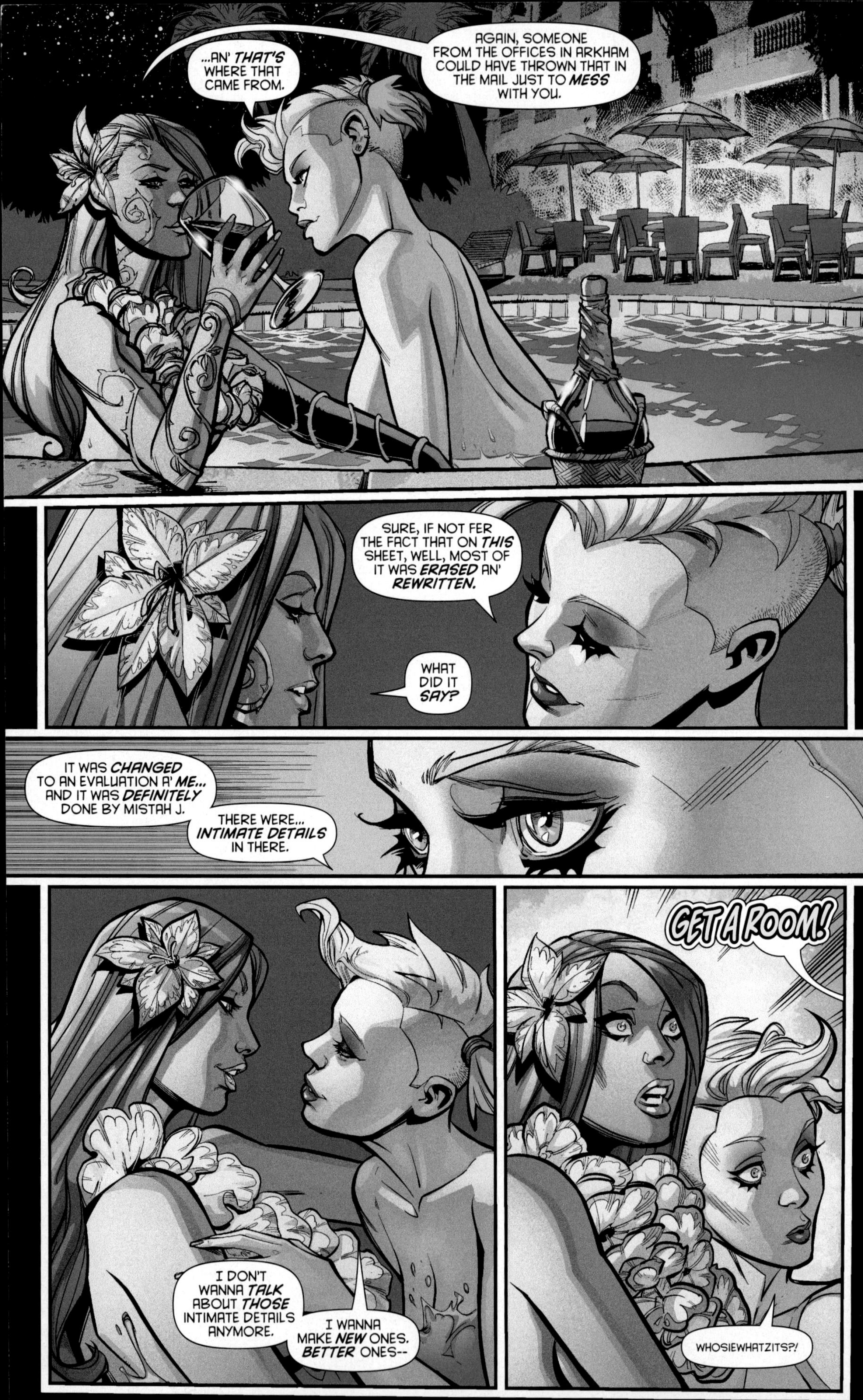

...AN' THAT'S WHERE THAT CAME FROM.
AGAIN, SOMEONE FROM THE OFFICES IN ARKHAM COULD HAVE THROWN THAT IN THE MAIL JUST TO MESS WITH YOU.
SURE, IF NOT FER THE FACT THAT ON THIS SHEET, WELL, MOST OF IT WAS ERASED AN' REWRITTEN.
WHAT DID IT SAY?
IT WAS CHANGED TO AN EVALUATION A' ME... AND IT WAS DEFINITELY DONE BY MISTAH J.
THERE WERE... INTIMATE DETAILS IN THERE.
I DON'T WANNA TALK ABOUT THOSE INTIMATE DETAILS ANYMORE.
I WANNA MAKE NEW ONES. BETTER ONES--
GET A ROOM!
WHOSIEWHATZITS?!

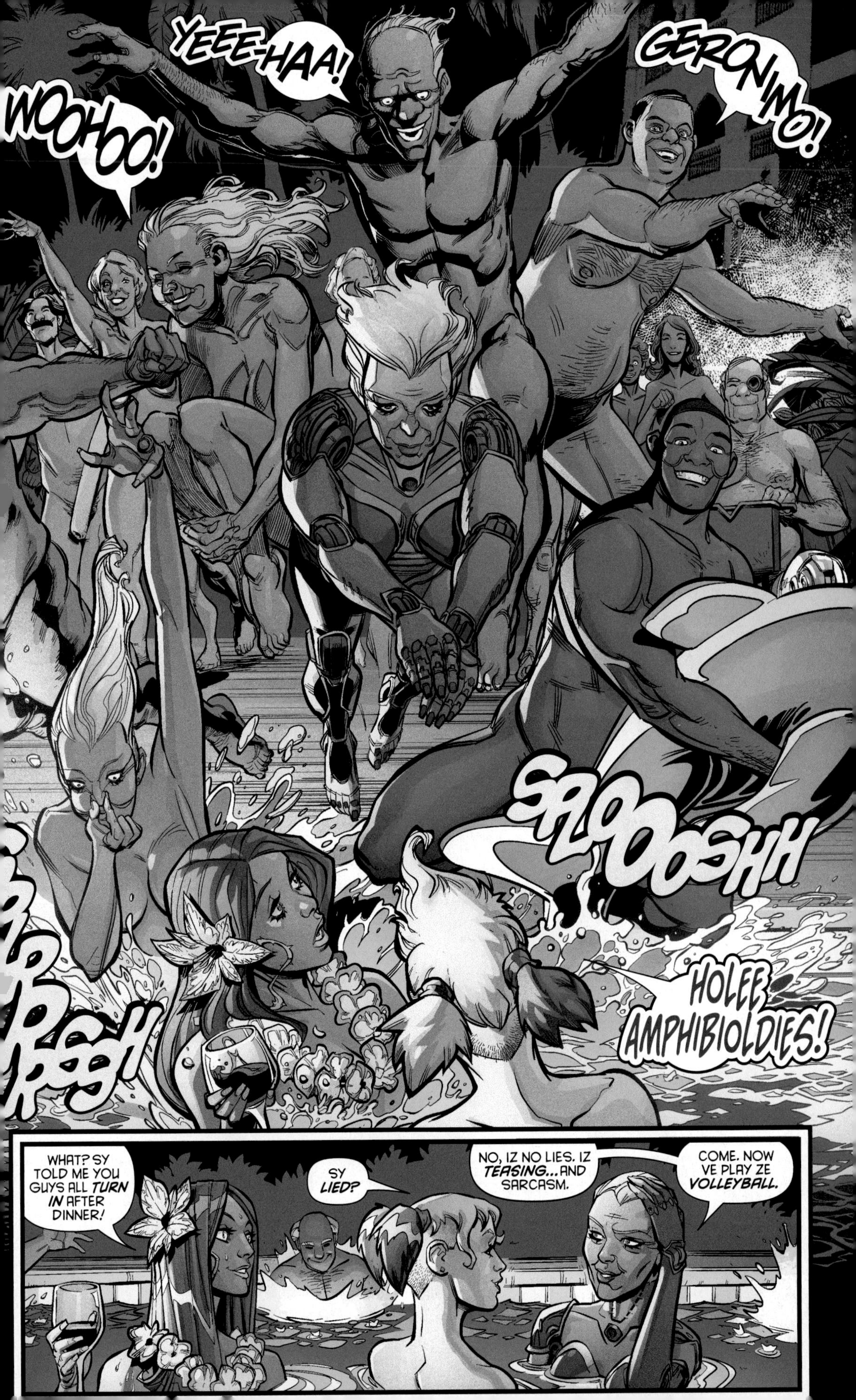
WOOHOO!
YEEE-HAA!
GERONIMO!
SPLOOOSHH
HOLEE AMPHIBIOLDIES!
WHAT? SY TOLD ME YOU GUYS ALL TURN IN AFTER DINNER!
SY LIED?
NO, IZ NO LIES. IZ TEASING...AND SARCASM.
COME. NOW VE PLAY ZE VOLLEYBALL.

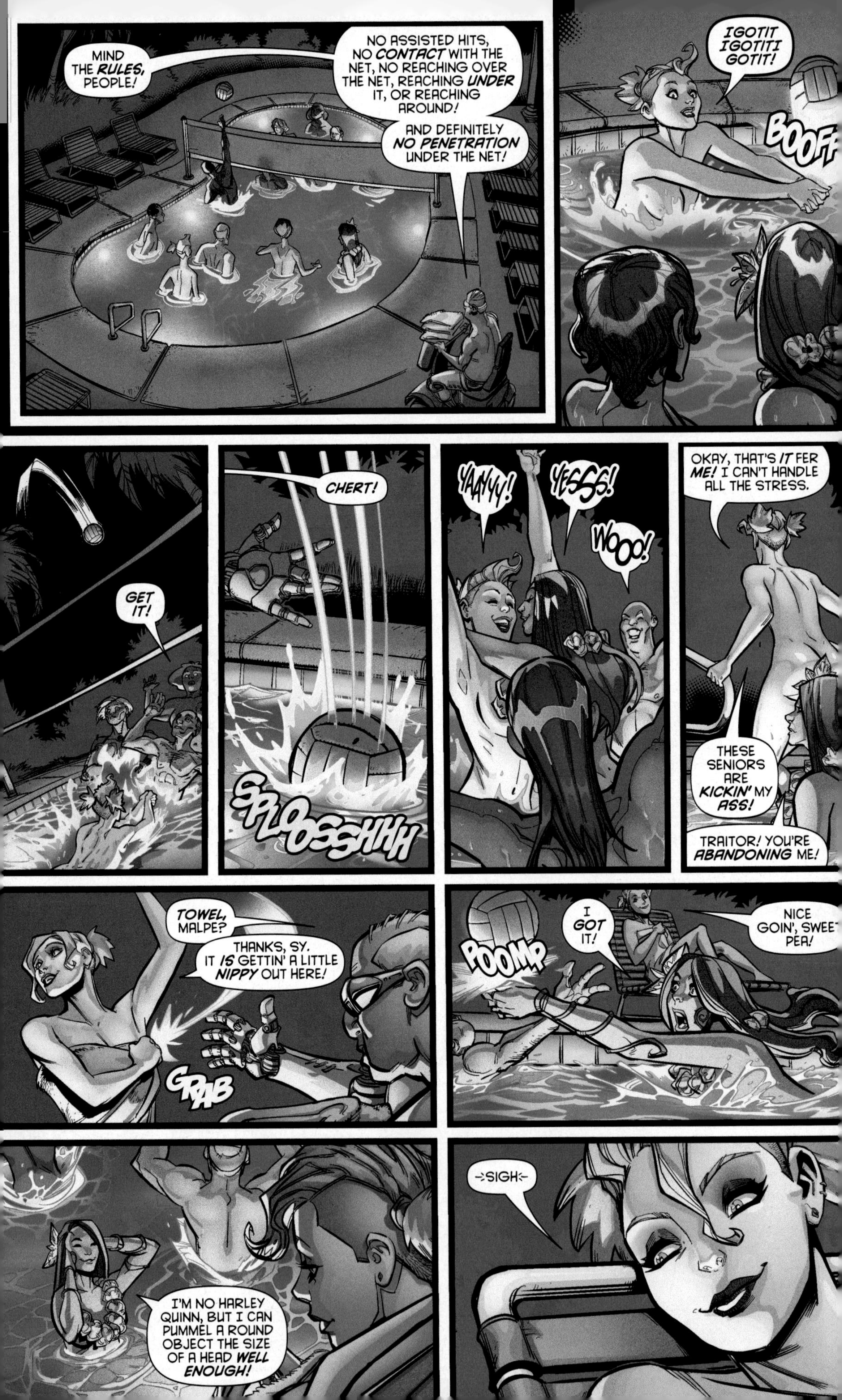

MIND THE RULES, PEOPLE!
NO ASSISTED HITS, NO CONTACT WITH THE NET, NO REACHING OVER THE NET, REACHING UNDER IT, OR REACHING AROUND!
AND DEFINITELY NO PENETRATION UNDER THE NET!
IGOTIT IGOTITI GOTIT!
BOOF!
GET IT!
CHERT!
SPLOOSSHHH
YAAYYY!
YESSS!
WOOO!
OKAY, THAT'S IT FER ME! I CAN'T HANDLE ALL THE STRESS.
THESE SENIORS ARE KICKIN' MY ASS!
TRAITOR! YOU'RE ABANDONING ME!
TOWEL, MALPE?
THANKS, SY. IT IS GETTIN' A LITTLE NIPPY OUT HERE!
GRAB
I GOT IT!
POOMP
NICE GOIN', SWEET PEA!
I'M NO HARLEY QUINN, BUT I CAN PUMMEL A ROUND OBJECT THE SIZE OF A HEAD WELL ENOUGH!
-SIGH-

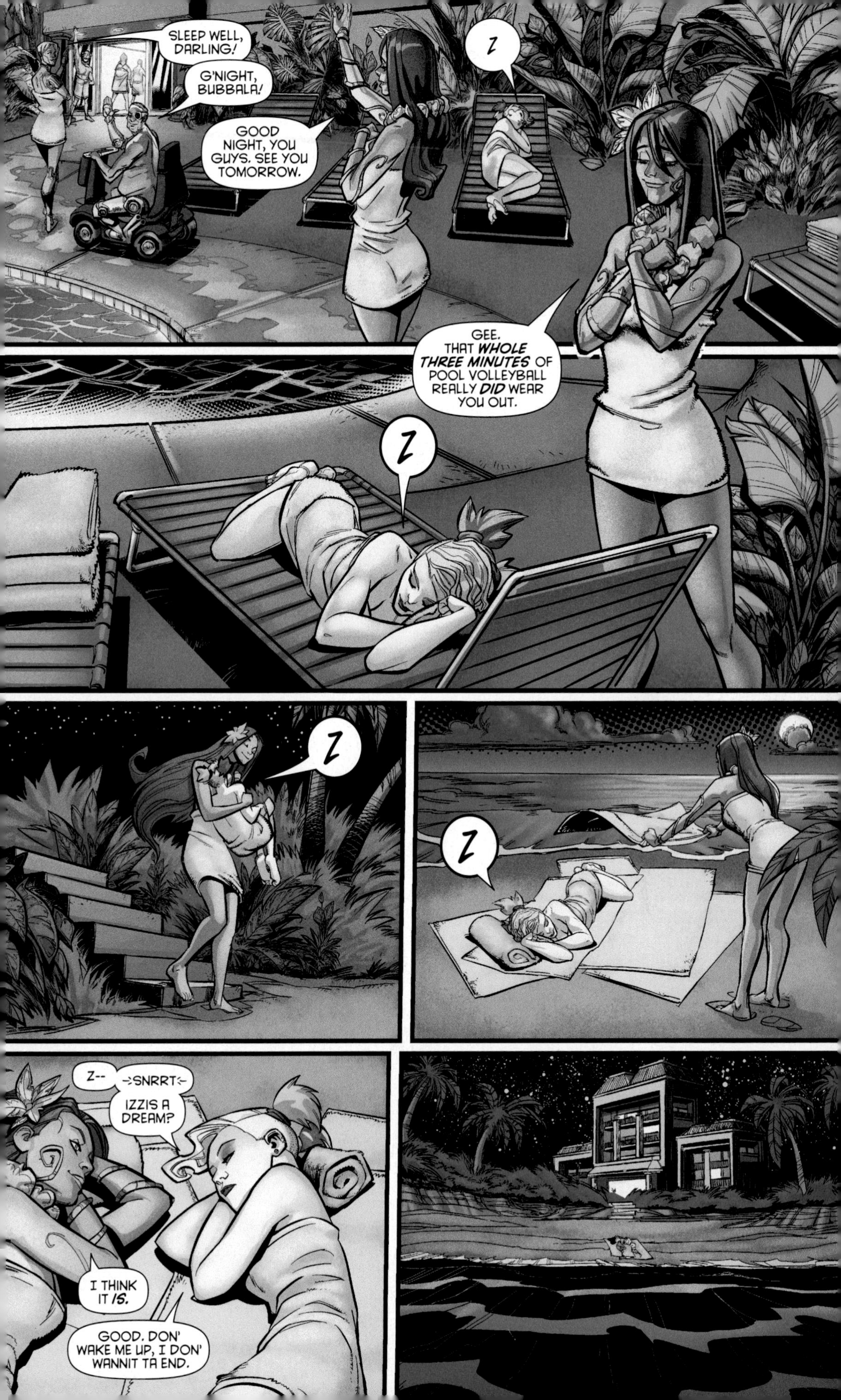
SLEEP WELL, DARLING!
G'NIGHT, BUBBALA!
GOOD NIGHT, YOU GUYS. SEE YOU TOMORROW.
Z
GEE. THAT *WHOLE THREE MINUTES* OF POOL VOLLEYBALL REALLY *DID* WEAR YOU OUT.
Z
Z
Z
Z--
-SNRRT-
IZZIS A DREAM?
I THINK IT *IS.*
GOOD. DON' WAKE ME UP, I DON' WANNIT TA END.

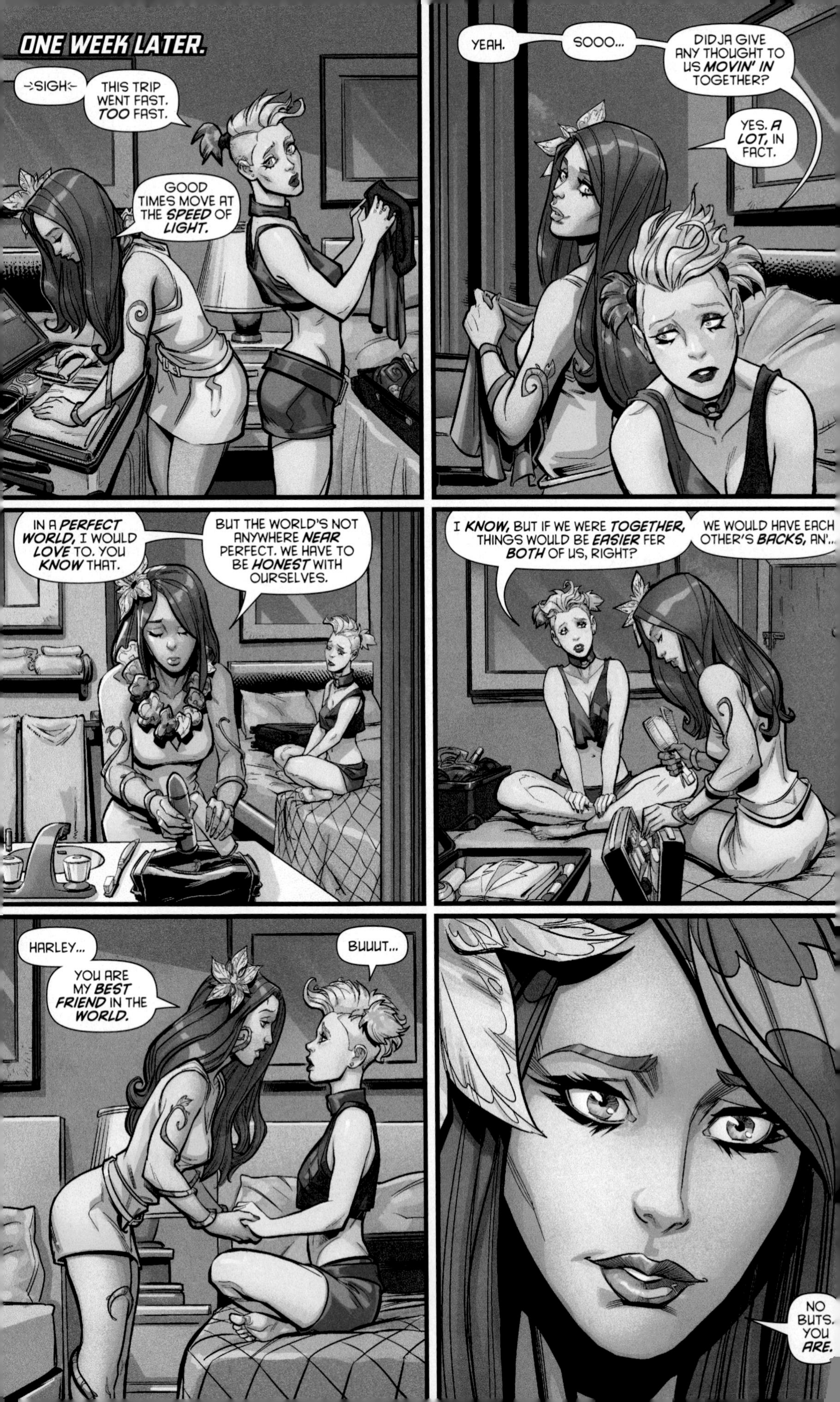
ONE WEEK LATER.
-SIGH-
THIS TRIP WENT FAST. TOO FAST.
GOOD TIMES MOVE AT THE SPEED OF LIGHT.
YEAH.
SOOO...
DIDJA GIVE ANY THOUGHT TO US MOVIN' IN TOGETHER?
YES. A LOT, IN FACT.
IN A PERFECT WORLD, I WOULD LOVE TO. YOU KNOW THAT.
BUT THE WORLD'S NOT ANYWHERE NEAR PERFECT. WE HAVE TO BE HONEST WITH OURSELVES.
I KNOW, BUT IF WE WERE TOGETHER, THINGS WOULD BE EASIER FER BOTH OF US, RIGHT?
WE WOULD HAVE EACH OTHER'S BACKS, AN'...
HARLEY...
YOU ARE MY BEST FRIEND IN THE WORLD.
BUUUT...
NO BUTS. YOU ARE.

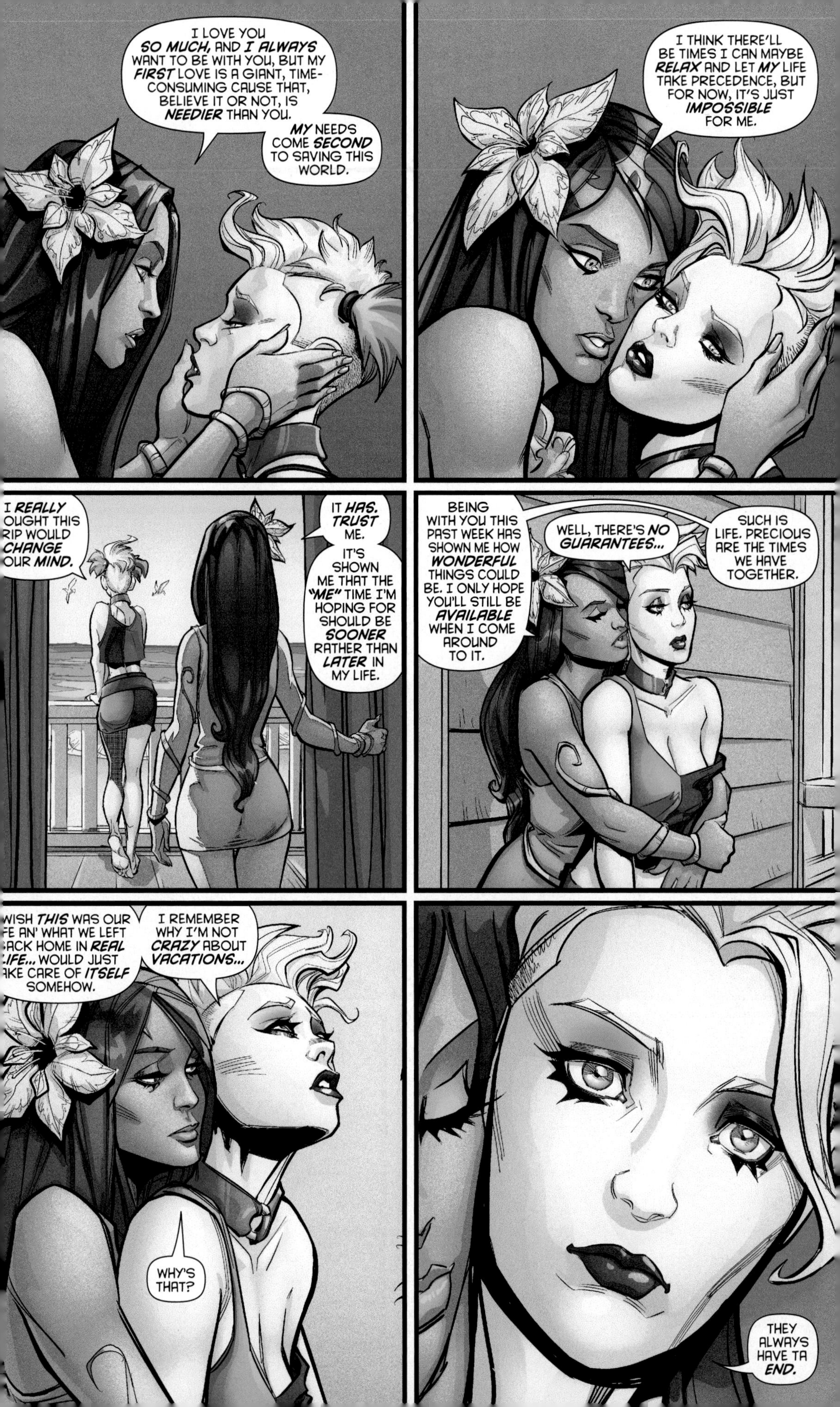

I LOVE YOU **SO MUCH,** AND **I ALWAYS** WANT TO BE WITH YOU, BUT MY **FIRST** LOVE IS A GIANT, TIME-CONSUMING CAUSE THAT, BELIEVE IT OR NOT, IS **NEEDIER** THAN YOU.
MY NEEDS COME **SECOND** TO SAVING THIS WORLD.
I THINK THERE'LL BE TIMES I CAN MAYBE **RELAX** AND LET **MY** LIFE TAKE PRECEDENCE, BUT FOR NOW, IT'S JUST **IMPOSSIBLE** FOR ME.
I **REALLY** OUGHT THIS RIP WOULD **CHANGE** OUR **MIND.**
IT **HAS. TRUST** ME.
IT'S SHOWN ME THAT THE **"ME"** TIME I'M HOPING FOR SHOULD BE **SOONER** RATHER THAN **LATER** IN MY LIFE.
BEING WITH YOU THIS PAST WEEK HAS SHOWN ME HOW **WONDERFUL** THINGS COULD BE. I ONLY HOPE YOU'LL STILL BE **AVAILABLE** WHEN I COME AROUND TO IT.
WELL, THERE'S **NO GUARANTEES...**
SUCH IS LIFE. PRECIOUS ARE THE TIMES WE HAVE TOGETHER.
WISH **THIS** WAS OUR FE AN' WHAT WE LEFT ACK HOME IN **REAL IFE...** WOULD JUST AKE CARE OF **ITSELF** SOMEHOW.
I REMEMBER WHY I'M NOT **CRAZY** ABOUT **VACATIONS...**
WHY'S THAT?
THEY ALWAYS HAVE TA **END.**

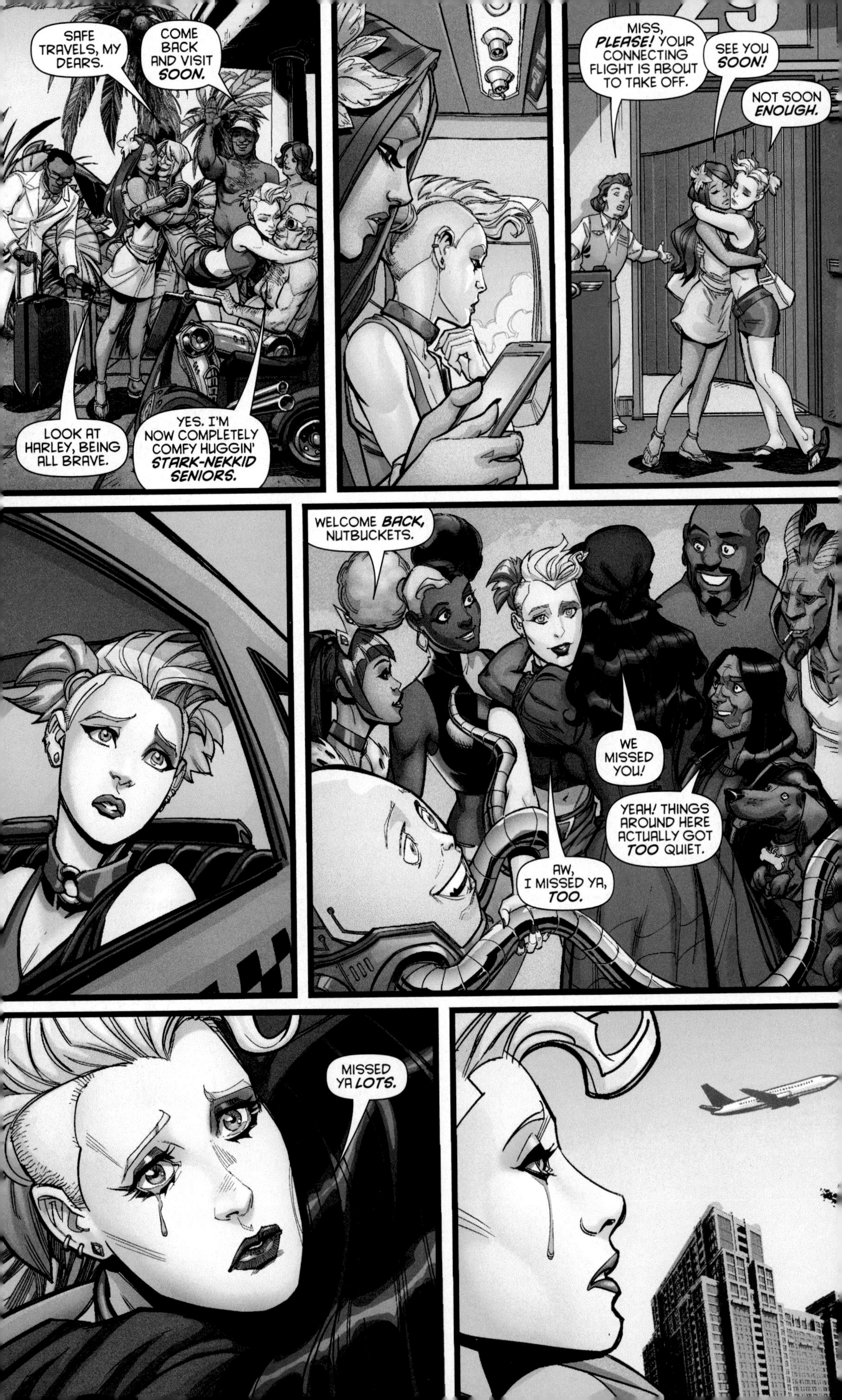
SAFE TRAVELS, MY DEARS.
COME BACK AND VISIT SOON.
LOOK AT HARLEY, BEING ALL BRAVE.
YES. I'M NOW COMPLETELY COMFY HUGGIN' STARK-NEKKID SENIORS.
MISS, PLEASE! YOUR CONNECTING FLIGHT IS ABOUT TO TAKE OFF.
SEE YOU SOON!
NOT SOON ENOUGH.
WELCOME BACK, NUTBUCKETS.
WE MISSED YOU!
YEAH! THINGS AROUND HERE ACTUALLY GOT TOO QUIET.
AW, I MISSED YA, TOO.
MISSED YA LOTS.

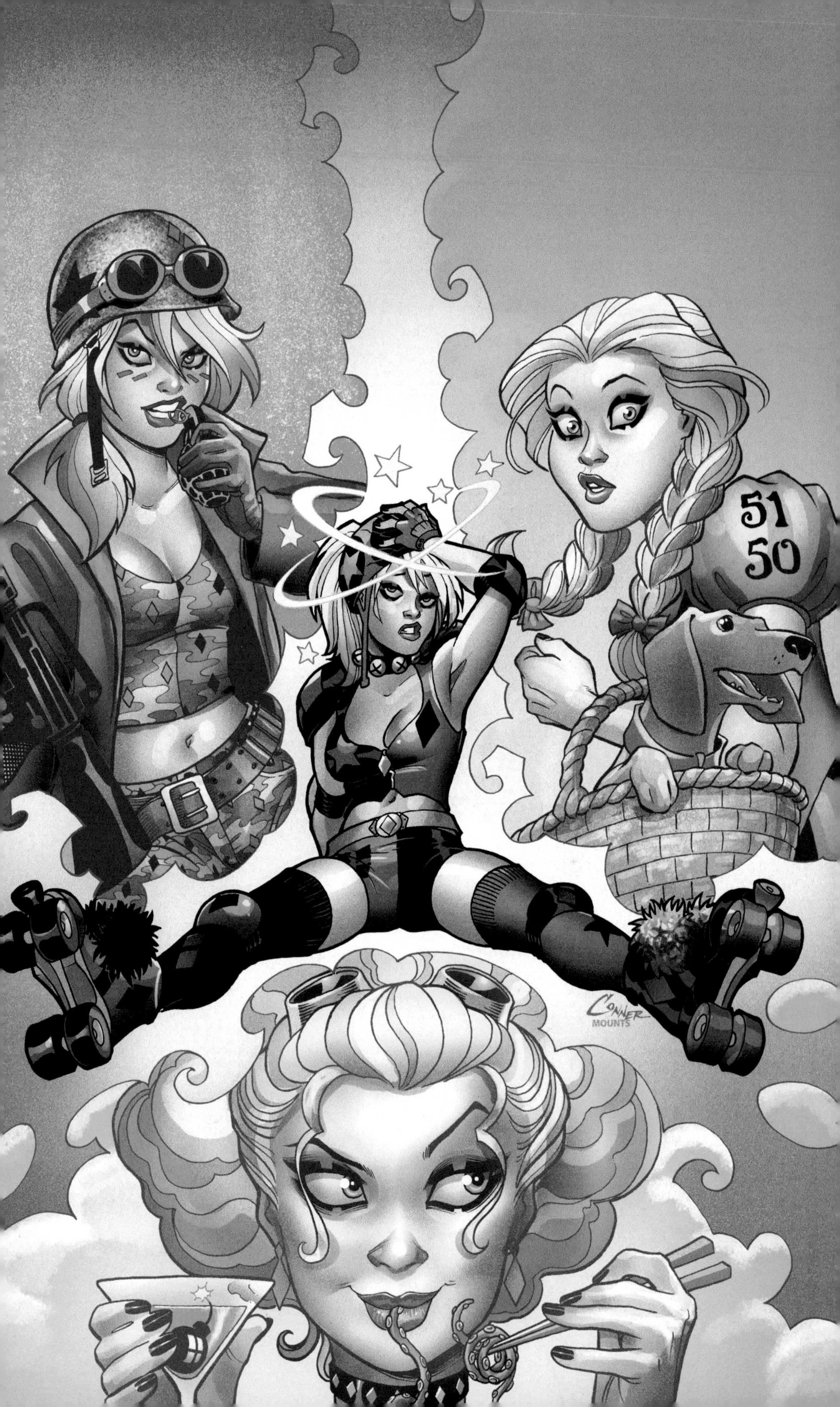

51
50
CONNER
MOUNTS

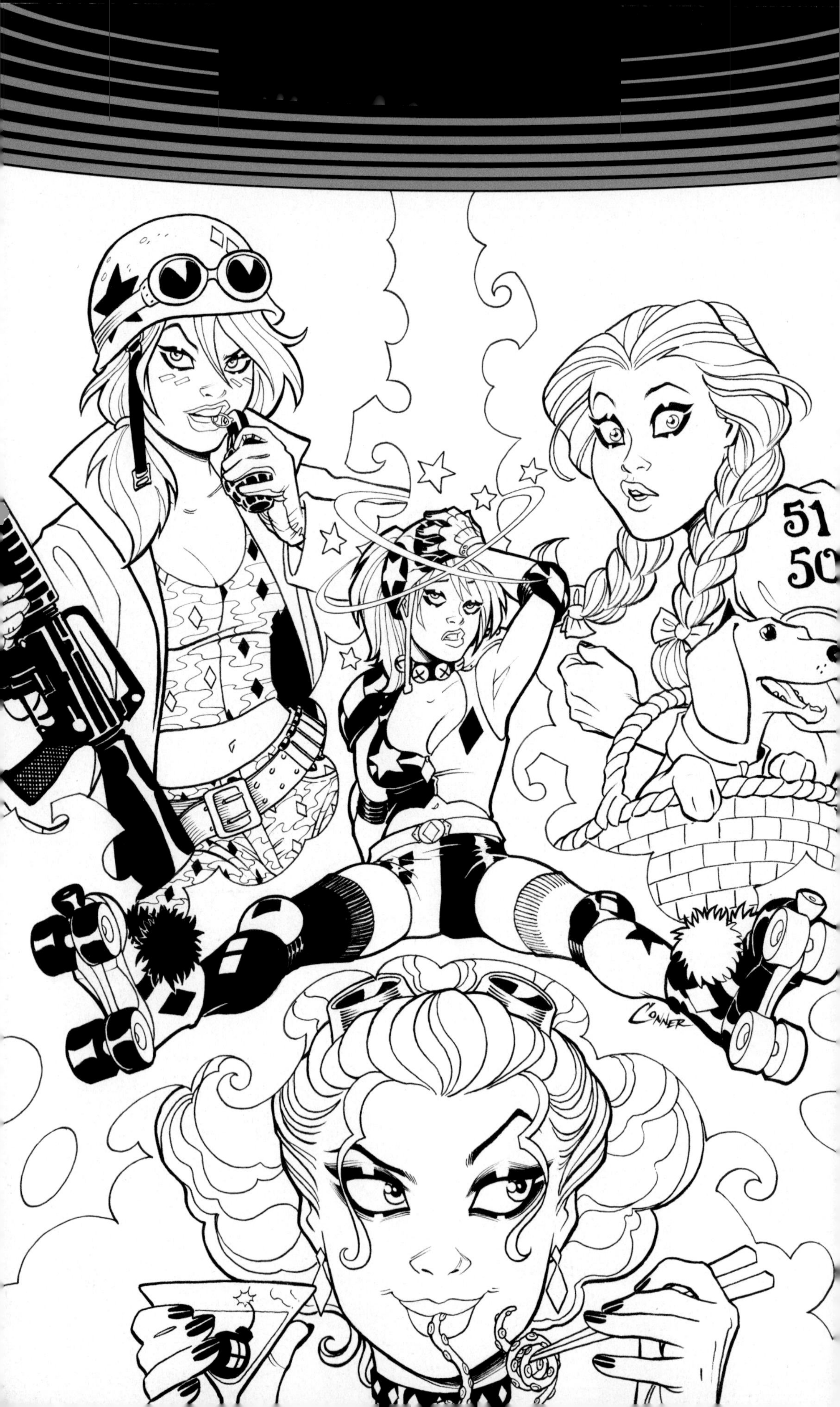
51
50
CONNER

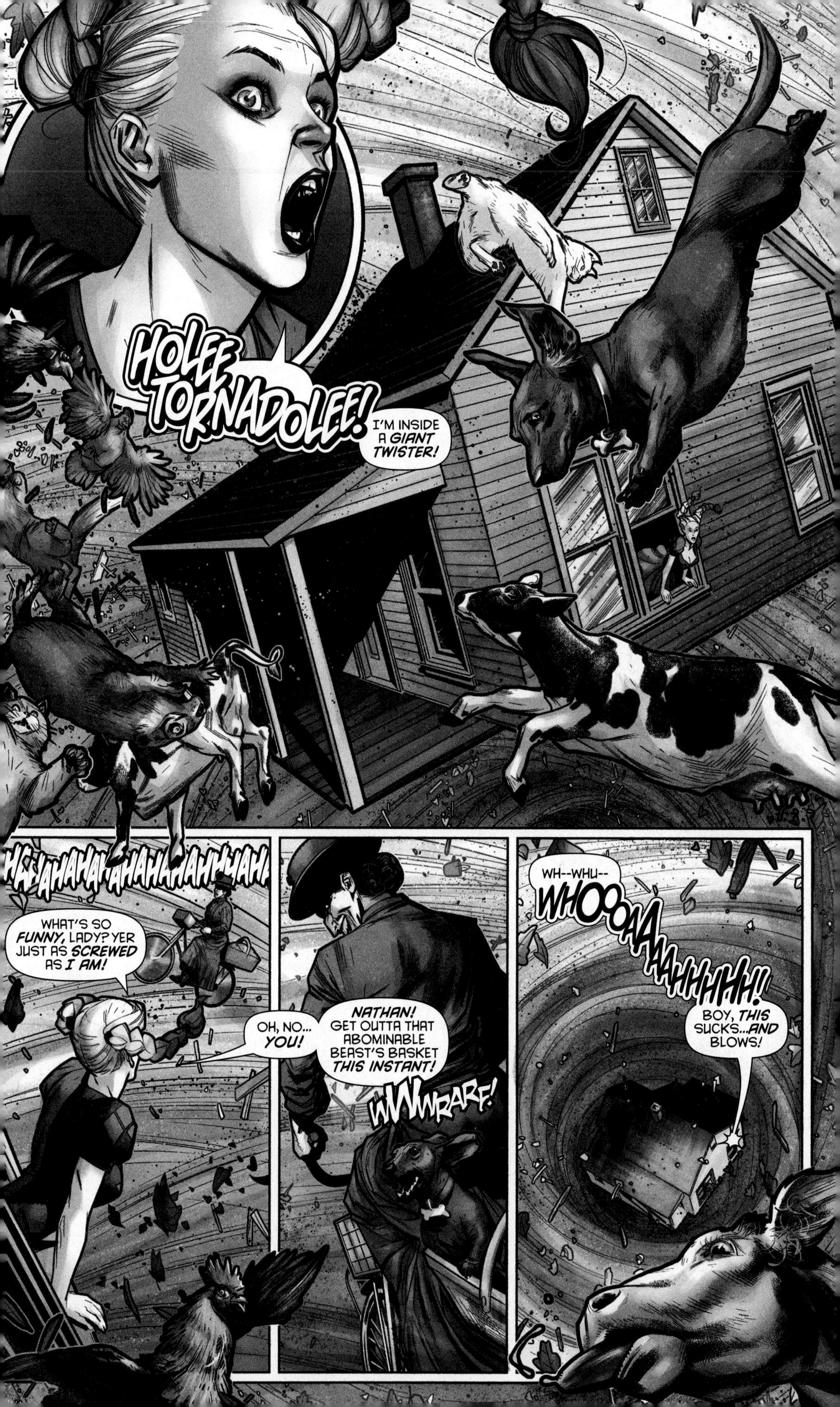

HOLEE TORNADOLEE!
I'M INSIDE A GIANT TWISTER!
HAHAHAHAHAHAHAHAHAHAHAHA
WHAT'S SO FUNNY, LADY? YER JUST AS SCREWED AS I AM!
OH, NO... YOU!
NATHAN! GET OUTTA THAT ABOMINABLE BEAST'S BASKET THIS INSTANT!
WWWRARF!
WH--WHU--
WHOOOAAAAHHHHHH!
BOY, THIS SUCKS...AND BLOWS!

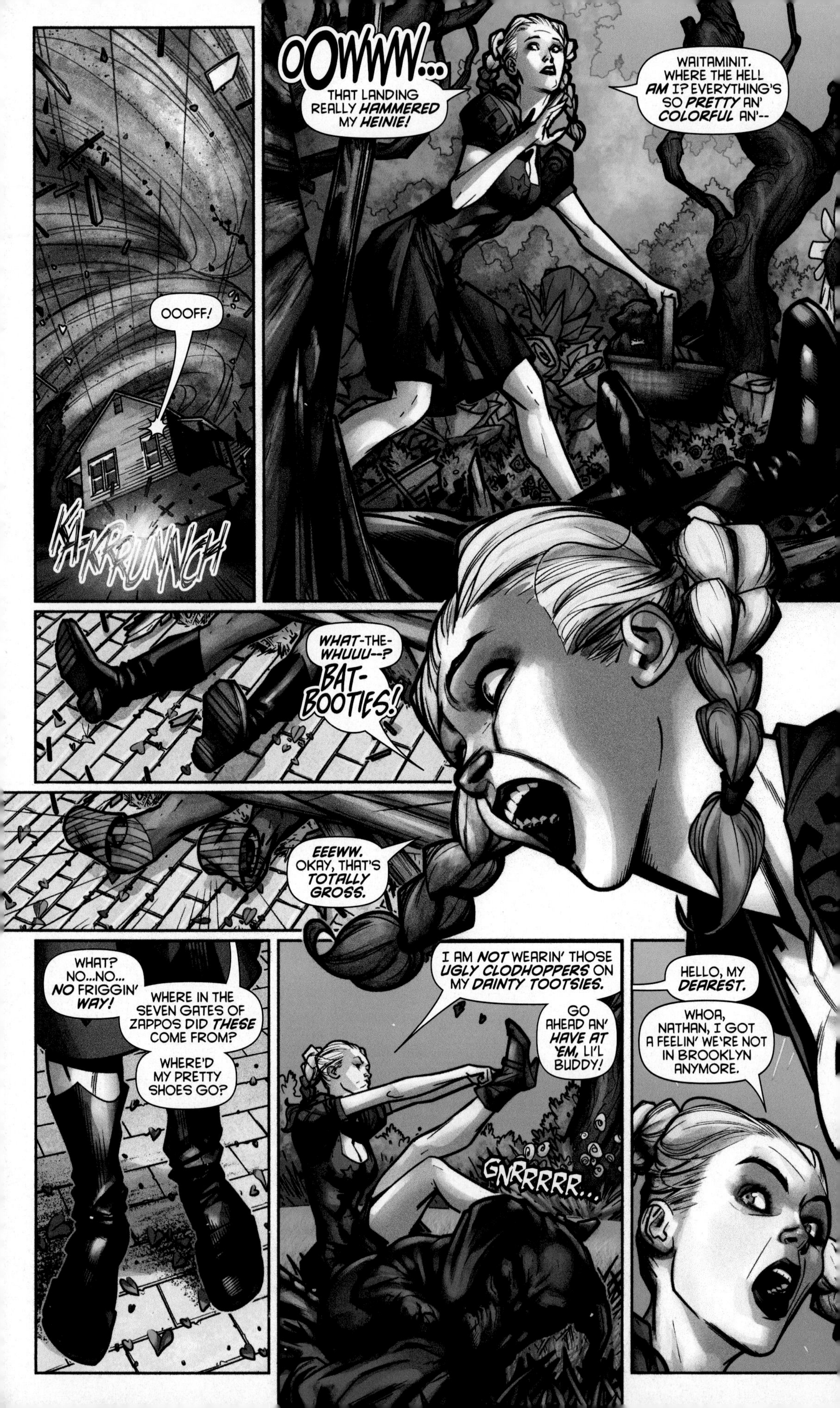

OOOFF!
KA-KRRUNNCH
OOWWW...
THAT LANDING REALLY HAMMERED MY HEINIE!
WAITAMINIT. WHERE THE HELL AM I? EVERYTHING'S SO PRETTY AN' COLORFUL AN'--
WHAT-THE-WHUUU--? BAT-BOOTIES!
EEEWW. OKAY, THAT'S TOTALLY GROSS.
WHAT? NO...NO... NO FRIGGIN' WAY!
WHERE IN THE SEVEN GATES OF ZAPPOS DID THESE COME FROM?
WHERE'D MY PRETTY SHOES GO?
I AM NOT WEARIN' THOSE UGLY CLODHOPPERS ON MY DAINTY TOOTSIES.
GO AHEAD AN' HAVE AT 'EM, LI'L BUDDY!
GNRRRRR...
HELLO, MY DEAREST.
WHOA, NATHAN, I GOT A FEELIN' WE'RE NOT IN BROOKLYN ANYMORE.

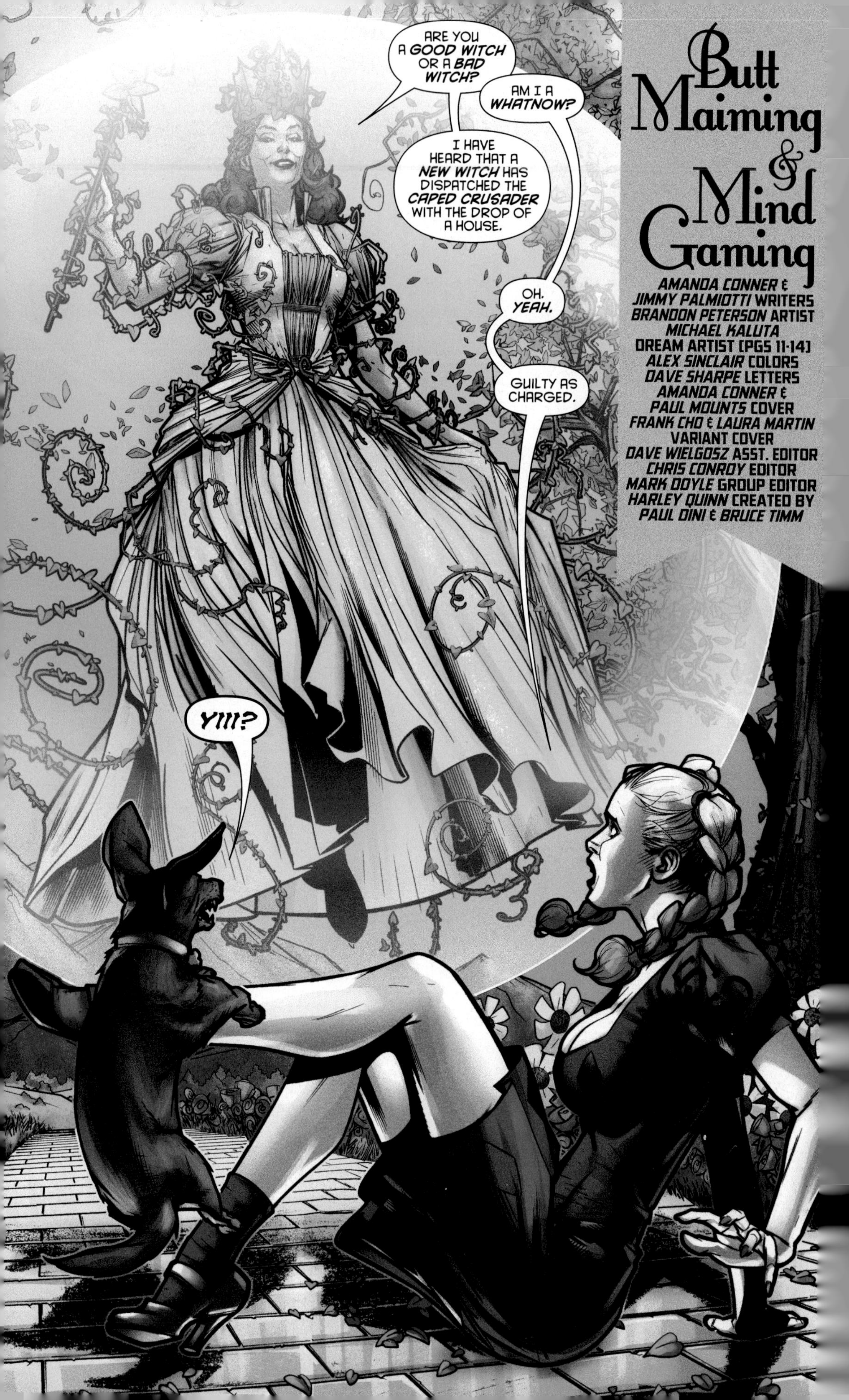
ARE YOU A GOOD WITCH OR A BAD WITCH?
AM I A WHATNOW?
I HAVE HEARD THAT A NEW WITCH HAS DISPATCHED THE CAPED CRUSADER WITH THE DROP OF A HOUSE.
OH. YEAH.
GUILTY AS CHARGED.
YIII?
Butt Maiming & Mind Gaming
AMANDA CONNER & JIMMY PALMIOTTI WRITERS
BRANDON PETERSON ARTIST
MICHAEL KALUTA DREAM ARTIST [PGS 11-14]
ALEX SINCLAIR COLORS
DAVE SHARPE LETTERS
AMANDA CONNER & PAUL MOUNTS COVER
FRANK CHO & LAURA MARTIN VARIANT COVER
DAVE WIELGOSZ ASST. EDITOR
CHRIS CONROY EDITOR
MARK DOYLE GROUP EDITOR
HARLEY QUINN CREATED BY PAUL DINI & BRUCE TIMM

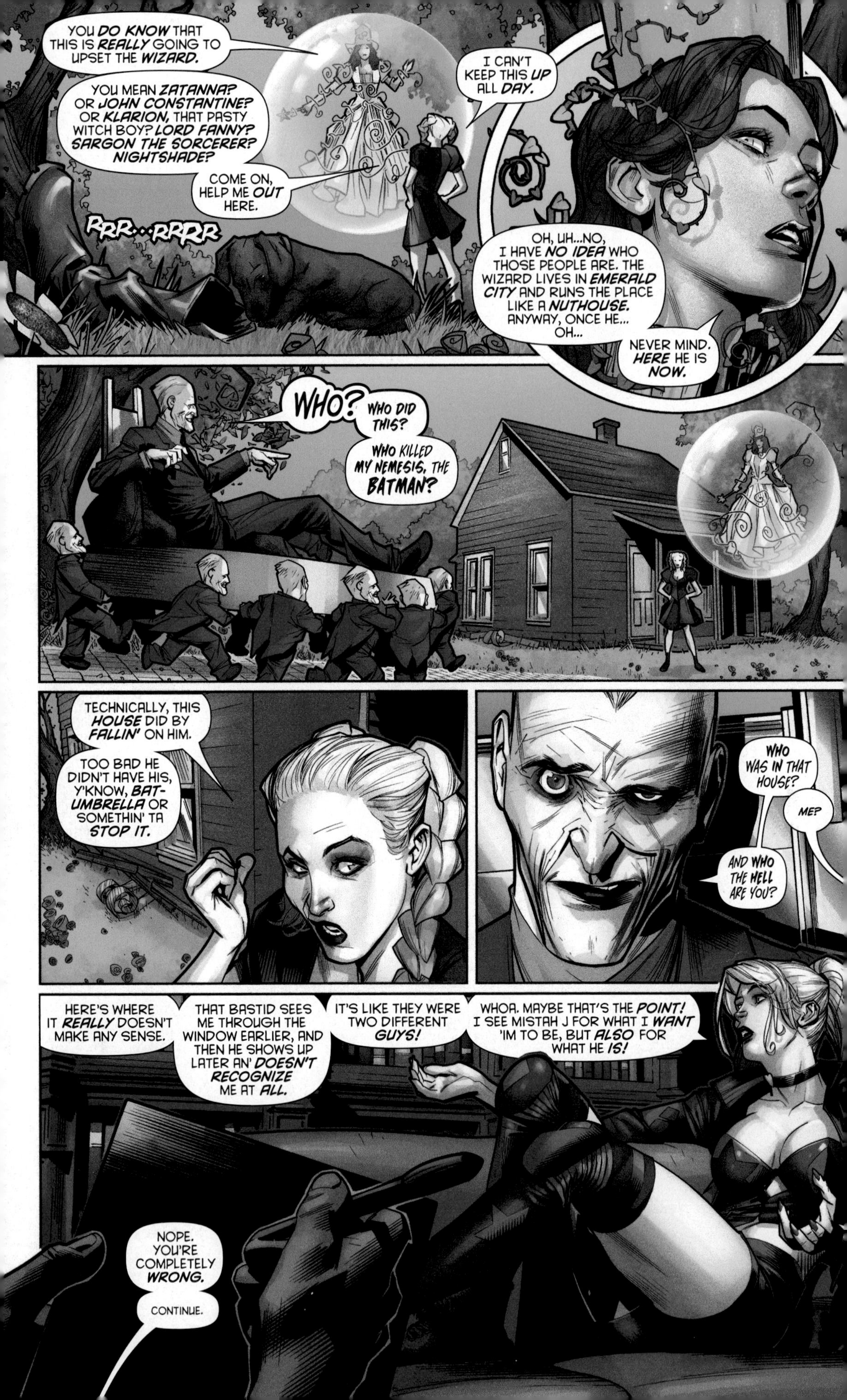

YOU DO KNOW THAT THIS IS REALLY GOING TO UPSET THE WIZARD.
YOU MEAN ZATANNA? OR JOHN CONSTANTINE? OR KLARION, THAT PASTY WITCH BOY? LORD FANNY? SARGON THE SORCERER? NIGHTSHADE?
COME ON, HELP ME OUT HERE.
I CAN'T KEEP THIS UP ALL DAY.
RRR...RRRR
OH, UH...NO, I HAVE NO IDEA WHO THOSE PEOPLE ARE. THE WIZARD LIVES IN EMERALD CITY AND RUNS THE PLACE LIKE A NUTHOUSE. ANYWAY, ONCE HE... OH...
NEVER MIND. HERE HE IS NOW.
WHO? WHO DID THIS?
WHO KILLED MY NEMESIS, THE BATMAN?
TECHNICALLY, THIS HOUSE DID BY FALLIN' ON HIM.
TOO BAD HE DIDN'T HAVE HIS, Y'KNOW, BAT-UMBRELLA OR SOMETHIN' TA STOP IT.
WHO WAS IN THAT HOUSE?
ME?
AND WHO THE HELL ARE YOU?
HERE'S WHERE IT REALLY DOESN'T MAKE ANY SENSE.
THAT BASTID SEES ME THROUGH THE WINDOW EARLIER, AND THEN HE SHOWS UP LATER AN' DOESN'T RECOGNIZE ME AT ALL.
IT'S LIKE THEY WERE TWO DIFFERENT GUYS!
WHOA. MAYBE THAT'S THE POINT! I SEE MISTAH J FOR WHAT I WANT 'IM TO BE, BUT ALSO FOR WHAT HE IS!
NOPE. YOU'RE COMPLETELY WRONG.
CONTINUE.

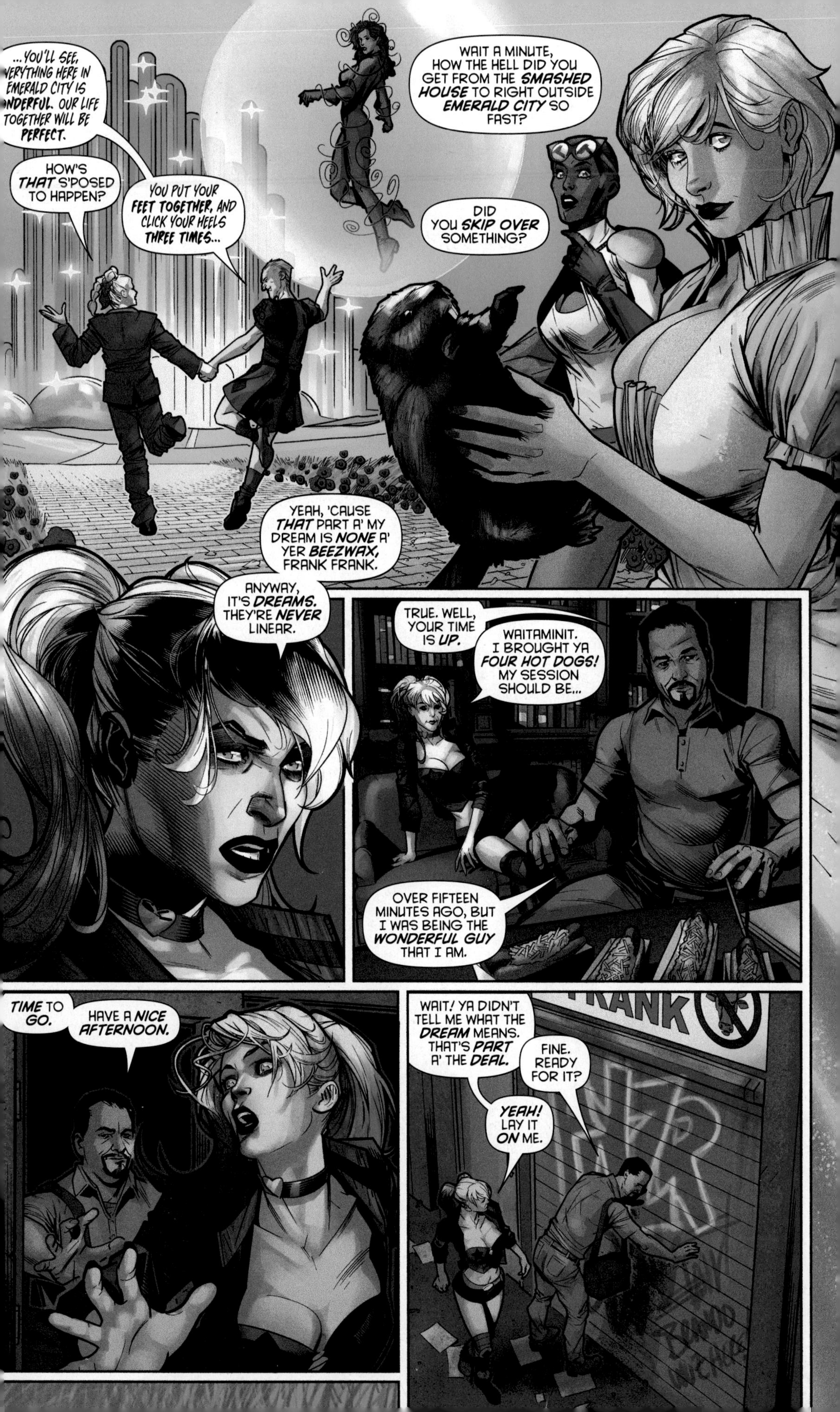
...YOU'LL SEE, EVERYTHING HERE IN EMERALD CITY IS WONDERFUL. OUR LIFE TOGETHER WILL BE PERFECT.
HOW'S THAT S'POSED TO HAPPEN?
YOU PUT YOUR FEET TOGETHER, AND CLICK YOUR HEELS THREE TIMES...
WAIT A MINUTE, HOW THE HELL DID YOU GET FROM THE SMASHED HOUSE TO RIGHT OUTSIDE EMERALD CITY SO FAST?
DID YOU SKIP OVER SOMETHING?
YEAH, 'CAUSE THAT PART A' MY DREAM IS NONE A' YER BEEZWAX, FRANK FRANK.
ANYWAY, IT'S DREAMS. THEY'RE NEVER LINEAR.
TRUE. WELL, YOUR TIME IS UP.
WAITAMINIT. I BROUGHT YA FOUR HOT DOGS! MY SESSION SHOULD BE...
OVER FIFTEEN MINUTES AGO, BUT I WAS BEING THE WONDERFUL GUY THAT I AM.
TIME TO GO.
HAVE A NICE AFTERNOON.
WAIT! YA DIDN'T TELL ME WHAT THE DREAM MEANS. THAT'S PART A' THE DEAL.
FINE. READY FOR IT?
YEAH! LAY IT ON ME.
FRANK

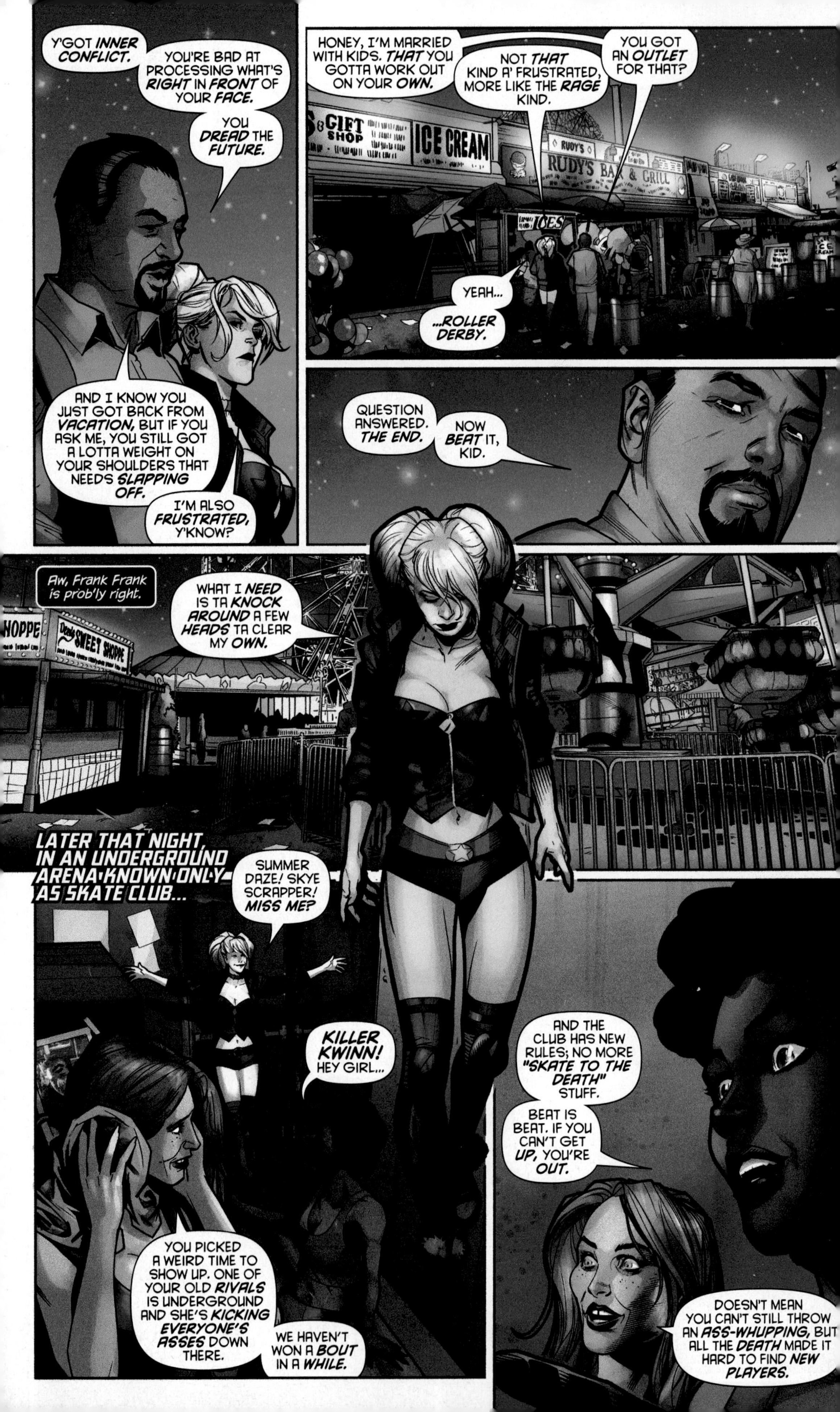
Y'GOT INNER CONFLICT.
YOU'RE BAD AT PROCESSING WHAT'S RIGHT IN FRONT OF YOUR FACE.
YOU DREAD THE FUTURE.
AND I KNOW YOU JUST GOT BACK FROM VACATION, BUT IF YOU ASK ME, YOU STILL GOT A LOTTA WEIGHT ON YOUR SHOULDERS THAT NEEDS SLAPPING OFF.
I'M ALSO FRUSTRATED, Y'KNOW?
HONEY, I'M MARRIED WITH KIDS. THAT YOU GOTTA WORK OUT ON YOUR OWN.
NOT THAT KIND A' FRUSTRATED, MORE LIKE THE RAGE KIND.
YOU GOT AN OUTLET FOR THAT?
GIFT SHOP
ICE CREAM
RUDY'S
RUDY'S BAR & GRILL
YEAH...
...ROLLER DERBY.
QUESTION ANSWERED. THE END.
NOW BEAT IT, KID.
Aw, Frank Frank is prob'ly right.
WHAT I NEED IS TA KNOCK AROUND A FEW HEADS TA CLEAR MY OWN.
SWEET SHOPPE
LATER THAT NIGHT, IN AN UNDERGROUND ARENA KNOWN ONLY AS SKATE CLUB...
SUMMER DAZE! SKYE SCRAPPER! MISS ME?
KILLER KWINN! HEY GIRL...
YOU PICKED A WEIRD TIME TO SHOW UP. ONE OF YOUR OLD RIVALS IS UNDERGROUND AND SHE'S KICKING EVERYONE'S ASSES DOWN THERE.
WE HAVEN'T WON A BOUT IN A WHILE.
AND THE CLUB HAS NEW RULES; NO MORE "SKATE TO THE DEATH" STUFF.
BEAT IS BEAT. IF YOU CAN'T GET UP, YOU'RE OUT.
DOESN'T MEAN YOU CAN'T STILL THROW AN ASS-WHUPPING, BUT ALL THE DEATH MADE IT HARD TO FIND NEW PLAYERS.

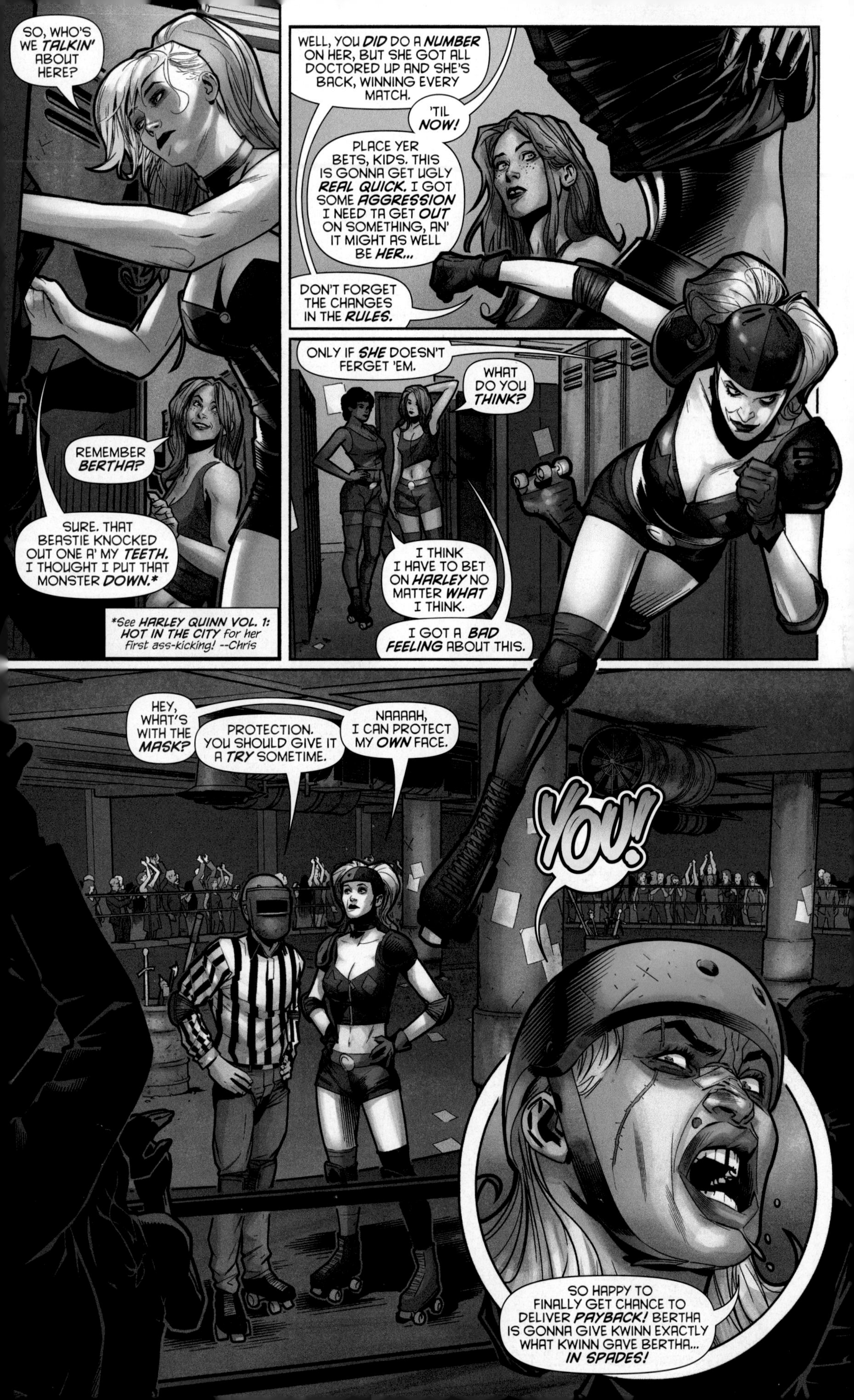
SO, WHO'S WE TALKIN' ABOUT HERE?
WELL, YOU DID DO A NUMBER ON HER, BUT SHE GOT ALL DOCTORED UP AND SHE'S BACK, WINNING EVERY MATCH.
'TIL NOW!
PLACE YER BETS, KIDS. THIS IS GONNA GET UGLY REAL QUICK. I GOT SOME AGGRESSION I NEED TA GET OUT ON SOMETHING, AN' IT MIGHT AS WELL BE HER...
DON'T FORGET THE CHANGES IN THE RULES.
REMEMBER BERTHA?
SURE. THAT BEASTIE KNOCKED OUT ONE A' MY TEETH. I THOUGHT I PUT THAT MONSTER DOWN.*
*See HARLEY QUINN VOL. 1: HOT IN THE CITY for her first ass-kicking! --Chris
ONLY IF SHE DOESN'T FERGET 'EM.
WHAT DO YOU THINK?
I THINK I HAVE TO BET ON HARLEY NO MATTER WHAT I THINK.
I GOT A BAD FEELING ABOUT THIS.
HEY, WHAT'S WITH THE MASK?
PROTECTION. YOU SHOULD GIVE IT A TRY SOMETIME.
NAAAAH, I CAN PROTECT MY OWN FACE.
YOU!
SO HAPPY TO FINALLY GET CHANCE TO DELIVER PAYBACK! BERTHA IS GONNA GIVE KWINN EXACTLY WHAT KWINN GAVE BERTHA... IN SPADES!

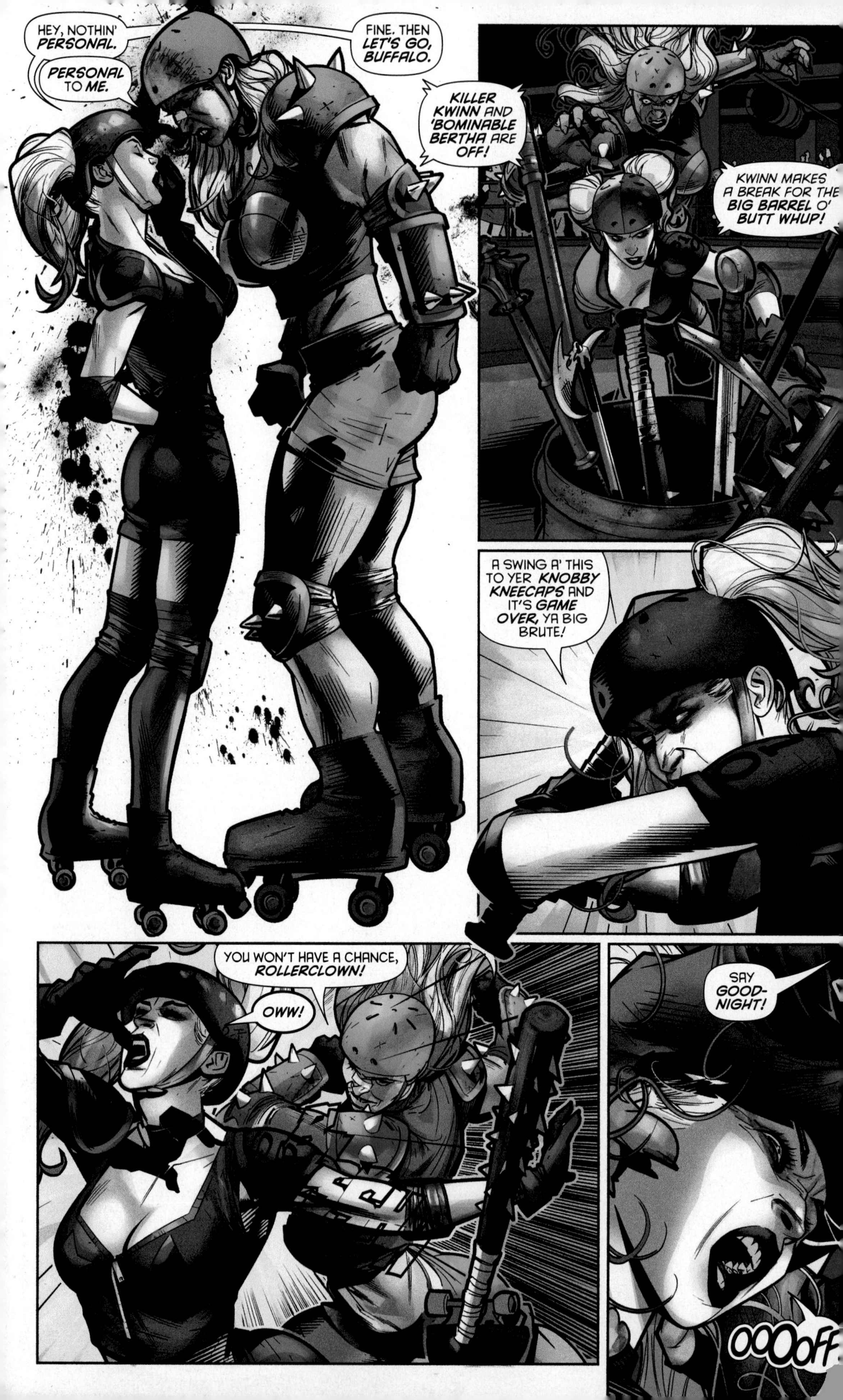
HEY, NOTHIN' PERSONAL.
FINE. THEN LET'S GO, BUFFALO.
PERSONAL TO ME.
KILLER KWINN AND 'BOMINABLE BERTHA ARE OFF!
KWINN MAKES A BREAK FOR THE BIG BARREL O' BUTT WHUP!
A SWING A' THIS TO YER KNOBBY KNEECAPS AND IT'S GAME OVER, YA BIG BRUTE!
YOU WON'T HAVE A CHANCE, ROLLERCLOWN!
OWW!
SAY GOOD-NIGHT!
OOOoFF

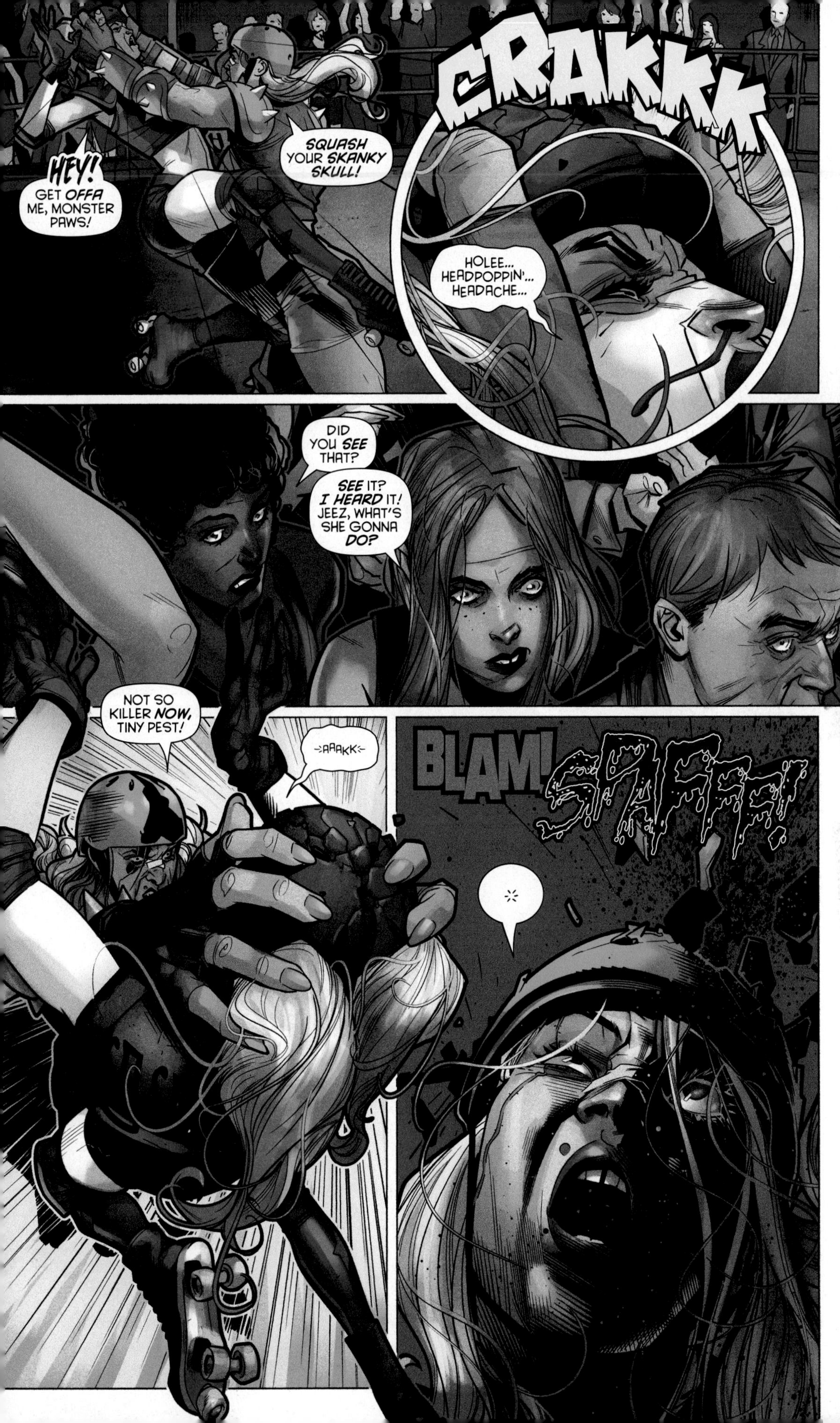
HEY! GET OFFA ME, MONSTER PAWS!
SQUASH YOUR SKANKY SKULL!
CRAKKK
HOLEE... HEADPOPPIN'... HEADACHE...
DID YOU SEE THAT?
SEE IT? I HEARD IT! JEEZ, WHAT'S SHE GONNA DO?
NOT SO KILLER NOW, TINY PEST!
AAAKK
BLAM!
SPAFFF!

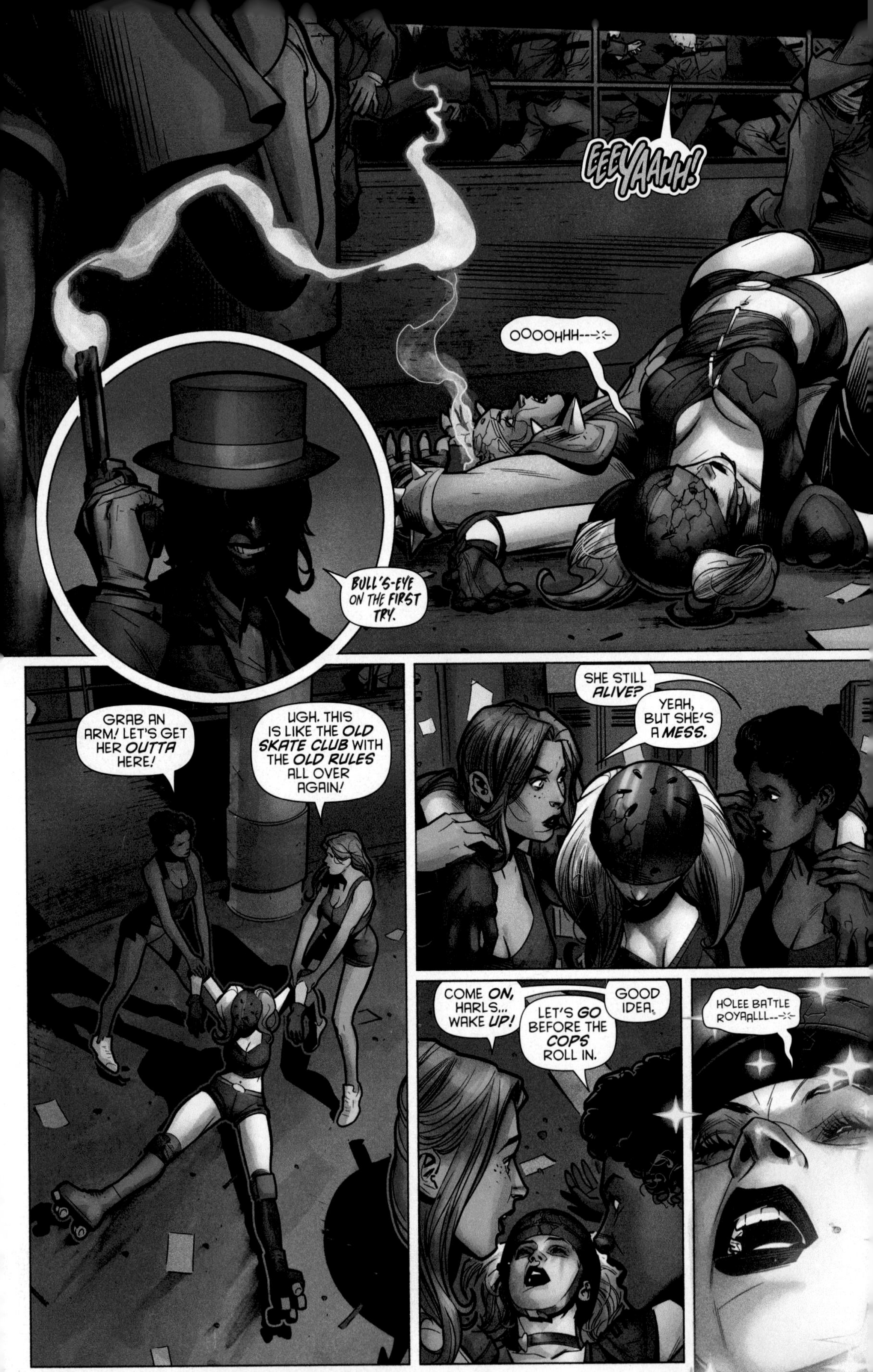

EEEYAAHH!
OOOOHHH---
BULL'S-EYE ON THE FIRST TRY.
GRAB AN ARM! LET'S GET HER OUTTA HERE!
UGH. THIS IS LIKE THE OLD SKATE CLUB WITH THE OLD RULES ALL OVER AGAIN!
SHE STILL ALIVE?
YEAH, BUT SHE'S A MESS.
COME ON, HARLS... WAKE UP!
GOOD IDEA.
LET'S GO BEFORE THE COPS ROLL IN.
HOLEE BATTLE ROYAALLL---

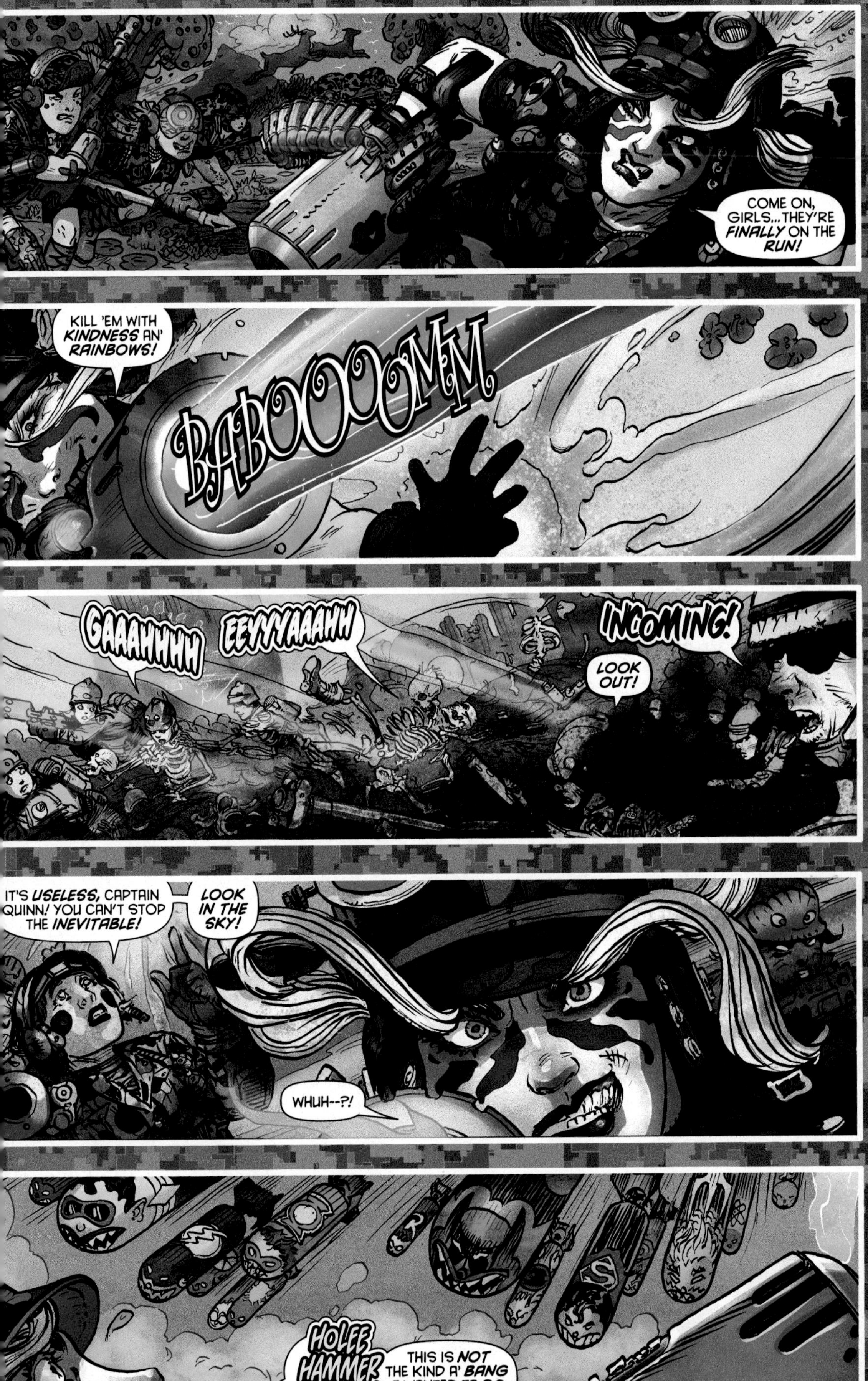

COME ON, GIRLS...THEY'RE *FINALLY* ON THE *RUN!*
KILL 'EM WITH *KINDNESS* AN' *RAINBOWS!*
BABOOOOMM
GAAAHHHH
EEYYYAAAHH
INCOMING!
LOOK OUT!
IT'S *USELESS,* CAPTAIN QUINN! YOU CAN'T STOP THE *INEVITABLE!*
LOOK IN THE SKY!
WHUH--?!
HOLEE HAMMER DOWN!
THIS IS *NOT* THE KIND A' *BANG* I WANTED TA GO *OUT* ON!

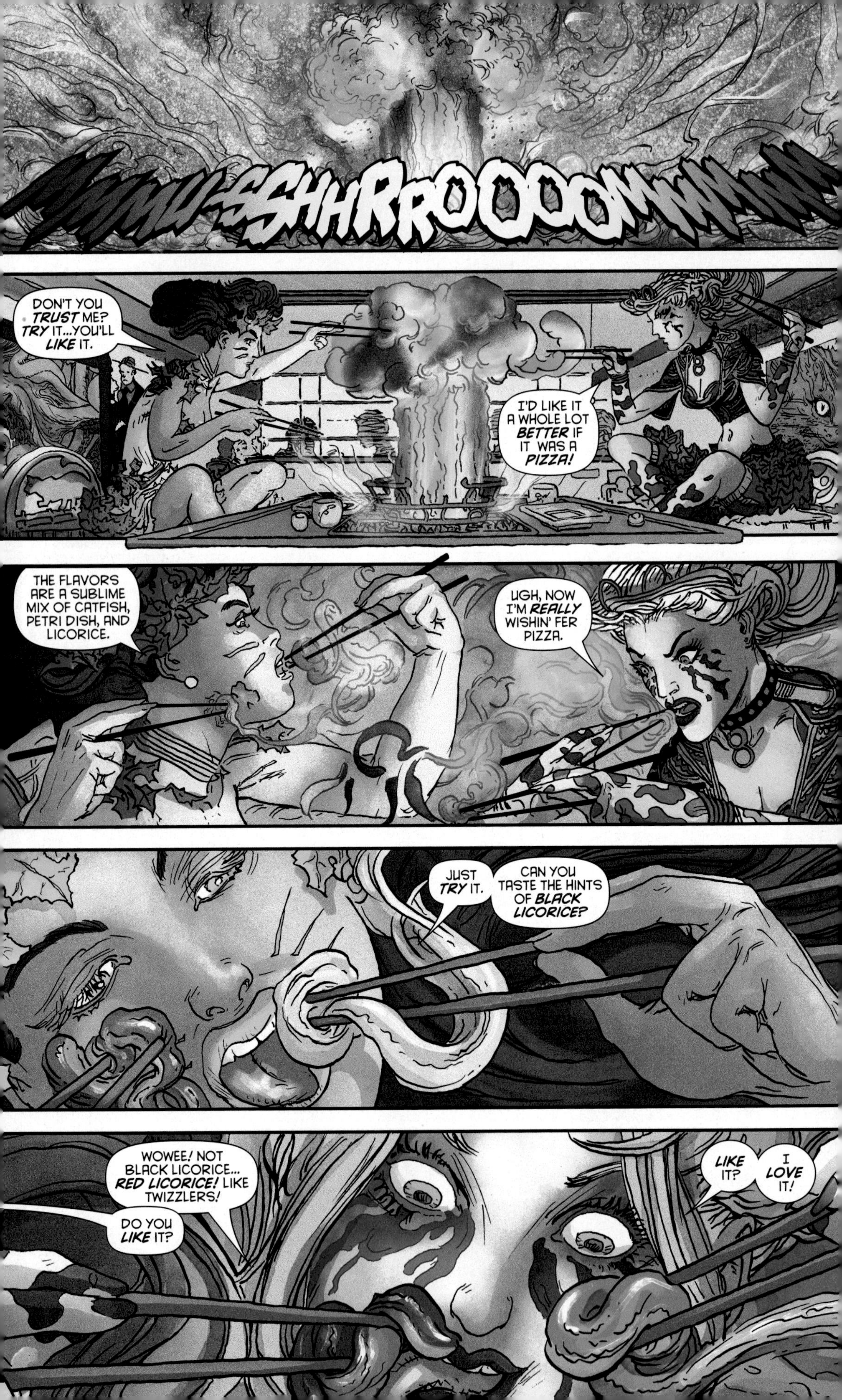
MMMMU-SSHHRROOOOOMMMMM
DON'T YOU TRUST ME? TRY IT...YOU'LL LIKE IT.
I'D LIKE IT A WHOLE LOT BETTER IF IT WAS A PIZZA!
THE FLAVORS ARE A SUBLIME MIX OF CATFISH, PETRI DISH, AND LICORICE.
UGH, NOW I'M REALLY WISHIN' FER PIZZA.
JUST TRY IT.
CAN YOU TASTE THE HINTS OF BLACK LICORICE?
WOWEE! NOT BLACK LICORICE... RED LICORICE! LIKE TWIZZLERS!
DO YOU LIKE IT?
LIKE IT?
I LOVE IT!

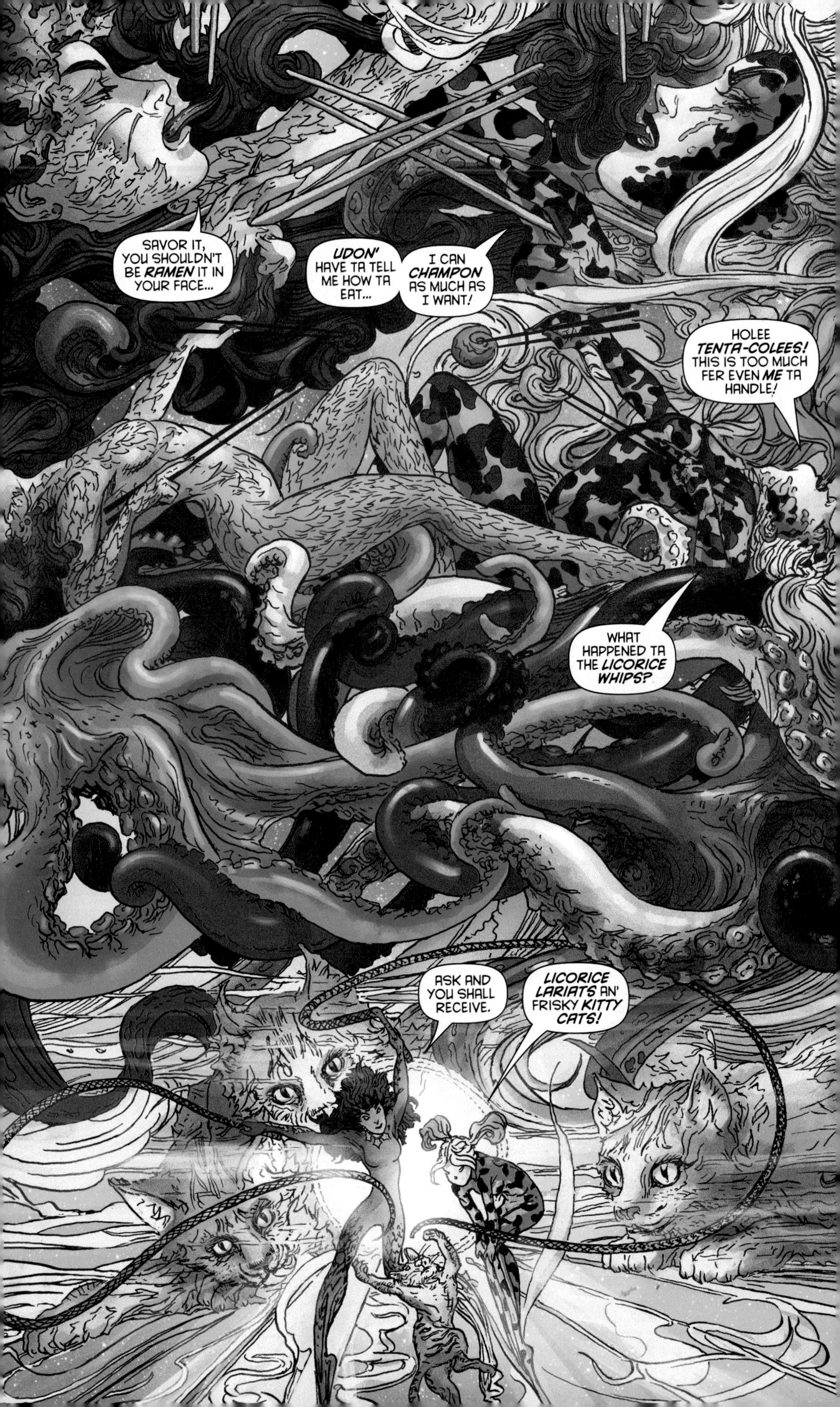
SAVOR IT, YOU SHOULDN'T BE RAMEN IT IN YOUR FACE...
UDON' HAVE TA TELL ME HOW TA EAT...
I CAN CHAMPON AS MUCH AS I WANT!
HOLEE TENTA-COLEES! THIS IS TOO MUCH FER EVEN ME TA HANDLE!
WHAT HAPPENED TA THE LICORICE WHIPS?
ASK AND YOU SHALL RECEIVE.
LICORICE LARIATS AN' FRISKY KITTY CATS!

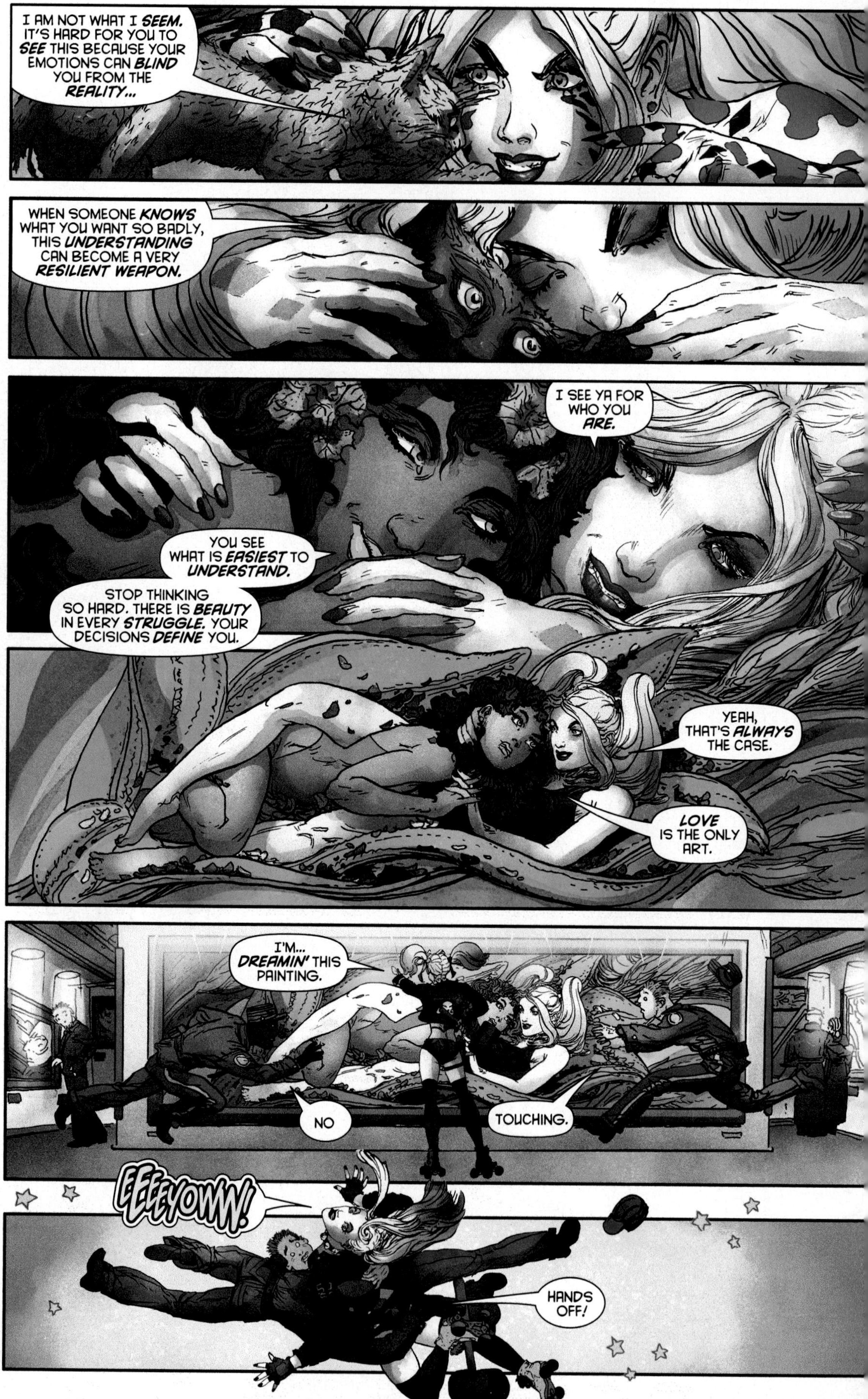
I AM NOT WHAT I SEEM. IT'S HARD FOR YOU TO SEE THIS BECAUSE YOUR EMOTIONS CAN BLIND YOU FROM THE REALITY...
WHEN SOMEONE KNOWS WHAT YOU WANT SO BADLY, THIS UNDERSTANDING CAN BECOME A VERY RESILIENT WEAPON.
I SEE YA FOR WHO YOU ARE.
YOU SEE WHAT IS EASIEST TO UNDERSTAND.
STOP THINKING SO HARD. THERE IS BEAUTY IN EVERY STRUGGLE. YOUR DECISIONS DEFINE YOU.
YEAH, THAT'S ALWAYS THE CASE.
LOVE IS THE ONLY ART.
I'M... DREAMIN' THIS PAINTING.
NO
TOUCHING.
EEEEEYOWW!
HANDS OFF!

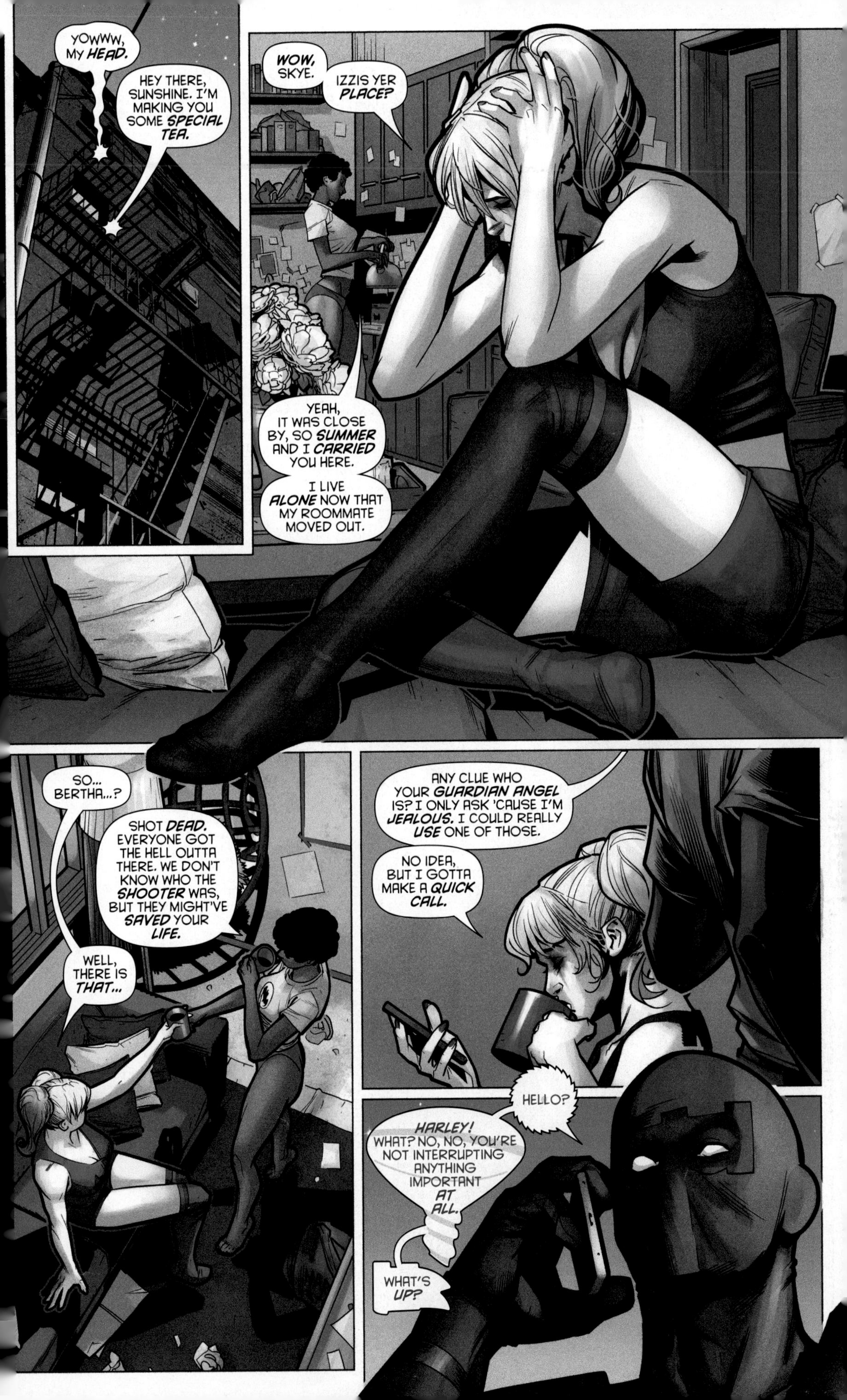
YOWWW, MY HEAD.
HEY THERE, SUNSHINE. I'M MAKING YOU SOME SPECIAL TEA.
WOW, SKYE.
IZZIS YER PLACE?
YEAH, IT WAS CLOSE BY, SO SUMMER AND I CARRIED YOU HERE.
I LIVE ALONE NOW THAT MY ROOMMATE MOVED OUT.
SO... BERTHA...?
SHOT DEAD. EVERYONE GOT THE HELL OUTTA THERE. WE DON'T KNOW WHO THE SHOOTER WAS, BUT THEY MIGHT'VE SAVED YOUR LIFE.
WELL, THERE IS THAT...
ANY CLUE WHO YOUR GUARDIAN ANGEL IS? I ONLY ASK 'CAUSE I'M JEALOUS. I COULD REALLY USE ONE OF THOSE.
NO IDEA, BUT I GOTTA MAKE A QUICK CALL.
HELLO?
HARLEY! WHAT? NO, NO, YOU'RE NOT INTERRUPTING ANYTHING IMPORTANT AT ALL.
WHAT'S UP?

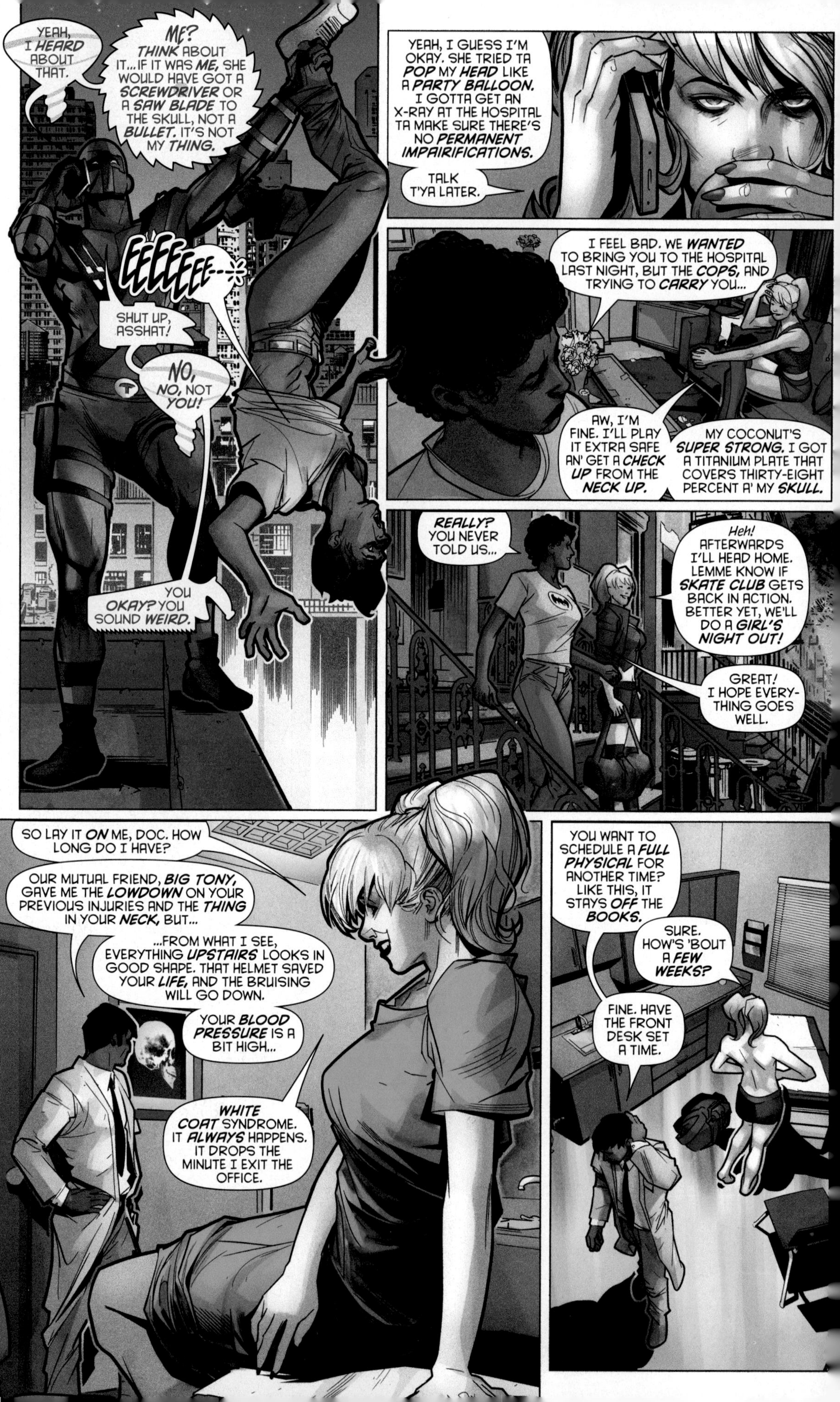

YEAH, I HEARD ABOUT THAT.
ME? THINK ABOUT IT... IF IT WAS ME, SHE WOULD HAVE GOT A SCREWDRIVER OR A SAW BLADE TO THE SKULL, NOT A BULLET. IT'S NOT MY THING.
EEEEEEE--*
SHUT UP, ASSHAT!
NO, NO, NOT YOU!
YOU OKAY? YOU SOUND WEIRD.
YEAH, I GUESS I'M OKAY. SHE TRIED TA POP MY HEAD LIKE A PARTY BALLOON. I GOTTA GET AN X-RAY AT THE HOSPITAL TA MAKE SURE THERE'S NO PERMANENT IMPAIRIFICATIONS.
TALK T'YA LATER.
I FEEL BAD. WE WANTED TO BRING YOU TO THE HOSPITAL LAST NIGHT, BUT THE COPS, AND TRYING TO CARRY YOU...
AW, I'M FINE. I'LL PLAY IT EXTRA SAFE AN' GET A CHECK UP FROM THE NECK UP.
MY COCONUT'S SUPER STRONG. I GOT A TITANIUM PLATE THAT COVERS THIRTY-EIGHT PERCENT A' MY SKULL.
REALLY? YOU NEVER TOLD US...
Heh! AFTERWARDS I'LL HEAD HOME. LEMME KNOW IF SKATE CLUB GETS BACK IN ACTION. BETTER YET, WE'LL DO A GIRL'S NIGHT OUT!
GREAT! I HOPE EVERYTHING GOES WELL.
SO LAY IT ON ME, DOC. HOW LONG DO I HAVE?
OUR MUTUAL FRIEND, BIG TONY, GAVE ME THE LOWDOWN ON YOUR PREVIOUS INJURIES AND THE THING IN YOUR NECK, BUT...
...FROM WHAT I SEE, EVERYTHING UPSTAIRS LOOKS IN GOOD SHAPE. THAT HELMET SAVED YOUR LIFE, AND THE BRUISING WILL GO DOWN.
YOUR BLOOD PRESSURE IS A BIT HIGH...
WHITE COAT SYNDROME. IT ALWAYS HAPPENS. IT DROPS THE MINUTE I EXIT THE OFFICE.
YOU WANT TO SCHEDULE A FULL PHYSICAL FOR ANOTHER TIME? LIKE THIS, IT STAYS OFF THE BOOKS.
SURE. HOW'S 'BOUT A FEW WEEKS?
FINE. HAVE THE FRONT DESK SET A TIME.

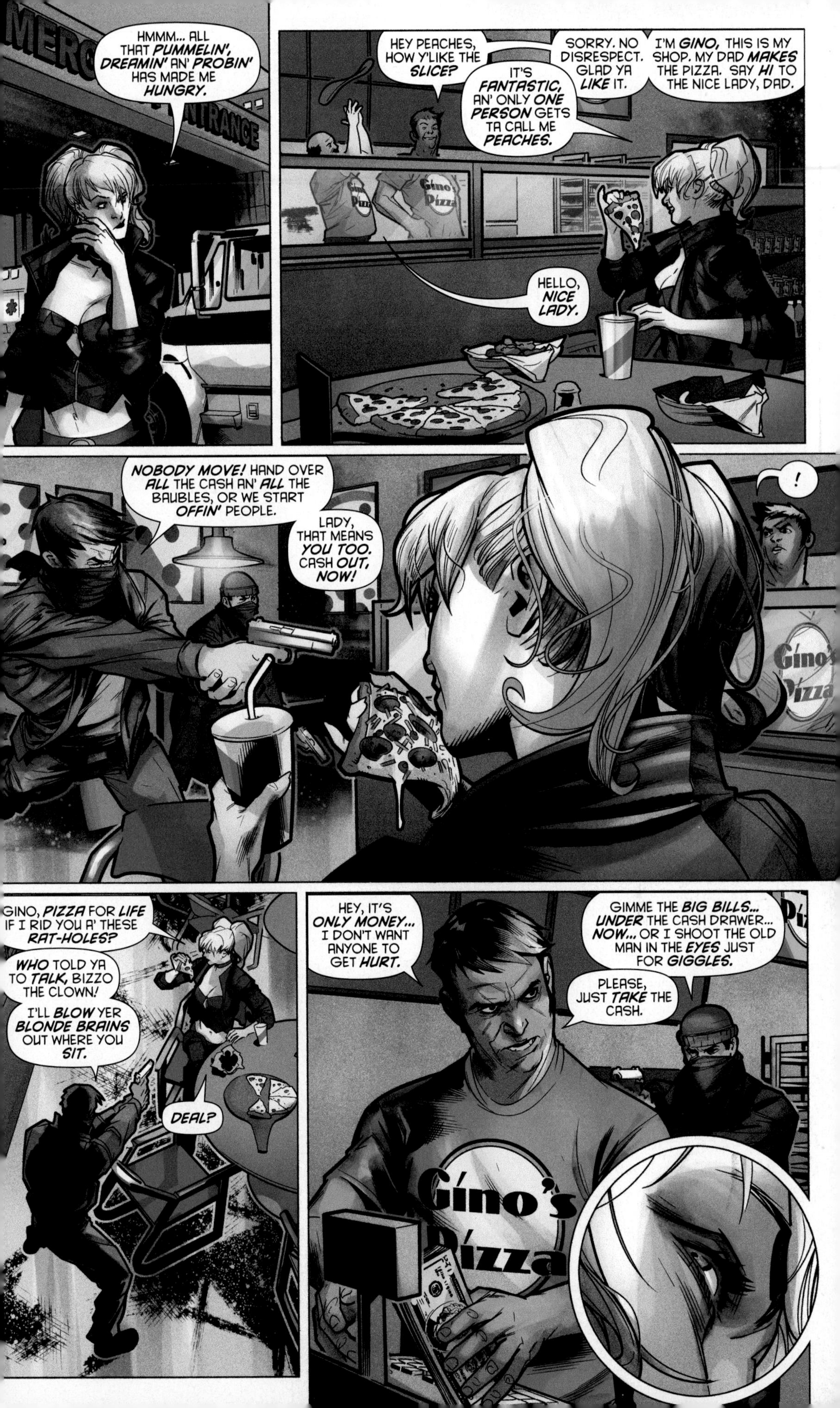

MERC
ENTRANCE
HMMM... ALL THAT PUMMELIN', DREAMIN' AN' PROBIN' HAS MADE ME HUNGRY.
HEY PEACHES, HOW Y'LIKE THE SLICE?
IT'S FANTASTIC, AN' ONLY ONE PERSON GETS TA CALL ME PEACHES.
SORRY. NO DISRESPECT. GLAD YA LIKE IT.
I'M GINO, THIS IS MY SHOP. MY DAD MAKES THE PIZZA. SAY HI TO THE NICE LADY, DAD.
Gino's Pizza
HELLO, NICE LADY.
NOBODY MOVE! HAND OVER ALL THE CASH AN' ALL THE BAUBLES, OR WE START OFFIN' PEOPLE.
LADY, THAT MEANS YOU TOO. CASH OUT, NOW!
!
Gino's Pizza
GINO, PIZZA FOR LIFE IF I RID YOU A' THESE RAT-HOLES?
WHO TOLD YA TO TALK, BIZZO THE CLOWN!
I'LL BLOW YER BLONDE BRAINS OUT WHERE YOU SIT.
DEAL?
HEY, IT'S ONLY MONEY... I DON'T WANT ANYONE TO GET HURT.
GIMME THE BIG BILLS... UNDER THE CASH DRAWER... NOW... OR I SHOOT THE OLD MAN IN THE EYES JUST FOR GIGGLES.
PLEASE, JUST TAKE THE CASH.
Gino's Pizza

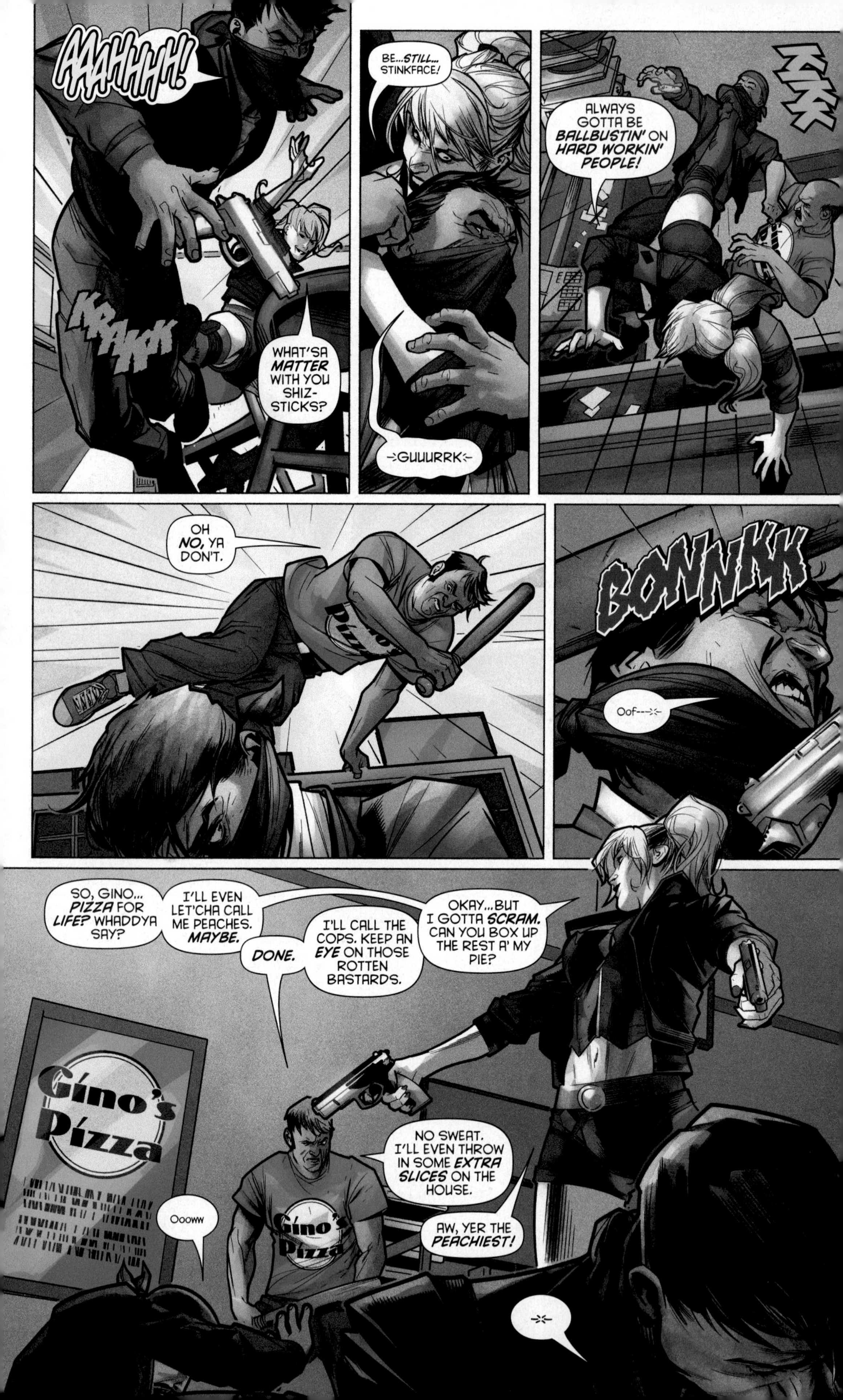
AAAHHHH!
KRAKK
WHAT'SA MATTER WITH YOU SHIZ-STICKS?
BE...STILL... STINKFACE!
GUUURRK
KKK
ALWAYS GOTTA BE BALLBUSTIN' ON HARD WORKIN' PEOPLE!
OH NO, YA DON'T.
BONNKK
Oof--
SO, GINO... PIZZA FOR LIFE? WHADDYA SAY?
I'LL EVEN LET'CHA CALL ME PEACHES. MAYBE.
DONE.
I'LL CALL THE COPS. KEEP AN EYE ON THOSE ROTTEN BASTARDS.
OKAY...BUT I GOTTA SCRAM. CAN YOU BOX UP THE REST A' MY PIE?
Gino's Pizza
NO SWEAT. I'LL EVEN THROW IN SOME EXTRA SLICES ON THE HOUSE.
Oooww
AW, YER THE PEACHIEST!

JEEZ LOWEEZ, WHATTA' FREAKIN' FORTY-EIGHT HOURS.

DIZZYIN' DREAMS, A ROLLER DERBY RUMP WHUPPIN', A NASTY NOGGIN FLOGGIN', AN' ALL DAMN DAY AT THE DOCTOR'S.

AM I THE PATHETIC-EST PERSON ON THE PLANET, OR WHAT?

WOW... I GUESS NOT.

SO...WHAT'S YER STORY, SKIPPER?

HUH?

HOW DIDJA WIND UP HERE... LIKE THIS?

AFTER MY WIFE DIED, I NEVER WENT BACK HOME. I JUST CAN'T...

SO, D'YA HAVE A HOME?

SHE WAS MY HOME. I'M JUST WAITING TO JOIN HER.

Awww...

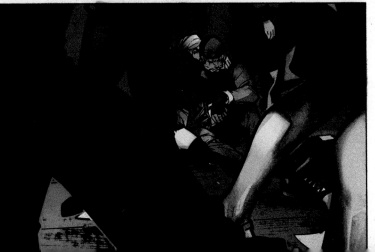

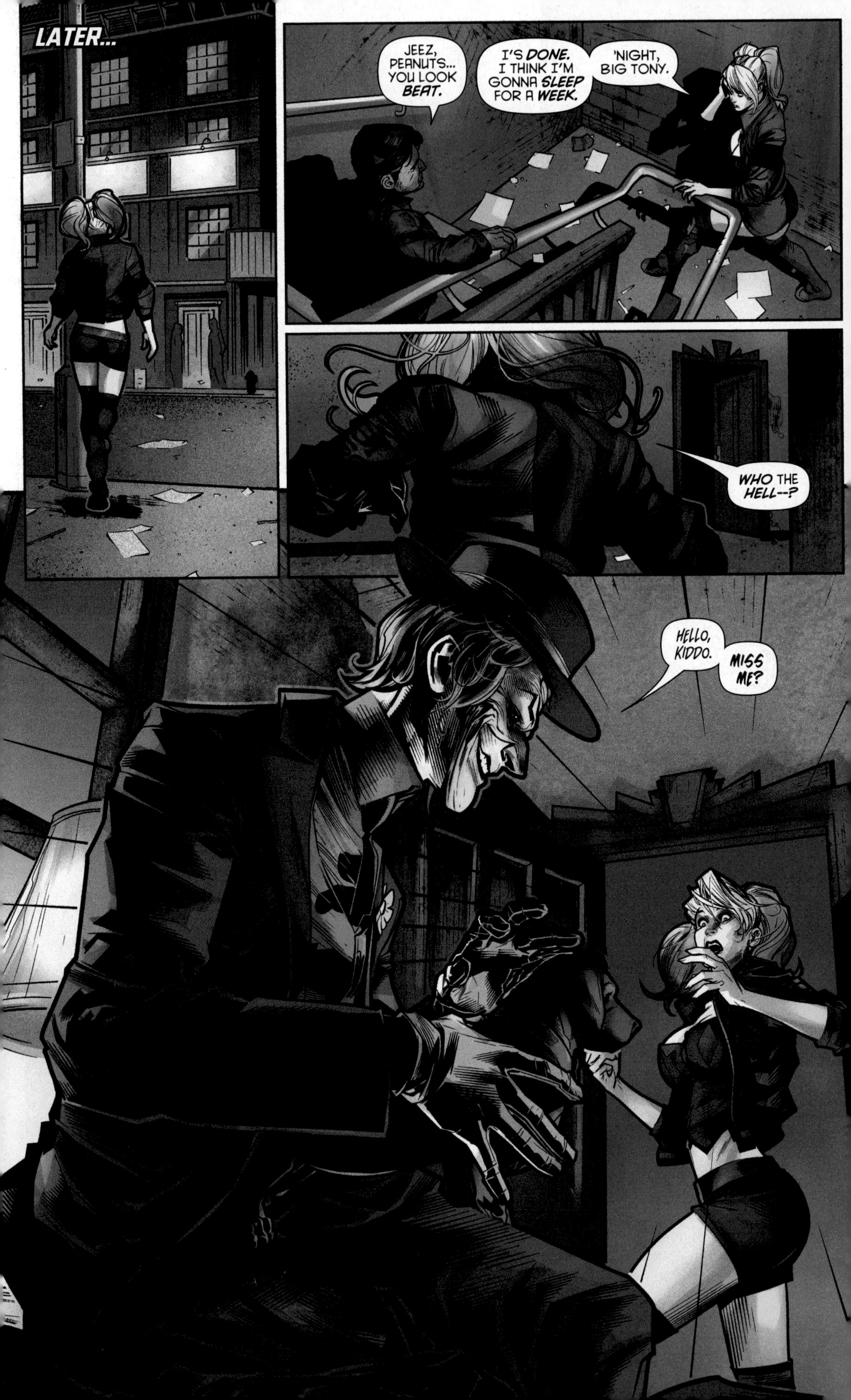
LATER...
JEEZ, PEANUTS... YOU LOOK BEAT.
I'S DONE. I THINK I'M GONNA SLEEP FOR A WEEK.
'NIGHT, BIG TONY.
WHO THE HELL--?
HELLO, KIDDO.
MISS ME?

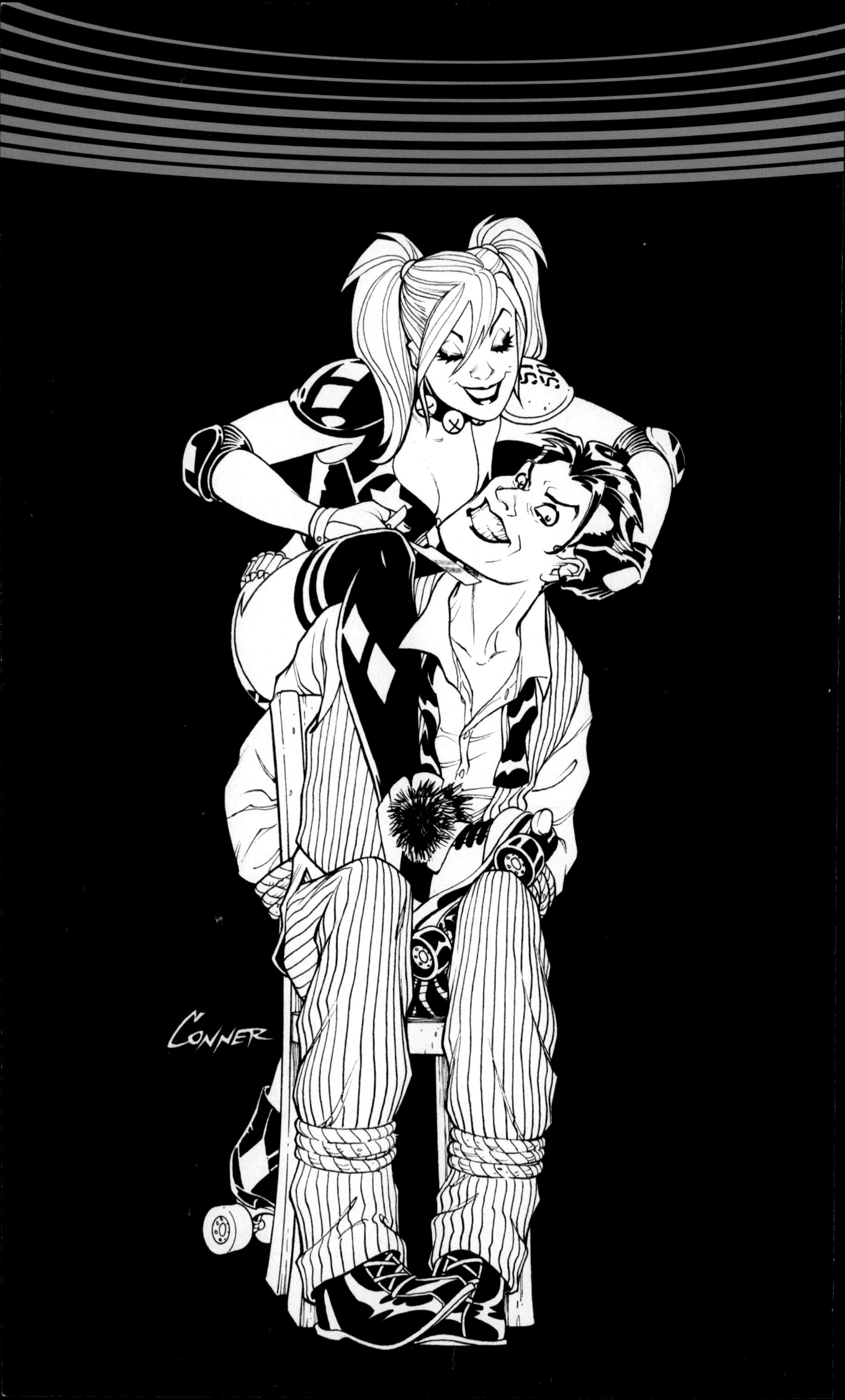
CONNER

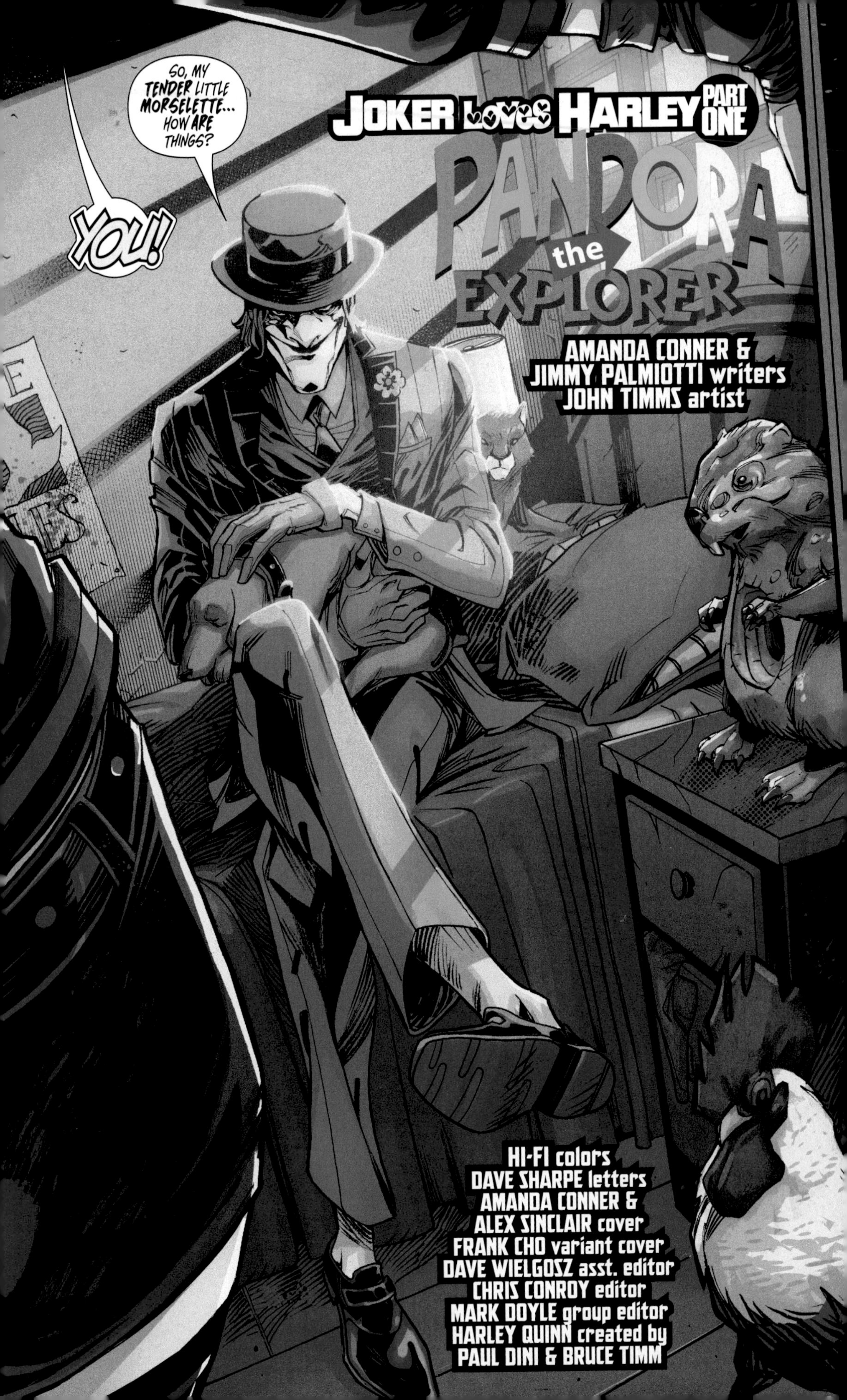
YOU!
SO, MY TENDER LITTLE MORSELETTE... HOW ARE THINGS?
JOKER LOVES HARLEY PART ONE
PANDORA the EXPLORER
AMANDA CONNER & JIMMY PALMIOTTI writers
JOHN TIMMS artist
HI-FI colors
DAVE SHARPE letters
AMANDA CONNER & ALEX SINCLAIR cover
FRANK CHO variant cover
DAVE WIELGOSZ asst. editor
CHRIS CONROY editor
MARK DOYLE group editor
HARLEY QUINN created by PAUL DINI & BRUCE TIMM

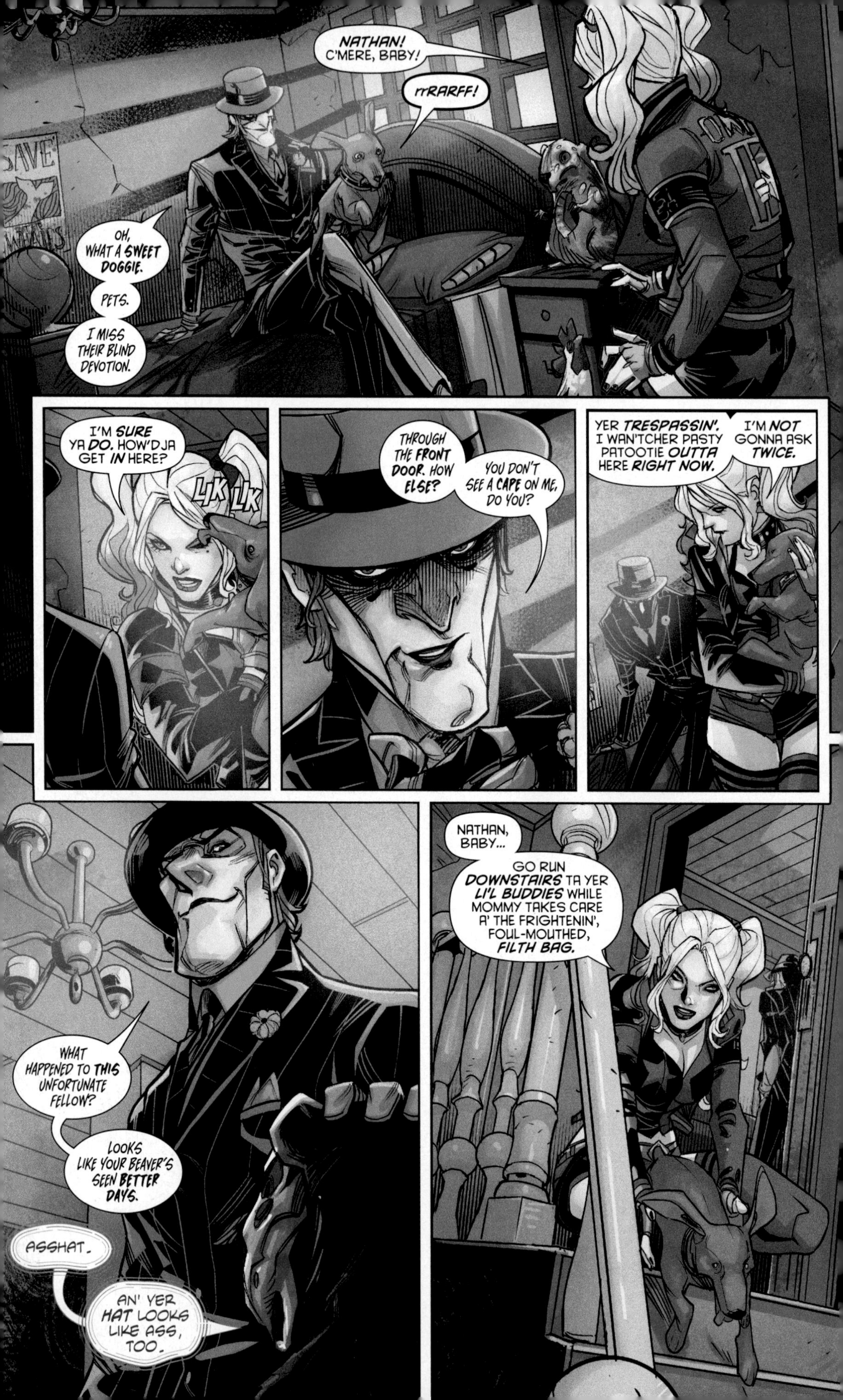

NATHAN! C'MERE, BABY!
rrRARFF!
OH, WHAT A SWEET DOGGIE.
PETS.
I MISS THEIR BLIND DEVOTION.
I'M SURE YA DO. HOW'DJA GET IN HERE?
LIK LK
THROUGH THE FRONT DOOR. HOW ELSE?
YOU DON'T SEE A CAPE ON ME, DO YOU?
YER TRESPASSIN'. I WAN'TCHER PASTY PATOOTIE OUTTA HERE RIGHT NOW.
I'M NOT GONNA ASK TWICE.
WHAT HAPPENED TO THIS UNFORTUNATE FELLOW?
LOOKS LIKE YOUR BEAVER'S SEEN BETTER DAYS.
ASSHAT.
AN' YER HAT LOOKS LIKE ASS, TOO.
NATHAN, BABY...
GO RUN DOWNSTAIRS TA YER LI'L BUDDIES WHILE MOMMY TAKES CARE A' THE FRIGHTENIN', FOUL-MOUTHED, FILTH BAG.

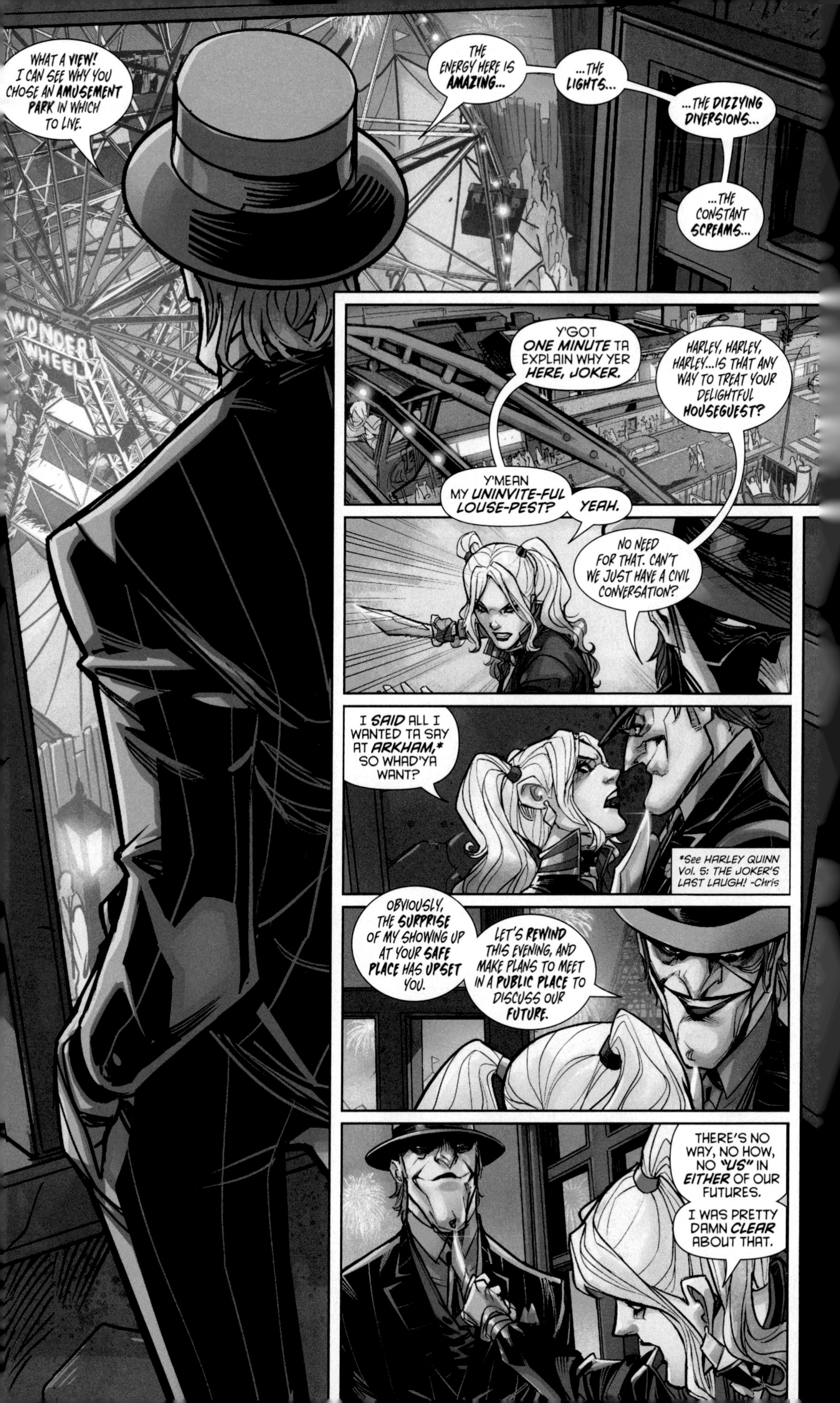
WHAT A VIEW! I CAN SEE WHY YOU CHOSE AN AMUSEMENT PARK IN WHICH TO LIVE.
THE ENERGY HERE IS AMAZING...
...THE LIGHTS...
...THE DIZZYING DIVERSIONS...
...THE CONSTANT SCREAMS...
WONDER WHEEL
Y'GOT ONE MINUTE TA EXPLAIN WHY YER HERE, JOKER.
HARLEY, HARLEY, HARLEY...IS THAT ANY WAY TO TREAT YOUR DELIGHTFUL HOUSEGUEST?
Y'MEAN MY UNINVITE-FUL LOUSE-PEST?
YEAH.
NO NEED FOR THAT. CAN'T WE JUST HAVE A CIVIL CONVERSATION?
I SAID ALL I WANTED TA SAY AT ARKHAM,* SO WHAD'YA WANT?
*See HARLEY QUINN Vol. 5: THE JOKER'S LAST LAUGH! -Chris
OBVIOUSLY, THE SURPRISE OF MY SHOWING UP AT YOUR SAFE PLACE HAS UPSET YOU.
LET'S REWIND THIS EVENING, AND MAKE PLANS TO MEET IN A PUBLIC PLACE TO DISCUSS OUR FUTURE.
THERE'S NO WAY, NO HOW, NO "US" IN EITHER OF OUR FUTURES.
I WAS PRETTY DAMN CLEAR ABOUT THAT.

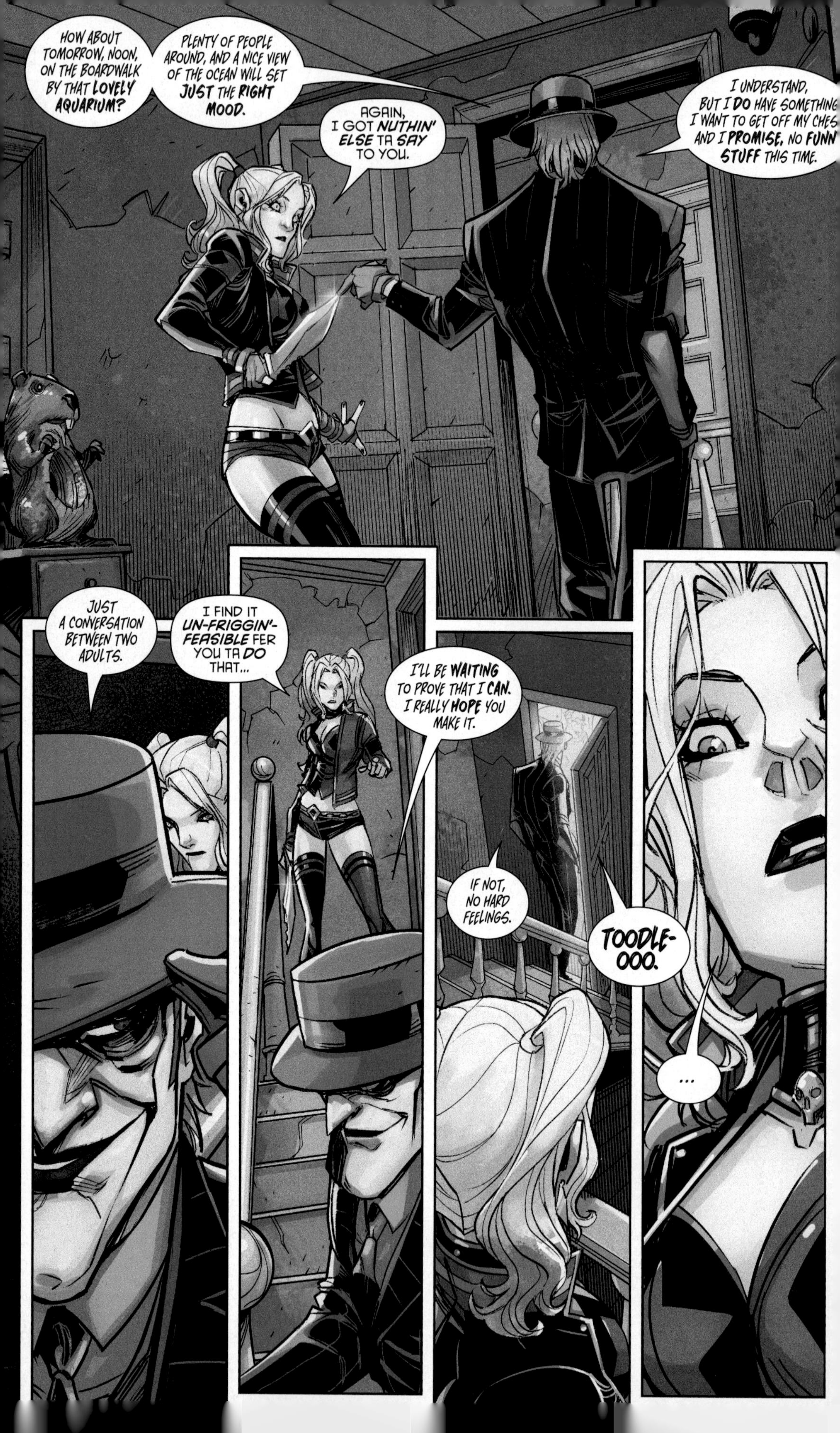

HOW ABOUT TOMORROW, NOON, ON THE BOARDWALK BY THAT LOVELY AQUARIUM?
PLENTY OF PEOPLE AROUND, AND A NICE VIEW OF THE OCEAN WILL SET JUST THE RIGHT MOOD.
AGAIN, I GOT NUTHIN' ELSE TA SAY TO YOU.
I UNDERSTAND, BUT I DO HAVE SOMETHING I WANT TO GET OFF MY CHES AND I PROMISE, NO FUNN STUFF THIS TIME.
JUST A CONVERSATION BETWEEN TWO ADULTS.
I FIND IT UN-FRIGGIN'-FEASIBLE FER YOU TA DO THAT...
I'LL BE WAITING TO PROVE THAT I CAN. I REALLY HOPE YOU MAKE IT.
IF NOT, NO HARD FEELINGS.
TOODLE-OOO.
...

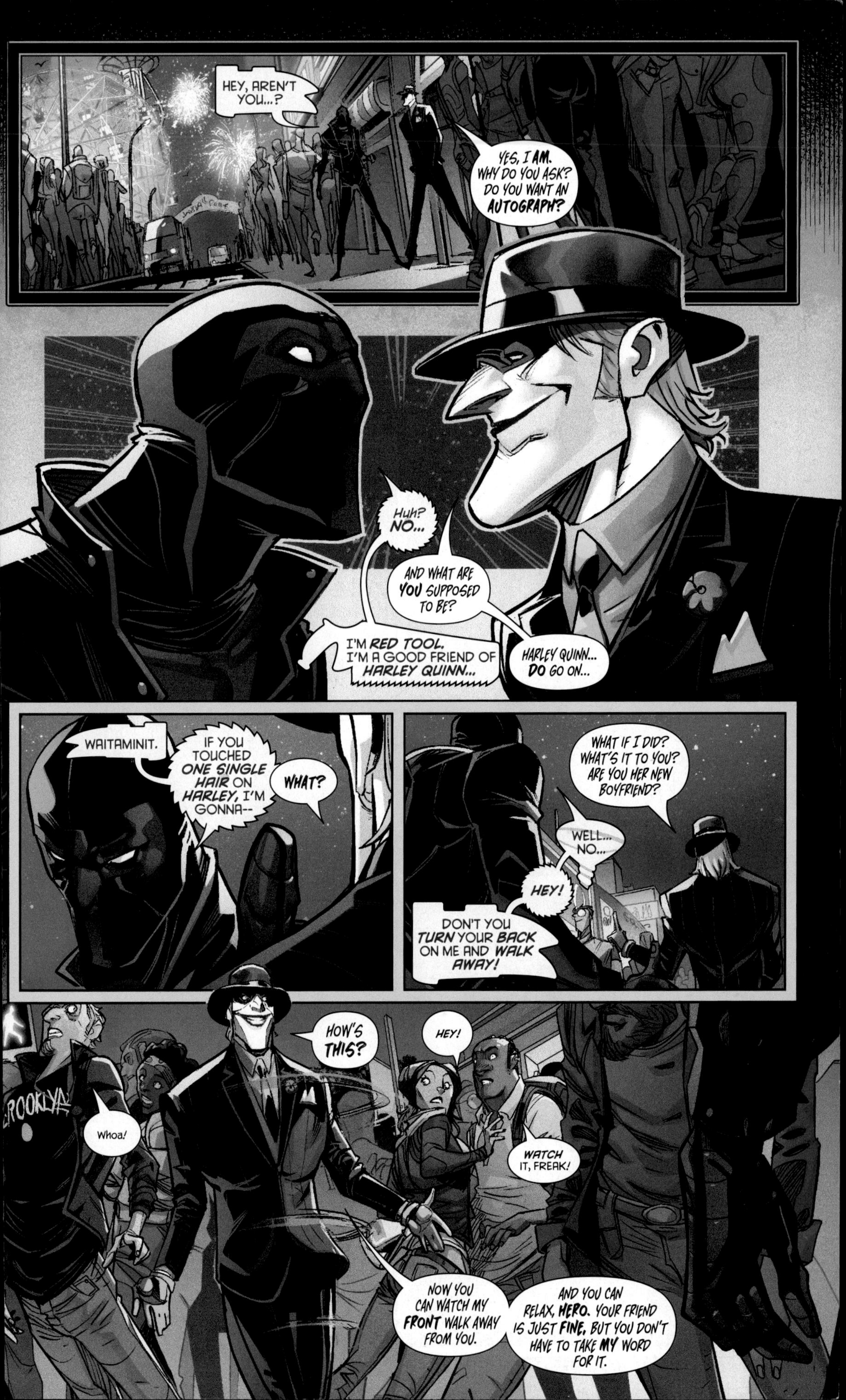
HEY, AREN'T YOU...?
YES, I AM. WHY DO YOU ASK? DO YOU WANT AN AUTOGRAPH?
Huh? NO...
AND WHAT ARE YOU SUPPOSED TO BE?
I'M RED TOOL. I'M A GOOD FRIEND OF HARLEY QUINN...
HARLEY QUINN... DO GO ON...
WAITAMINIT.
IF YOU TOUCHED ONE SINGLE HAIR ON HARLEY, I'M GONNA--
WHAT?
WHAT IF I DID? WHAT'S IT TO YOU? ARE YOU HER NEW BOYFRIEND?
WELL... NO...
HEY!
DON'T YOU TURN YOUR BACK ON ME AND WALK AWAY!
HOW'S THIS?
HEY!
Whoa!
WATCH IT, FREAK!
NOW YOU CAN WATCH MY FRONT WALK AWAY FROM YOU.
AND YOU CAN RELAX, HERO. YOUR FRIEND IS JUST FINE, BUT YOU DON'T HAVE TO TAKE MY WORD FOR IT.

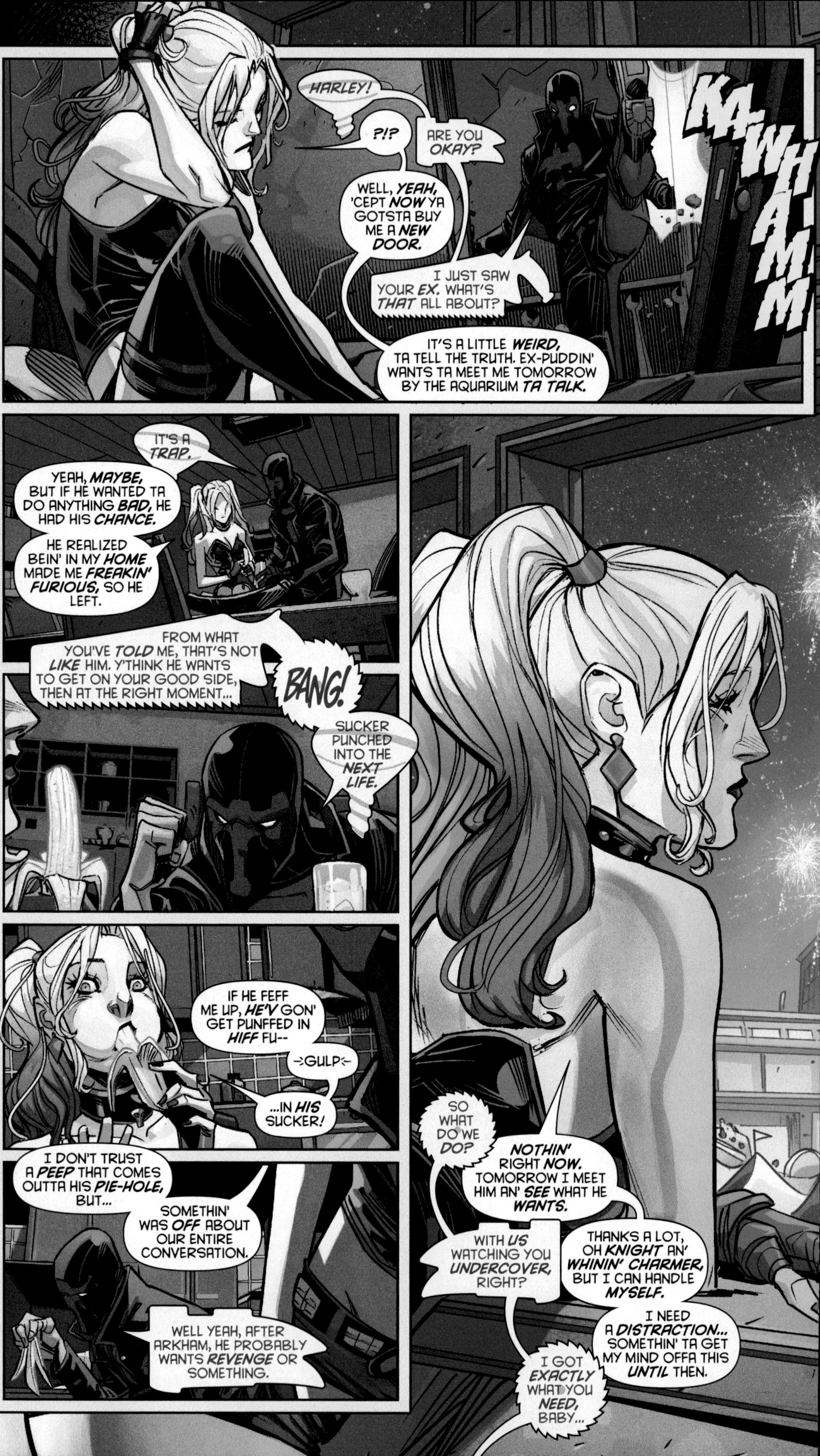
HARLEY!
?!?
ARE YOU OKAY?
WELL, YEAH, 'CEPT NOW YA GOTSTA BUY ME A NEW DOOR.
KA-WHAMM
I JUST SAW YOUR EX. WHAT'S THAT ALL ABOUT?
IT'S A LITTLE WEIRD, TA TELL THE TRUTH. EX-PUDDIN' WANTS TA MEET ME TOMORROW BY THE AQUARIUM TA TALK.
IT'S A TRAP.
YEAH, MAYBE, BUT IF HE WANTED TA DO ANYTHING BAD, HE HAD HIS CHANCE.
HE REALIZED BEIN' IN MY HOME MADE ME FREAKIN' FURIOUS, SO HE LEFT.
FROM WHAT YOU'VE TOLD ME, THAT'S NOT LIKE HIM. Y'THINK HE WANTS TO GET ON YOUR GOOD SIDE, THEN AT THE RIGHT MOMENT...
BANG!
SUCKER PUNCHED INTO THE NEXT LIFE.
IF HE FEFF ME UP, HE'V GON' GET PUNFFED IN HIFF FU--
-GULP-
...IN HIS SUCKER!
I DON'T TRUST A PEEP THAT COMES OUTTA HIS PIE-HOLE, BUT...
SOMETHIN' WAS OFF ABOUT OUR ENTIRE CONVERSATION.
WELL YEAH, AFTER ARKHAM, HE PROBABLY WANTS REVENGE OR SOMETHING.
SO WHAT DO WE DO?
NOTHIN' RIGHT NOW. TOMORROW I MEET HIM AN' SEE WHAT HE WANTS.
WITH US WATCHING YOU UNDERCOVER, RIGHT?
THANKS A LOT, OH KNIGHT AN' WHININ' CHARMER, BUT I CAN HANDLE MYSELF.
I NEED A DISTRACTION... SOMETHIN' TA GET MY MIND OFFA THIS UNTIL THEN.
I GOT EXACTLY WHAT YOU NEED, BABY...

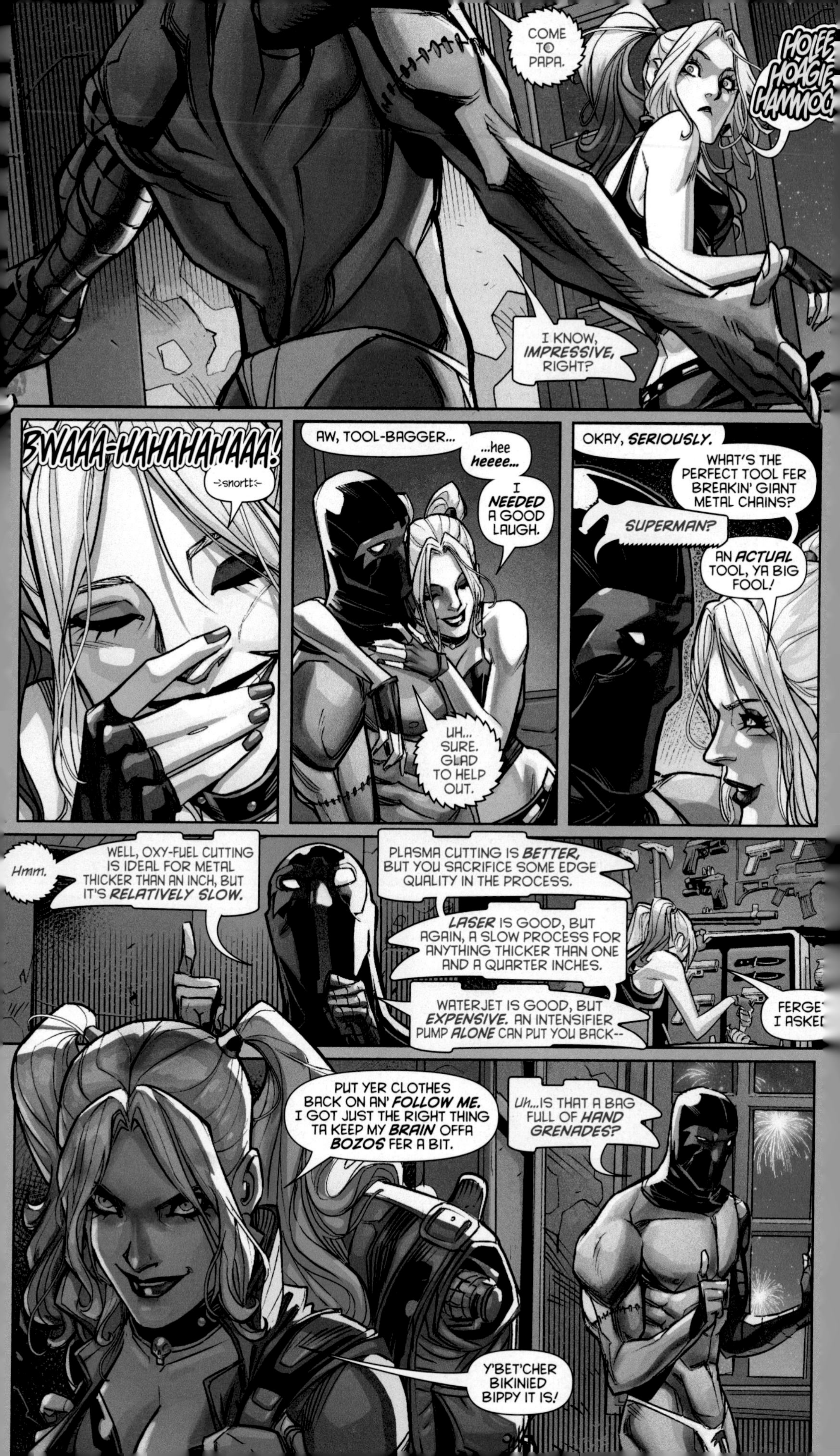
COME TO PAPA.
HOLEE HOAGIE HAMMOC
I KNOW, IMPRESSIVE, RIGHT?
BWAAA-HAHAHAHAAA!
snortt
AW, TOOL-BAGGER...
...hee heeee...
I NEEDED A GOOD LAUGH.
UH... SURE. GLAD TO HELP OUT.
OKAY, SERIOUSLY.
WHAT'S THE PERFECT TOOL FER BREAKIN' GIANT METAL CHAINS?
SUPERMAN?
AN ACTUAL TOOL, YA BIG FOOL!
Hmm.
WELL, OXY-FUEL CUTTING IS IDEAL FOR METAL THICKER THAN AN INCH, BUT IT'S RELATIVELY SLOW.
PLASMA CUTTING IS BETTER, BUT YOU SACRIFICE SOME EDGE QUALITY IN THE PROCESS.
LASER IS GOOD, BUT AGAIN, A SLOW PROCESS FOR ANYTHING THICKER THAN ONE AND A QUARTER INCHES.
WATERJET IS GOOD, BUT EXPENSIVE. AN INTENSIFIER PUMP ALONE CAN PUT YOU BACK--
FERGE I ASKED
PUT YER CLOTHES BACK ON AN' FOLLOW ME. I GOT JUST THE RIGHT THING TA KEEP MY BRAIN OFFA BOZOS FER A BIT.
Uh...IS THAT A BAG FULL OF HAND GRENADES?
Y'BET'CHER BIKINIED BIPPY IT IS!

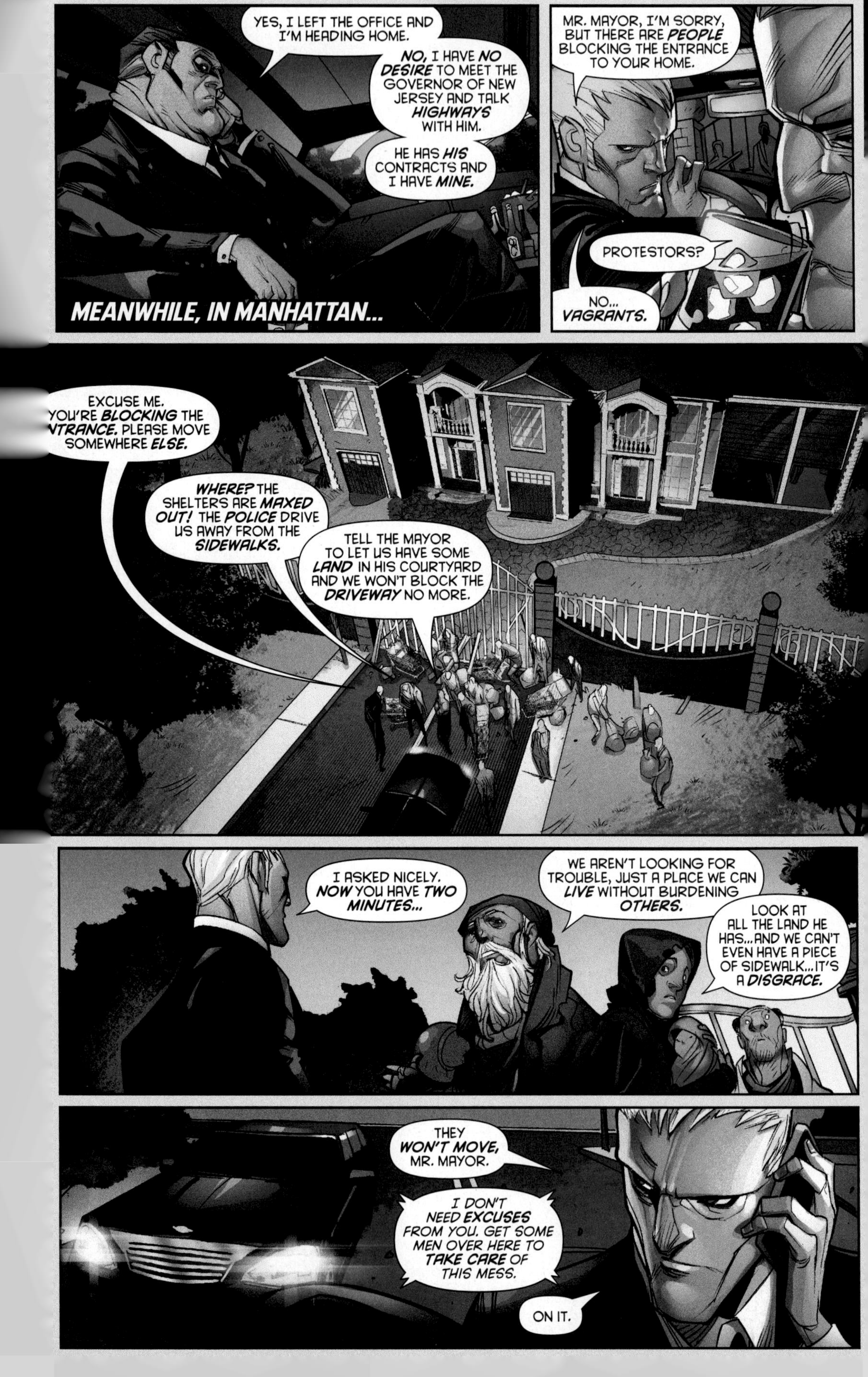
YES, I LEFT THE OFFICE AND I'M HEADING HOME.
NO, I HAVE NO DESIRE TO MEET THE GOVERNOR OF NEW JERSEY AND TALK HIGHWAYS WITH HIM.
HE HAS HIS CONTRACTS AND I HAVE MINE.
MEANWHILE, IN MANHATTAN...
MR. MAYOR, I'M SORRY, BUT THERE ARE PEOPLE BLOCKING THE ENTRANCE TO YOUR HOME.
PROTESTORS?
NO... VAGRANTS.
EXCUSE ME. YOU'RE BLOCKING THE NTRANCE. PLEASE MOVE SOMEWHERE ELSE.
WHERE? THE SHELTERS ARE MAXED OUT! THE POLICE DRIVE US AWAY FROM THE SIDEWALKS.
TELL THE MAYOR TO LET US HAVE SOME LAND IN HIS COURTYARD AND WE WON'T BLOCK THE DRIVEWAY NO MORE.
I ASKED NICELY. NOW YOU HAVE TWO MINUTES...
WE AREN'T LOOKING FOR TROUBLE, JUST A PLACE WE CAN LIVE WITHOUT BURDENING OTHERS.
LOOK AT ALL THE LAND HE HAS...AND WE CAN'T EVEN HAVE A PIECE OF SIDEWALK...IT'S A DISGRACE.
THEY WON'T MOVE, MR. MAYOR.
I DON'T NEED EXCUSES FROM YOU. GET SOME MEN OVER HERE TO TAKE CARE OF THIS MESS.
ON IT.

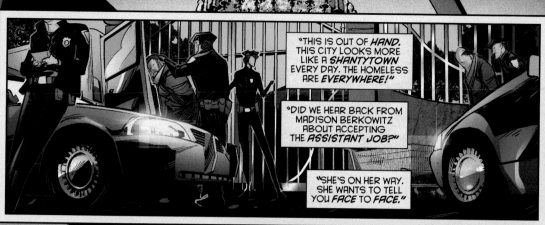

"THIS IS OUT OF *HAND*. THIS CITY LOOKS MORE LIKE A *SHANTYTOWN* EVERY DAY. THE HOMELESS ARE *EVERYWHERE!*"

"DID WE HEAR BACK FROM MADISON BERKOWITZ ABOUT ACCEPTING THE *ASSISTANT JOB?*"

"SHE'S ON HER WAY. SHE WANTS TO TELL YOU *FACE* TO *FACE*."

MAYOR DePERTO, I HOPE I'M NOT INTERRUPTING.

MADISON... WHAT AN *UNEXPECTED SURPRISE*. PLEASE... COME *IN*.

MAY I GET YOU A BEVERAGE?

WATER, PLEASE. ICE. I WANT TO TELL YOU IN PERSON THAT I *ACCEPT* THE JOB AS YOUR NEW ASSISTANT, BUT THERE ARE SOME *DETAILS*. I WANT US TO BE ON THE *SAME PAGE* FROM THE START.

GO ON.

I *GREW UP* IN THIS CITY. THE *MIDWOOD* SECTION OF BROOKLYN. I REMEMBER WHAT A *WAR ZONE* IT USED TO BE, AND I'LL DO *ANYTHING POSSIBLE* TO CLEAN IT UP.

I *WANT* THIS JOB BECAUSE IT'LL GIVE ME THE POWER AND INFLUENCE TO ACTUALLY MAKE A *DIFFERENCE*.

I *KNOW* WHY YOU PICKED ME, SIR. IT'S BECAUSE I CAN LOOK THE *OTHER WAY* TO GET THINGS DONE. MY REPUTATION IS BUILT ON CONFIDENCE AND EFFECTIVENESS.

MAY I BE *FRANK?*

MORE THAN YOU'RE *ALREADY* BEING? SURE, WHY NOT.

YOU HAVE A CHIEF OF POLICE WHO'S *OUT* OF *CONTROL*, ENLISTING CHARACTERS LIKE *HARLEY QUINN* TO DO HIS DIRTY WORK.

IT'S BEEN PRETTY EFFECTIVE *SO FAR*, BUT YOU AND I *BOTH KNOW* IT'S HEADED FOR *DISASTER*.

I PROPOSE WE TAKE *ADVANTAGE* OF THIS, AND MAKE SOME BIG MOVES THAT'LL *GUARANTEE* YOU RE-ELECTION.

WHAT *BIG MOVES* ARE YOU *TALKING ABOUT?*

WELL, THE *FIRST* IS TO TAKE CARE OF THE *HOMELESS* ISSUE HERE IN THE CITY. I HAVE A *PLAN* IN MIND THAT CAN GET RID OF THIS PROBLEM *ONCE* AND *FOR ALL*.

THIS I GOTTA HEAR. GO ON.

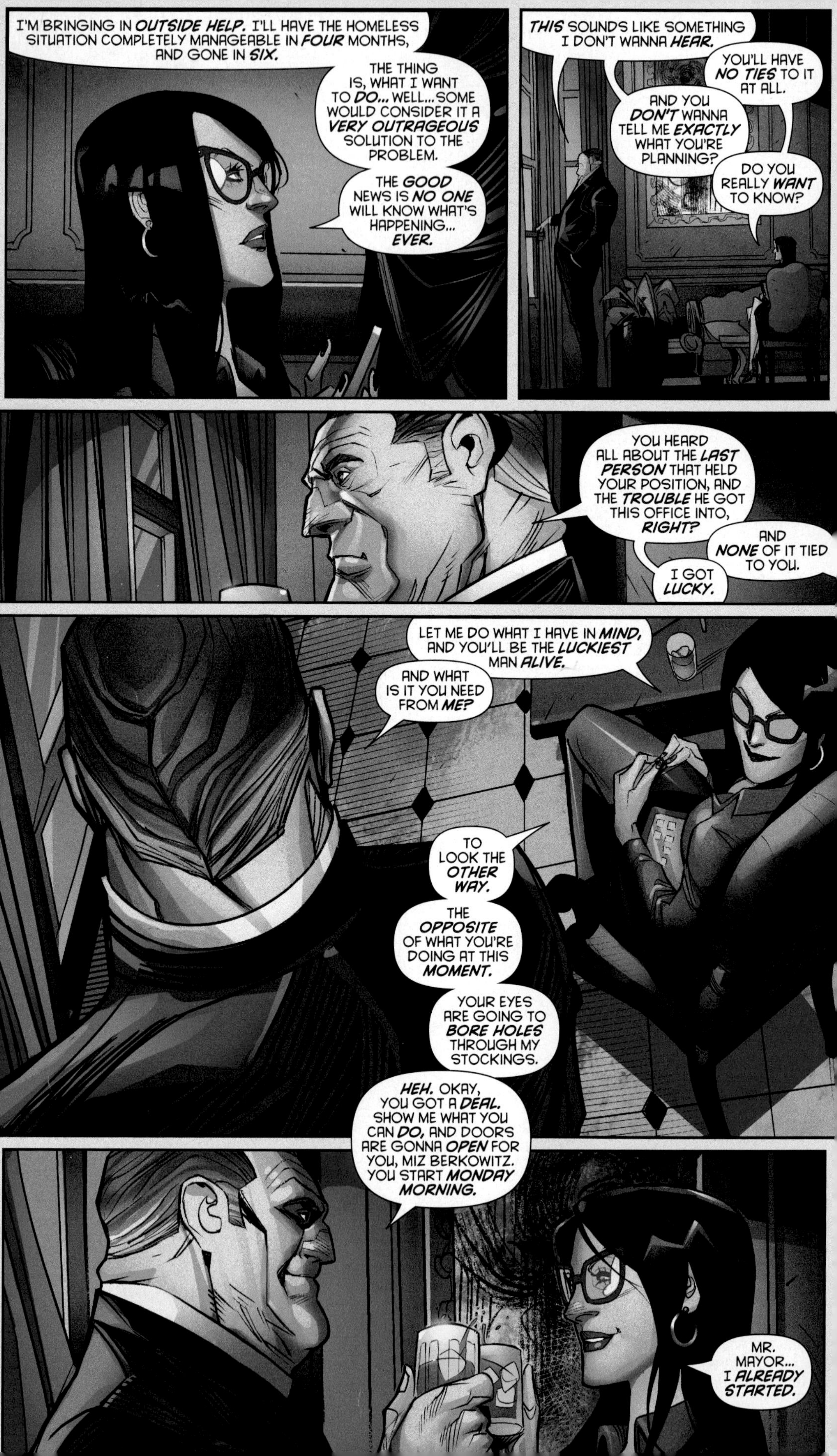
I'M BRINGING IN OUTSIDE HELP. I'LL HAVE THE HOMELESS SITUATION COMPLETELY MANAGEABLE IN FOUR MONTHS, AND GONE IN SIX.
THE THING IS, WHAT I WANT TO DO... WELL... SOME WOULD CONSIDER IT A VERY OUTRAGEOUS SOLUTION TO THE PROBLEM.
THE GOOD NEWS IS NO ONE WILL KNOW WHAT'S HAPPENING... EVER.
THIS SOUNDS LIKE SOMETHING I DON'T WANNA HEAR.
YOU'LL HAVE NO TIES TO IT AT ALL.
AND YOU DON'T WANNA TELL ME EXACTLY WHAT YOU'RE PLANNING?
DO YOU REALLY WANT TO KNOW?
YOU HEARD ALL ABOUT THE LAST PERSON THAT HELD YOUR POSITION, AND THE TROUBLE HE GOT THIS OFFICE INTO, RIGHT?
I GOT LUCKY.
AND NONE OF IT TIED TO YOU.
LET ME DO WHAT I HAVE IN MIND, AND YOU'LL BE THE LUCKIEST MAN ALIVE.
AND WHAT IS IT YOU NEED FROM ME?
TO LOOK THE OTHER WAY.
THE OPPOSITE OF WHAT YOU'RE DOING AT THIS MOMENT.
YOUR EYES ARE GOING TO BORE HOLES THROUGH MY STOCKINGS.
HEH. OKAY, YOU GOT A DEAL. SHOW ME WHAT YOU CAN DO, AND DOORS ARE GONNA OPEN FOR YOU, MIZ BERKOWITZ. YOU START MONDAY MORNING.
MR. MAYOR... I ALREADY STARTED.

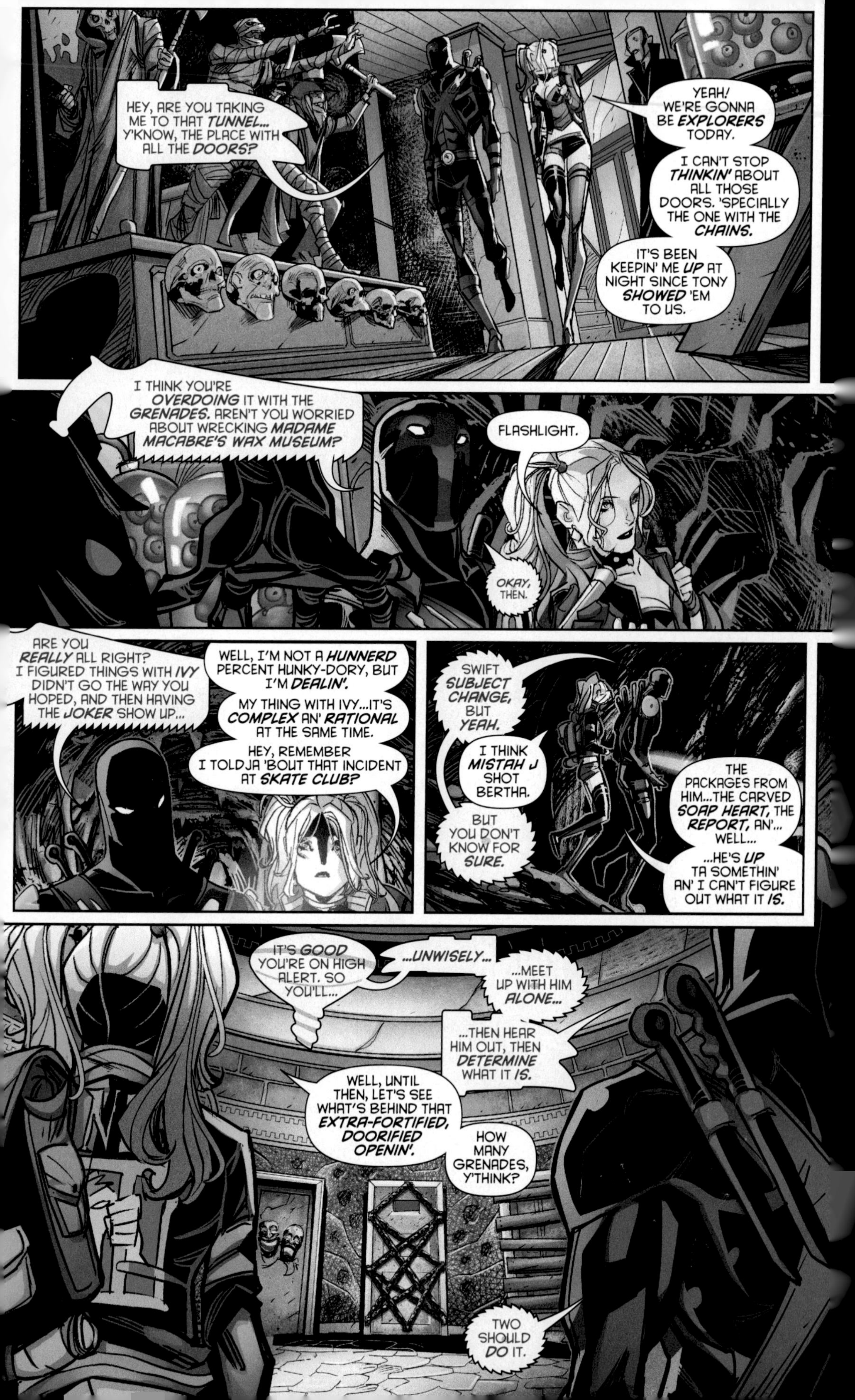

HEY, ARE YOU TAKING ME TO THAT TUNNEL... Y'KNOW, THE PLACE WITH ALL THE DOORS?
YEAH! WE'RE GONNA BE EXPLORERS TODAY.
I CAN'T STOP THINKIN' ABOUT ALL THOSE DOORS. 'SPECIALLY THE ONE WITH THE CHAINS.
IT'S BEEN KEEPIN' ME UP AT NIGHT SINCE TONY SHOWED 'EM TO US.
I THINK YOU'RE OVERDOING IT WITH THE GRENADES. AREN'T YOU WORRIED ABOUT WRECKING MADAME MACABRE'S WAX MUSEUM?
FLASHLIGHT.
OKAY, THEN.
ARE YOU REALLY ALL RIGHT? I FIGURED THINGS WITH IVY DIDN'T GO THE WAY YOU HOPED, AND THEN HAVING THE JOKER SHOW UP...
WELL, I'M NOT A HUNNERD PERCENT HUNKY-DORY, BUT I'M DEALIN'.
MY THING WITH IVY...IT'S COMPLEX AN' RATIONAL AT THE SAME TIME.
HEY, REMEMBER I TOLDJA 'BOUT THAT INCIDENT AT SKATE CLUB?
SWIFT SUBJECT CHANGE, BUT YEAH.
I THINK MISTAH J SHOT BERTHA.
BUT YOU DON'T KNOW FOR SURE.
THE PACKAGES FROM HIM...THE CARVED SOAP HEART, THE REPORT, AN'... WELL...
...HE'S UP TA SOMETHIN' AN' I CAN'T FIGURE OUT WHAT IT IS.
IT'S GOOD YOU'RE ON HIGH ALERT. SO YOU'LL...
...UNWISELY...
...MEET UP WITH HIM ALONE...
...THEN HEAR HIM OUT, THEN DETERMINE WHAT IT IS.
WELL, UNTIL THEN, LET'S SEE WHAT'S BEHIND THAT EXTRA-FORTIFIED, DOORIFIED OPENIN'.
HOW MANY GRENADES, Y'THINK?
TWO SHOULD DO IT.

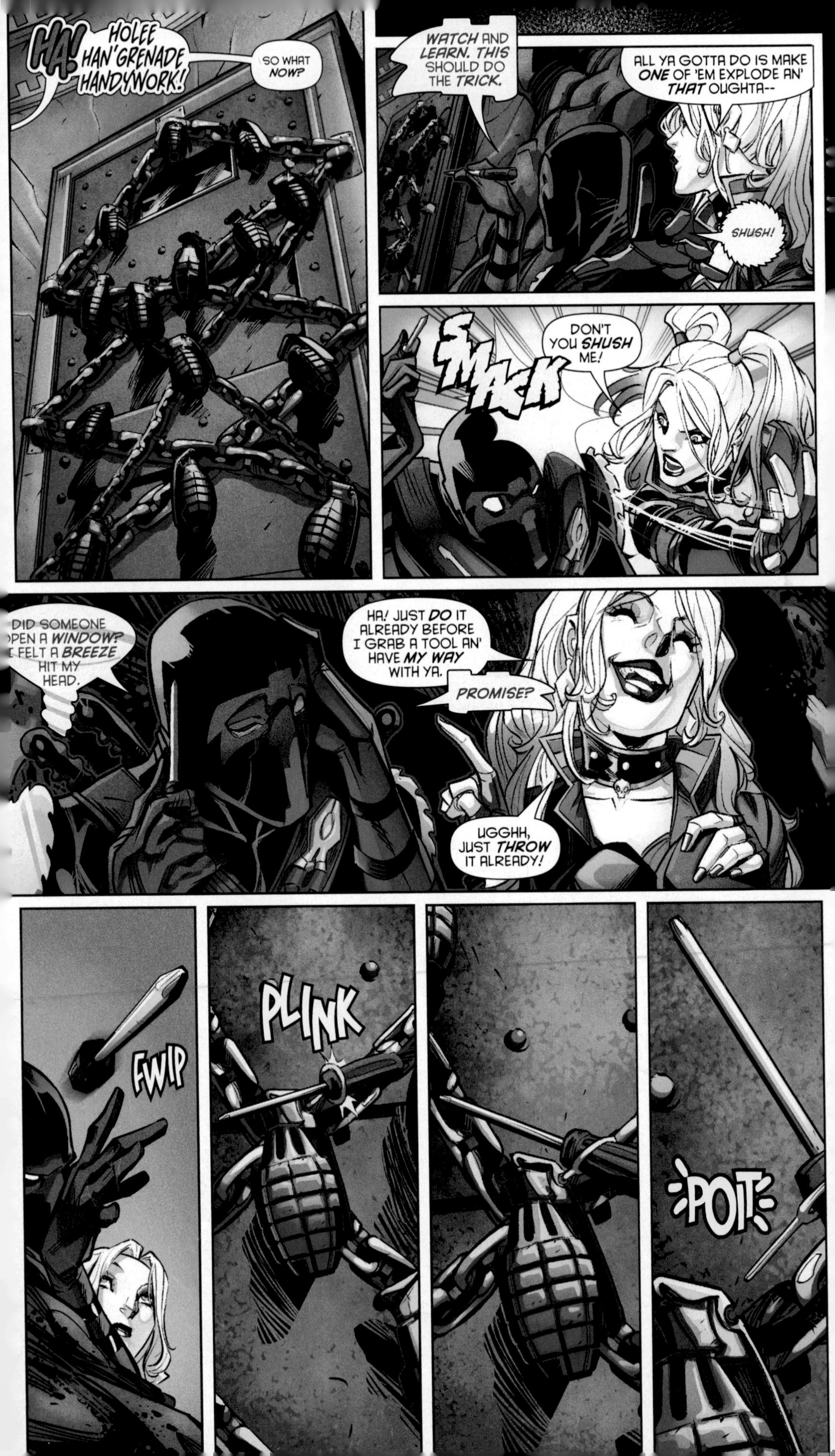

HA!
HOLEE HAN'GRENADE HANDYWORK!
SO WHAT NOW?
WATCH AND LEARN. THIS SHOULD DO THE TRICK.
ALL YA GOTTA DO IS MAKE ONE OF 'EM EXPLODE AN' THAT OUGHTA--
SHUSH!
SMACK
DON'T YOU SHUSH ME!
DID SOMEONE OPEN A WINDOW? I FELT A BREEZE HIT MY HEAD.
HA! JUST DO IT ALREADY BEFORE I GRAB A TOOL AN' HAVE MY WAY WITH YA.
PROMISE?
UGGHH, JUST THROW IT ALREADY!
FWIP
PLINK
POIT

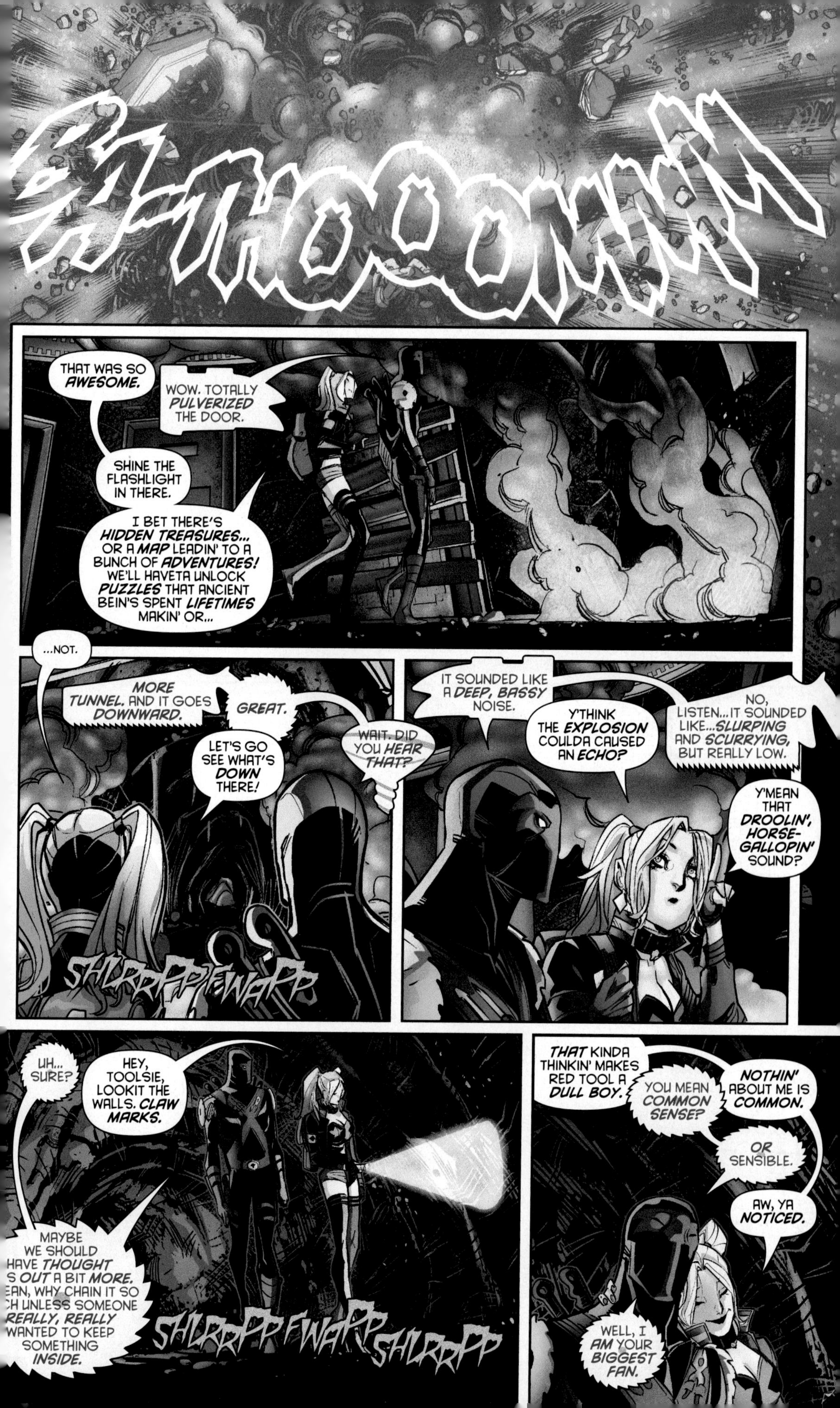

KA-THOOOMM
THAT WAS SO AWESOME.
WOW. TOTALLY PULVERIZED THE DOOR.
SHINE THE FLASHLIGHT IN THERE.
I BET THERE'S HIDDEN TREASURES... OR A MAP LEADIN' TO A BUNCH OF ADVENTURES! WE'LL HAVETA UNLOCK PUZZLES THAT ANCIENT BEIN'S SPENT LIFETIMES MAKIN' OR...
...NOT.
MORE TUNNEL. AND IT GOES DOWNWARD.
GREAT.
LET'S GO SEE WHAT'S DOWN THERE!
WAIT. DID YOU HEAR THAT?
SHLRRPP FWAPP
IT SOUNDED LIKE A DEEP, BASSY NOISE.
Y'THINK THE EXPLOSION COULDA CAUSED AN ECHO?
NO, LISTEN...IT SOUNDED LIKE...SLURPING AND SCURRYING, BUT REALLY LOW.
Y'MEAN THAT DROOLIN', HORSE-GALLOPIN' SOUND?
UH... SURE?
HEY, TOOLSIE, LOOKIT THE WALLS. CLAW MARKS.
MAYBE WE SHOULD HAVE THOUGHT S OUT A BIT MORE. EAN, WHY CHAIN IT SO CH UNLESS SOMEONE REALLY, REALLY WANTED TO KEEP SOMETHING INSIDE.
SHLRRPP FWAPP SHLRRPP
THAT KINDA THINKIN' MAKES RED TOOL A DULL BOY.
YOU MEAN COMMON SENSE?
NOTHIN' ABOUT ME IS COMMON.
OR SENSIBLE.
AW, YA NOTICED.
WELL, I AM YOUR BIGGEST FAN.

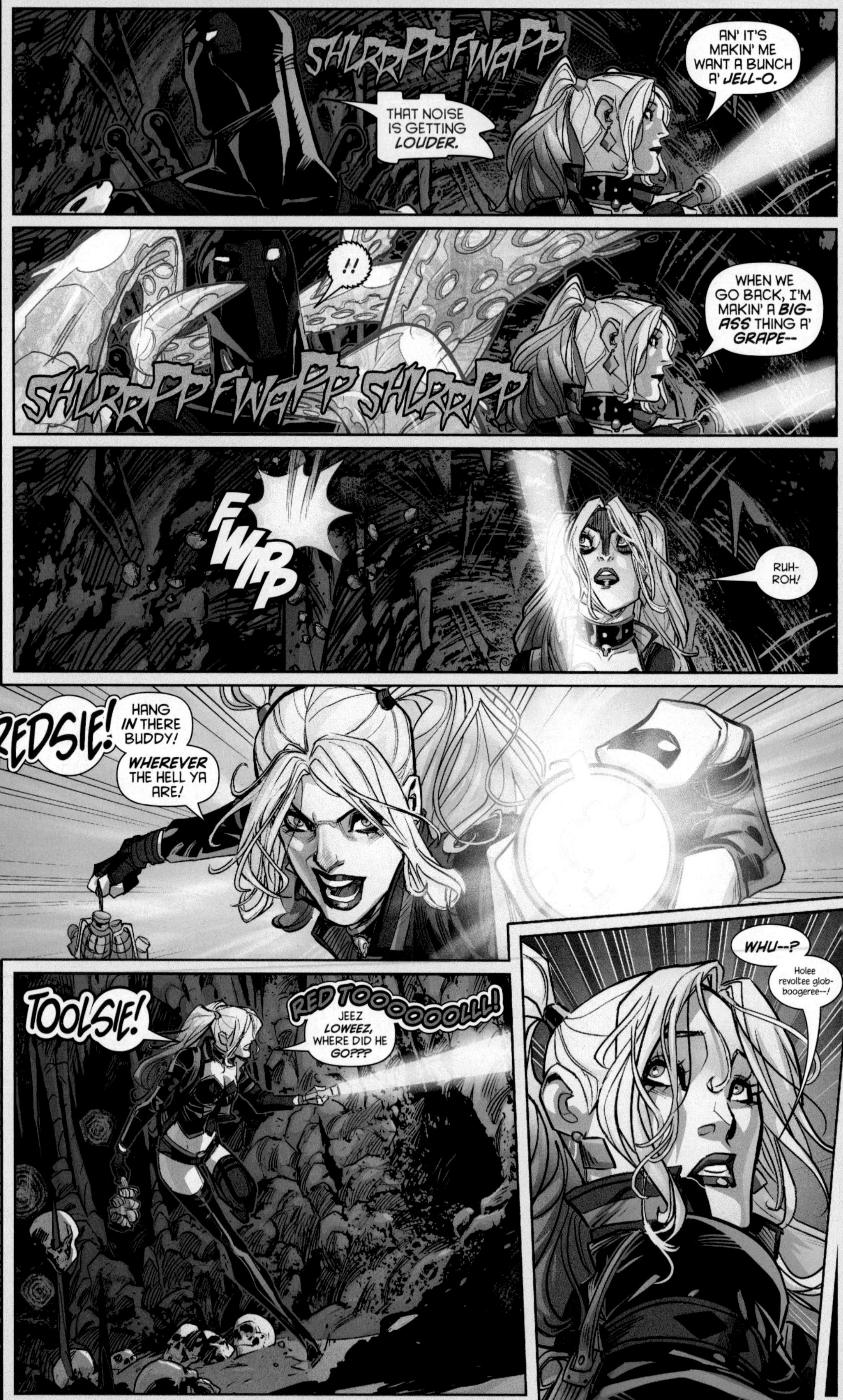
SHLRRPP FWAPP
AN' IT'S MAKIN' ME WANT A BUNCH A' JELL-O.
THAT NOISE IS GETTING LOUDER.
!!
WHEN WE GO BACK, I'M MAKIN' A BIG-ASS THING A' GRAPE--
SHLRRPP FWAPP SHLRRPP
FWIPP
RUH-ROH!
REDSIE!
HANG IN THERE BUDDY!
WHEREVER THE HELL YA ARE!
TOOLSIE!
RED TOOOOOOOOLLL!
JEEZ LOWEEZ, WHERE DID HE GO???
WHU--?
Holee revoltee glob-boogeree--!

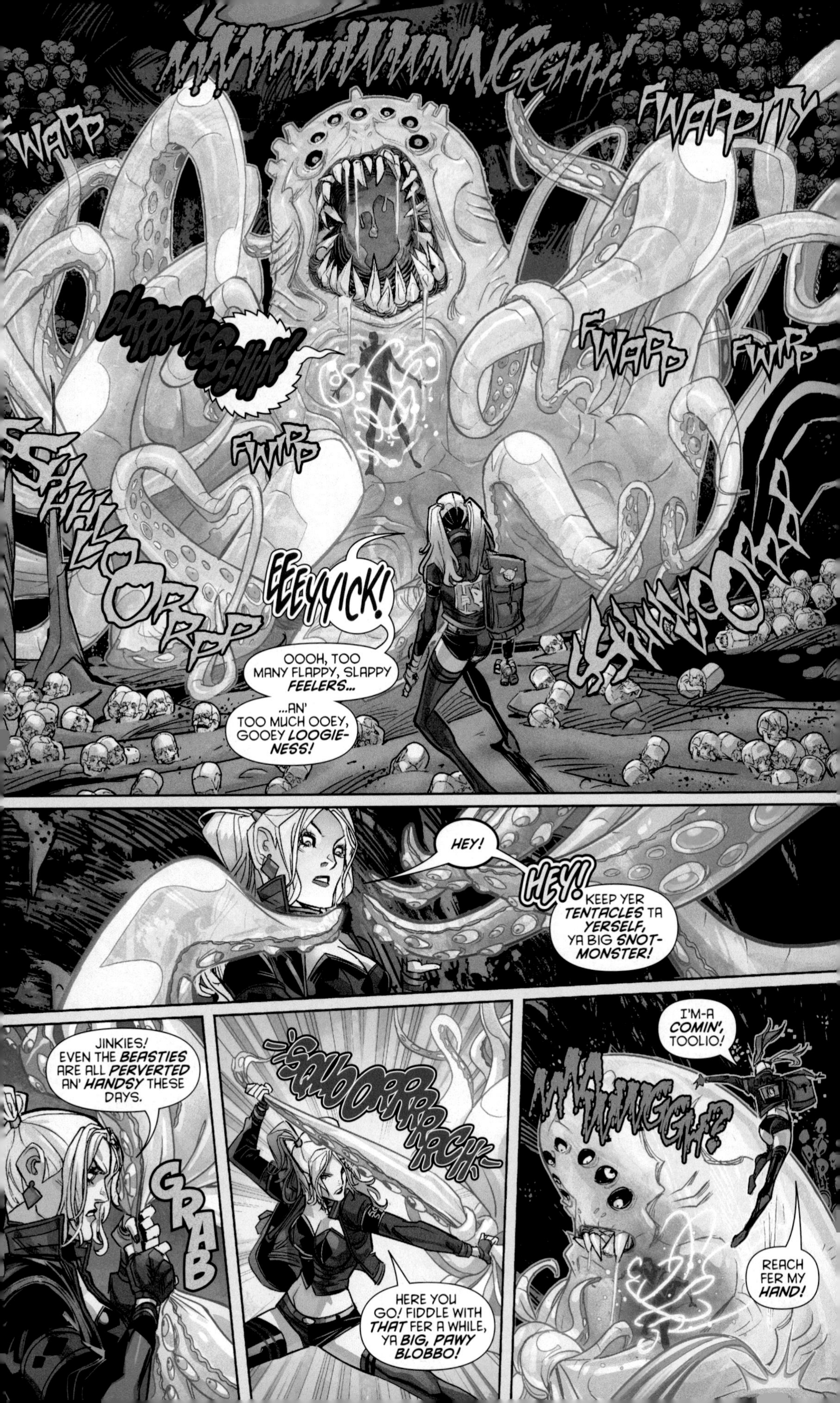
MMMMMMMMNGGHH!
WARP
FWAPPITY
BLARRDTSSSHHK!
FWARP
FWIRP
FWIRP
SHHLOORRPP
EEEEYYICK!
OOOH, TOO MANY FLAPPY, SLAPPY FEELERS...
...AN' TOO MUCH OOEY, GOOEY LOOGIENESS!
HEY!
HEY!
KEEP YER TENTACLES TA YERSELF, YA BIG SNOT-MONSTER!
JINKIES! EVEN THE BEASTIES ARE ALL PERVERTED AN' HANDSY THESE DAYS.
GRAB
SQUOORRRRCH
HERE YOU GO! FIDDLE WITH THAT FER A WHILE, YA BIG, PAWY BLOBBO!
I'M-A COMIN', TOOLIO!
REACH FER MY HAND!

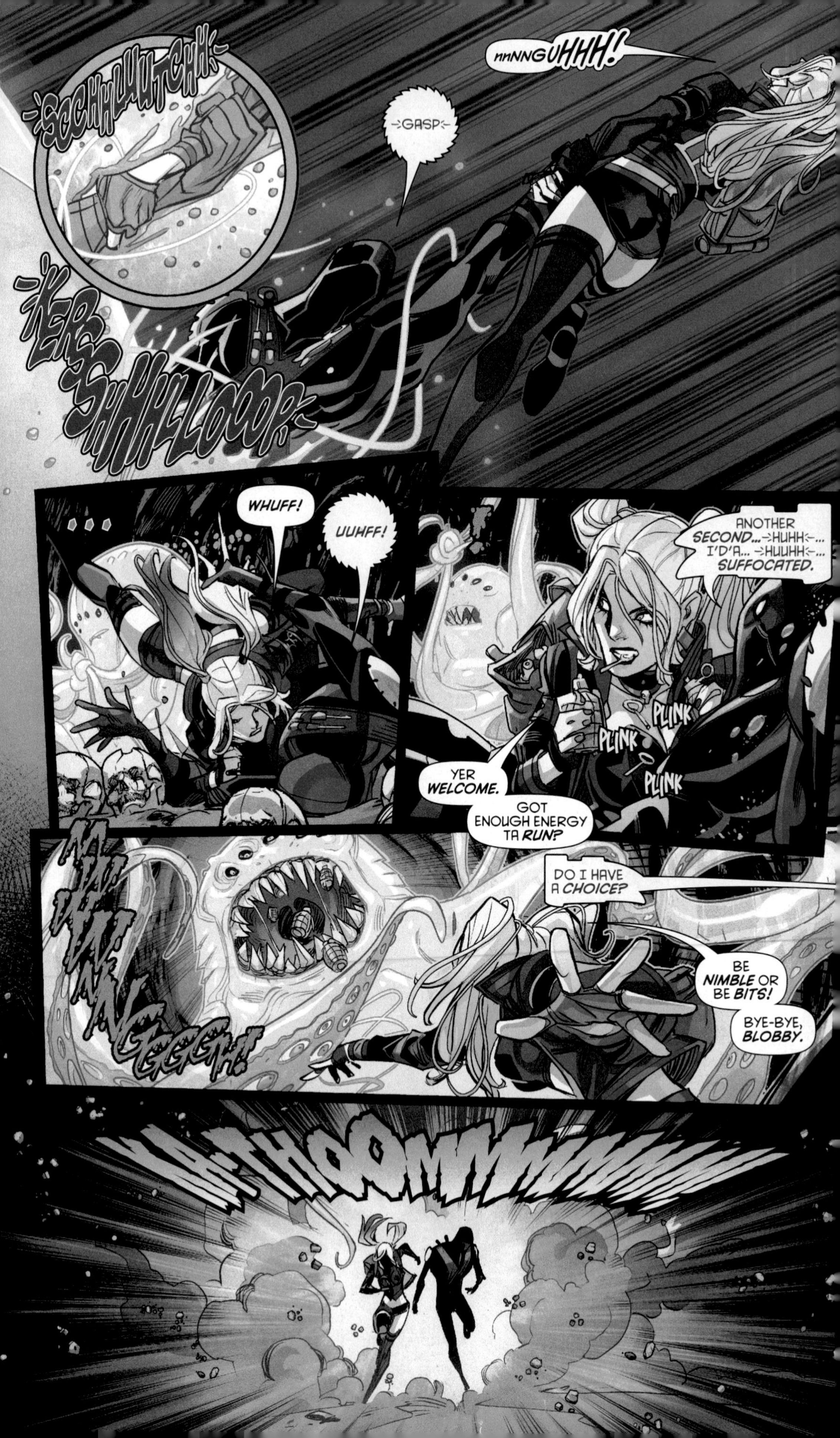

SCCHHLUUTCHH
nnNNGUHHH!
GASP
KERSSHHHLOOOP!
WHUFF!
UUHFF!
ANOTHER SECOND... HUHH... I'D'A... HUUHH... SUFFOCATED.
YER WELCOME.
GOT ENOUGH ENERGY TA RUN?
PLINK
PLINK
PLINK
DO I HAVE A CHOICE?
BE NIMBLE OR BE BITS!
BYE-BYE, BLOBBY.
THOOMMM

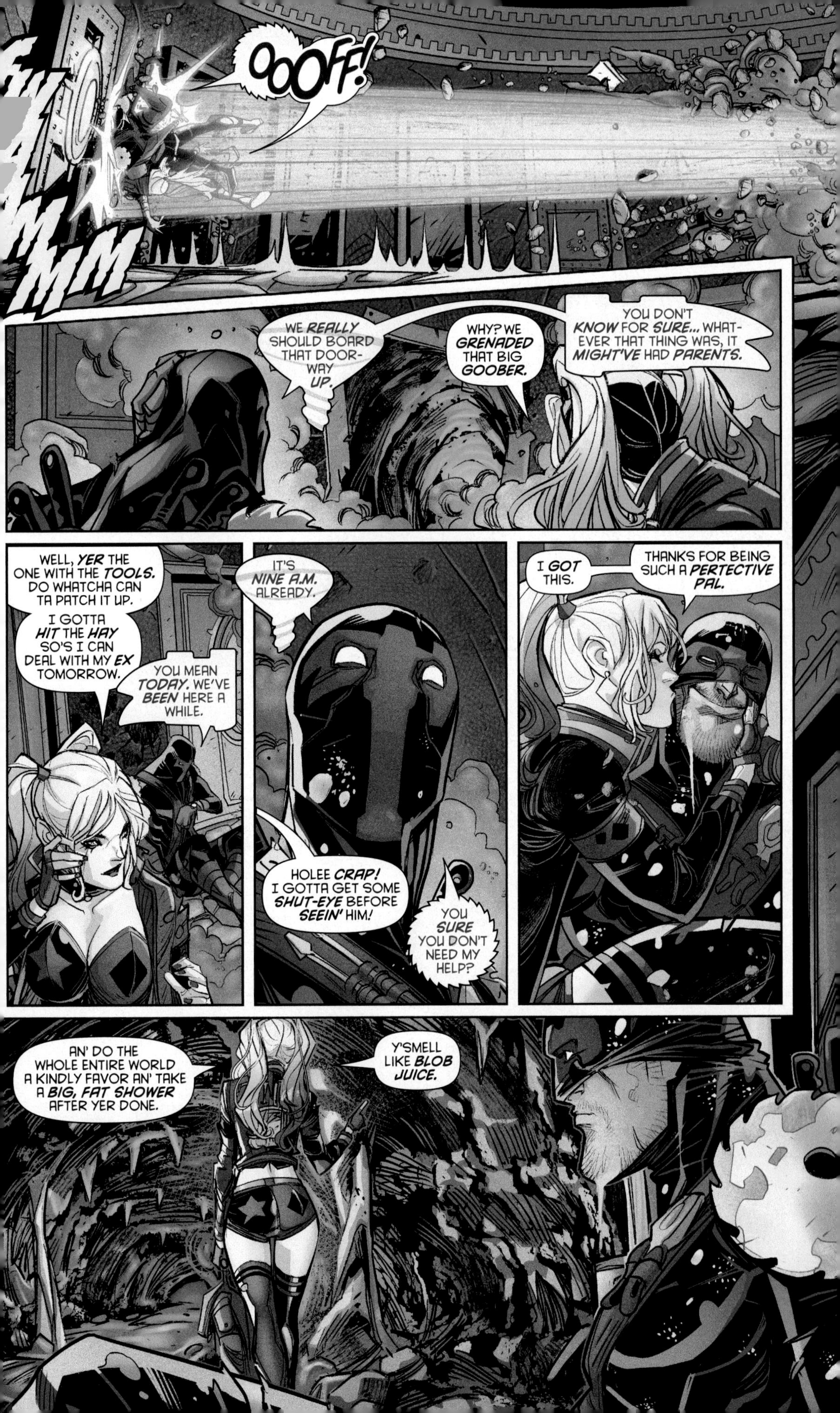

FWAMMM
OOOFF!
WE REALLY SHOULD BOARD THAT DOORWAY UP.
WHY? WE GRENADED THAT BIG GOOBER.
YOU DON'T KNOW FOR SURE... WHATEVER THAT THING WAS, IT MIGHT'VE HAD PARENTS.
WELL, YER THE ONE WITH THE TOOLS. DO WHATCHA CAN TA PATCH IT UP.
I GOTTA HIT THE HAY SO'S I CAN DEAL WITH MY EX TOMORROW.
YOU MEAN TODAY. WE'VE BEEN HERE A WHILE.
IT'S NINE A.M. ALREADY.
HOLEE CRAP! I GOTTA GET SOME SHUT-EYE BEFORE SEEIN' HIM!
YOU SURE YOU DON'T NEED MY HELP?
I GOT THIS.
THANKS FOR BEING SUCH A PERTECTIVE PAL.
AN' DO THE WHOLE ENTIRE WORLD A KINDLY FAVOR AN' TAKE A BIG, FAT SHOWER AFTER YER DONE.
Y'SMELL LIKE BLOB JUICE.

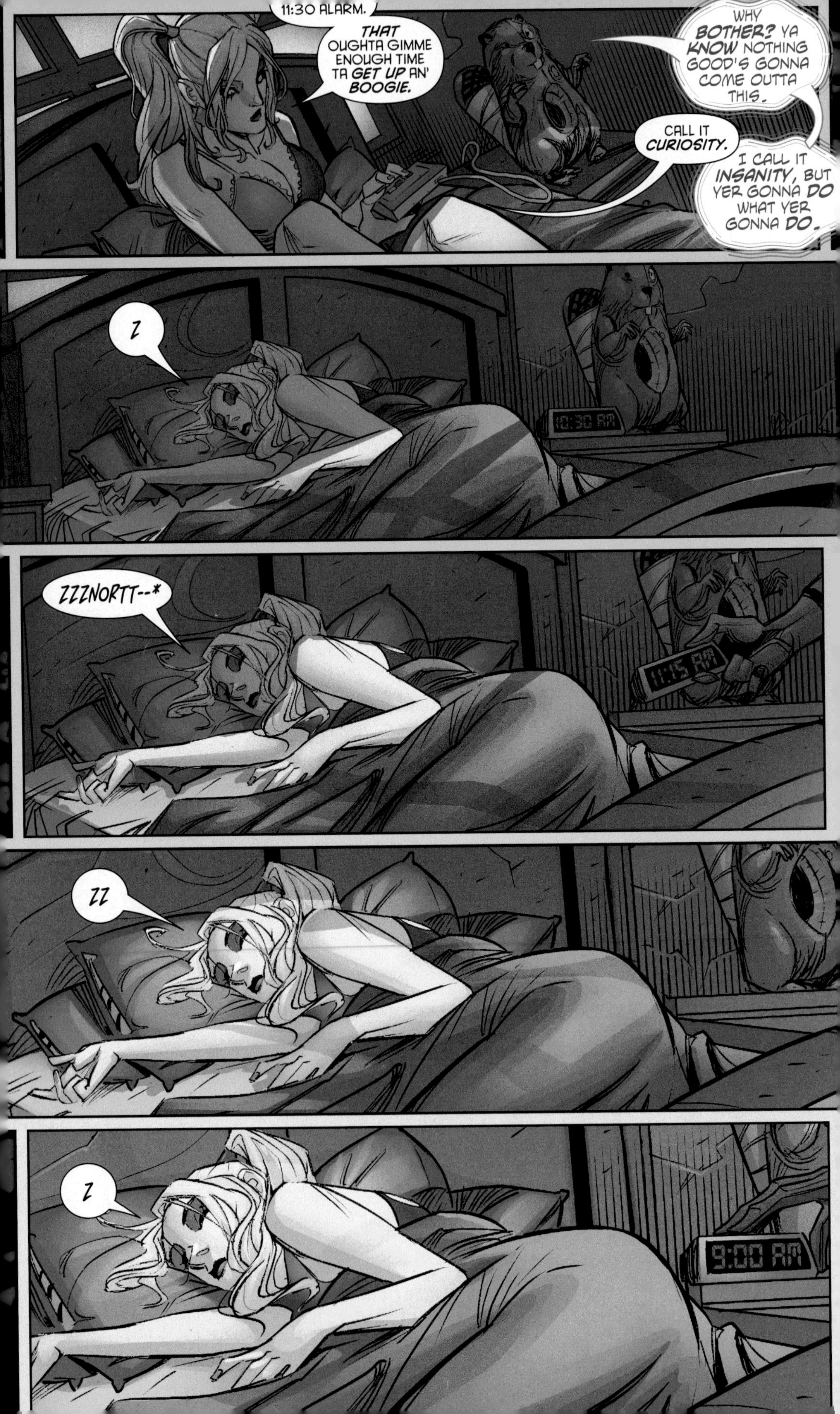

11:30 ALARM.
THAT OUGHTA GIMME ENOUGH TIME TA GET UP AN' BOOGIE.
WHY BOTHER? YA KNOW NOTHING GOOD'S GONNA COME OUTTA THIS.
CALL IT CURIOSITY.
I CALL IT INSANITY, BUT YER GONNA DO WHAT YER GONNA DO.
Z
10:30 AM
ZZZNORTT--*
ZZ
Z
9:00 AM

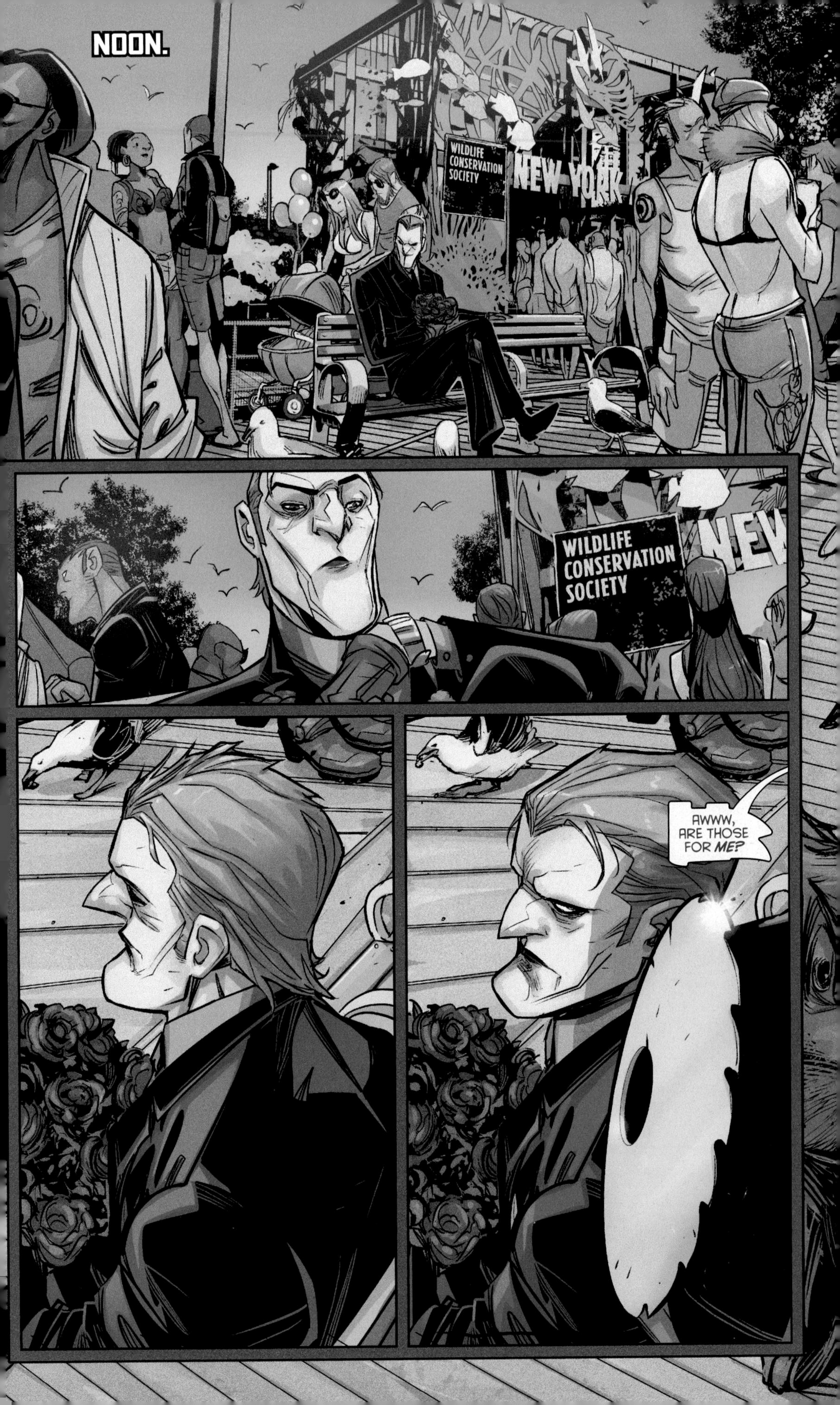
NOON.
WILDLIFE CONSERVATION SOCIETY
NEW YORK
WILDLIFE CONSERVATION SOCIETY
AWWW, ARE THOSE FOR *ME?*

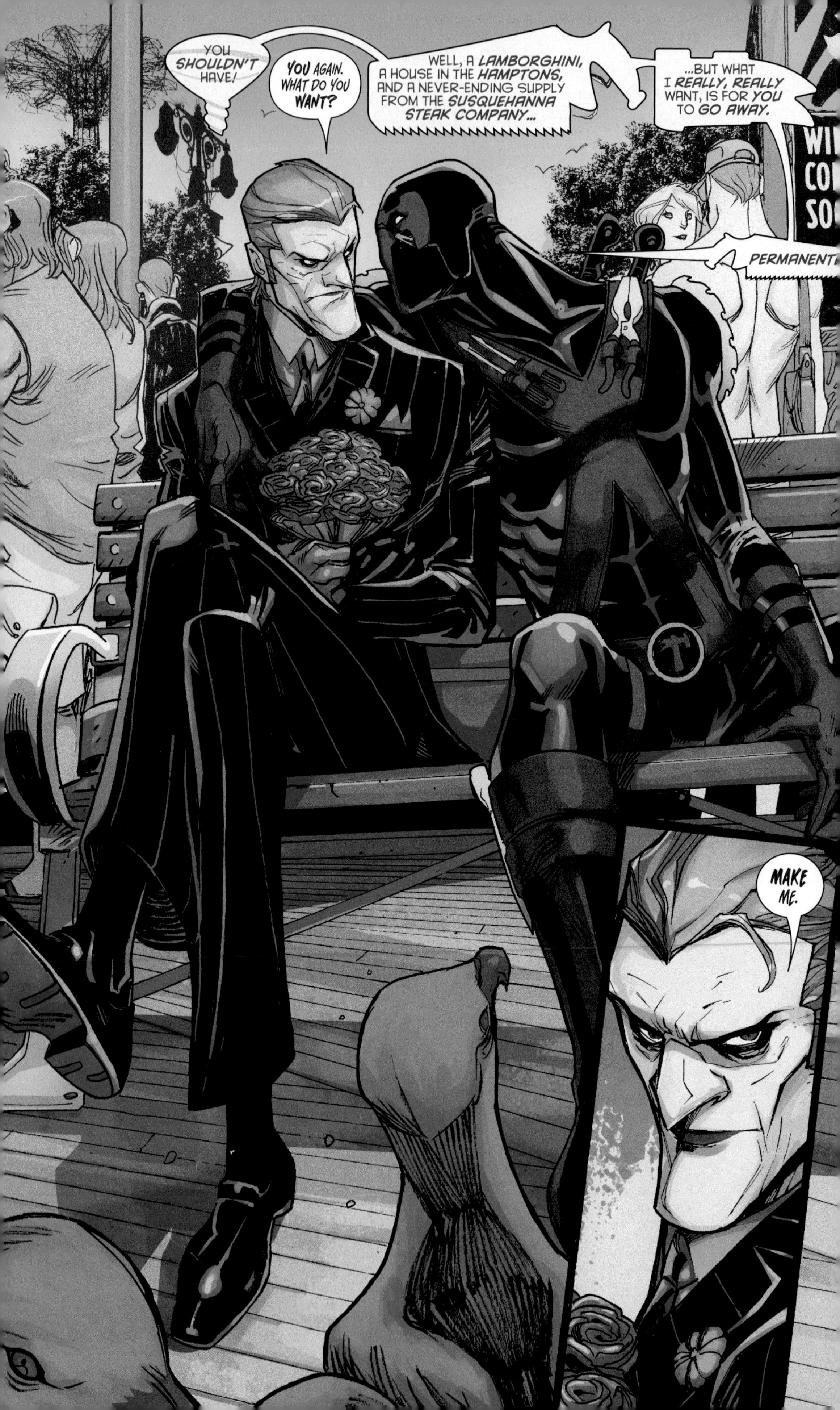

YOU SHOULDN'T HAVE!
YOU AGAIN. WHAT DO YOU WANT?
WELL, A LAMBORGHINI, A HOUSE IN THE HAMPTONS, AND A NEVER-ENDING SUPPLY FROM THE SUSQUEHANNA STEAK COMPANY...
...BUT WHAT I REALLY, REALLY WANT, IS FOR YOU TO GO AWAY.
PERMANENT
MAKE ME.

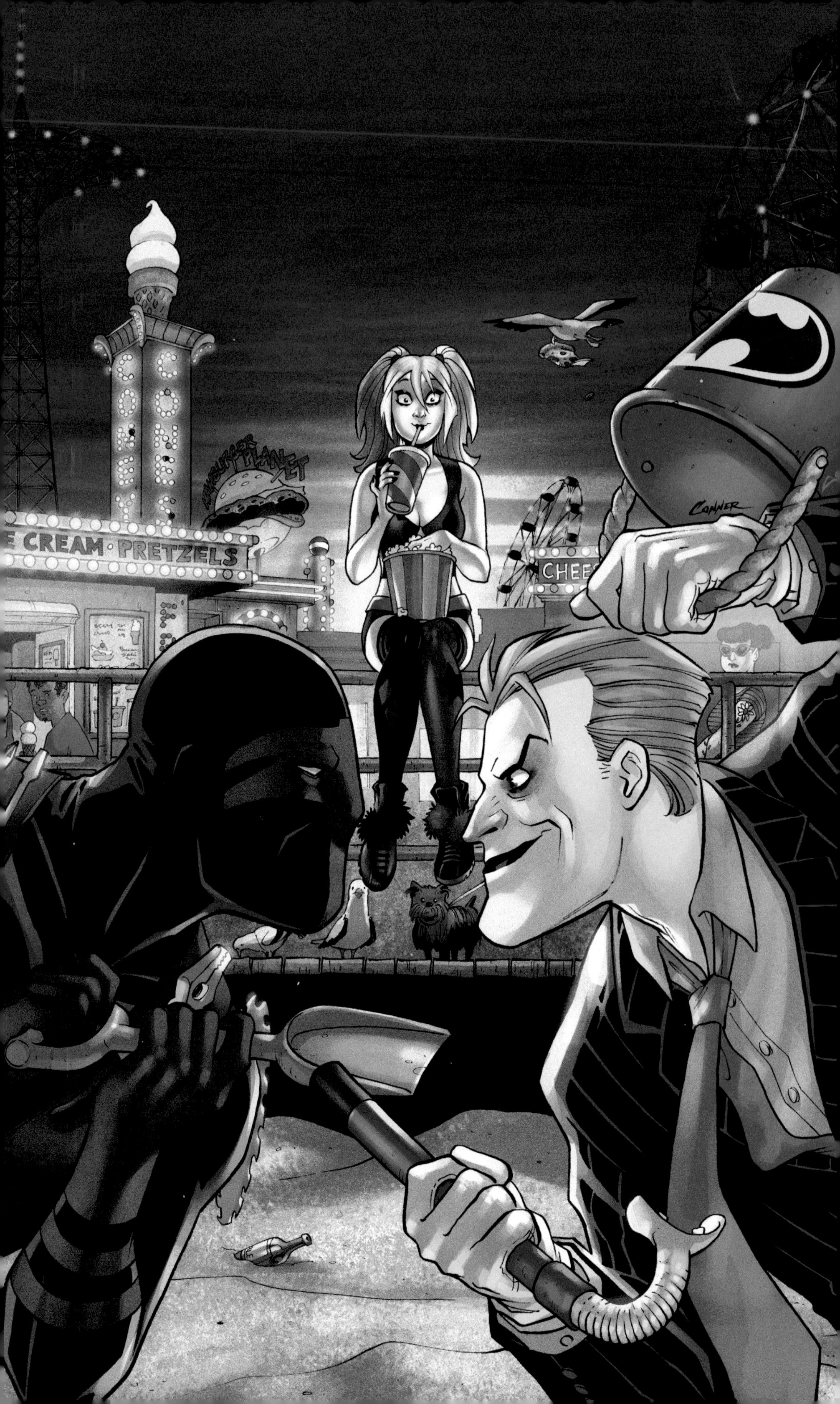

E CREAM · PRETZELS
CHEES
CONNER

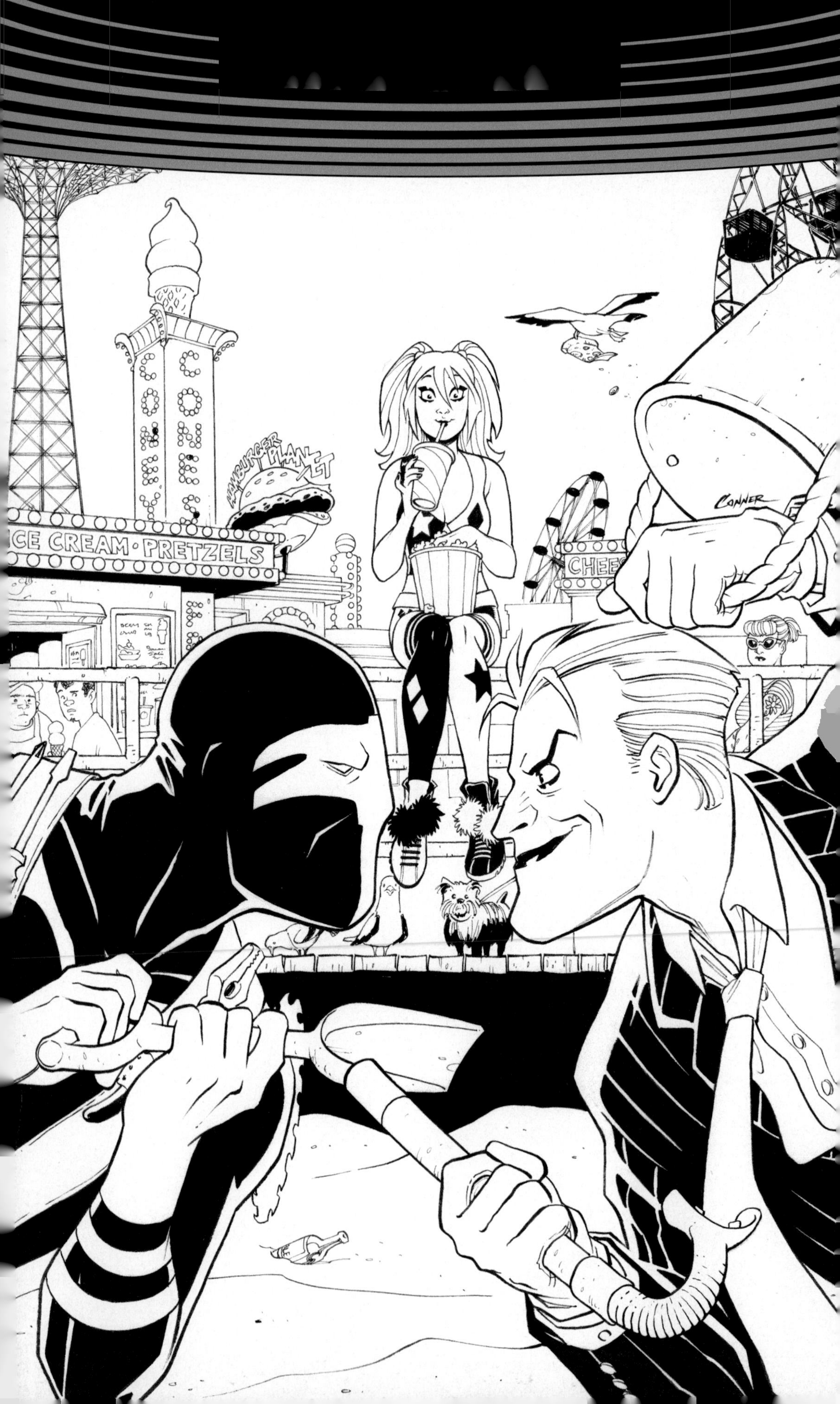
HAMBURGER PLANET
CE CREAM · PRETZELS
CHEES
CONNER

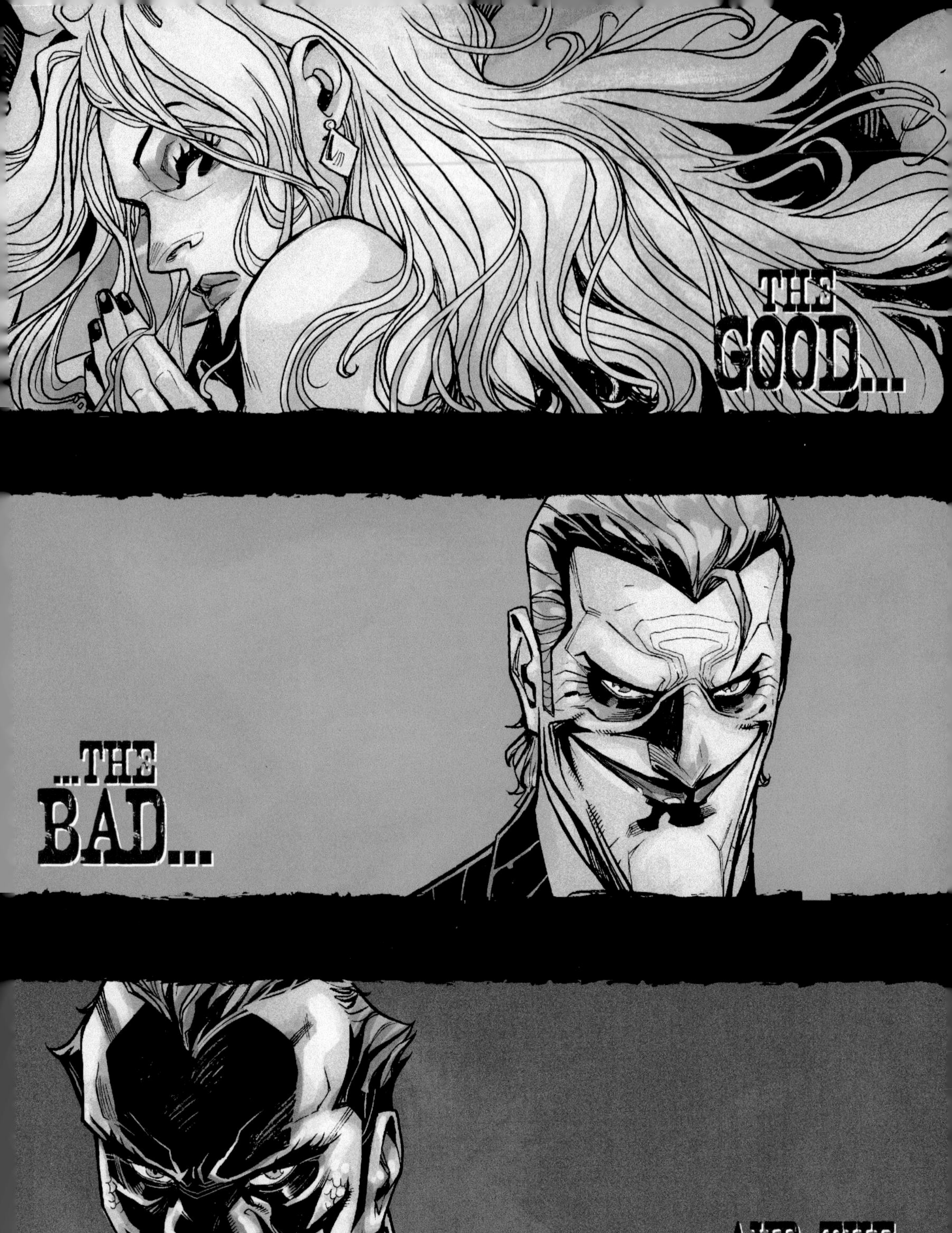
THE GOOD...
...THE BAD...
...AND THE HUNGRY!

JIMMY PALMIOTTI & AMANDA CONNER WRITERS JOHN TIMMS ARTIST
CHAD HARDIN DREAM ARTIST (Pgs 8-10) HI-FI COLORS DAVE SHARPE LETTERS
AMANDA CONNER & ALEX SINCLAIR COVER FRANK CHO & LAURA MARTIN VARIANT COVER
DAVE WIELGOSZ ASST. EDITOR CHRIS CONROY EDITOR MARK DOYLE GROUP EDITOR
HARLEY QUINN CREATED BY PAUL DINI & BRUCE TIMM

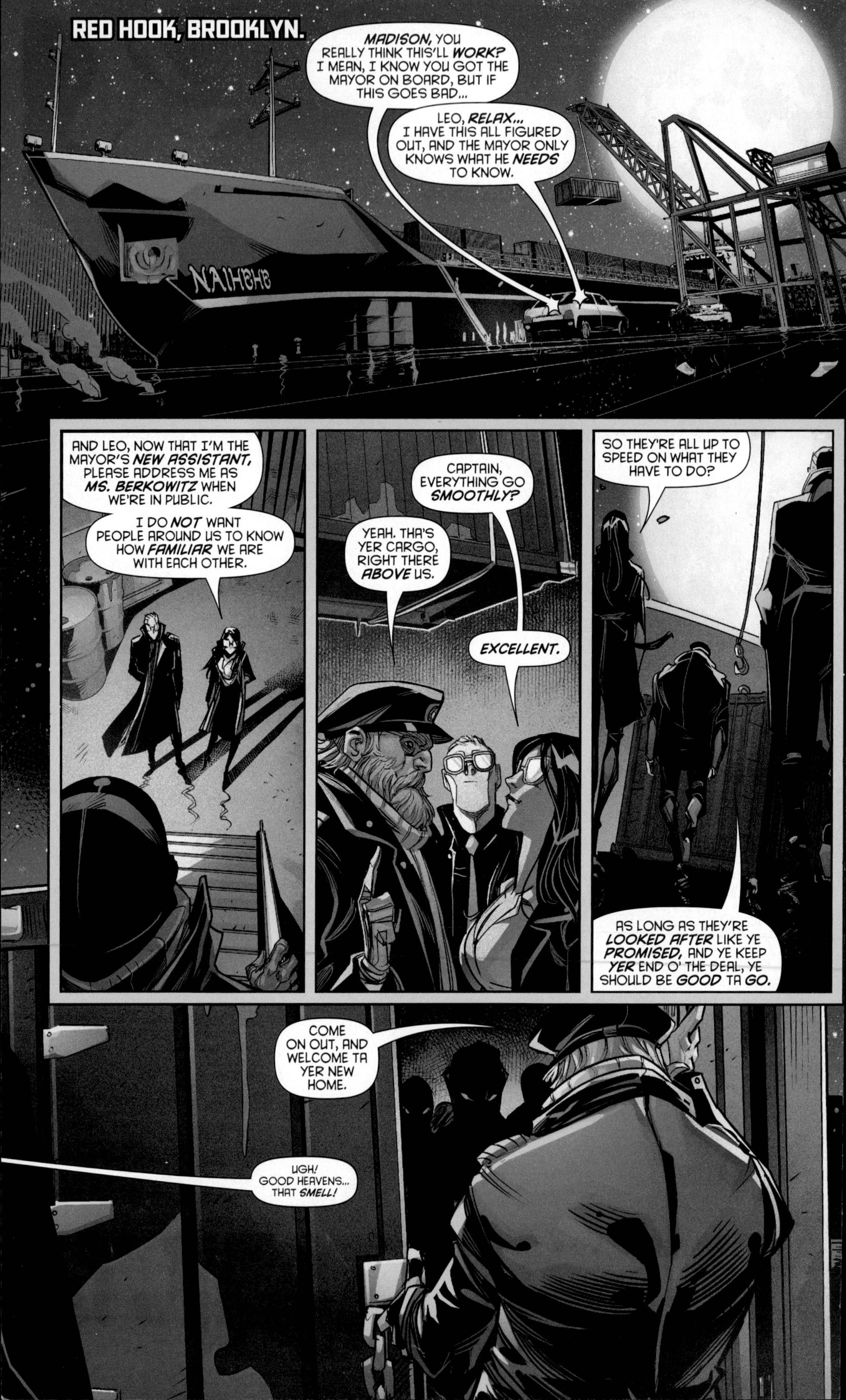

RED HOOK, BROOKLYN.
MADISON, YOU REALLY THINK THIS'LL WORK? I MEAN, I KNOW YOU GOT THE MAYOR ON BOARD, BUT IF THIS GOES BAD...
LEO, RELAX... I HAVE THIS ALL FIGURED OUT, AND THE MAYOR ONLY KNOWS WHAT HE NEEDS TO KNOW.
AND LEO, NOW THAT I'M THE MAYOR'S NEW ASSISTANT, PLEASE ADDRESS ME AS MS. BERKOWITZ WHEN WE'RE IN PUBLIC.
I DO NOT WANT PEOPLE AROUND US TO KNOW HOW FAMILIAR WE ARE WITH EACH OTHER.
CAPTAIN, EVERYTHING GO SMOOTHLY?
YEAH. THA'S YER CARGO, RIGHT THERE ABOVE US.
EXCELLENT.
SO THEY'RE ALL UP TO SPEED ON WHAT THEY HAVE TO DO?
AS LONG AS THEY'RE LOOKED AFTER LIKE YE PROMISED, AND YE KEEP YER END O' THE DEAL, YE SHOULD BE GOOD TA GO.
COME ON OUT, AND WELCOME TA YER NEW HOME.
UGH! GOOD HEAVENS... THAT SMELL!

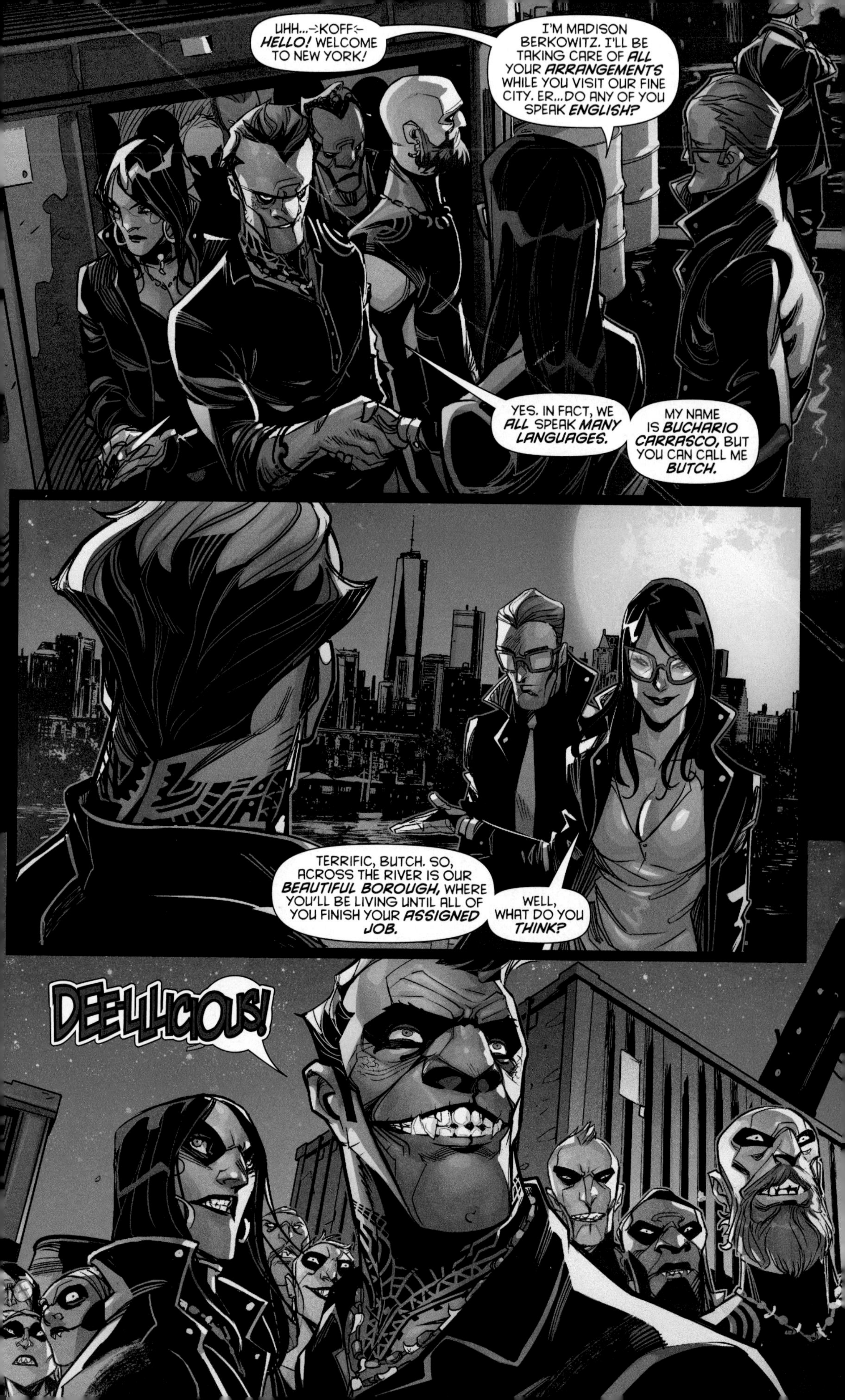
UHH...>KOFF< HELLO! WELCOME TO NEW YORK!
I'M MADISON BERKOWITZ. I'LL BE TAKING CARE OF ALL YOUR ARRANGEMENTS WHILE YOU VISIT OUR FINE CITY. ER...DO ANY OF YOU SPEAK ENGLISH?
YES. IN FACT, WE ALL SPEAK MANY LANGUAGES.
MY NAME IS BUCHARIO CARRASCO, BUT YOU CAN CALL ME BUTCH.
TERRIFIC, BUTCH. SO, ACROSS THE RIVER IS OUR BEAUTIFUL BOROUGH, WHERE YOU'LL BE LIVING UNTIL ALL OF YOU FINISH YOUR ASSIGNED JOB.
WELL, WHAT DO YOU THINK?
DEE-LLLICIOUS!

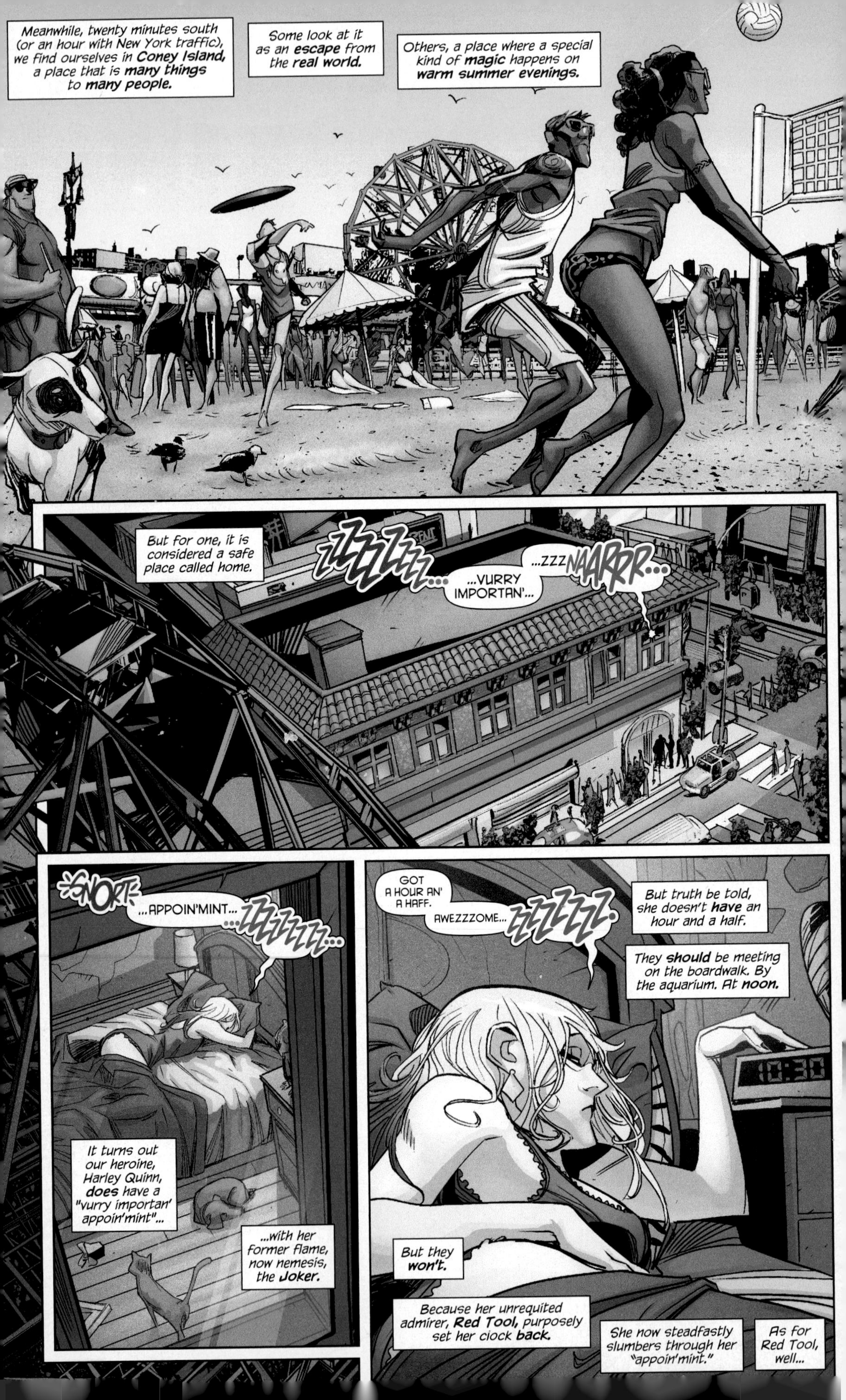

Meanwhile, twenty minutes south (or an hour with New York traffic), we find ourselves in Coney Island, a place that is many things to many people.
Some look at it as an escape from the real world.
Others, a place where a special kind of magic happens on warm summer evenings.
But for one, it is considered a safe place called home.
ZZZZZzzz...
...VURRY IMPORTAN'...
...ZZZNAARRR...
SNORT
...APPOIN'MINT...
...ZZZZZzzzz...
GOT A HOUR AN' A HAFF.
AWEZZZOME...
ZZZZZZZ.
But truth be told, she doesn't have an hour and a half.
They should be meeting on the boardwalk. By the aquarium. At noon.
It turns out our heroine, Harley Quinn, does have a "vurry importan' appoin'mint"...
...with her former flame, now nemesis, the Joker.
But they won't.
Because her unrequited admirer, Red Tool, purposely set her clock back.
She now steadfastly slumbers through her "appoin'mint."
As for Red Tool, well...

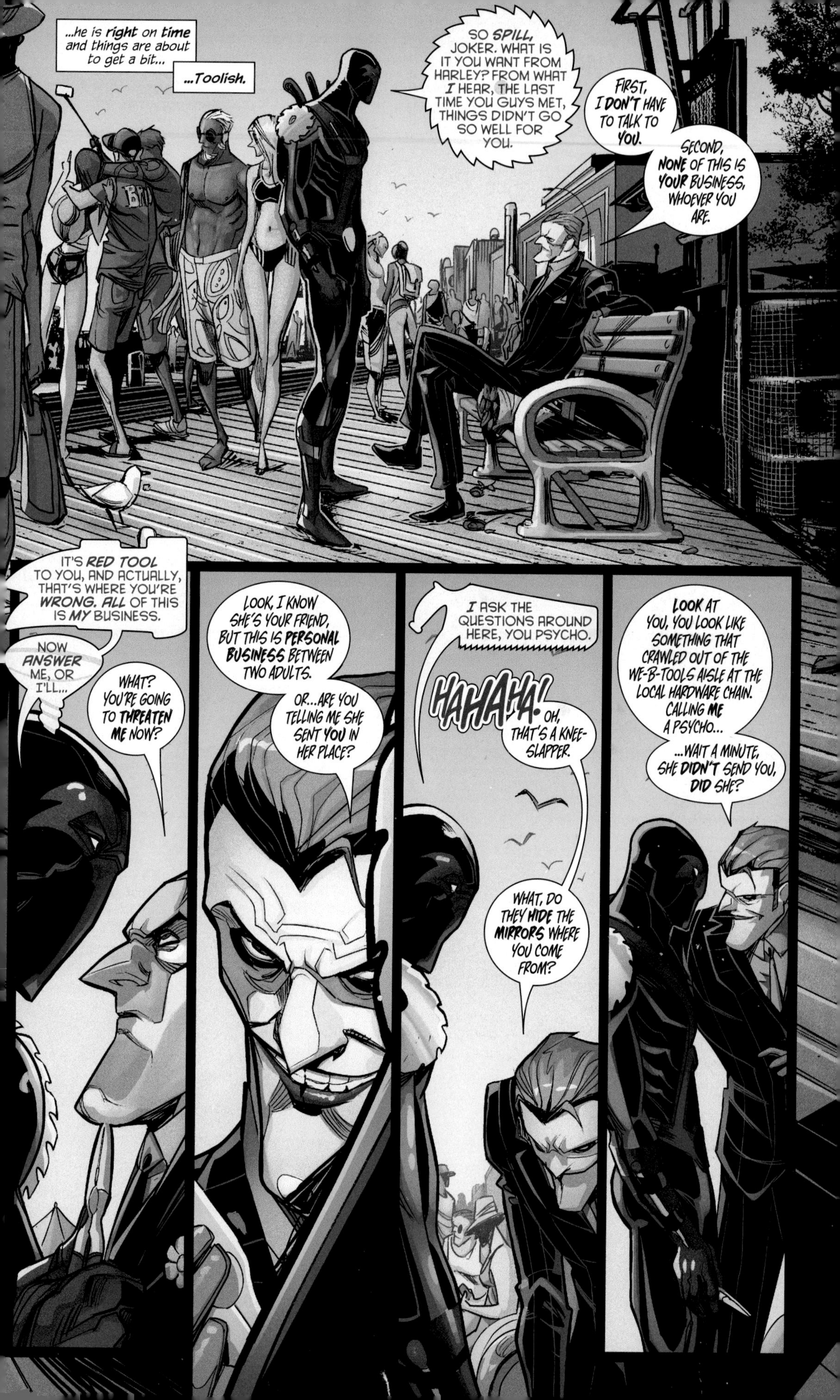
...he is right on time and things are about to get a bit...
...Toolish.
SO SPILL, JOKER. WHAT IS IT YOU WANT FROM HARLEY? FROM WHAT I HEAR, THE LAST TIME YOU GUYS MET, THINGS DIDN'T GO SO WELL FOR YOU.
FIRST, I DON'T HAVE TO TALK TO YOU.
SECOND, NONE OF THIS IS YOUR BUSINESS, WHOEVER YOU ARE.
IT'S RED TOOL TO YOU, AND ACTUALLY, THAT'S WHERE YOU'RE WRONG. ALL OF THIS IS MY BUSINESS.
NOW ANSWER ME, OR I'LL...
WHAT? YOU'RE GOING TO THREATEN ME NOW?
LOOK, I KNOW SHE'S YOUR FRIEND, BUT THIS IS PERSONAL BUSINESS BETWEEN TWO ADULTS.
OR...ARE YOU TELLING ME SHE SENT YOU IN HER PLACE?
I ASK THE QUESTIONS AROUND HERE, YOU PSYCHO.
HAHAHA!
OH, THAT'S A KNEE-SLAPPER.
WHAT, DO THEY HIDE THE MIRRORS WHERE YOU COME FROM?
LOOK AT YOU, YOU LOOK LIKE SOMETHING THAT CRAWLED OUT OF THE WE-B-TOOLS AISLE AT THE LOCAL HARDWARE CHAIN. CALLING ME A PSYCHO...
...WAIT A MINUTE, SHE DIDN'T SEND YOU, DID SHE?

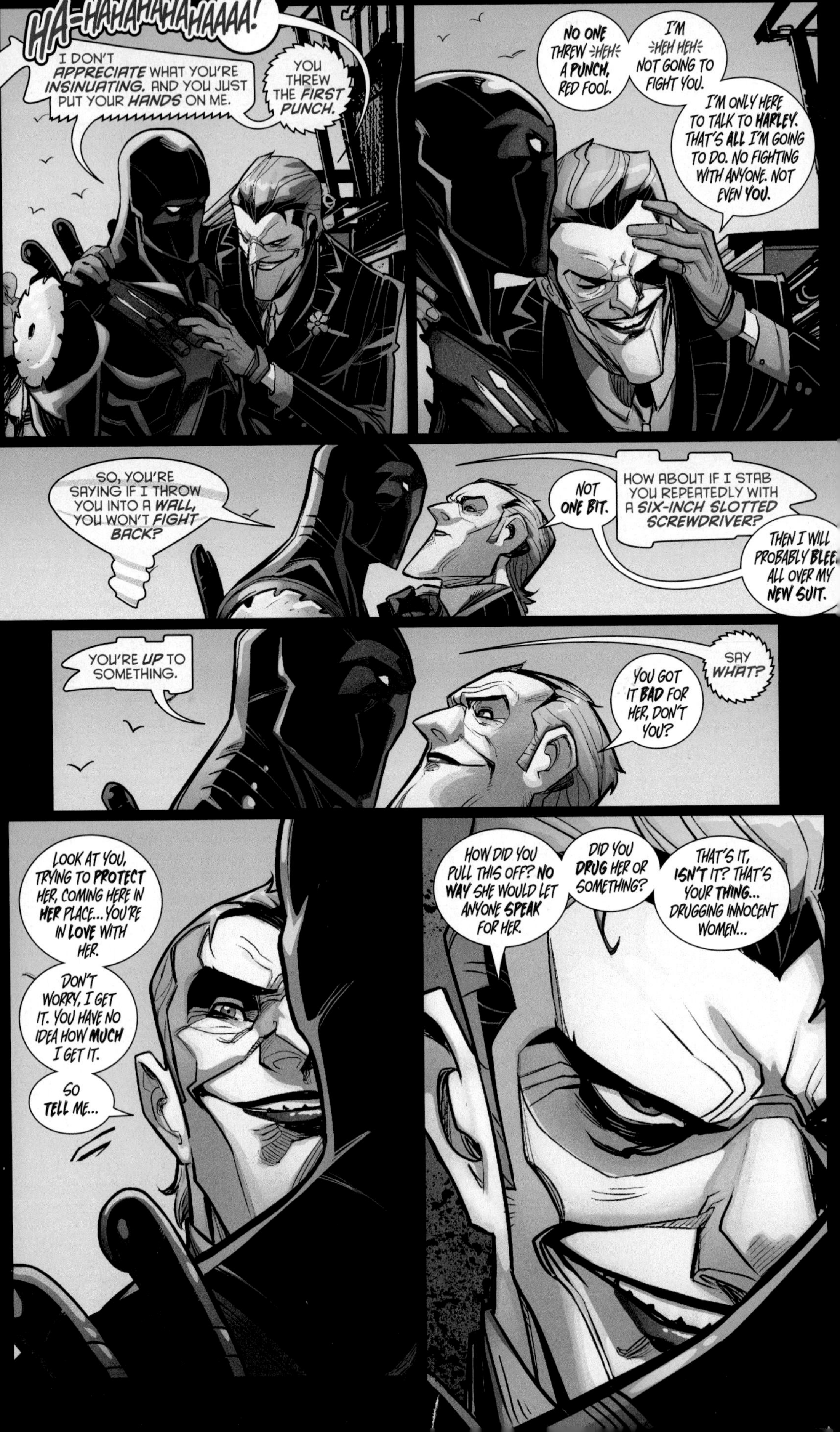
HA-HAHAHAHAHAAAA!
I DON'T APPRECIATE WHAT YOU'RE INSINUATING. AND YOU JUST PUT YOUR HANDS ON ME.
YOU THREW THE FIRST PUNCH.
NO ONE THREW ≈HEH≈ A PUNCH, RED FOOL.
I'M ≈HEH HEH≈ NOT GOING TO FIGHT YOU.
I'M ONLY HERE TO TALK TO HARLEY. THAT'S ALL I'M GOING TO DO. NO FIGHTING WITH ANYONE. NOT EVEN YOU.
SO, YOU'RE SAYING IF I THROW YOU INTO A WALL, YOU WON'T FIGHT BACK?
NOT ONE BIT.
HOW ABOUT IF I STAB YOU REPEATEDLY WITH A SIX-INCH SLOTTED SCREWDRIVER?
THEN I WILL PROBABLY BLEE ALL OVER MY NEW SUIT.
YOU'RE UP TO SOMETHING.
SAY WHAT?
YOU GOT IT BAD FOR HER, DON'T YOU?
LOOK AT YOU, TRYING TO PROTECT HER, COMING HERE IN HER PLACE... YOU'RE IN LOVE WITH HER.
DON'T WORRY, I GET IT. YOU HAVE NO IDEA HOW MUCH I GET IT.
SO TELL ME...
HOW DID YOU PULL THIS OFF? NO WAY SHE WOULD LET ANYONE SPEAK FOR HER.
DID YOU DRUG HER OR SOMETHING?
THAT'S IT, ISN'T IT? THAT'S YOUR THING... DRUGGING INNOCENT WOMEN...

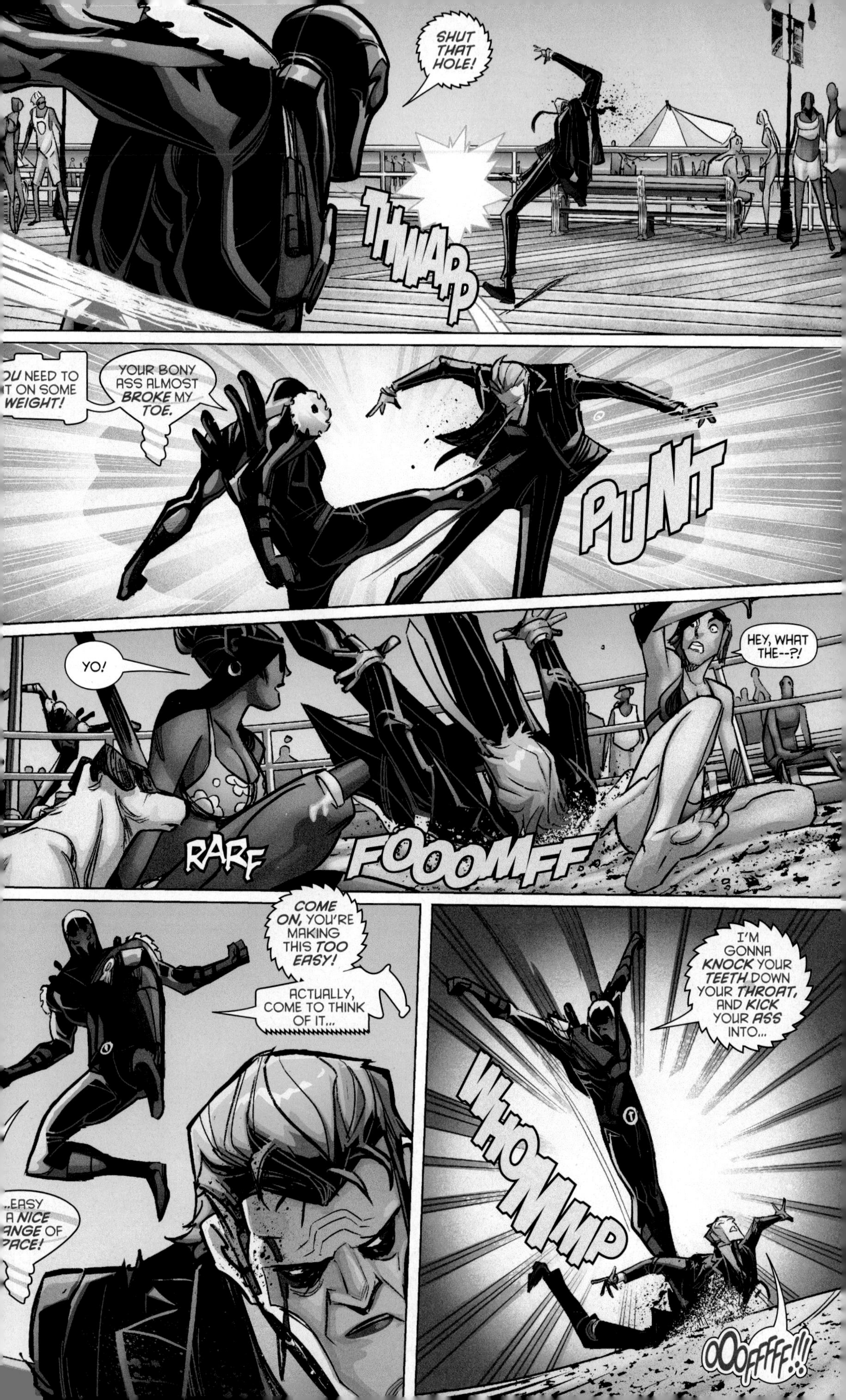

SHUT THAT HOLE!
THWAPP
OU NEED TO T ON SOME WEIGHT!
YOUR BONY ASS ALMOST BROKE MY TOE.
PUNT
YO!
HEY, WHAT THE--?!
RARF
FOOOOMFF
COME ON, YOU'RE MAKING THIS TOO EASY!
ACTUALLY, COME TO THINK OF IT...
..EASY A NICE ANGE OF PACE!
I'M GONNA KNOCK YOUR TEETH DOWN YOUR THROAT, AND KICK YOUR ASS INTO...
WHOMMMP
OOOFFFFF!!!

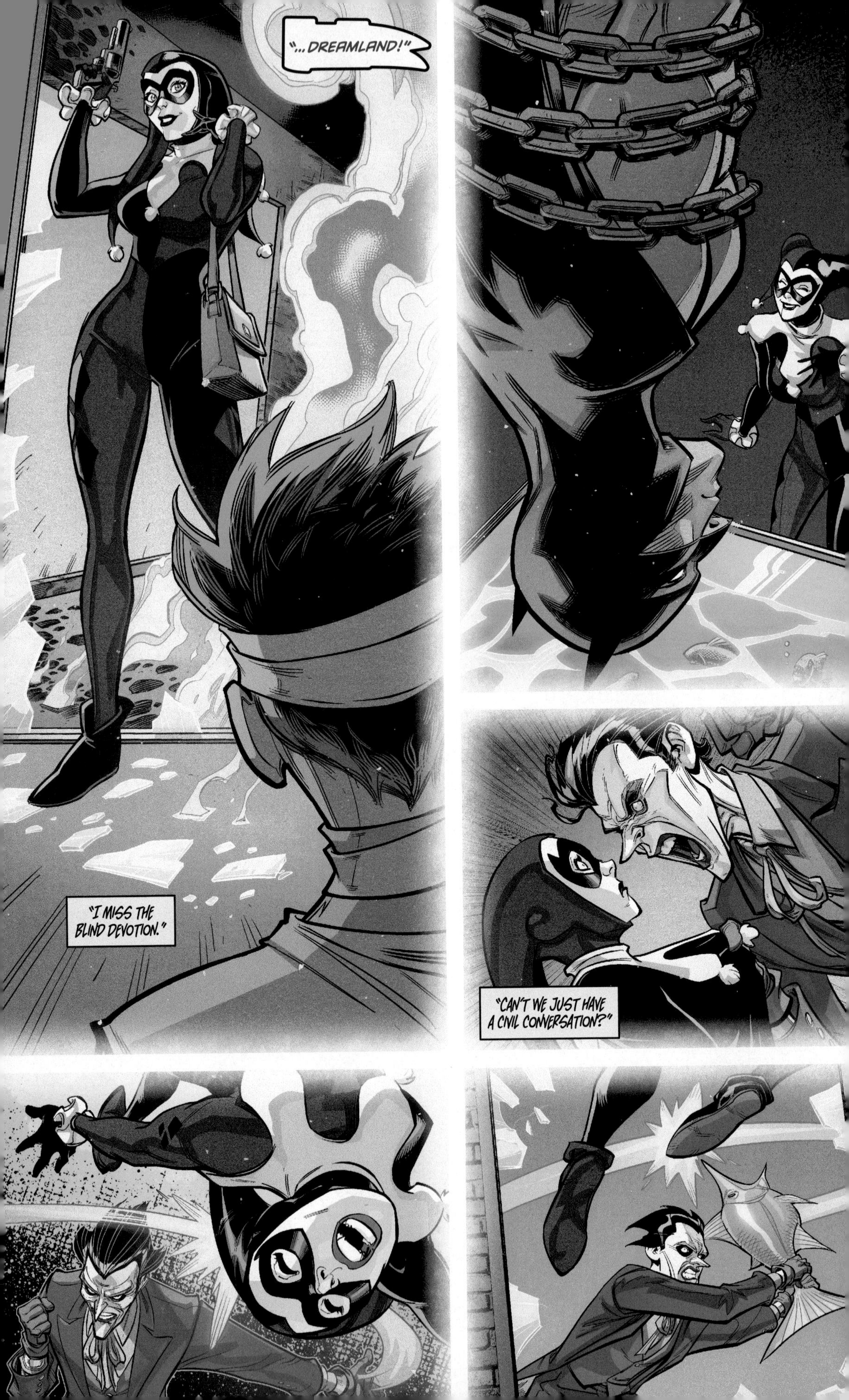
"...DREAMLAND!"
"I MISS THE BLIND DEVOTION."
"CAN'T WE JUST HAVE A CIVIL CONVERSATION?"

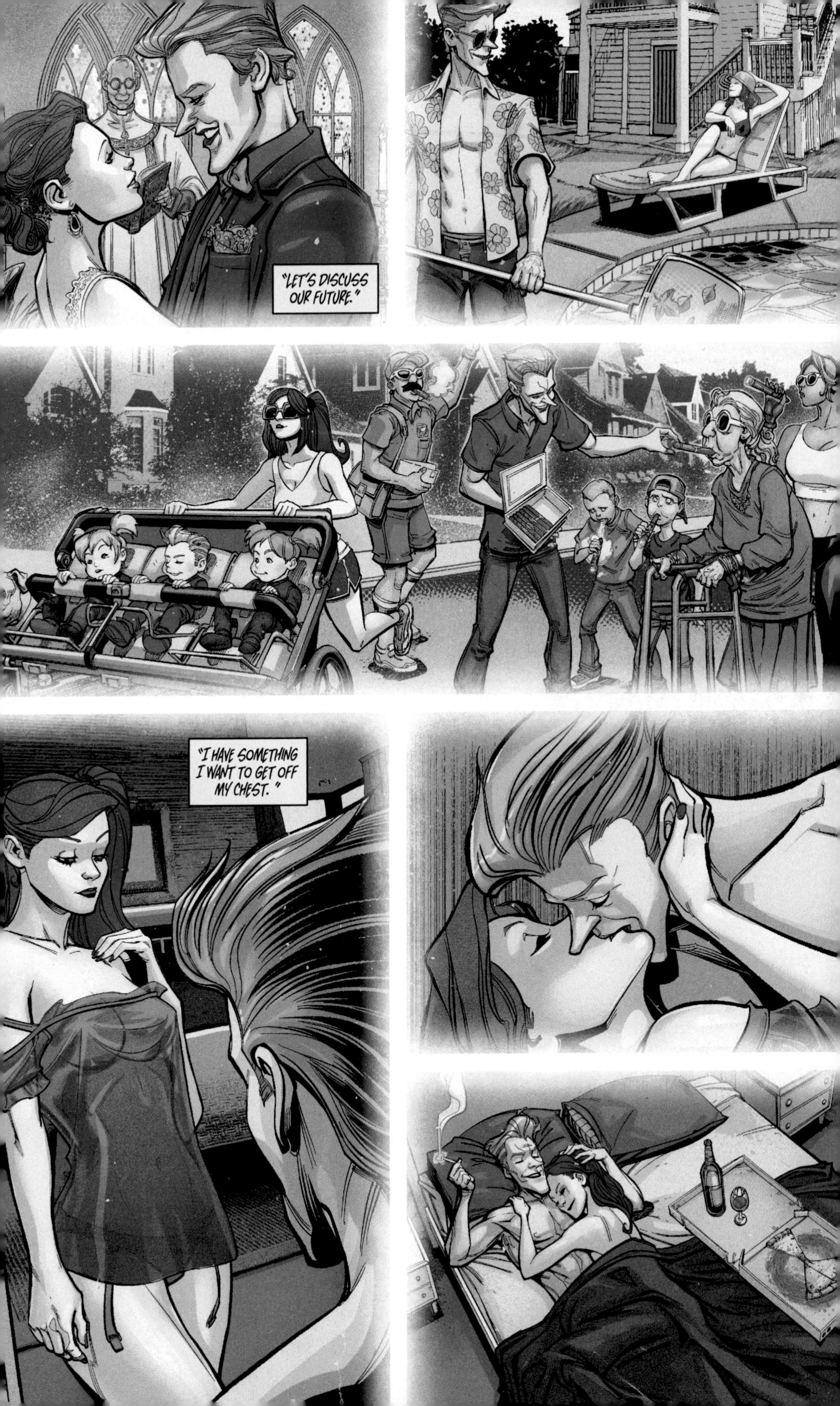
"LET'S DISCUSS OUR FUTURE."
"I HAVE SOMETHING I WANT TO GET OFF MY CHEST."

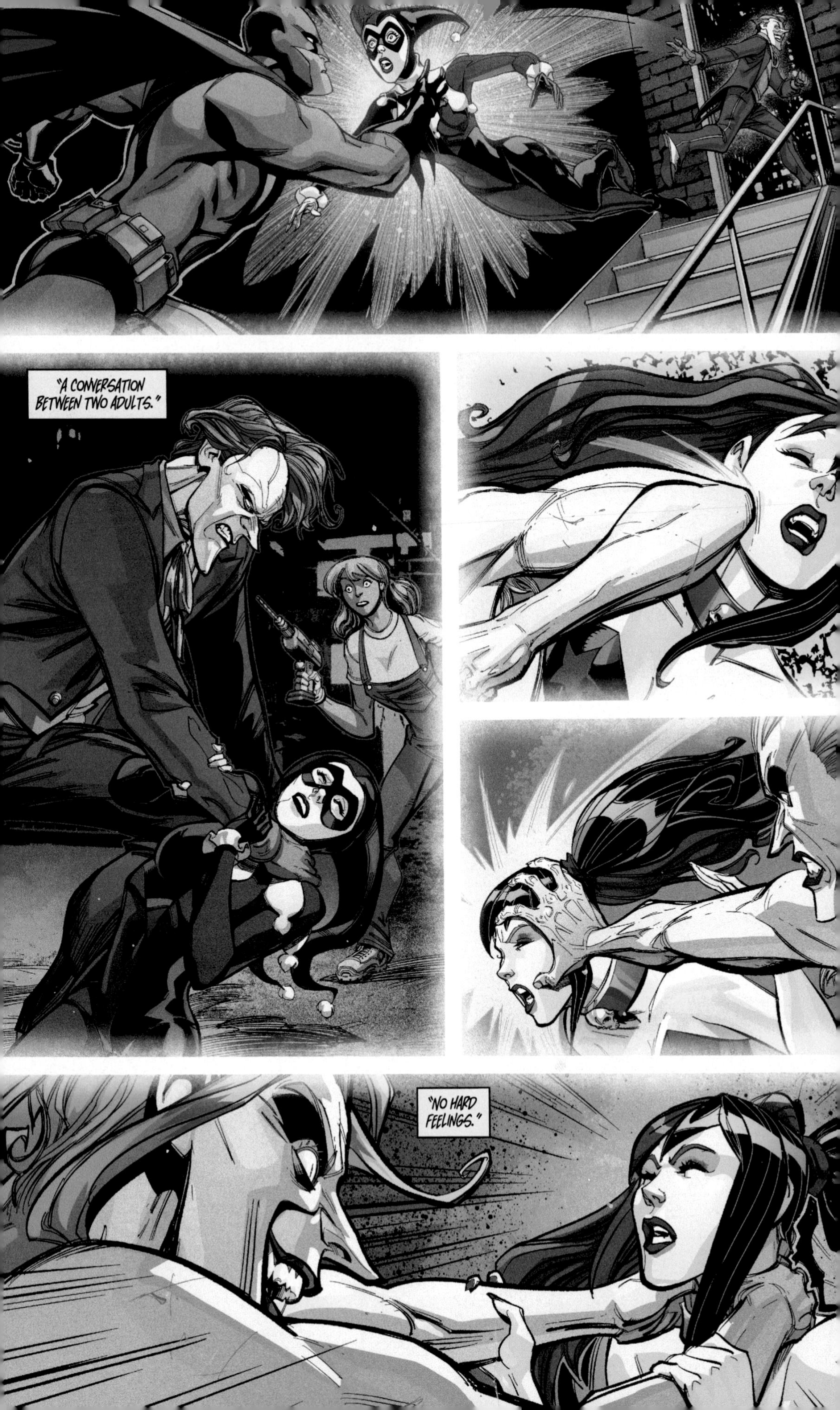
"A CONVERSATION BETWEEN TWO ADULTS."
"NO HARD FEELINGS."

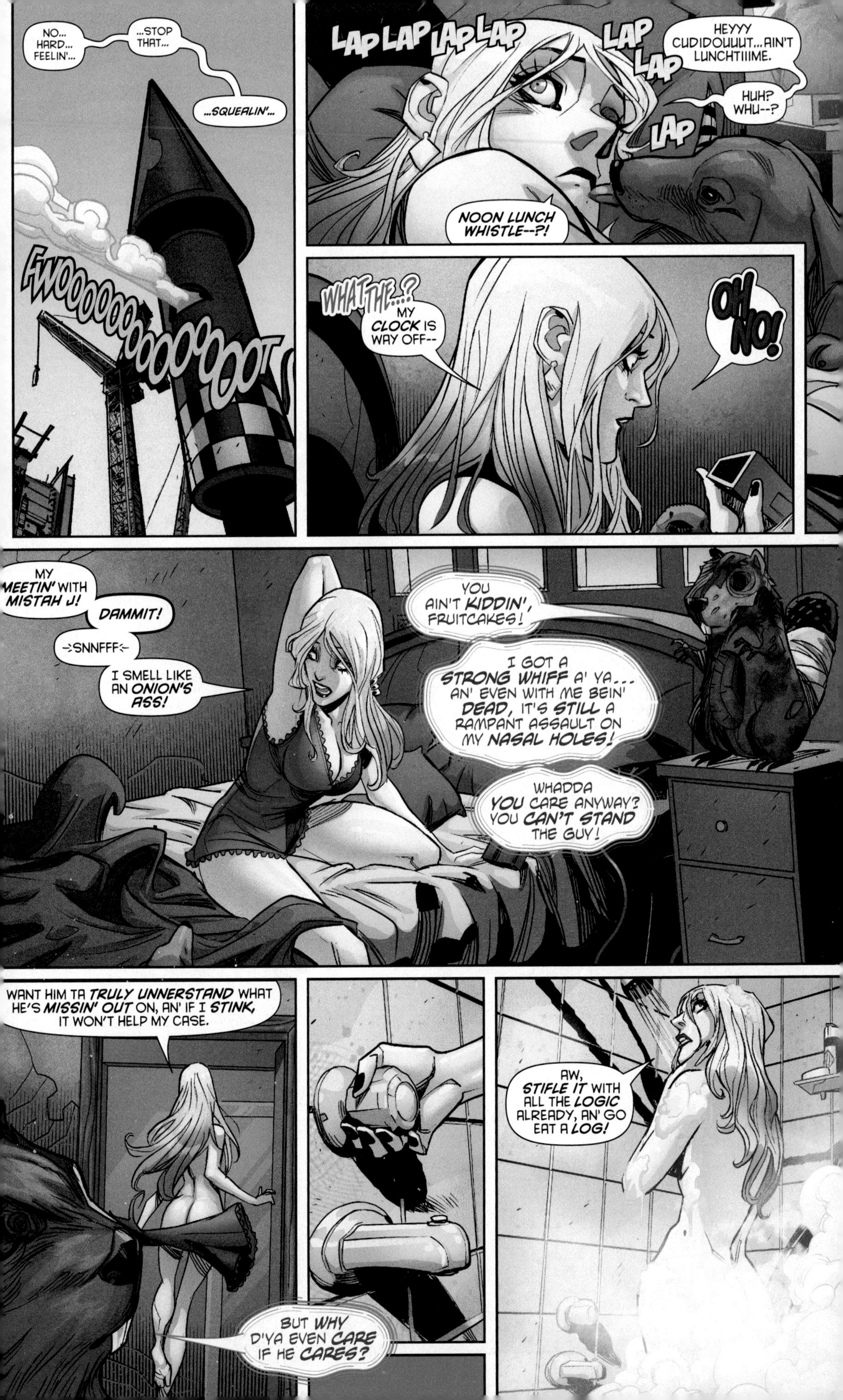
NO... HARD... FEELIN'...
...STOP THAT...
...SQUEALIN'...
FWOOOOOOOOOOOOOOOT
LAP LAP LAP LAP
LAP LAP
HEYYY CUDIDOUUUT...AIN'T LUNCHTIIIME.
HUH? WHU--?
LAP
NOON LUNCH WHISTLE--?!
WHAT THE...?
MY CLOCK IS WAY OFF--
OH NO!
MY MEETIN' WITH MISTAH J!
DAMMIT!
SNNFFF
I SMELL LIKE AN ONION'S ASS!
YOU AIN'T KIDDIN', FRUITCAKES!
I GOT A STRONG WHIFF A' YA... AN' EVEN WITH ME BEIN' DEAD, IT'S STILL A RAMPANT ASSAULT ON MY NASAL HOLES!
WHADDA YOU CARE ANYWAY? YOU CAN'T STAND THE GUY!
WANT HIM TA TRULY UNNERSTAND WHAT HE'S MISSIN' OUT ON, AN' IF I STINK, IT WON'T HELP MY CASE.
BUT WHY D'YA EVEN CARE IF HE CARES?
AW, STIFLE IT WITH ALL THE LOGIC ALREADY, AN' GO EAT A LOG!

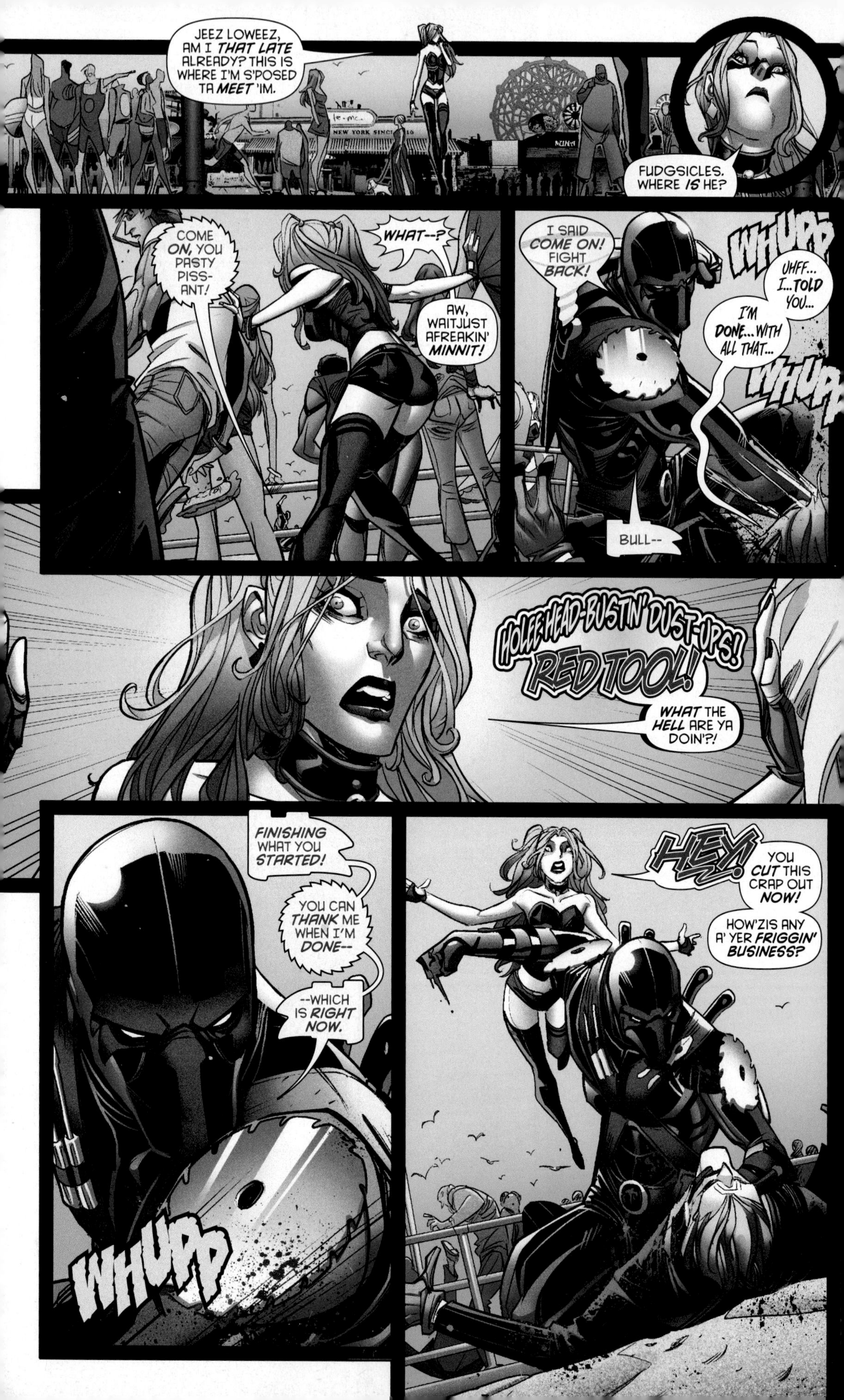
JEEZ LOWEEZ, AM I THAT LATE ALREADY? THIS IS WHERE I'M S'POSED TA MEET 'IM.
NEW YORK
FUDGSICLES. WHERE IS HE?
COME ON, YOU PASTY PISS-ANT!
WHAT--?
AW, WAITJUST AFREAKIN' MINNIT!
I SAID COME ON! FIGHT BACK!
WHUPP
UHFF... I...TOLD YOU...
I'M DONE...WITH ALL THAT...
WHUPP
BULL--
HOLEE HEAD-BUSTIN' DUST-UPS! RED TOOL!
WHAT THE HELL ARE YA DOIN'?!
FINISHING WHAT YOU STARTED!
YOU CAN THANK ME WHEN I'M DONE--
--WHICH IS RIGHT NOW.
WHUPP
HEY!
YOU CUT THIS CRAP OUT NOW!
HOW'ZIS ANY A' YER FRIGGIN' BUSINESS?

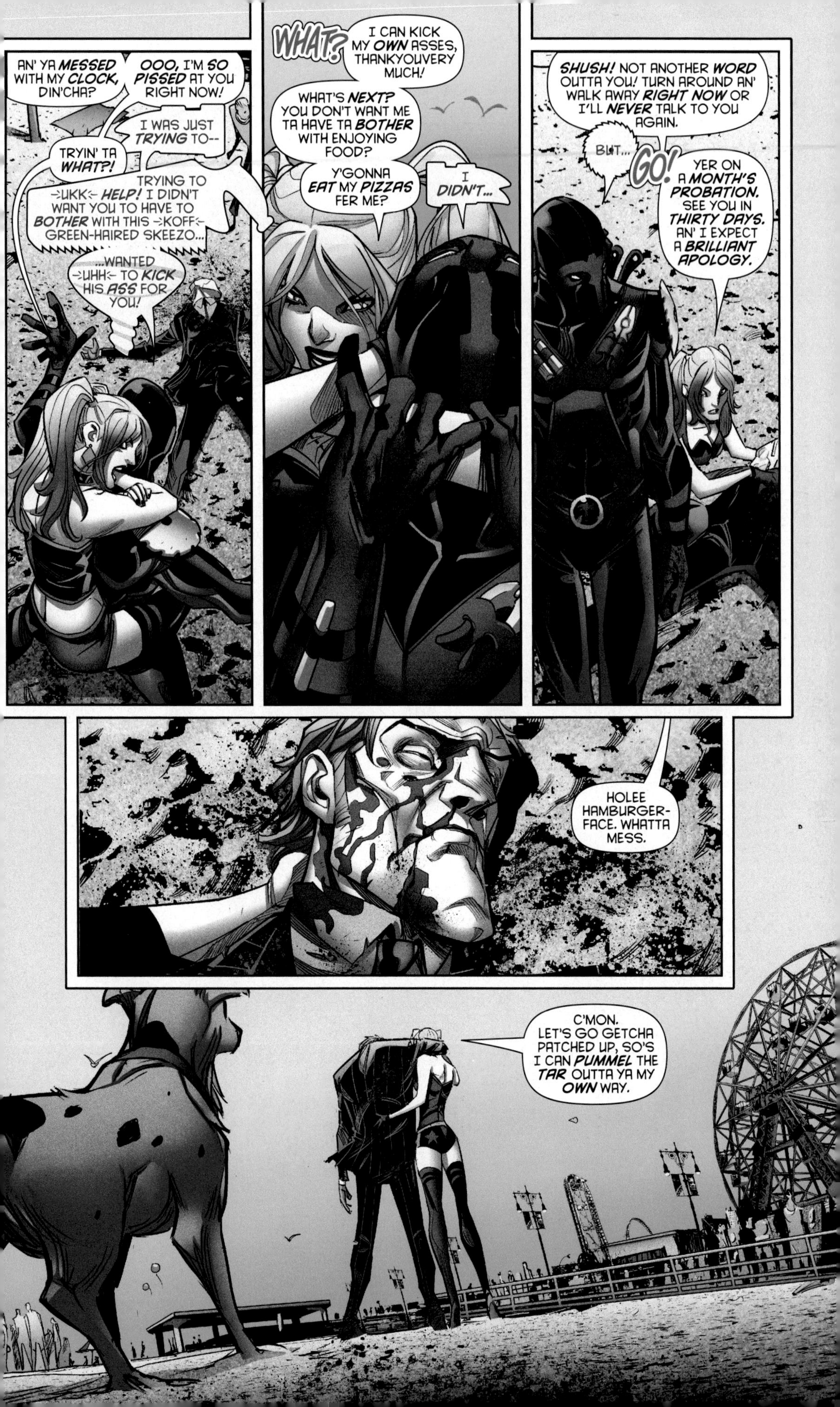
AN' YA MESSED WITH MY CLOCK, DIN'CHA?
OOO, I'M SO PISSED AT YOU RIGHT NOW!
I WAS JUST TRYING TO--
TRYIN' TA WHAT?!
TRYING TO -UKK- HELP! I DIDN'T WANT YOU TO HAVE TO BOTHER WITH THIS -KOFF- GREEN-HAIRED SKEEZO...
...WANTED -UHH- TO KICK HIS ASS FOR YOU!
WHAT?
I CAN KICK MY OWN ASSES, THANKYOUVERY MUCH!
WHAT'S NEXT? YOU DON'T WANT ME TA HAVE TA BOTHER WITH ENJOYING FOOD?
Y'GONNA EAT MY PIZZAS FER ME?
I DIDN'T...
SHUSH! NOT ANOTHER WORD OUTTA YOU! TURN AROUND AN' WALK AWAY RIGHT NOW OR I'LL NEVER TALK TO YOU AGAIN.
BUT...
GO!
YER ON A MONTH'S PROBATION. SEE YOU IN THIRTY DAYS. AN' I EXPECT A BRILLIANT APOLOGY.
HOLEE HAMBURGER-FACE. WHATTA MESS.
C'MON. LET'S GO GETCHA PATCHED UP, SO'S I CAN PUMMEL THE TAR OUTTA YA MY OWN WAY.

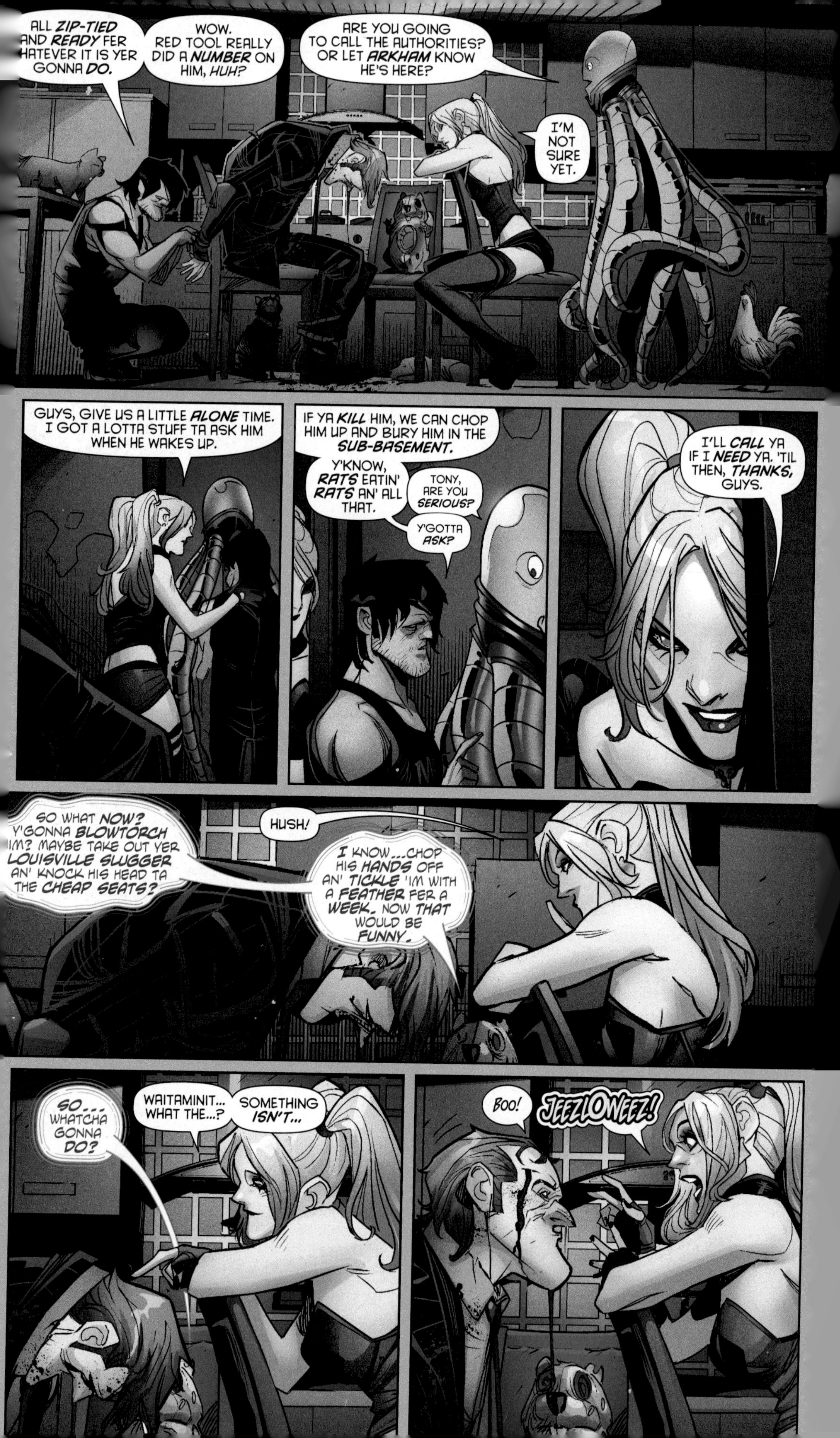

ALL ZIP-TIED AND READY FER WHATEVER IT IS YER GONNA DO.
WOW. RED TOOL REALLY DID A NUMBER ON HIM, HUH?
ARE YOU GOING TO CALL THE AUTHORITIES? OR LET ARKHAM KNOW HE'S HERE?
I'M NOT SURE YET.
GUYS, GIVE US A LITTLE ALONE TIME. I GOT A LOTTA STUFF TA ASK HIM WHEN HE WAKES UP.
IF YA KILL HIM, WE CAN CHOP HIM UP AND BURY HIM IN THE SUB-BASEMENT.
Y'KNOW, RATS EATIN' RATS AN' ALL THAT.
TONY, ARE YOU SERIOUS?
Y'GOTTA ASK?
I'LL CALL YA IF I NEED YA. 'TIL THEN, THANKS, GUYS.
SO WHAT NOW? Y'GONNA BLOWTORCH 'IM? MAYBE TAKE OUT YER LOUISVILLE SLUGGER AN' KNOCK HIS HEAD TA THE CHEAP SEATS?
HUSH!
I KNOW...CHOP HIS HANDS OFF AN' TICKLE 'IM WITH A FEATHER FER A WEEK. NOW THAT WOULD BE FUNNY.
SO... WHATCHA GONNA DO?
WAITAMINIT... WHAT THE...?
SOMETHING ISN'T...
BOO!
JEEZLOWEEZ!

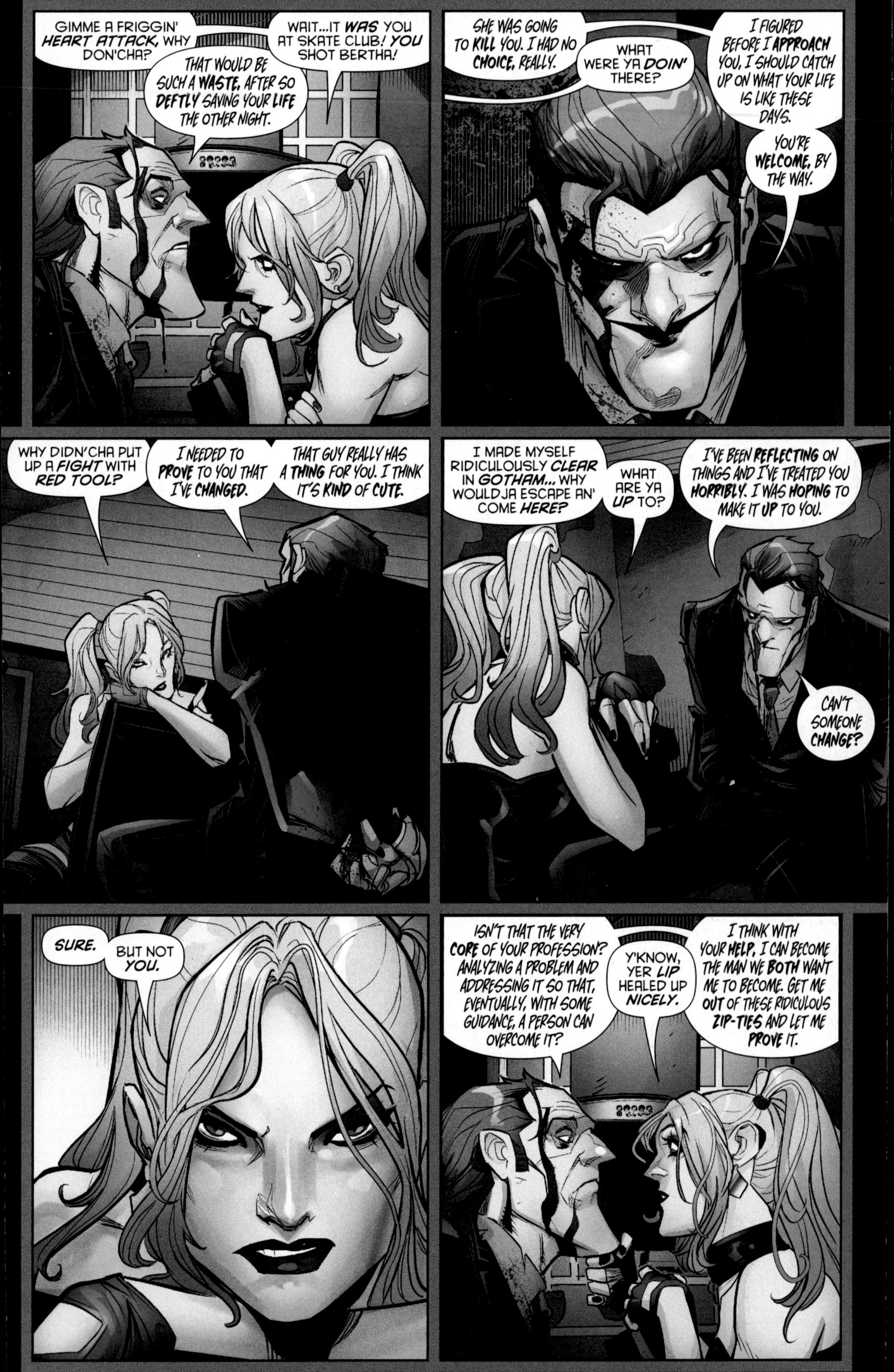

GIMME A FRIGGIN' HEART ATTACK, WHY DON'CHA?
THAT WOULD BE SUCH A WASTE, AFTER SO DEFTLY SAVING YOUR LIFE THE OTHER NIGHT.
WAIT...IT WAS YOU AT SKATE CLUB! YOU SHOT BERTHA!
SHE WAS GOING TO KILL YOU. I HAD NO CHOICE, REALLY.
WHAT WERE YA DOIN' THERE?
I FIGURED BEFORE I APPROACH YOU, I SHOULD CATCH UP ON WHAT YOUR LIFE IS LIKE THESE DAYS.
YOU'RE WELCOME, BY THE WAY.
WHY DIDN'CHA PUT UP A FIGHT WITH RED TOOL?
I NEEDED TO PROVE TO YOU THAT I'VE CHANGED.
THAT GUY REALLY HAS A THING FOR YOU. I THINK IT'S KIND OF CUTE.
I MADE MYSELF RIDICULOUSLY CLEAR IN GOTHAM... WHY WOULDJA ESCAPE AN' COME HERE?
WHAT ARE YA UP TO?
I'VE BEEN REFLECTING ON THINGS AND I'VE TREATED YOU HORRIBLY. I WAS HOPING TO MAKE IT UP TO YOU.
CAN'T SOMEONE CHANGE?
SURE.
BUT NOT YOU.
ISN'T THAT THE VERY CORE OF YOUR PROFESSION? ANALYZING A PROBLEM AND ADDRESSING IT SO THAT, EVENTUALLY, WITH SOME GUIDANCE, A PERSON CAN OVERCOME IT?
Y'KNOW, YER LIP HEALED UP NICELY.
I THINK WITH YOUR HELP, I CAN BECOME THE MAN WE BOTH WANT ME TO BECOME. GET ME OUT OF THESE RIDICULOUS ZIP-TIES AND LET ME PROVE IT.

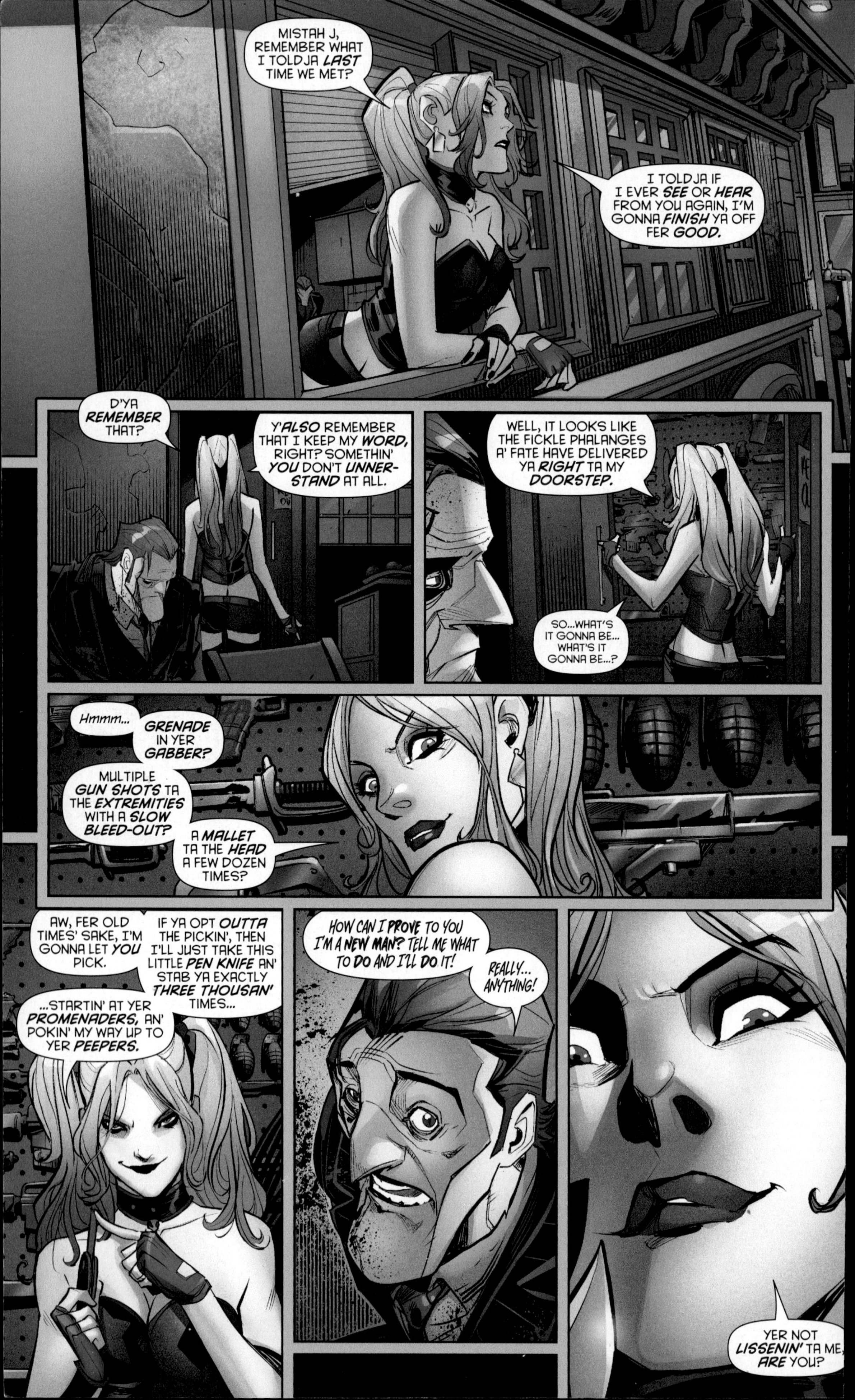
MISTAH J, REMEMBER WHAT I TOLDJA LAST TIME WE MET?
I TOLDJA IF I EVER SEE OR HEAR FROM YOU AGAIN, I'M GONNA FINISH YA OFF FER GOOD.
D'YA REMEMBER THAT?
Y'ALSO REMEMBER THAT I KEEP MY WORD, RIGHT? SOMETHIN' YOU DON'T UNNER-STAND AT ALL.
WELL, IT LOOKS LIKE THE FICKLE PHALANGES A' FATE HAVE DELIVERED YA RIGHT TA MY DOORSTEP.
SO...WHAT'S IT GONNA BE... WHAT'S IT GONNA BE...?
Hmmm...
GRENADE IN YER GABBER?
MULTIPLE GUN SHOTS TA THE EXTREMITIES WITH A SLOW BLEED-OUT?
A MALLET TA THE HEAD A FEW DOZEN TIMES?
AW, FER OLD TIMES' SAKE, I'M GONNA LET YOU PICK.
IF YA OPT OUTTA THE PICKIN', THEN I'LL JUST TAKE THIS LITTLE PEN KNIFE AN' STAB YA EXACTLY THREE THOUSAN' TIMES...
...STARTIN' AT YER PROMENADERS, AN' POKIN' MY WAY UP TO YER PEEPERS.
HOW CAN I PROVE TO YOU I'M A NEW MAN? TELL ME WHAT TO DO AND I'LL DO IT!
REALLY... ANYTHING!
YER NOT LISSENIN' TA ME, ARE YOU?

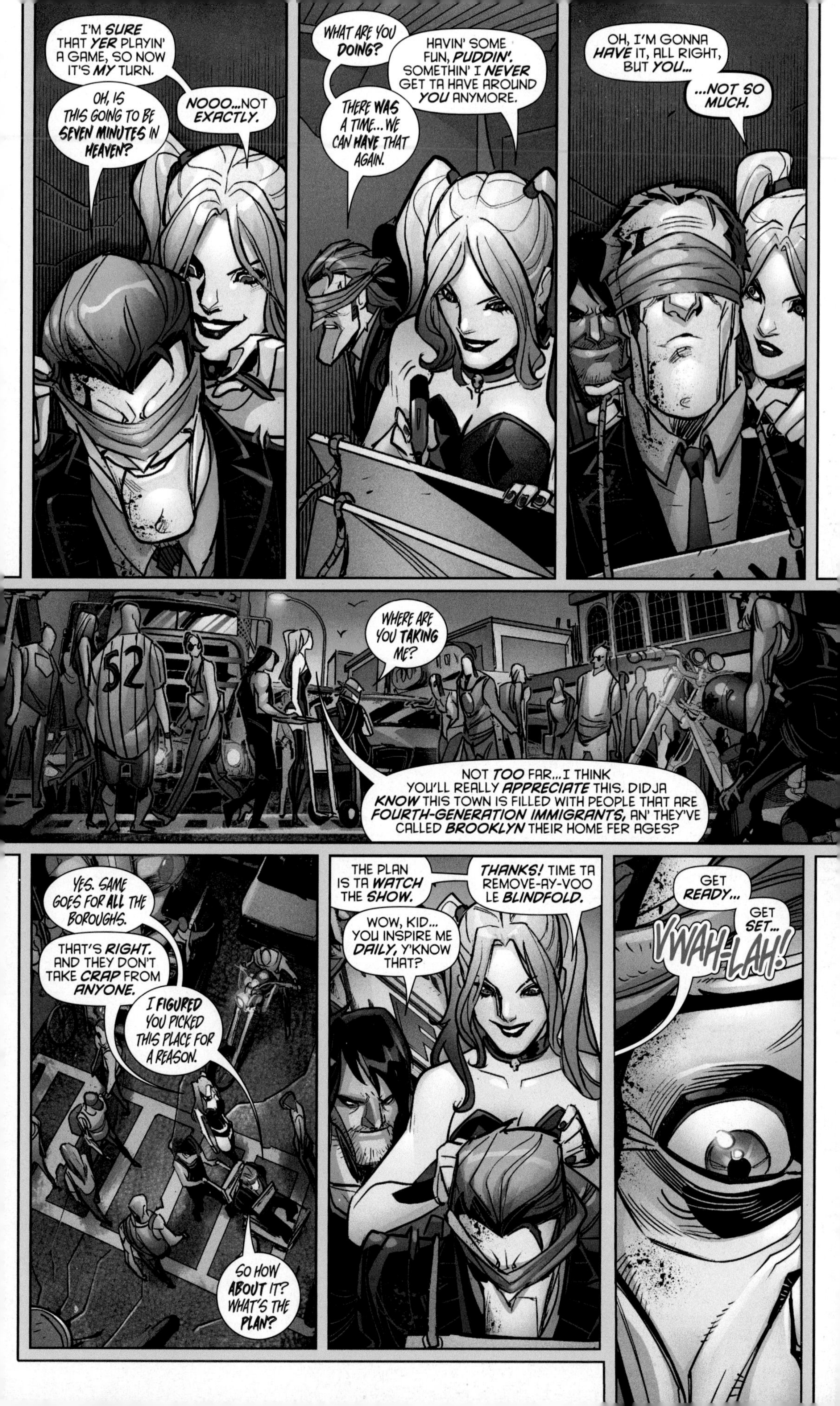

I'M SURE THAT YER PLAYIN' A GAME, SO NOW IT'S MY TURN.
OH, IS THIS GOING TO BE SEVEN MINUTES IN HEAVEN?
NOOO...NOT EXACTLY.
WHAT ARE YOU DOING?
HAVIN' SOME FUN, PUDDIN'. SOMETHIN' I NEVER GET TA HAVE AROUND YOU ANYMORE.
THERE WAS A TIME... WE CAN HAVE THAT AGAIN.
OH, I'M GONNA HAVE IT, ALL RIGHT, BUT YOU...
...NOT SO MUCH.
52
WHERE ARE YOU TAKING ME?
NOT TOO FAR...I THINK YOU'LL REALLY APPRECIATE THIS. DIDJA KNOW THIS TOWN IS FILLED WITH PEOPLE THAT ARE FOURTH-GENERATION IMMIGRANTS, AN' THEY'VE CALLED BROOKLYN THEIR HOME FER AGES?
YES. SAME GOES FOR ALL THE BOROUGHS.
THAT'S RIGHT. AND THEY DON'T TAKE CRAP FROM ANYONE.
I FIGURED YOU PICKED THIS PLACE FOR A REASON.
SO HOW ABOUT IT? WHAT'S THE PLAN?
THE PLAN IS TA WATCH THE SHOW.
WOW, KID... YOU INSPIRE ME DAILY, Y'KNOW THAT?
THANKS! TIME TA REMOVE-AY-VOO LE BLINDFOLD.
GET READY...
GET SET...
VWAH-LAH!

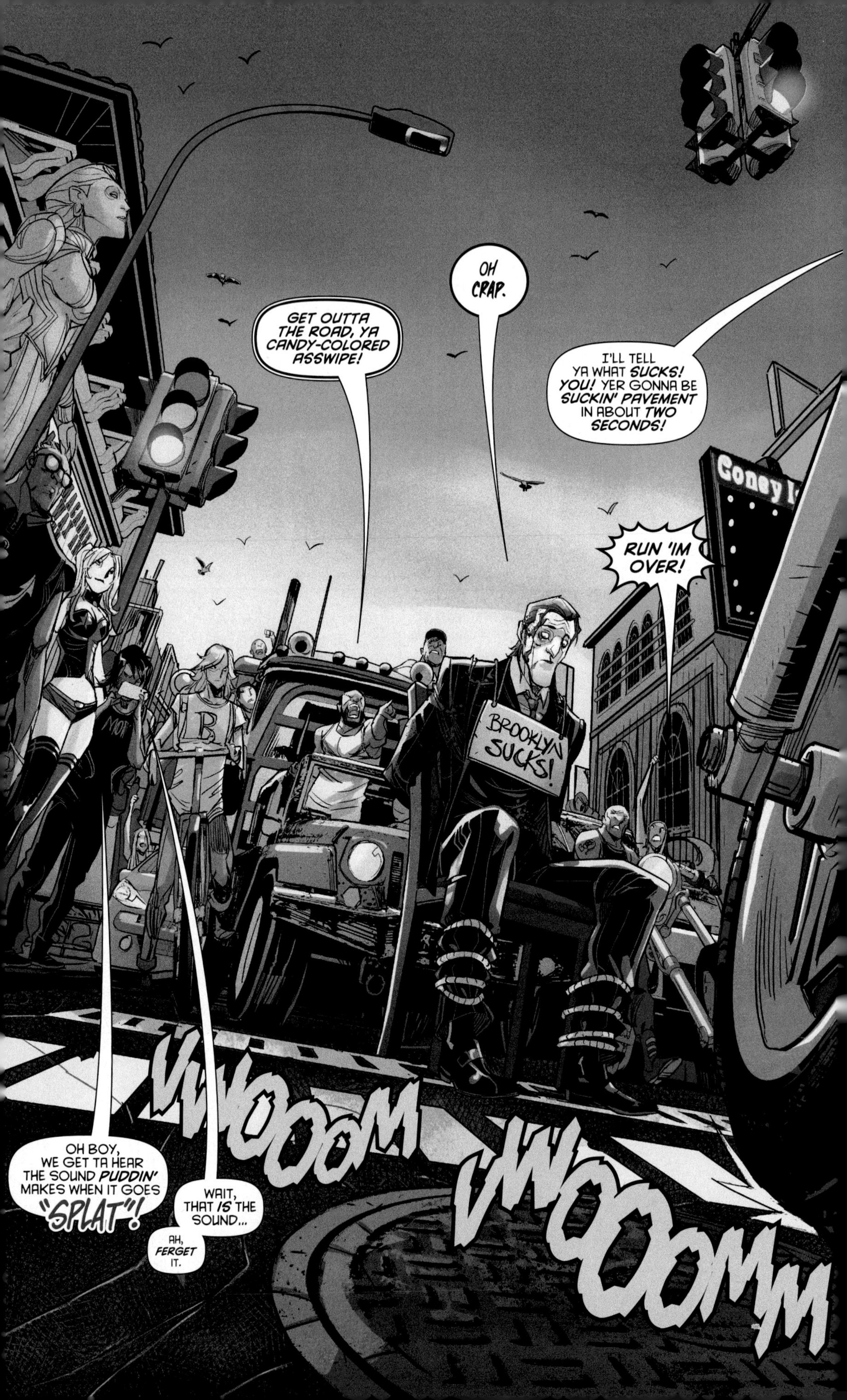
GET OUTTA THE ROAD, YA CANDY-COLORED ASSWIPE!
OH CRAP.
I'LL TELL YA WHAT SUCKS! YOU! YER GONNA BE SUCKIN' PAVEMENT IN ABOUT TWO SECONDS!
Coney I
RUN 'IM OVER!
BROOKLYN SUCKS!
VWOOOM
VWOOOMM
OH BOY, WE GET TA HEAR THE SOUND PUDDIN' MAKES WHEN IT GOES "SPLAT"!
WAIT, THAT IS THE SOUND...
AH, FERGET IT.

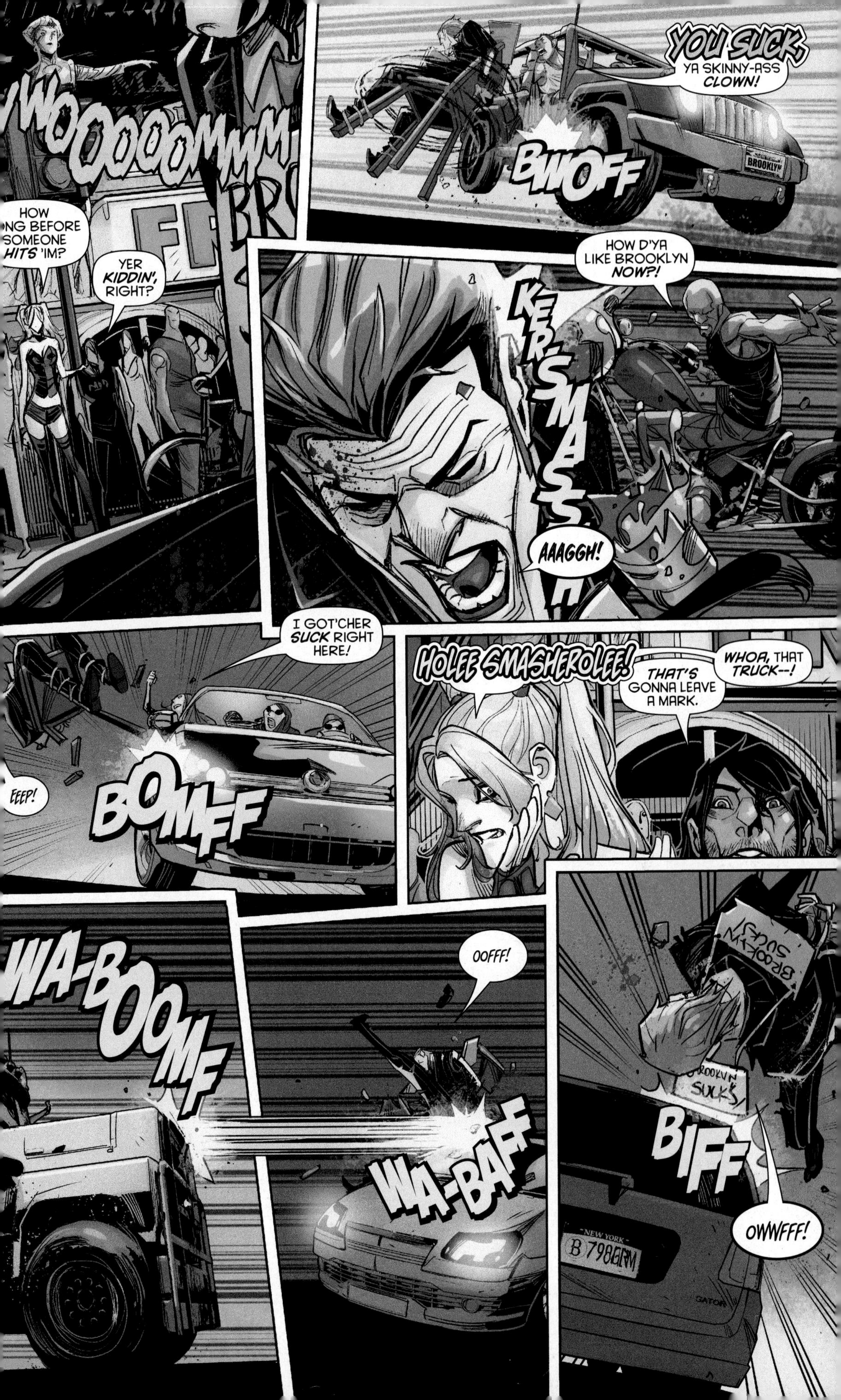
WOOOOOMMM
BR
FR
HOW
NG BEFORE
SOMEONE
HITS 'IM?
YER
KIDDIN',
RIGHT?
YOU SUCK,
YA SKINNY-ASS
CLOWN!
BWOFF
BROOKLYN
HOW D'YA
LIKE BROOKLYN
NOW?!
KER-SMASSH
AAAGGH!
I GOT'CHER
SUCK RIGHT
HERE!
EEEP!
BOMFF
HOLEE SMASHEROLEE!
WHOA, THAT
TRUCK--!
THAT'S
GONNA LEAVE
A MARK.
WA-BOOOMF
OOFFF!
WA-BAFF
BROOKLYN
SUCKS!
BIFF
NEW YORK
B 798GRM
OWWFFF!

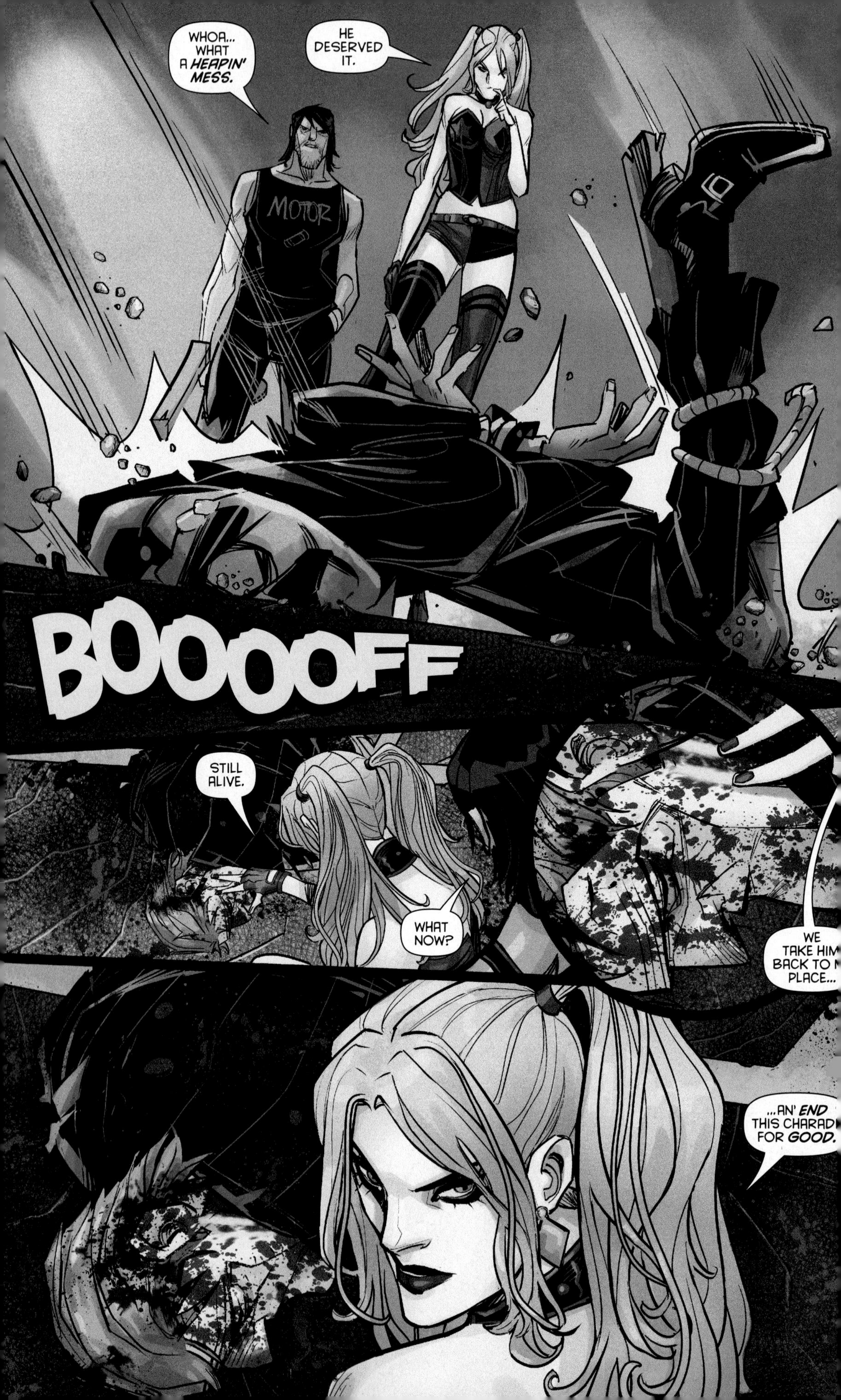

WHOA... WHAT A HEAPIN' MESS.
HE DESERVED IT.
MOTOR
BOOOOFF
STILL ALIVE.
WHAT NOW?
WE TAKE HIM BACK TO M PLACE...
...AN' END THIS CHARAD FOR GOOD.

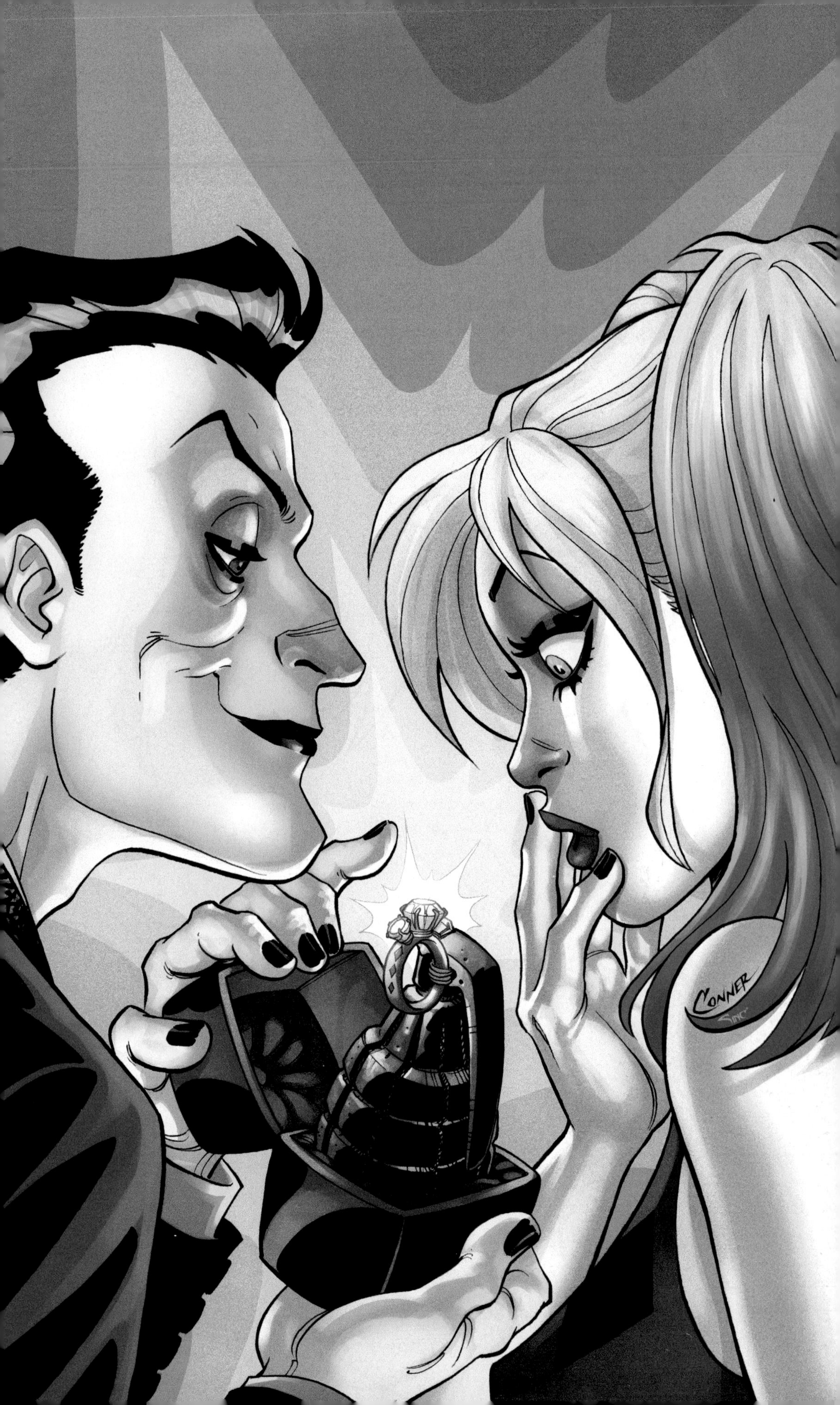
CONNER

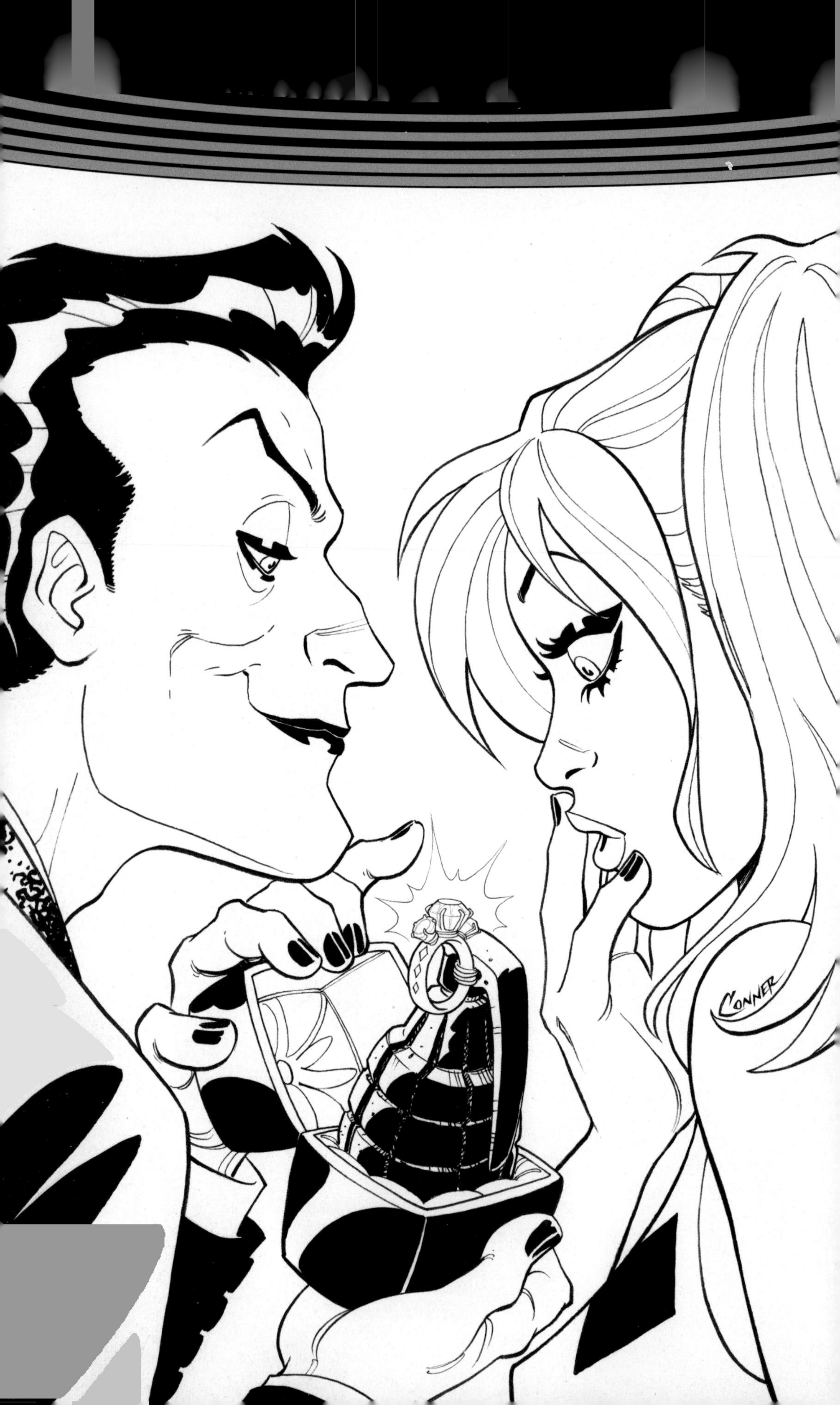

CONNER

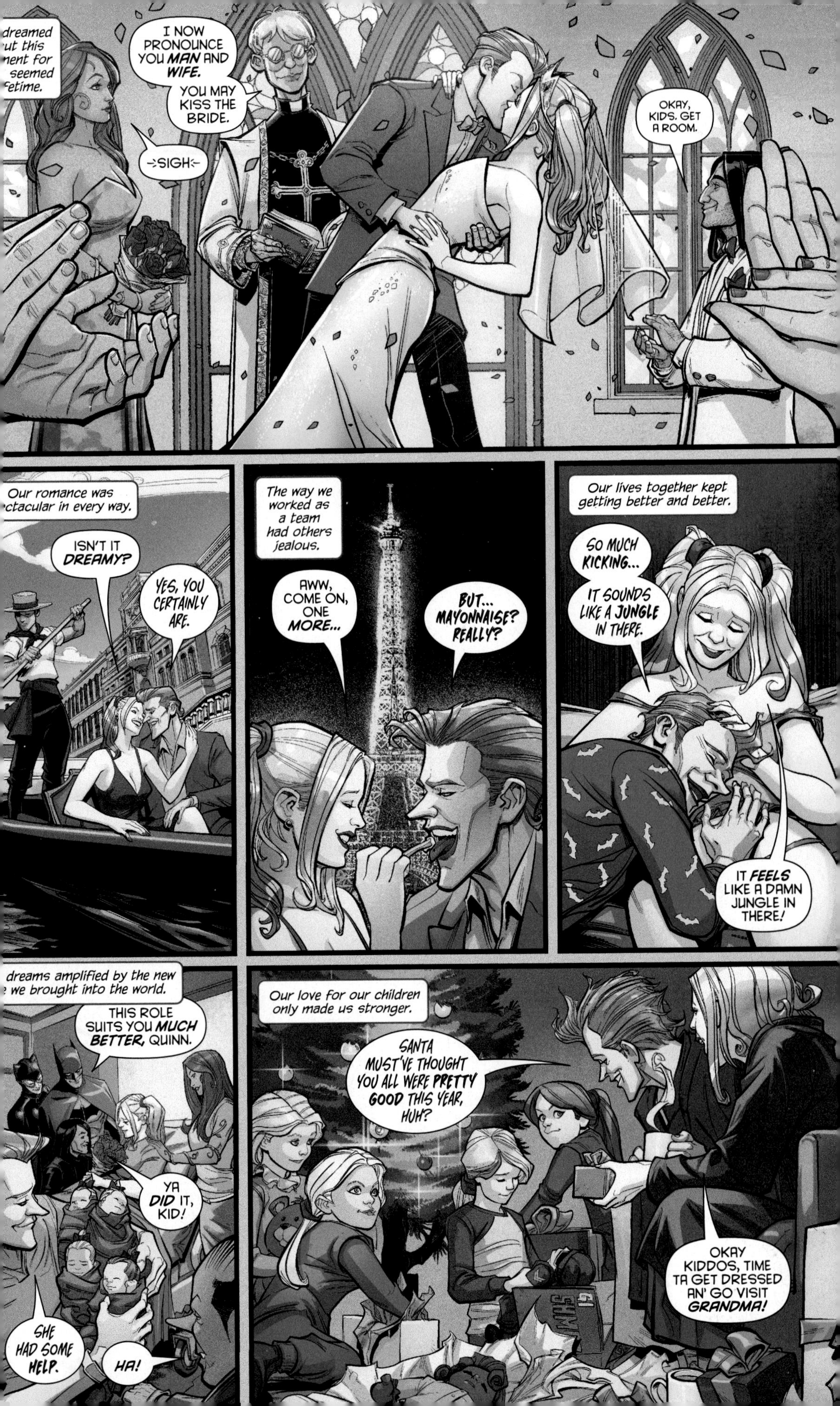
dreamed
ut this
nent for
seemed
fetime.
I NOW PRONOUNCE YOU MAN AND WIFE.
YOU MAY KISS THE BRIDE.
SIGH
OKAY, KIDS. GET A ROOM.
Our romance was
ctacular in every way.
ISN'T IT DREAMY?
YES, YOU CERTAINLY ARE.
The way we worked as a team had others jealous.
AWW, COME ON, ONE MORE...
BUT... MAYONNAISE? REALLY?
Our lives together kept getting better and better.
SO MUCH KICKING...
IT SOUNDS LIKE A JUNGLE IN THERE.
IT FEELS LIKE A DAMN JUNGLE IN THERE!
dreams amplified by the new
we brought into the world.
THIS ROLE SUITS YOU MUCH BETTER, QUINN.
YA DID IT, KID!
SHE HAD SOME HELP.
HA!
Our love for our children only made us stronger.
SANTA MUST'VE THOUGHT YOU ALL WERE PRETTY GOOD THIS YEAR, HUH?
OKAY KIDDOS, TIME TA GET DRESSED AN' GO VISIT GRANDMA!

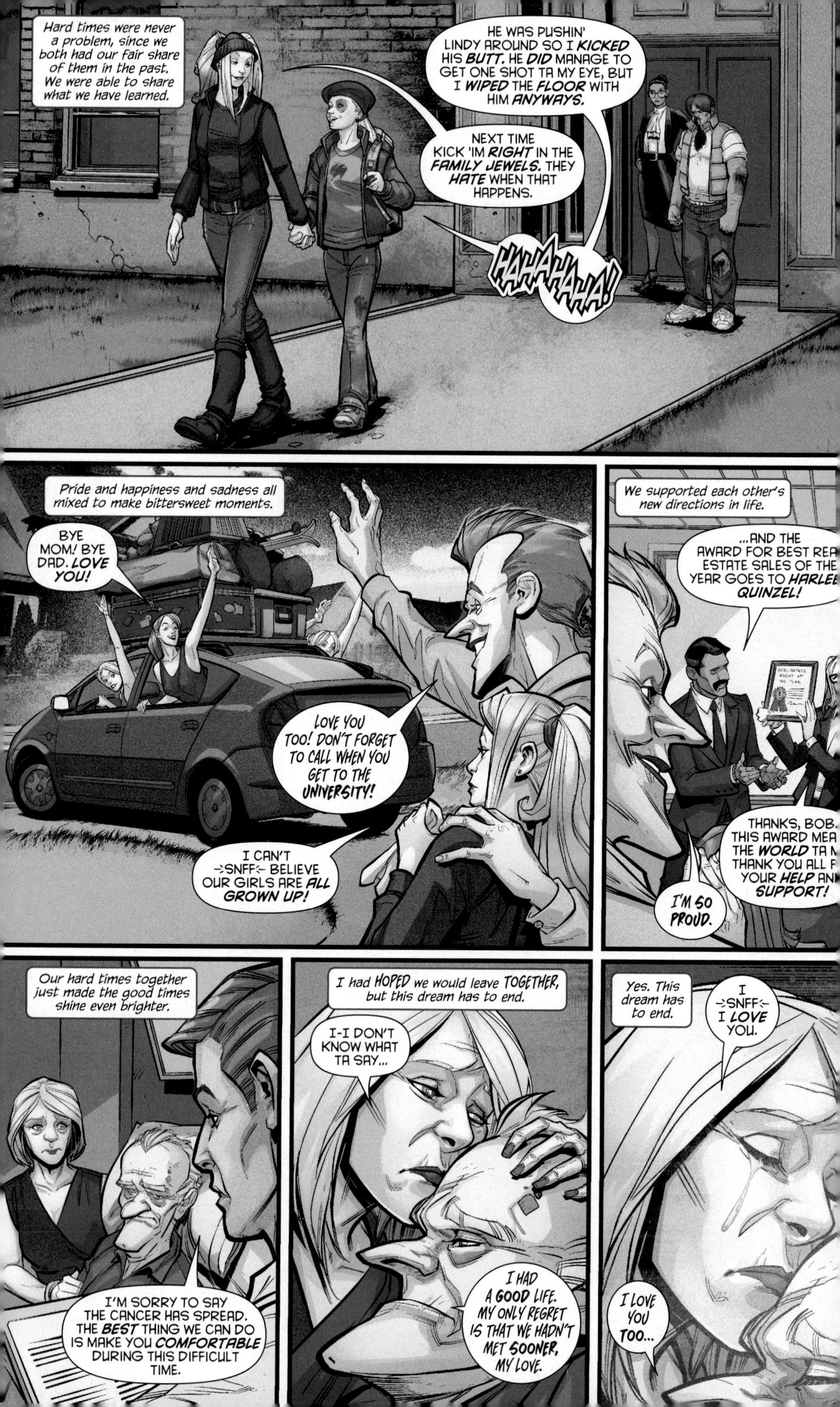

Hard times were never a problem, since we both had our fair share of them in the past. We were able to share what we have learned.
HE WAS PUSHIN' LINDY AROUND SO I KICKED HIS BUTT. HE DID MANAGE TO GET ONE SHOT TA MY EYE, BUT I WIPED THE FLOOR WITH HIM ANYWAYS.
NEXT TIME KICK 'IM RIGHT IN THE FAMILY JEWELS. THEY HATE WHEN THAT HAPPENS.
HAHAHAHA!
Pride and happiness and sadness all mixed to make bittersweet moments.
BYE MOM! BYE DAD. LOVE YOU!
LOVE YOU TOO! DON'T FORGET TO CALL WHEN YOU GET TO THE UNIVERSITY!
I CAN'T -SNFF- BELIEVE OUR GIRLS ARE ALL GROWN UP!
We supported each other's new directions in life.
...AND THE AWARD FOR BEST REA ESTATE SALES OF THE YEAR GOES TO HARLEE QUINZEL!
THANKS, BOB. THIS AWARD MEA THE WORLD TA M THANK YOU ALL F YOUR HELP AN SUPPORT!
I'M SO PROUD.
Our hard times together just made the good times shine even brighter.
I'M SORRY TO SAY THE CANCER HAS SPREAD. THE BEST THING WE CAN DO IS MAKE YOU COMFORTABLE DURING THIS DIFFICULT TIME.
I had HOPED we would leave TOGETHER, but this dream has to end.
I-I DON'T KNOW WHAT TA SAY...
I HAD A GOOD LIFE. MY ONLY REGRET IS THAT WE HADN'T MET SOONER, MY LOVE.
Yes. This dream has to end.
I -SNFF- I LOVE YOU.
I LOVE YOU TOO...

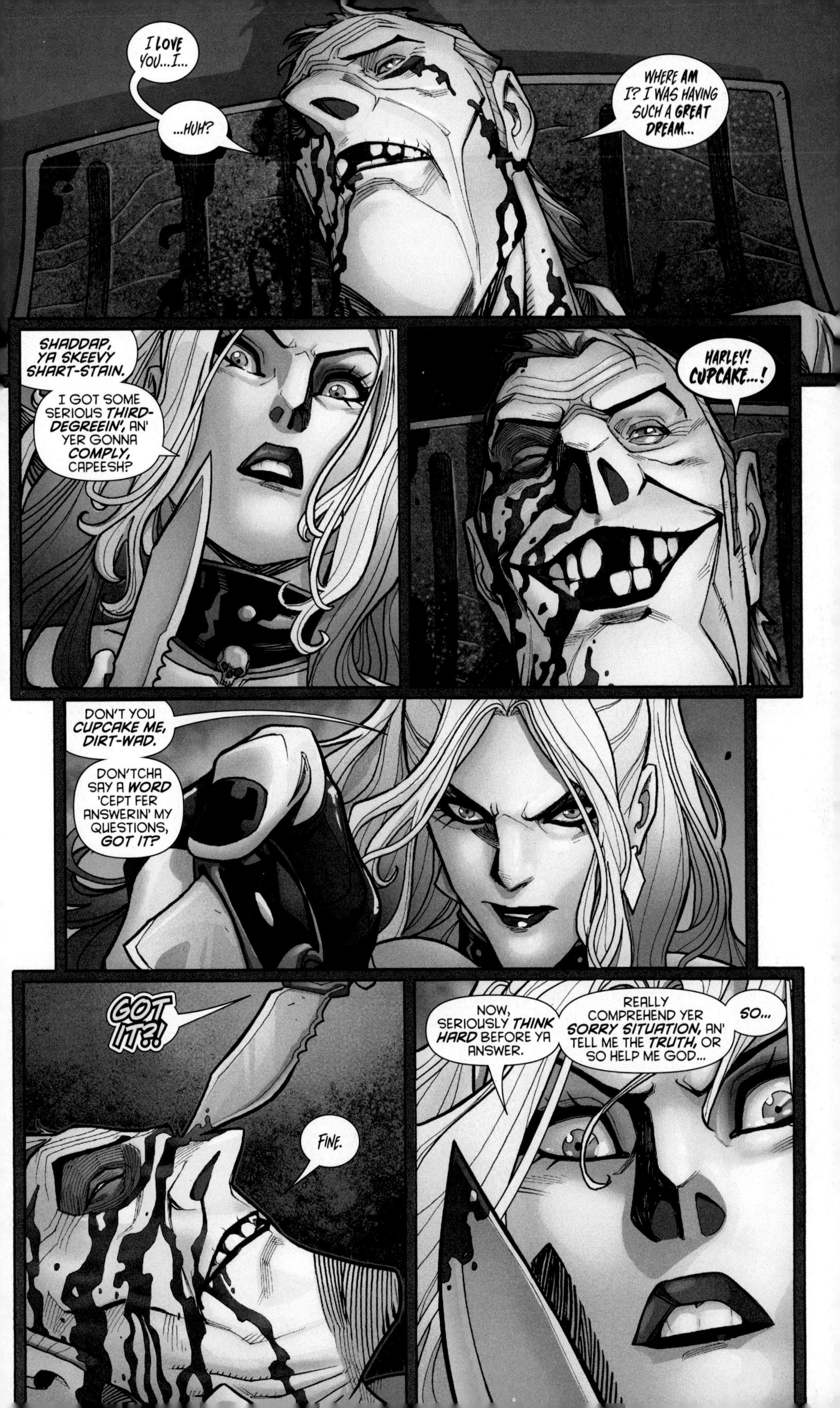
I LOVE YOU...I...
...HUH?
WHERE AM I? I WAS HAVING SUCH A GREAT DREAM...
SHADDAP, YA SKEEVY SHART-STAIN.
I GOT SOME SERIOUS THIRD-DEGREEIN', AN' YER GONNA COMPLY, CAPEESH?
HARLEY! CUPCAKE...!
DON'T YOU CUPCAKE ME, DIRT-WAD.
DON'TCHA SAY A WORD 'CEPT FER ANSWERIN' MY QUESTIONS, GOT IT?
GOT IT?!
FINE.
SO...
REALLY COMPREHEND YER SORRY SITUATION, AN' TELL ME THE TRUTH, OR SO HELP ME GOD...
NOW, SERIOUSLY THINK HARD BEFORE YA ANSWER.

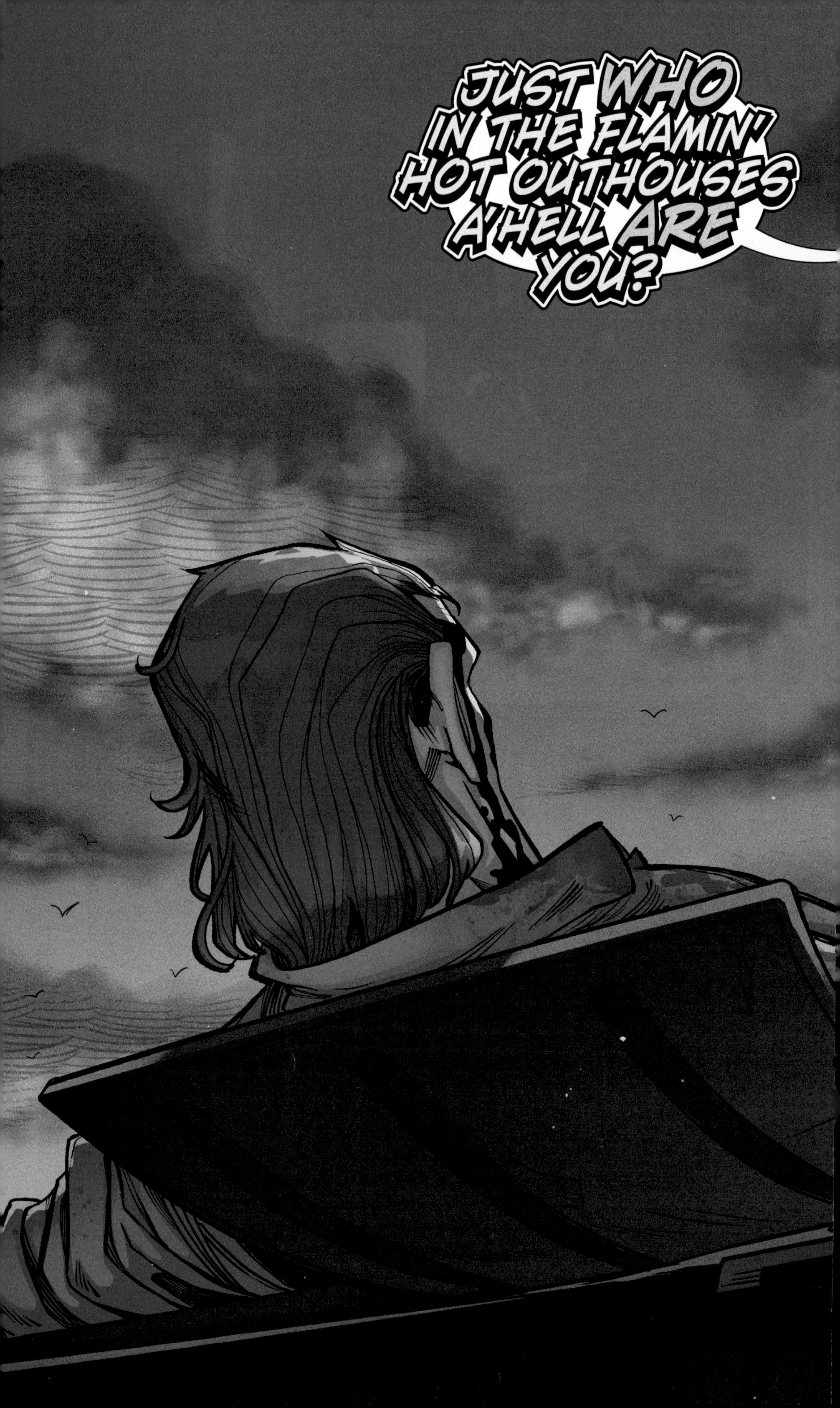
JUST WHO IN THE FLAMIN' HOT OUTHOUSES A'HELL ARE YOU?

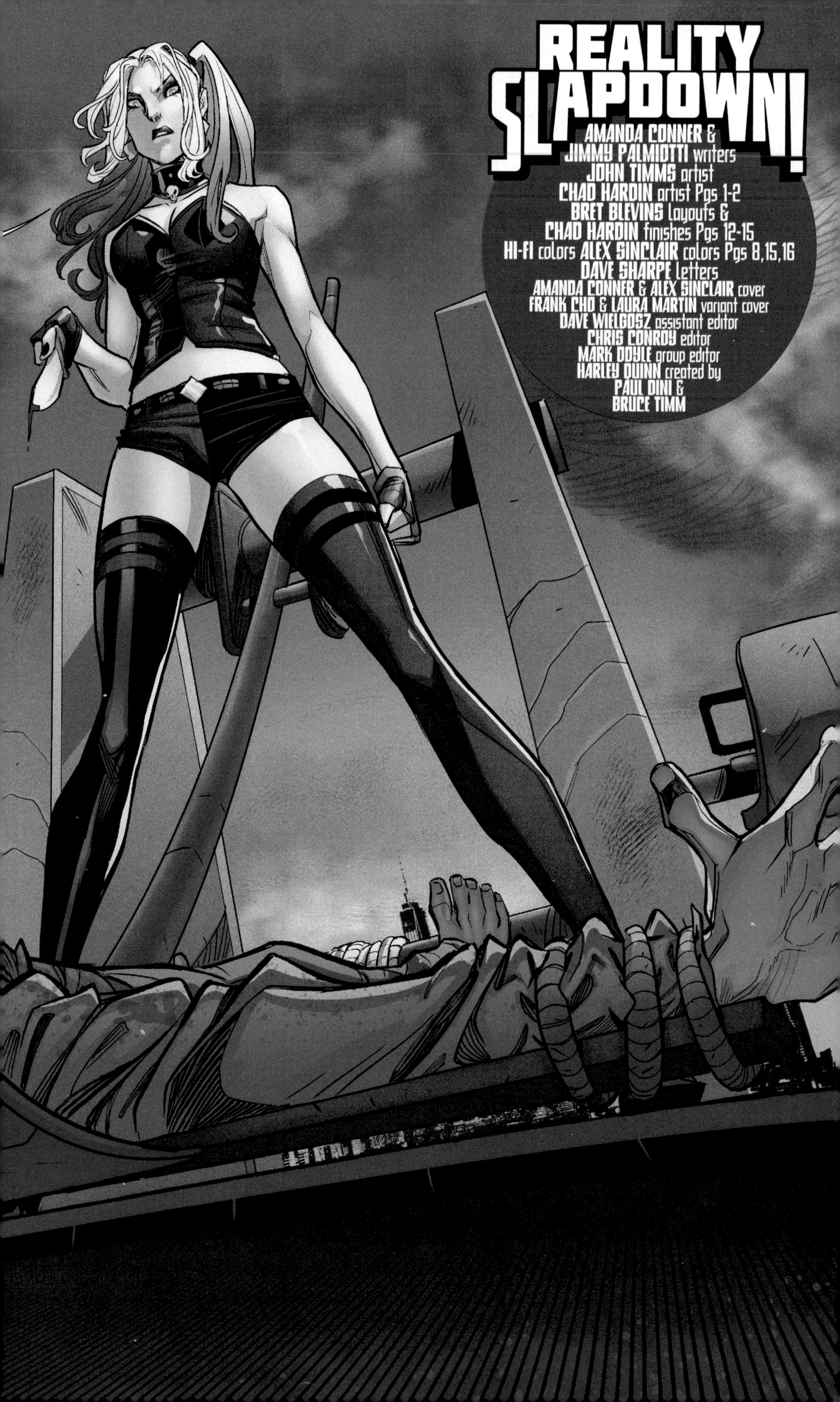

REALITY SLAPDOWN!
AMANDA CONNER & JIMMY PALMIOTTI writers
JOHN TIMMS artist
CHAD HARDIN artist Pgs 1-2
BRET BLEVINS layouts & CHAD HARDIN finishes Pgs 12-15
HI-FI colors ALEX SINCLAIR colors Pgs 8,15,16
DAVE SHARPE letters
AMANDA CONNER & ALEX SINCLAIR cover
FRANK CHO & LAURA MARTIN variant cover
DAVE WIELGOSZ assistant editor
CHRIS CONROY editor
MARK DOYLE group editor
HARLEY QUINN created by PAUL DINI & BRUCE TIMM

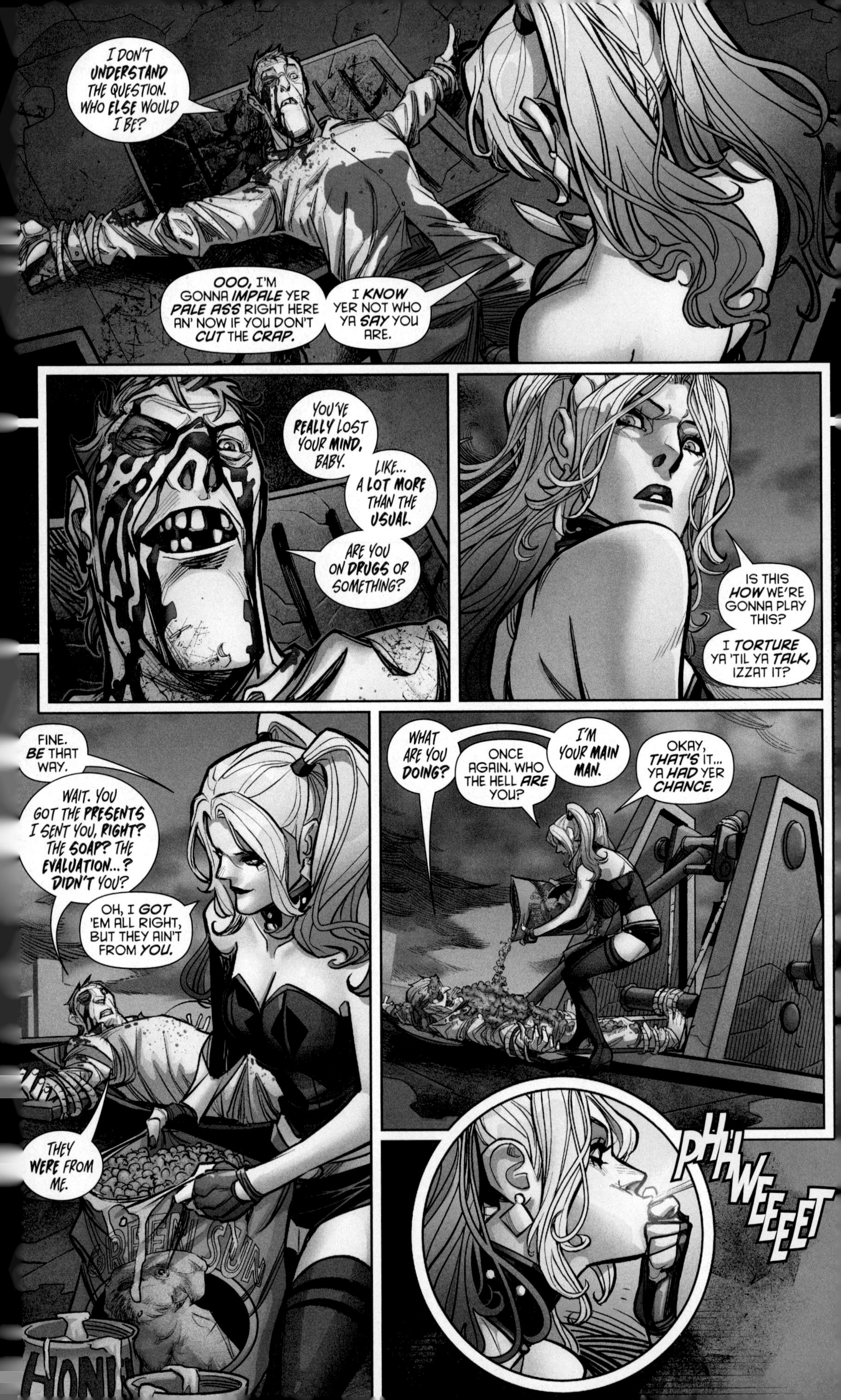
I DON'T UNDERSTAND THE QUESTION. WHO ELSE WOULD I BE?
I KNOW YER NOT WHO YA SAY YOU ARE.
OOO, I'M GONNA IMPALE YER PALE ASS RIGHT HERE AN' NOW IF YOU DON'T CUT THE CRAP.
YOU'VE REALLY LOST YOUR MIND, BABY.
LIKE... A LOT MORE THAN THE USUAL.
ARE YOU ON DRUGS OR SOMETHING?
IS THIS HOW WE'RE GONNA PLAY THIS?
I TORTURE YA 'TIL YA TALK, IZZAT IT?
FINE. BE THAT WAY.
WAIT. YOU GOT THE PRESENTS I SENT YOU, RIGHT? THE SOAP? THE EVALUATION...? DIDN'T YOU?
OH, I GOT 'EM ALL RIGHT, BUT THEY AIN'T FROM YOU.
THEY WERE FROM ME.
GREEN SUN
WHAT ARE YOU DOING?
I'M YOUR MAIN MAN.
ONCE AGAIN. WHO THE HELL ARE YOU?
OKAY, THAT'S IT... YA HAD YER CHANCE.
PHHWEEEEET

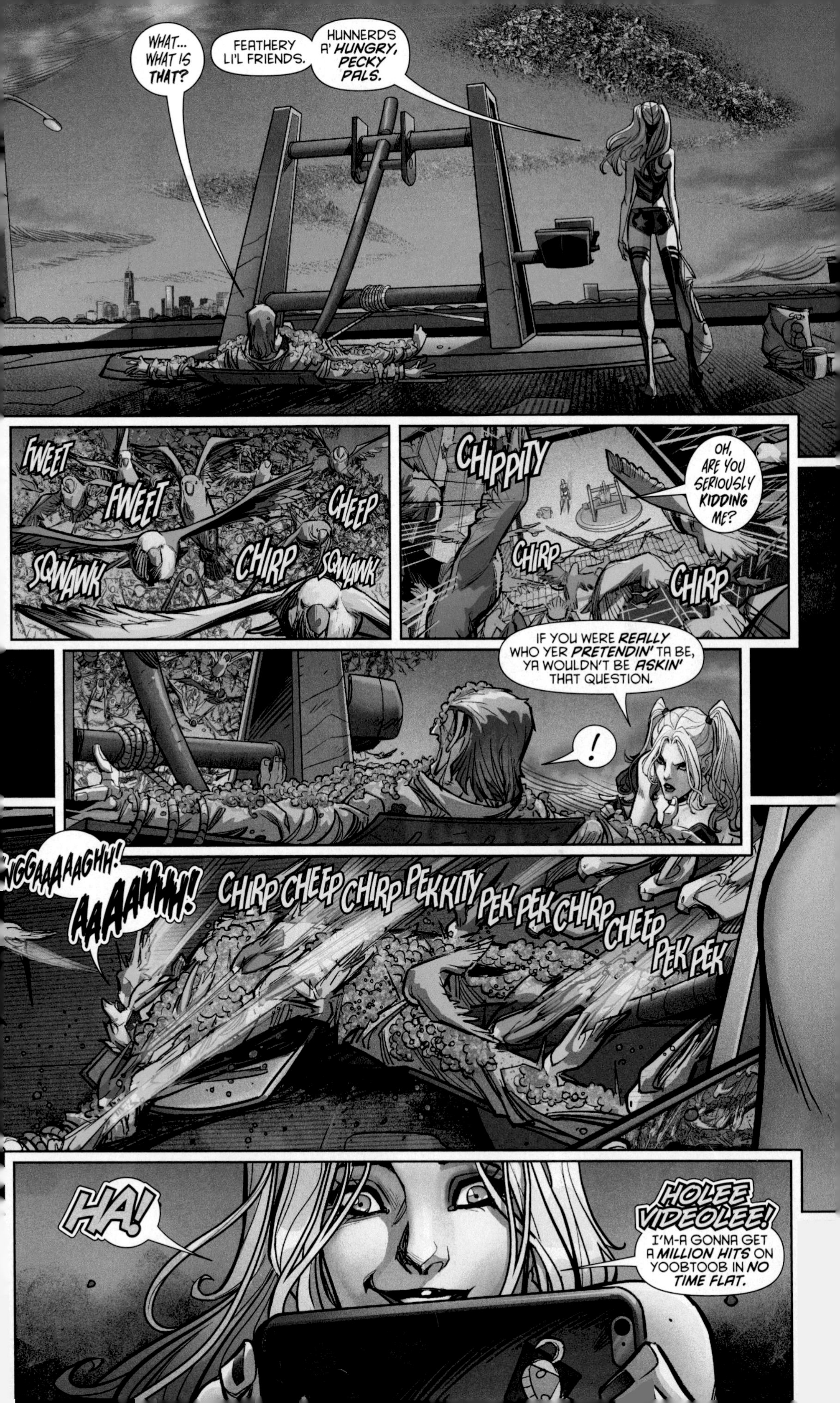
WHAT... WHAT IS THAT?
FEATHERY LI'L FRIENDS.
HUNNERDS A' HUNGRY, PECKY PALS.
FWEET
FWEET
CHEEP
SQWAWK
CHIRP
SQWAWK
CHIPPITY
OH, ARE YOU SERIOUSLY KIDDING ME?
CHIRP
CHIRP
IF YOU WERE REALLY WHO YER PRETENDIN' TA BE, YA WOULDN'T BE ASKIN' THAT QUESTION.
!
NGGAAAAAGHH!
AAAAHHH!
CHIRP CHEEP CHIRP PEKKITY PEK PEK CHIRP CHEEP PEK PEK
HA!
HOLEE VIDEOLEE!
I'M-A GONNA GET A MILLION HITS ON YOOBTOOB IN NO TIME FLAT.

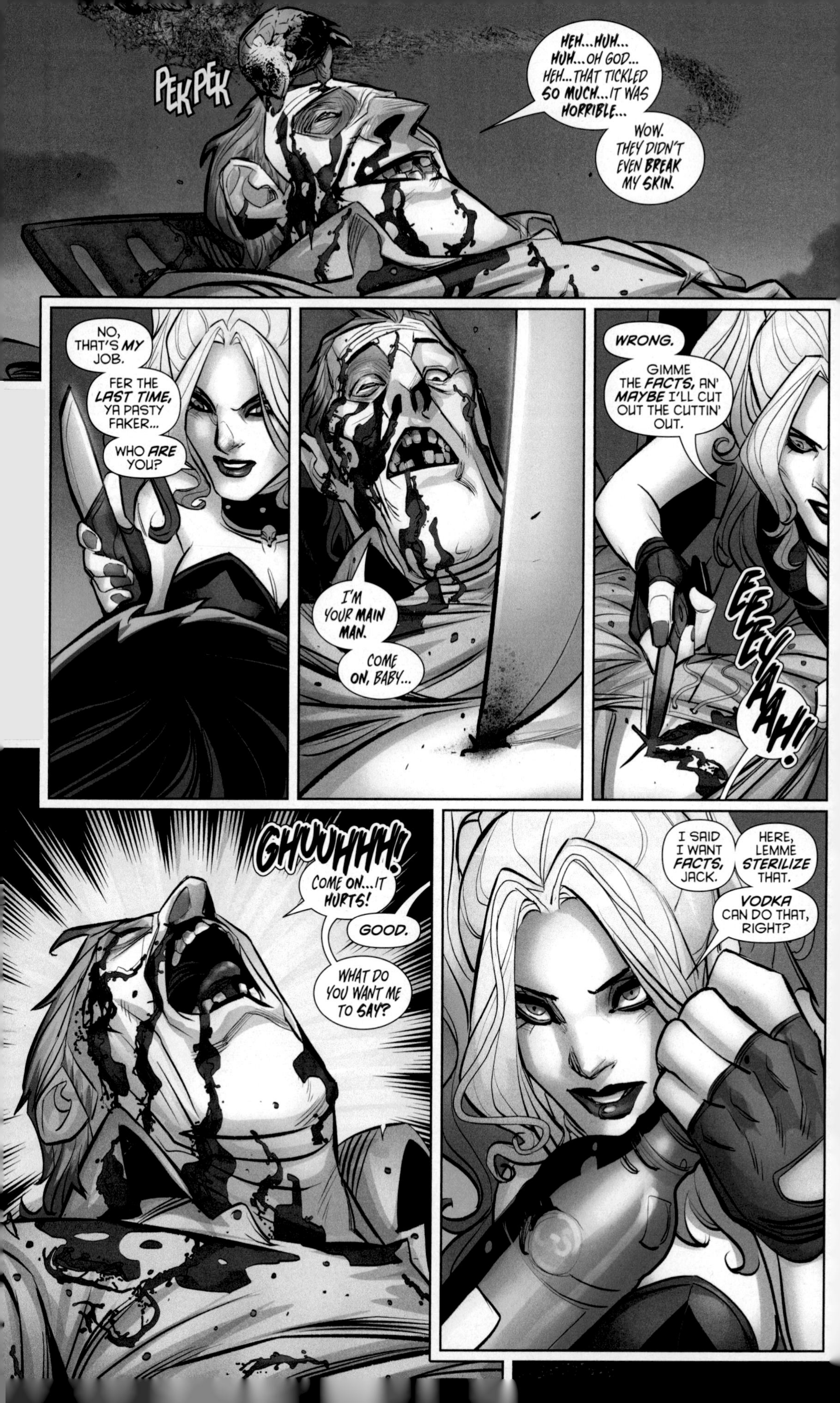
PEK PEK
HEH...HUH... HUH...OH GOD... HEH...THAT TICKLED SO MUCH...IT WAS HORRIBLE...
WOW. THEY DIDN'T EVEN BREAK MY SKIN.
NO, THAT'S MY JOB.
FER THE LAST TIME, YA PASTY FAKER...
WHO ARE YOU?
I'M YOUR MAIN MAN.
COME ON, BABY...
WRONG.
GIMME THE FACTS, AN' MAYBE I'LL CUT OUT THE CUTTIN' OUT.
EEEYAAAH!!
GHUUHHH!
COME ON...IT HURTS!
GOOD.
WHAT DO YOU WANT ME TO SAY?
I SAID I WANT FACTS, JACK.
HERE, LEMME STERILIZE THAT.
VODKA CAN DO THAT, RIGHT?

* (asterisk)

GHAAAAAAHHH!

~glug glug~

UHHGH... YOU... YOU'RE DONE, RIGHT?

TELL ME YOU'RE DONE.

AW, SWEETIE... I'VE BARELY BEGUN.

NOTICE ANYTHING DIFFERENT?

TONY AN' I BANDAGED YA UP AFTER YER TRAFFIC MISHAP. AN' WE TOOK OFF YER BLOODY DUDS...

...INCLUDIN' YER PANTS.

OH NO.

OH YES.

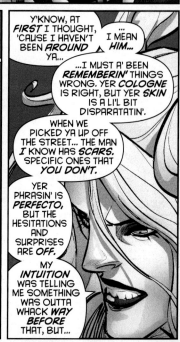

Y'KNOW, AT FIRST I THOUGHT, 'CAUSE I HAVEN'T BEEN AROUND YA...

...I MEAN HIM...

...I MUST A' BEEN REMEMBERIN' THINGS WRONG. YER COLOGNE IS RIGHT, BUT YER SKIN IS A LI'L BIT DISPARATATIN'.

WHEN WE PICKED YA UP OFF THE STREET... THE MAN I KNOW HAS SCARS. SPECIFIC ONES THAT YOU DON'T.

YER PHRASIN' IS PERFECTO, BUT THE HESITATIONS AND SURPRISES ARE OFF.

MY INTUITION WAS TELLING ME SOMETHING WAS OUTTA WHACK WAY BEFORE THAT, BUT...

WHAT CONVINCED ME A HUNNERD PERCENT WAS WHEN WE BROUGHT YER BUSTED-ASS SELF BACK HERE AND CHANGED YER CLOTHES.

YOU GOT THE FACIAL SURGERY DEAD ON. THE TEETH. THE EYES. THE NOSE IS ON THE NOSE.

THE MANNERISMS A[R]E MASTERFUL.

THAT CONFIDENT STRIDE... TRULY, UNDOUBTEDLY, SINCERE[LY] ASTOUNDIFYIN'.

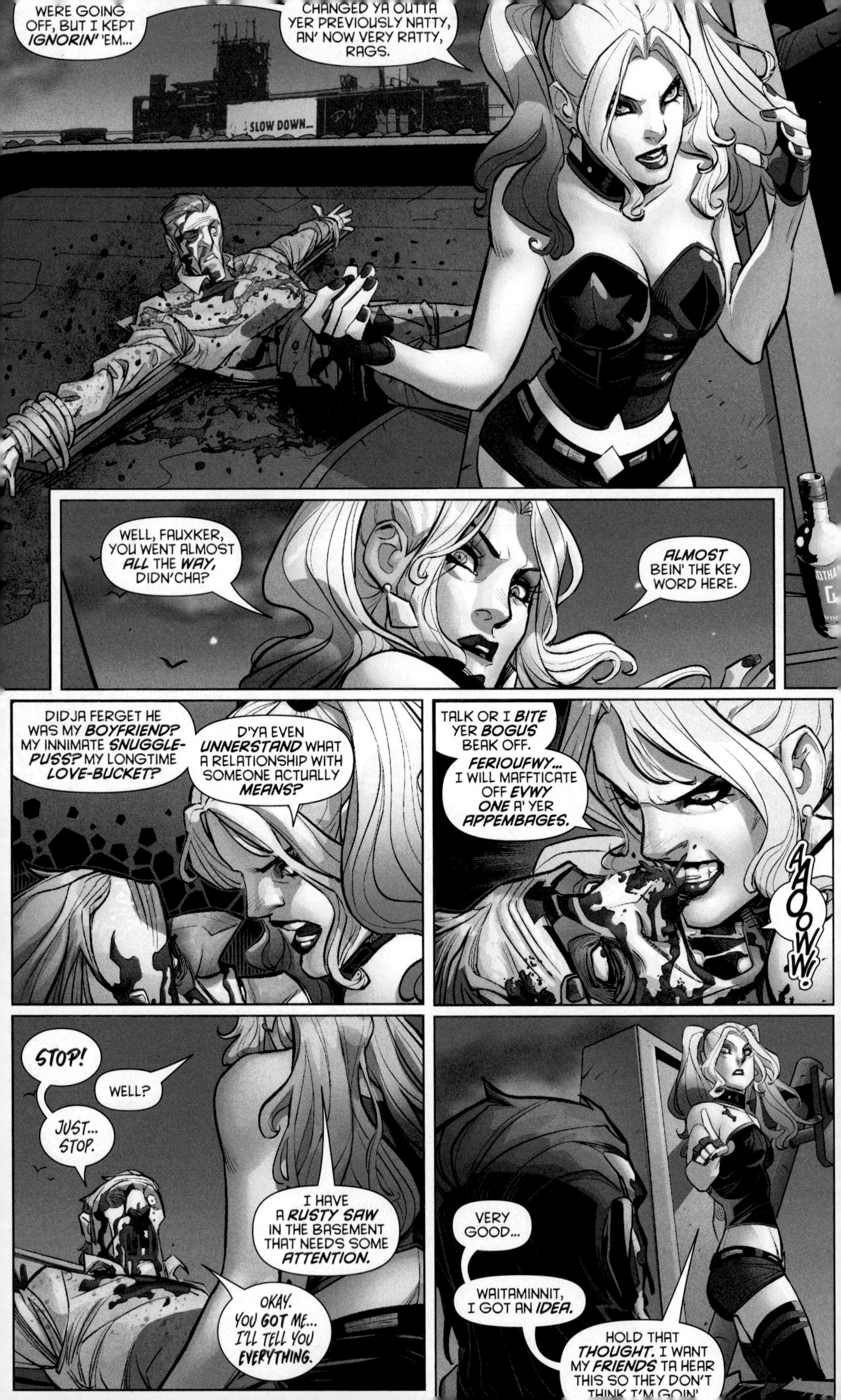
WERE GOING OFF, BUT I KEPT IGNORIN' 'EM...
CHANGED YA OUTTA YER PREVIOUSLY NATTY, AN' NOW VERY RATTY, RAGS.
SLOW DOWN...
WELL, FAUXKER, YOU WENT ALMOST ALL THE WAY, DIDN'CHA?
ALMOST BEIN' THE KEY WORD HERE.
DIDJA FERGET HE WAS MY BOYFRIEND? MY INNIMATE SNUGGLE-PUSS? MY LONGTIME LOVE-BUCKET?
D'YA EVEN UNNERSTAND WHAT A RELATIONSHIP WITH SOMEONE ACTUALLY MEANS?
TALK OR I BITE YER BOGUS BEAK OFF.
FERIOUFWY... I WILL MAFFTICATE OFF EVWY ONE A' YER APPEMBAGES.
AHOOWW!
STOP!
WELL?
JUST... STOP.
I HAVE A RUSTY SAW IN THE BASEMENT THAT NEEDS SOME ATTENTION.
OKAY. YOU GOT ME... I'LL TELL YOU EVERYTHING.
VERY GOOD...
WAITAMINNIT, I GOT AN IDEA.
HOLD THAT THOUGHT. I WANT MY FRIENDS TA HEAR THIS SO THEY DON'T

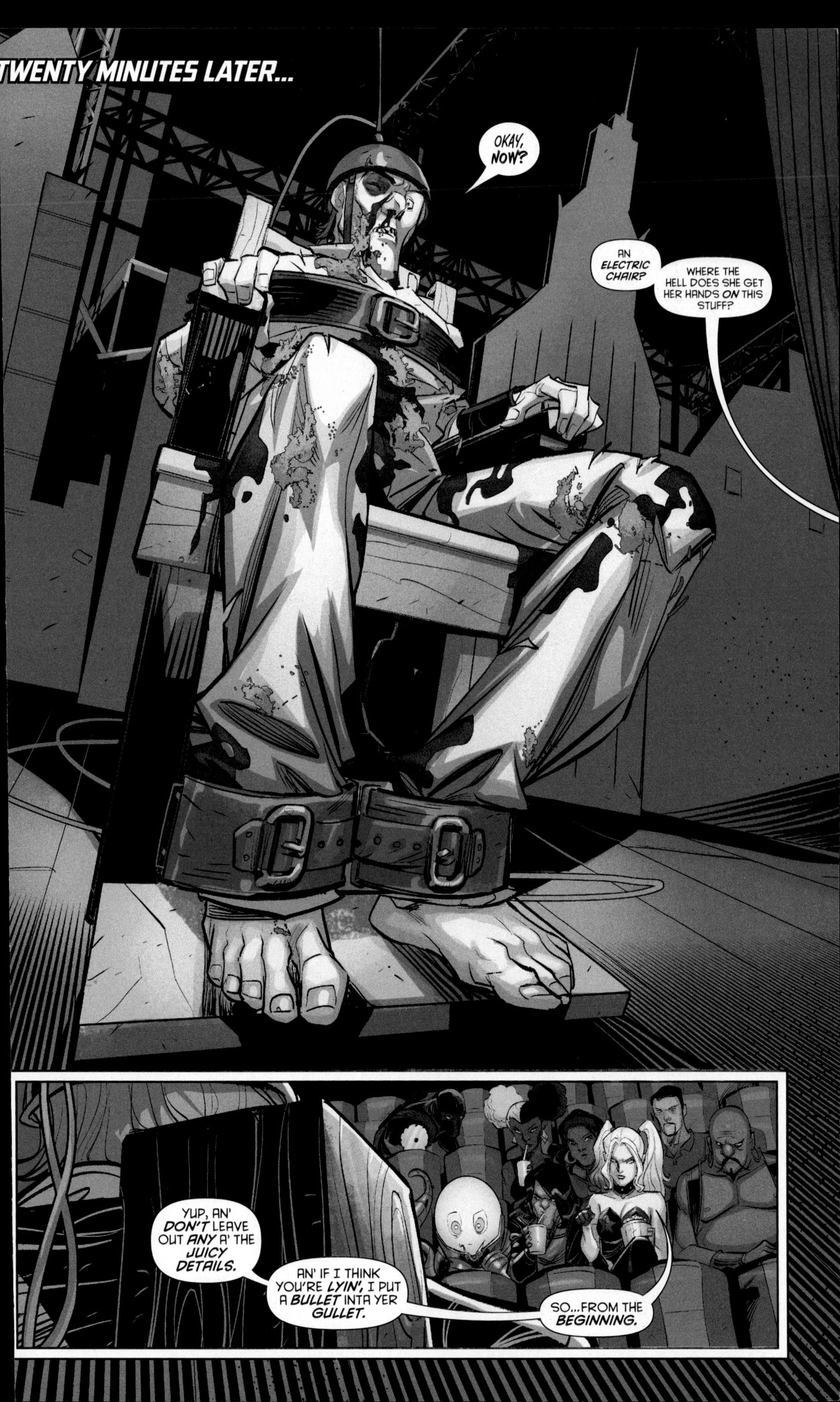
TWENTY MINUTES LATER...
OKAY, NOW?
AN ELECTRIC CHAIR?
WHERE THE HELL DOES SHE GET HER HANDS ON THIS STUFF?
YUP, AN' DON'T LEAVE OUT ANY A' THE JUICY DETAILS.
AN' IF I THINK YOU'RE LYIN', I PUT A BULLET INTA YER GULLET.
SO...FROM THE BEGINNING.

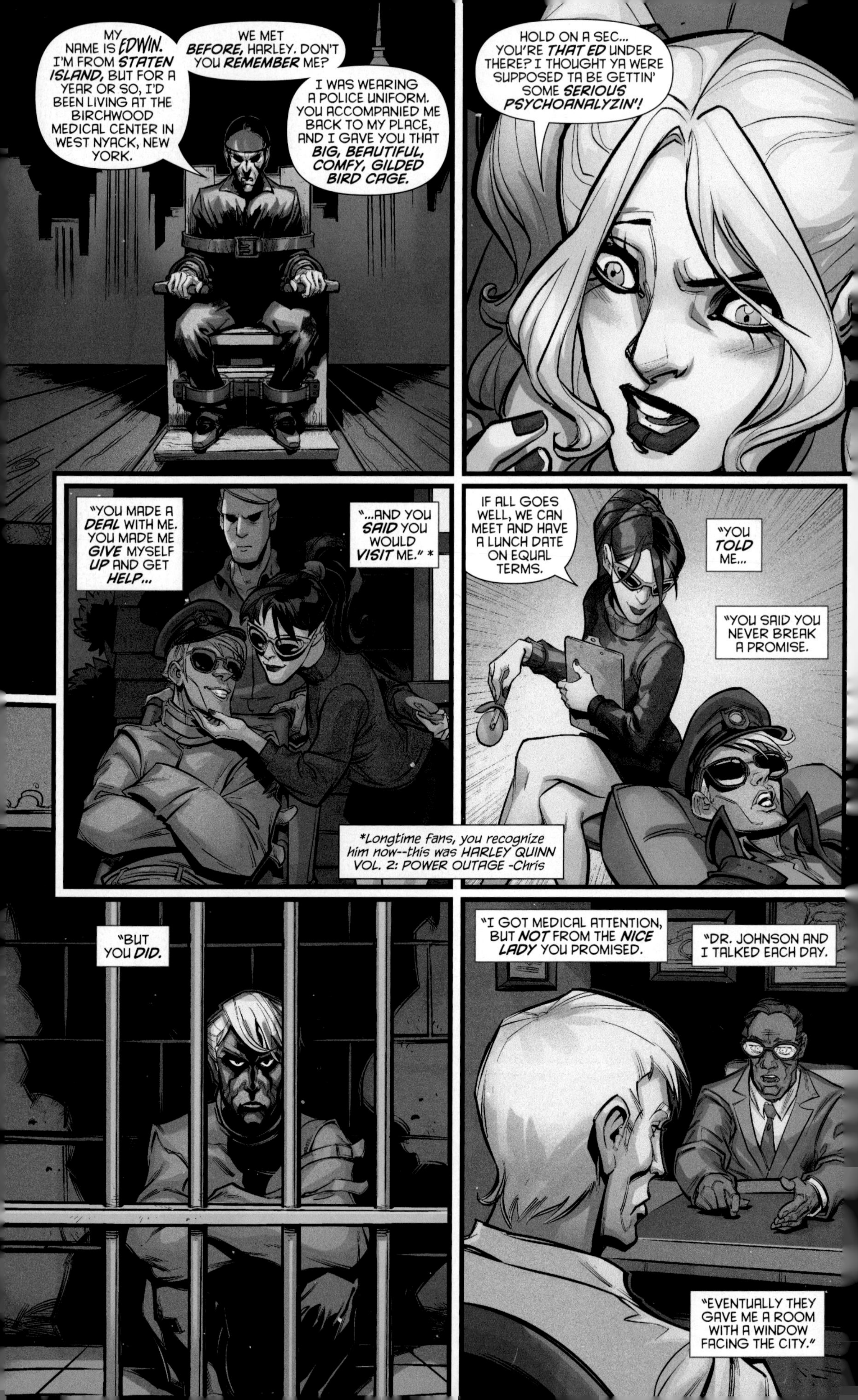
MY NAME IS EDWIN. I'M FROM STATEN ISLAND, BUT FOR A YEAR OR SO, I'D BEEN LIVING AT THE BIRCHWOOD MEDICAL CENTER IN WEST NYACK, NEW YORK.
WE MET BEFORE, HARLEY. DON'T YOU REMEMBER ME?
I WAS WEARING A POLICE UNIFORM. YOU ACCOMPANIED ME BACK TO MY PLACE, AND I GAVE YOU THAT BIG, BEAUTIFUL, COMFY, GILDED BIRD CAGE.
HOLD ON A SEC... YOU'RE THAT ED UNDER THERE? I THOUGHT YA WERE SUPPOSED TA BE GETTIN' SOME SERIOUS PSYCHOANALYZIN'!
"YOU MADE A DEAL WITH ME. YOU MADE ME GIVE MYSELF UP AND GET HELP...
"...AND YOU SAID YOU WOULD VISIT ME." *
IF ALL GOES WELL, WE CAN MEET AND HAVE A LUNCH DATE ON EQUAL TERMS.
"YOU TOLD ME...
"YOU SAID YOU NEVER BREAK A PROMISE.
*Longtime fans, you recognize him now--this was HARLEY QUINN VOL. 2: POWER OUTAGE -Chris
"BUT YOU DID.
"I GOT MEDICAL ATTENTION, BUT NOT FROM THE NICE LADY YOU PROMISED.
"DR. JOHNSON AND I TALKED EACH DAY.
"EVENTUALLY THEY GAVE ME A ROOM WITH A WINDOW FACING THE CITY."

"SOON THEY GAVE ME *RESPONSIBILITIES*, AND I BECAME THE *FOREMAN* OF THE *MAILROOM*.

"HAVING THINGS IN *ORDER* AND *ORGANIZED* WAS GREAT FOR ME. I FELT LIKE I WAS *CONTRIBUTING* SOMETHING...

"...UNTIL THAT DAY...

"THERE WAS THIS PACKAGE FROM *GOTHAM* THAT PIQUED MY *CURIOSITY*. IT WAS ADDRESSED TO A *CERTAIN SOMEONE* IN THE HOSPITAL. A *FELLOW PATIENT*.

"I PUT IT ASIDE AND TOOK IT BACK TO MY ROOM LATER THAT NIGHT TO *STUDY* IT.

"I REALIZED THAT THE NOTE WAS FROM *THE JOKER HIMSELF*, AND THE RETURN ADDRESS WAS *OUTSIDE* ARKHAM. THE JOKER HAD SOMEONE HANDLING HIS MAIL... I'D FOUND A *CORRESPONDENCE ADDRESS*.

"*HE* WAS THE PERSON THAT KNEW YOU THE *BEST*... I COULDN'T RESIST, SO I *WROTE* HIM.

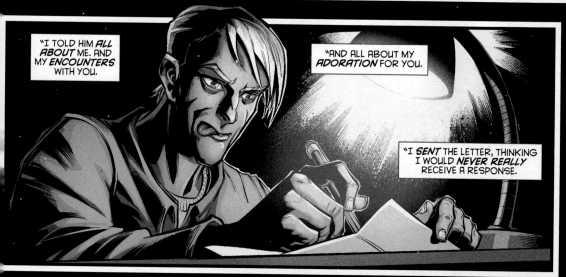

"I TOLD HIM *ALL ABOUT* ME. AND MY *ENCOUNTERS* WITH YOU.

"AND ALL ABOUT MY *ADORATION* FOR YOU.

"I *SENT* THE LETTER, THINKING I WOULD *NEVER REALLY* RECEIVE A RESPONSE.

"A WEEK LATER I *ACTUALLY* GOT A LETTER BACK! AND *ANOTHER*. AND THEN *ANOTHER*.

"I COULDN'T *BELIEVE* MY LUCK! WE BECAME FAST FRIENDS, AND HE EVEN HAD *SUGGESTIONS* ON HOW I MIGHT BE ABLE TO *GET TOGETHER* WITH YOU."

WHAT AN *AWESOME GUY!*

NO! *NO!* HE WAS *USING* YOU!

Y'*THINK?*

TAKING *LOVE ADVICE* FROM A *PSYCHO. NOT A GOOD PLAN...*

SHHBEQUIET, LET 'IM *FINISH*...

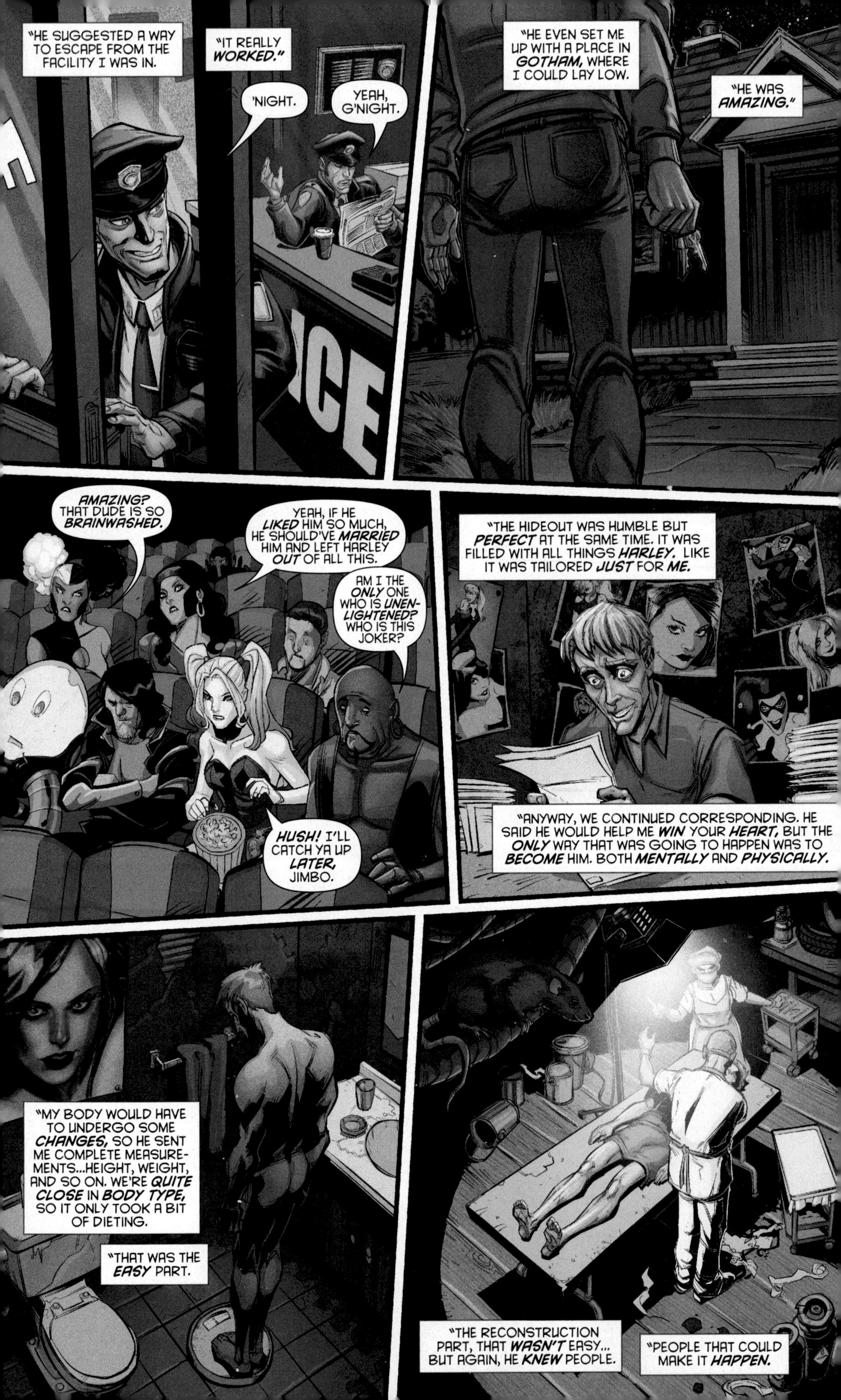
"HE SUGGESTED A WAY TO ESCAPE FROM THE FACILITY I WAS IN.
"IT REALLY *WORKED."*
'NIGHT.
YEAH, G'NIGHT.
ICE
"HE EVEN SET ME UP WITH A PLACE IN *GOTHAM,* WHERE I COULD LAY LOW.
"HE WAS *AMAZING."*
AMAZING? THAT DUDE IS SO *BRAINWASHED.*
YEAH, IF HE *LIKED* HIM SO MUCH, HE SHOULD'VE *MARRIED* HIM AND LEFT HARLEY *OUT* OF ALL THIS.
AM I THE *ONLY* ONE WHO IS *UNEN-LIGHTENED?* WHO IS THIS JOKER?
HUSH! I'LL CATCH YA UP *LATER,* JIMBO.
"THE HIDEOUT WAS HUMBLE BUT *PERFECT* AT THE SAME TIME. IT WAS FILLED WITH ALL THINGS *HARLEY.* LIKE IT WAS TAILORED *JUST* FOR *ME.*
"ANYWAY, WE CONTINUED CORRESPONDING. HE SAID HE WOULD HELP ME *WIN* YOUR *HEART,* BUT THE *ONLY* WAY THAT WAS GOING TO HAPPEN WAS TO *BECOME* HIM. BOTH *MENTALLY* AND *PHYSICALLY.*
"MY BODY WOULD HAVE TO UNDERGO SOME *CHANGES,* SO HE SENT ME COMPLETE MEASURE-MENTS...HEIGHT, WEIGHT, AND SO ON. WE'RE *QUITE CLOSE* IN *BODY TYPE,* SO IT ONLY TOOK A BIT OF DIETING.
"THAT WAS THE *EASY* PART.
"THE RECONSTRUCTION PART, THAT *WASN'T* EASY... BUT AGAIN, HE *KNEW* PEOPLE.
"PEOPLE THAT COULD MAKE IT *HAPPEN.*

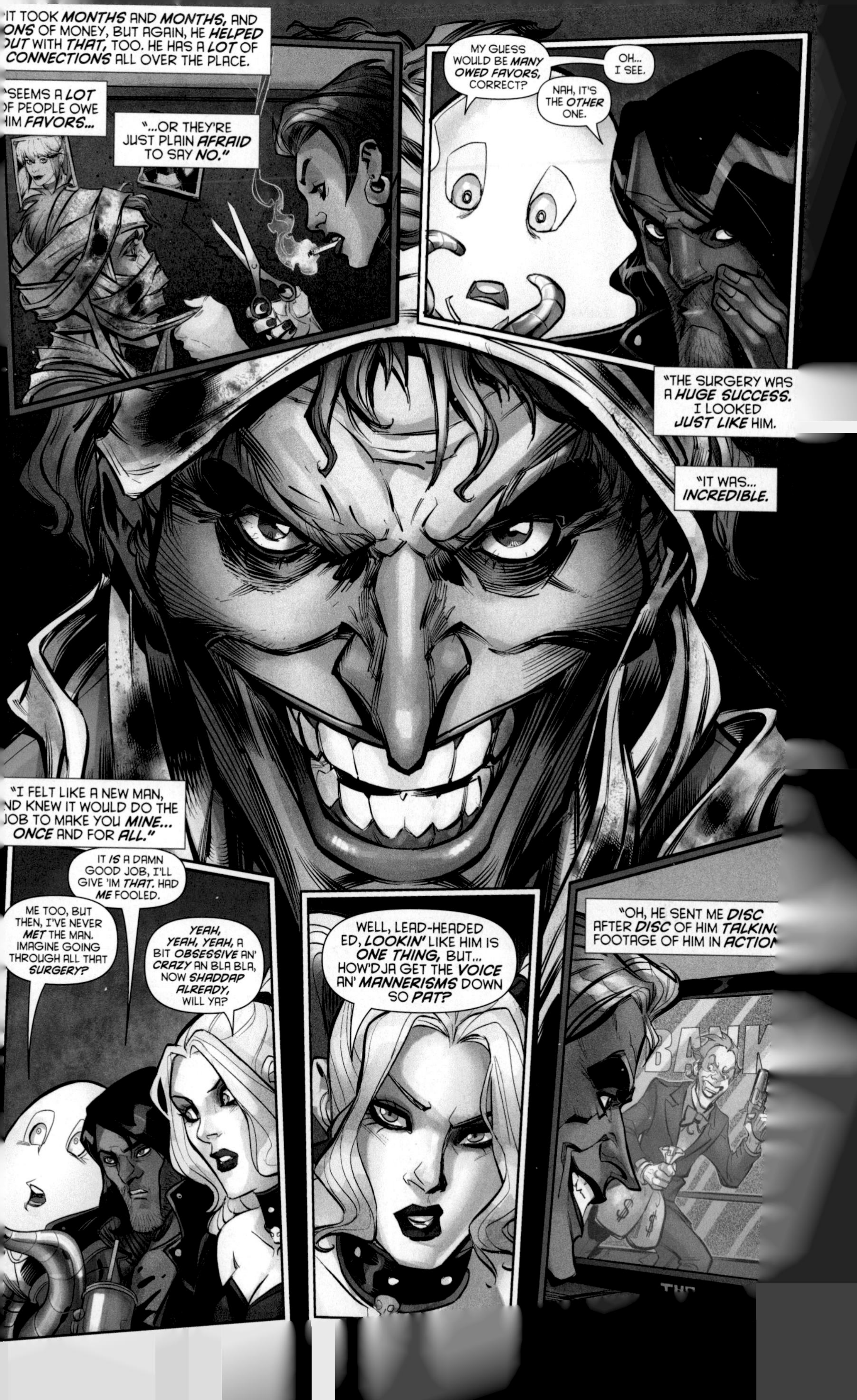
"IT TOOK MONTHS AND MONTHS, AND TONS OF MONEY, BUT AGAIN, HE HELPED OUT WITH THAT, TOO. HE HAS A LOT OF CONNECTIONS ALL OVER THE PLACE.
"SEEMS A LOT OF PEOPLE OWE HIM FAVORS...
"...OR THEY'RE JUST PLAIN AFRAID TO SAY NO."
MY GUESS WOULD BE MANY OWED FAVORS, CORRECT?
OH... I SEE.
NAH, IT'S THE OTHER ONE.
"THE SURGERY WAS A HUGE SUCCESS. I LOOKED JUST LIKE HIM.
"IT WAS... INCREDIBLE.
"I FELT LIKE A NEW MAN, AND KNEW IT WOULD DO THE JOB TO MAKE YOU MINE... ONCE AND FOR ALL."
IT IS A DAMN GOOD JOB, I'LL GIVE 'IM THAT. HAD ME FOOLED.
ME TOO, BUT THEN, I'VE NEVER MET THE MAN. IMAGINE GOING THROUGH ALL THAT SURGERY?
YEAH, YEAH, YEAH, A BIT OBSESSIVE AN' CRAZY AN BLA BLA, NOW SHADDAP ALREADY, WILL YA?
WELL, LEAD-HEADED ED, LOOKIN' LIKE HIM IS ONE THING, BUT... HOW'DJA GET THE VOICE AN' MANNERISMS DOWN SO PAT?
"OH, HE SENT ME DISC AFTER DISC OF HIM TALKING FOOTAGE OF HIM IN ACTION

"HE EVEN TOLD ME THE LOCATION OF THE *CHEMICAL* THAT WOULD BLEACH MY SKIN TO MATCH *YOURS.*

"AS I WENT THROUGH THIS TRANSFORMATION, HE TOLD ME HE WOULD SEND *PERSONAL MEMENTOS* TO YOU...

"...IN HOPES OF *WARMING* YOU *UP* TO THE IDEA OF ME RE-ENTERING YOUR LIFE, AND CLAIMING I WAS A *NEW MAN.*

"WE WROTE TO EACH OTHER, TALKING ABOUT HOW YOU MIGHT *REACT,* AND HOW TO *HANDLE* IT.

"HE ADVISED ME TO T[R] MY *NEW SELF* OUT FO[R] COUPLE OF *TEST RUN*[S]

"I MUST SAY, KNOWING YOU AND I WOULD HAVE *MATCHING SKIN COLORS* EXCITED THE *HELL* OUT OF ME.

"I SUITED UP AND WENT ON A *ONE-MAN CRIME SPREE.* I ROBBED BANKS, I EVEN BLEW UP AN OFFICE BUILDING IN DOWNTOWN GOTHAM. IT WAS *SPECTACULAR. LIBERATING.*

"I *LOOKED* LIKE HIM...I *FELT* LIKE HIM...I *WAS* HIM.

"AND I WAS READY FOR THE *FINAL PERFORMANCE.*"

THIRTY-FOUR PEOPLE *DIED* IN THAT EXPLOSION. IT WAS ALL OVER THE NEWS.

G'WAN, FINISH YER STORY...

GREAT ERRA!

OH... OH *MY.*

"AFTER THAT, I CAME TO CONEY TO STUDY *YOU* A[ND] YOUR NEW *FRIENDS,* LIKE THAT *RED TOOL* IDIOT

"IT WAS TIME TO *APPROACH* YOU, USING EVERYTHING THE JOKER GAVE ME.

"I EVEN GOT TO SAVE YOUR LIFE AT THE *SKATE CLUB.* THAT WOMAN WAS ABOUT TO *KILL* YOU.

"IT WAS *THRILLING!*"

I REALLY HAD YOU *CONVINCED,* DIDN'T I?

UNTIL... WELL, UNTIL *NOW.*

SO. HERE WE *ARE.*

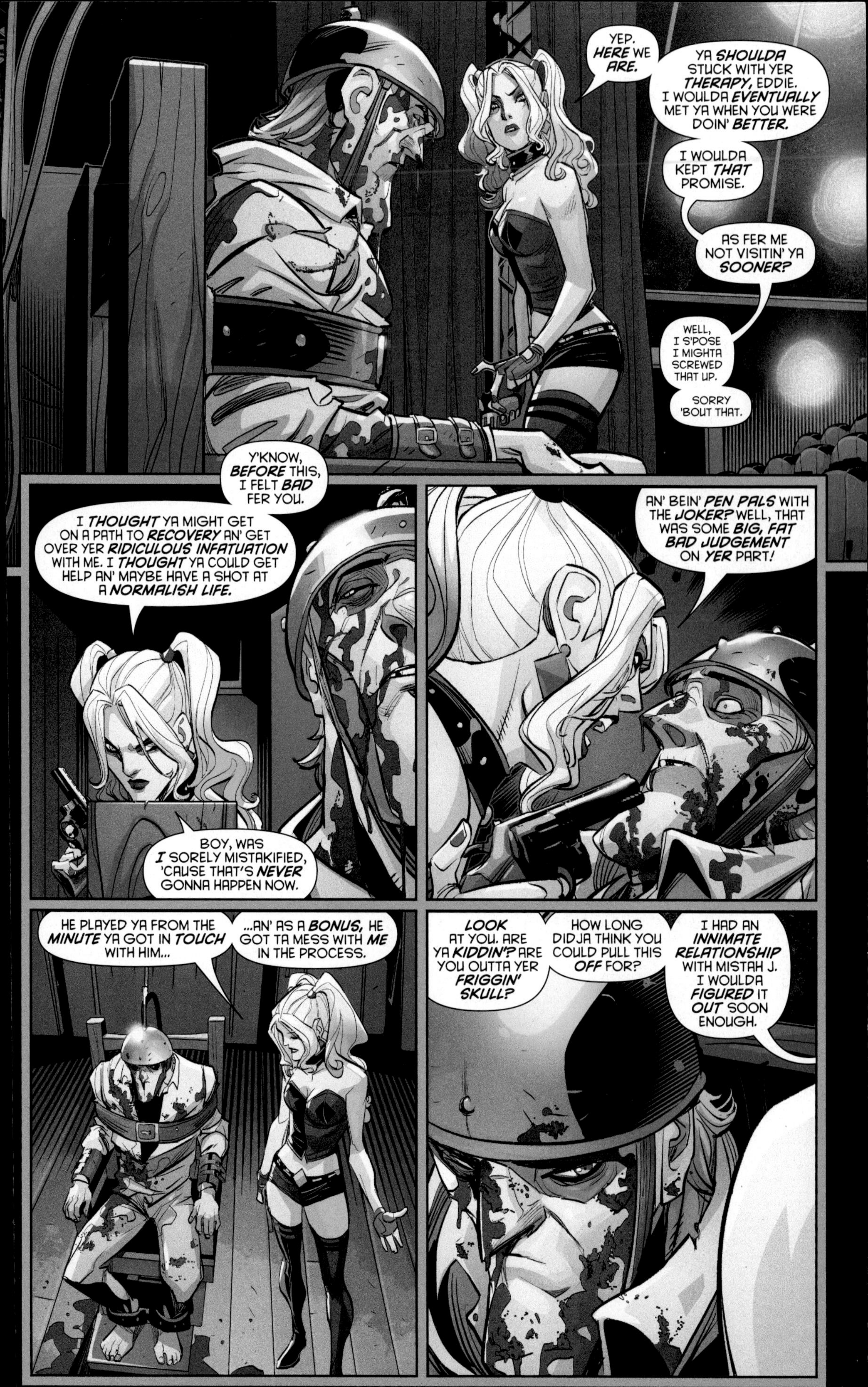
YEP. HERE WE ARE.
YA SHOULDA STUCK WITH YER THERAPY, EDDIE. I WOULDA EVENTUALLY MET YA WHEN YOU WERE DOIN' BETTER.
I WOULDA KEPT THAT PROMISE.
AS FER ME NOT VISITIN' YA SOONER?
WELL, I S'POSE I MIGHTA SCREWED THAT UP.
SORRY 'BOUT THAT.
Y'KNOW, BEFORE THIS, I FELT BAD FER YOU.
I THOUGHT YA MIGHT GET ON A PATH TO RECOVERY AN' GET OVER YER RIDICULOUS INFATUATION WITH ME. I THOUGHT YA COULD GET HELP AN' MAYBE HAVE A SHOT AT A NORMALISH LIFE.
BOY, WAS I SORELY MISTAKIFIED, 'CAUSE THAT'S NEVER GONNA HAPPEN NOW.
AN' BEIN' PEN PALS WITH THE JOKER? WELL, THAT WAS SOME BIG, FAT BAD JUDGEMENT ON YER PART!
HE PLAYED YA FROM THE MINUTE YA GOT IN TOUCH WITH HIM...
...AN' AS A BONUS, HE GOT TA MESS WITH ME IN THE PROCESS.
LOOK AT YOU. ARE YA KIDDIN'? ARE YOU OUTTA YER FRIGGIN' SKULL?
HOW LONG DIDJA THINK YOU COULD PULL THIS OFF FOR?
I HAD AN INNIMATE RELATIONSHIP WITH MISTAH J. I WOULDA FIGURED IT OUT SOON ENOUGH.

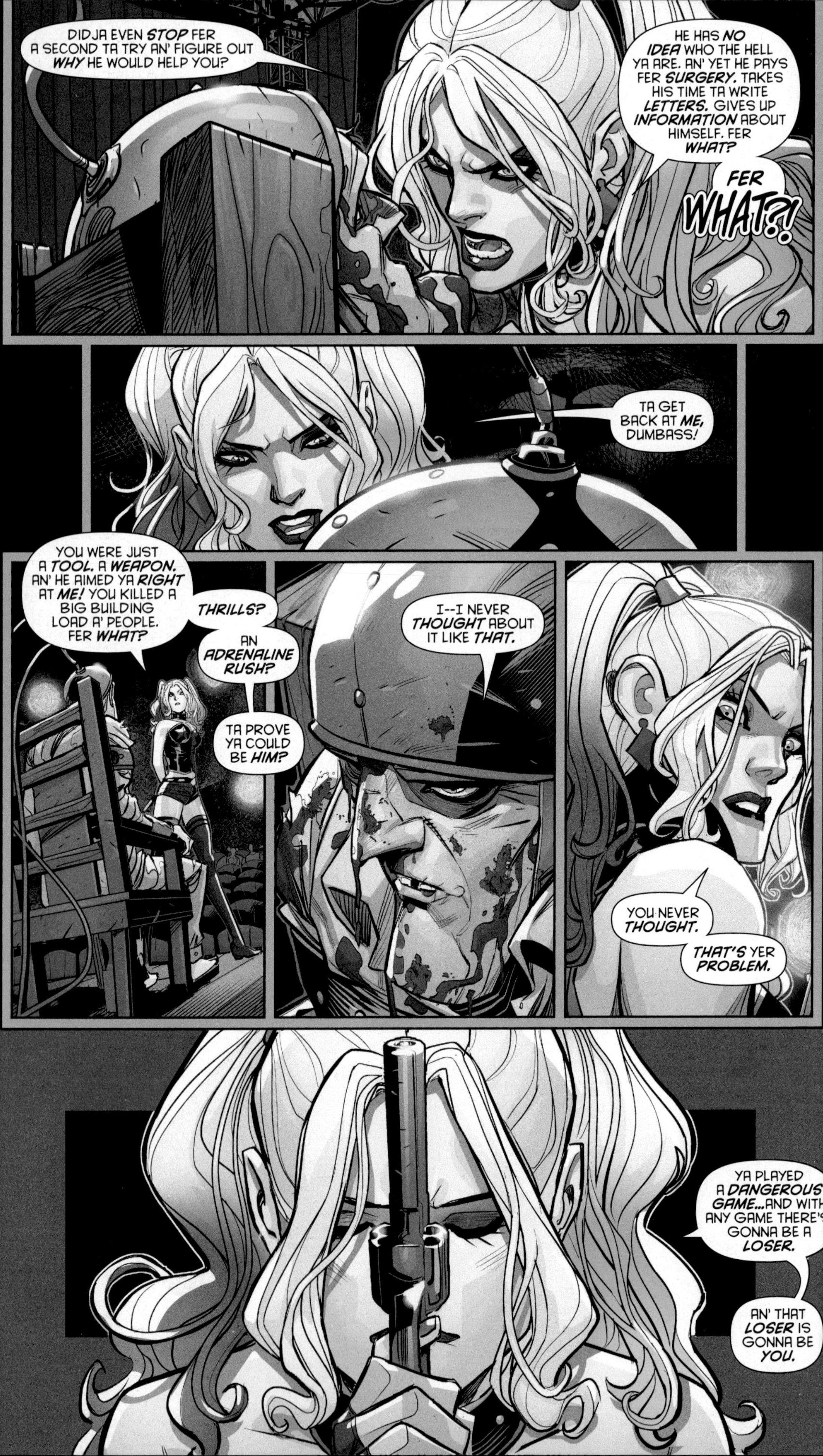
DIDJA EVEN STOP FER A SECOND TA TRY AN' FIGURE OUT WHY HE WOULD HELP YOU?
HE HAS NO IDEA WHO THE HELL YA ARE. AN' YET HE PAYS FER SURGERY. TAKES HIS TIME TA WRITE LETTERS. GIVES UP INFORMATION ABOUT HIMSELF. FER WHAT?
FER WHAT?!
TA GET BACK AT ME, DUMBASS!
YOU WERE JUST A TOOL. A WEAPON. AN' HE AIMED YA RIGHT AT ME! YOU KILLED A BIG BUILDING LOAD A' PEOPLE. FER WHAT?
THRILLS?
AN ADRENALINE RUSH?
TA PROVE YA COULD BE HIM?
I--I NEVER THOUGHT ABOUT IT LIKE THAT.
YOU NEVER THOUGHT.
THAT'S YER PROBLEM.
YA PLAYED A DANGEROUS GAME...AND WITH ANY GAME THERE'S GONNA BE A LOSER.
AN' THAT LOSER IS GONNA BE YOU.

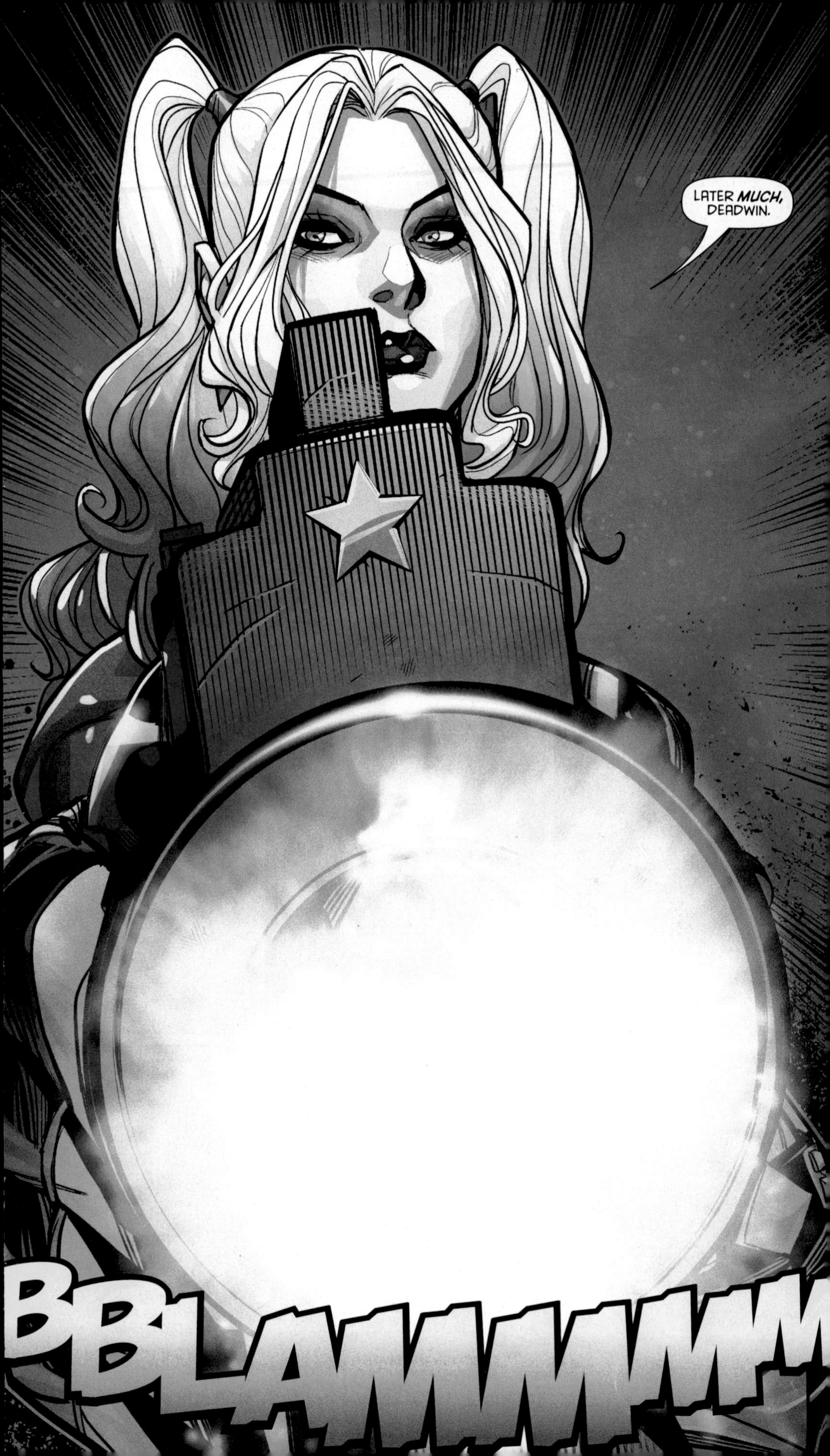

LATER MUCH, DEADWIN.
BBLAMMMMM

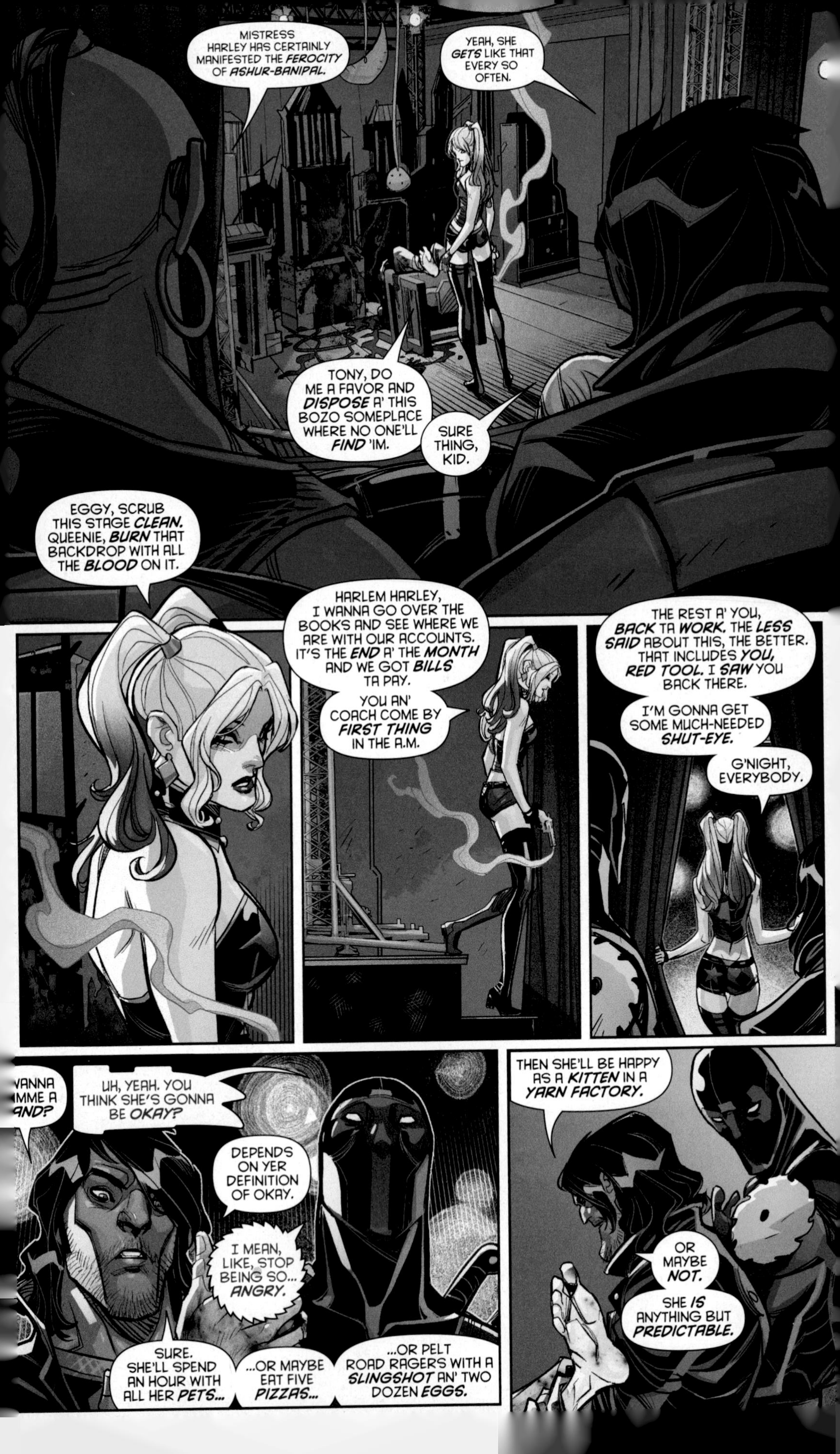
MISTRESS HARLEY HAS CERTAINLY MANIFESTED THE FEROCITY OF ASHUR-BANIPAL.
YEAH, SHE GETS LIKE THAT EVERY SO OFTEN.
TONY, DO ME A FAVOR AND DISPOSE A' THIS BOZO SOMEPLACE WHERE NO ONE'LL FIND 'IM.
SURE THING, KID.
EGGY, SCRUB THIS STAGE CLEAN. QUEENIE, BURN THAT BACKDROP WITH ALL THE BLOOD ON IT.
HARLEM HARLEY, I WANNA GO OVER THE BOOKS AND SEE WHERE WE ARE WITH OUR ACCOUNTS. IT'S THE END A' THE MONTH AND WE GOT BILLS TA PAY.
YOU AN' COACH COME BY FIRST THING IN THE A.M.
THE REST A' YOU, BACK TA WORK. THE LESS SAID ABOUT THIS, THE BETTER. THAT INCLUDES YOU, RED TOOL. I SAW YOU BACK THERE.
I'M GONNA GET SOME MUCH-NEEDED SHUT-EYE.
G'NIGHT, EVERYBODY.
UH, YEAH. YOU THINK SHE'S GONNA BE OKAY?
DEPENDS ON YER DEFINITION OF OKAY.
I MEAN, LIKE, STOP BEING SO... ANGRY.
SURE. SHE'LL SPEND AN HOUR WITH ALL HER PETS...
...OR MAYBE EAT FIVE PIZZAS...
...OR PELT ROAD RAGERS WITH A SLINGSHOT AN' TWO DOZEN EGGS.
THEN SHE'LL BE HAPPY AS A KITTEN IN A YARN FACTORY.
OR MAYBE NOT.
SHE IS ANYTHING BUT PREDICTABLE.

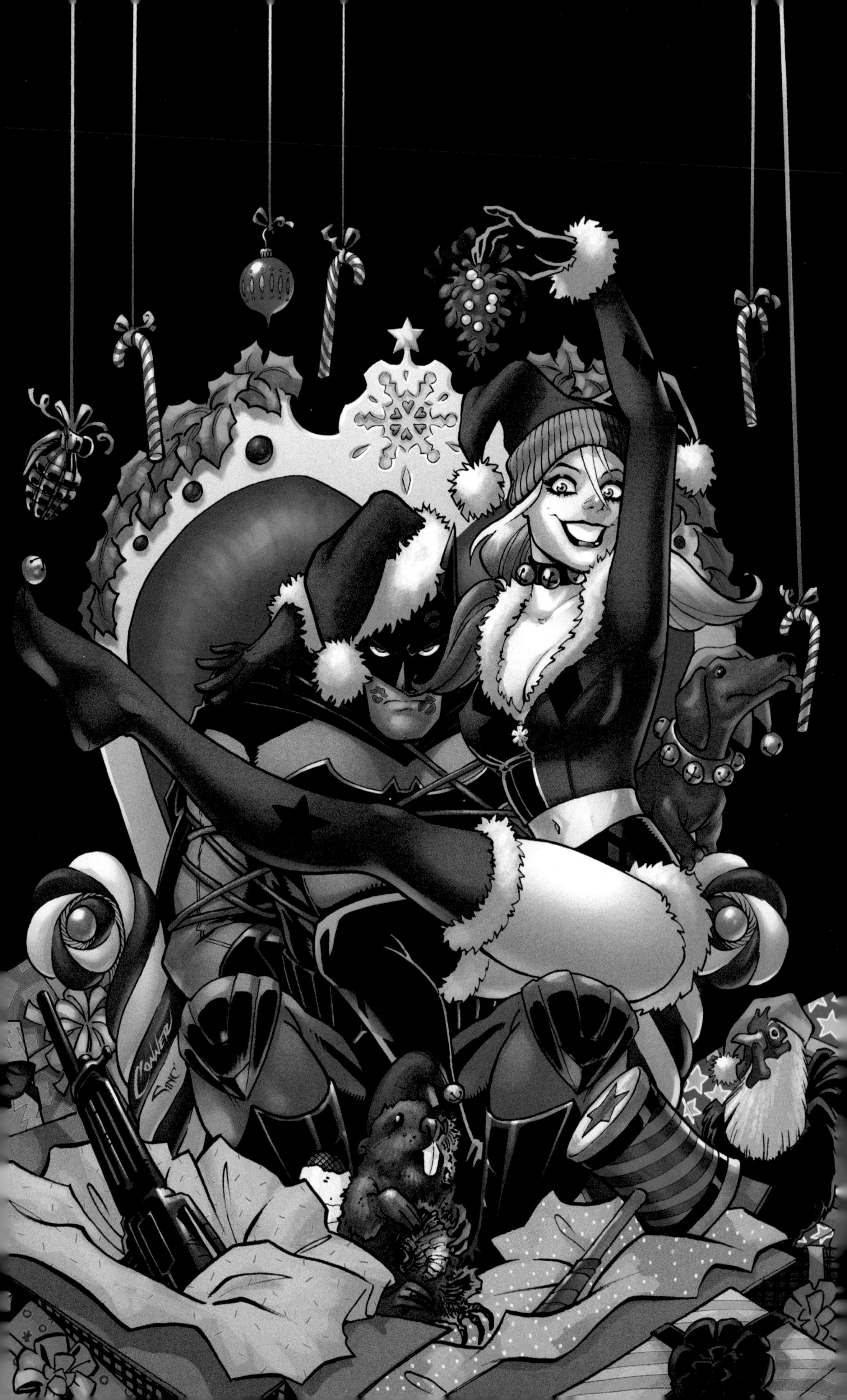

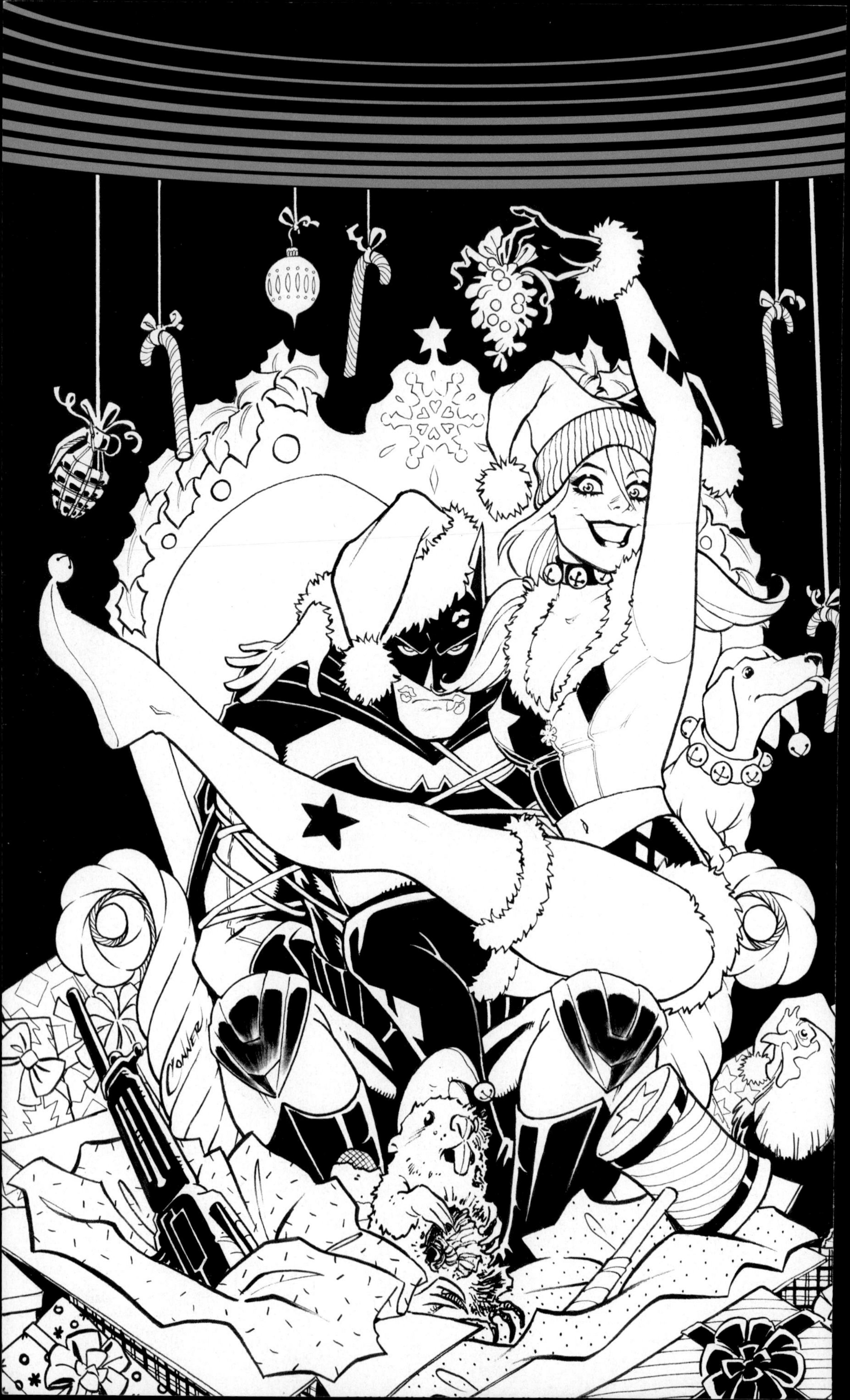
CONNER

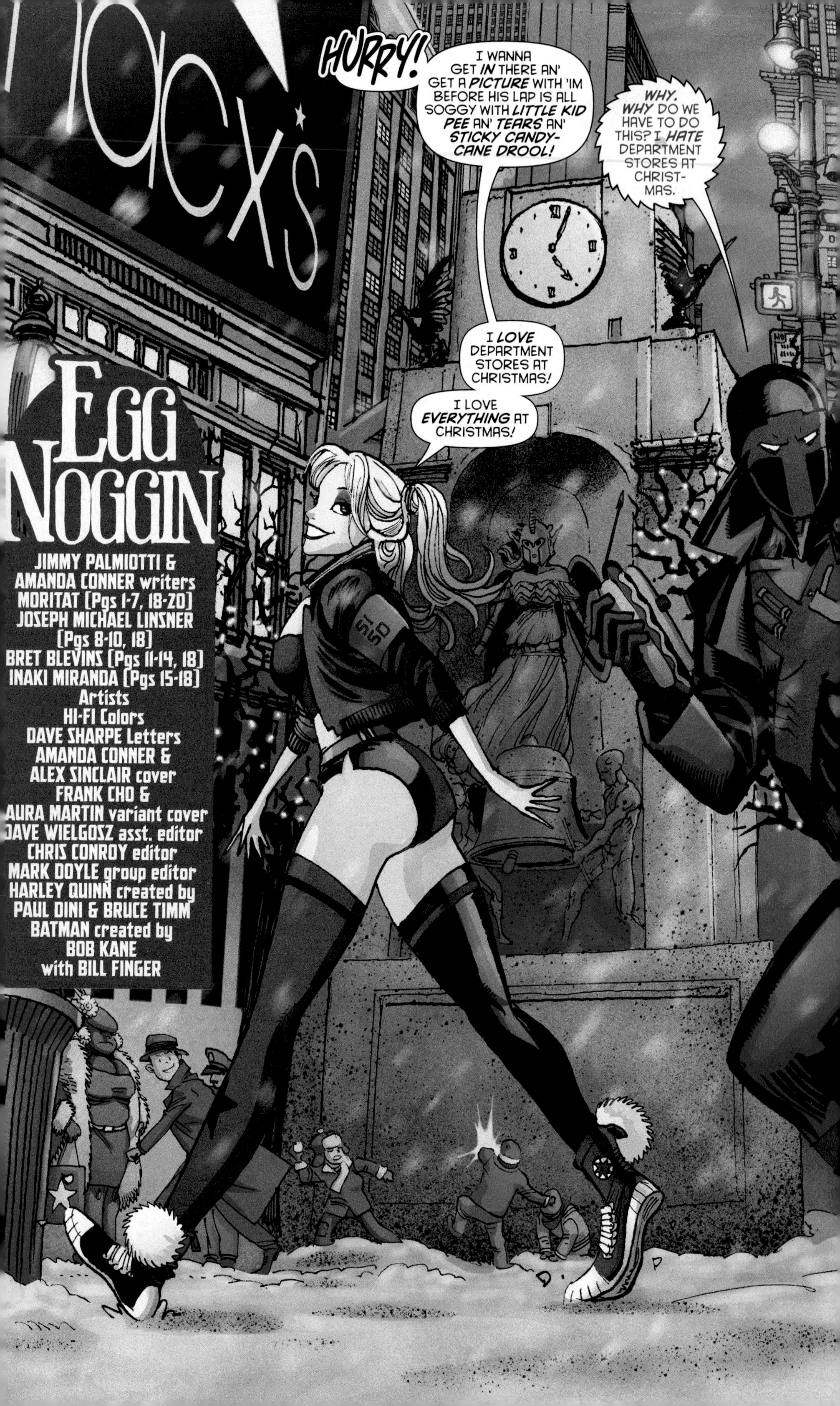
HURRY!
I WANNA GET IN THERE AN' GET A PICTURE WITH 'IM BEFORE HIS LAP IS ALL SOGGY WITH LITTLE KID PEE AN' TEARS AN' STICKY CANDY-CANE DROOL!
WHY. WHY DO WE HAVE TO DO THIS? I HATE DEPARTMENT STORES AT CHRIST-MAS.
I LOVE DEPARTMENT STORES AT CHRISTMAS!
I LOVE EVERYTHING AT CHRISTMAS!
EGG NOGGIN
JIMMY PALMIOTTI & AMANDA CONNER writers
MORITAT [Pgs 1-7, 18-20]
JOSEPH MICHAEL LINSNER [Pgs 8-10, 18]
BRET BLEVINS [Pgs 11-14, 18]
INAKI MIRANDA [Pgs 15-18]
Artists
HI-FI Colors
DAVE SHARPE Letters
AMANDA CONNER & ALEX SINCLAIR cover
FRANK CHO & AURA MARTIN variant cover
DAVE WIELGOSZ asst. editor
CHRIS CONROY editor
MARK DOYLE group editor
HARLEY QUINN created by PAUL DINI & BRUCE TIMM
BATMAN created by BOB KANE with BILL FINGER

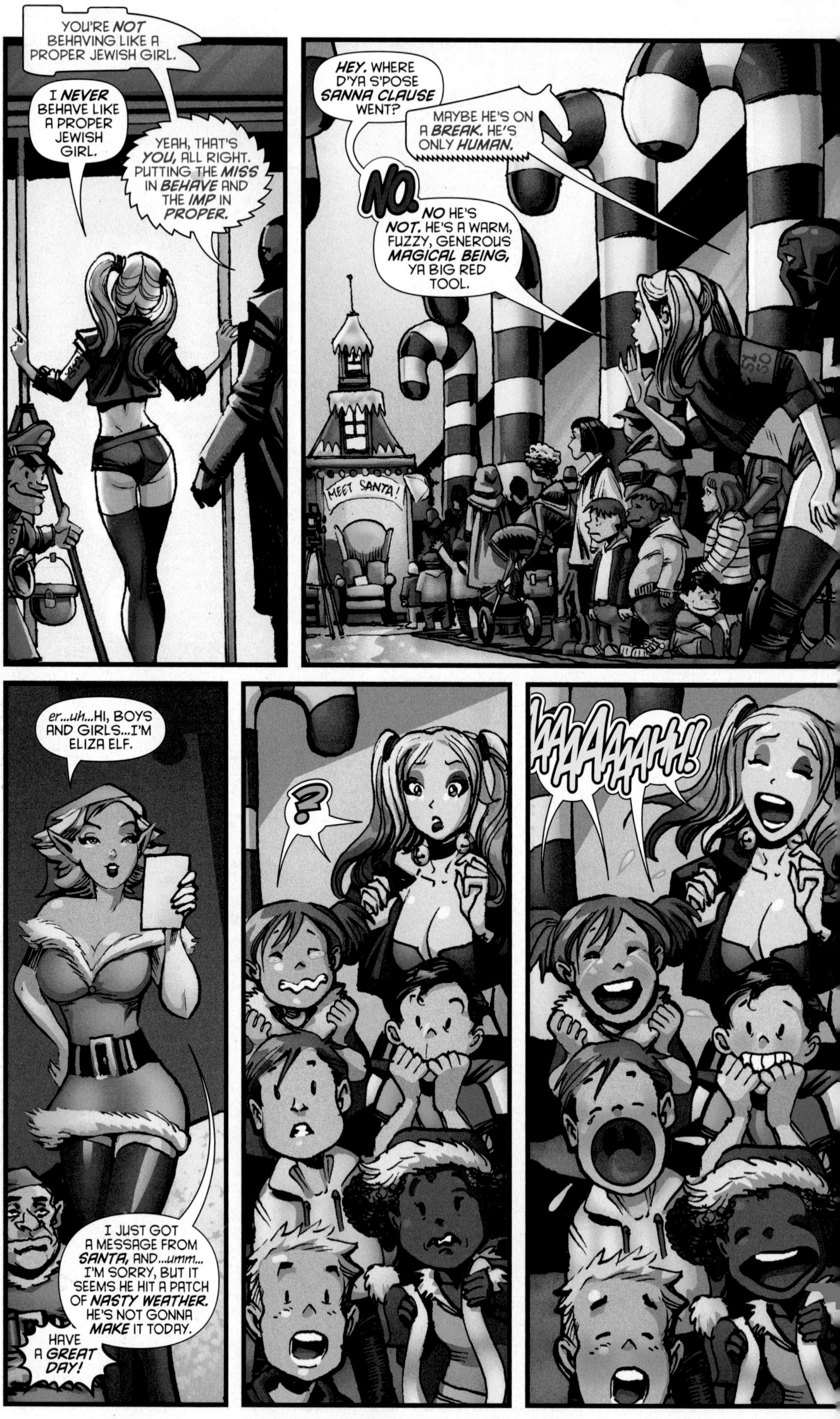

YOU'RE NOT BEHAVING LIKE A PROPER JEWISH GIRL.
I NEVER BEHAVE LIKE A PROPER JEWISH GIRL.
YEAH, THAT'S YOU, ALL RIGHT. PUTTING THE MISS IN BEHAVE AND THE IMP IN PROPER.
HEY. WHERE D'YA S'POSE SANNA CLAUSE WENT?
MAYBE HE'S ON A BREAK. HE'S ONLY HUMAN.
NO.
NO HE'S NOT. HE'S A WARM, FUZZY, GENEROUS MAGICAL BEING, YA BIG RED TOOL.
MEET SANTA!
er...uh...HI, BOYS AND GIRLS...I'M ELIZA ELF.
I JUST GOT A MESSAGE FROM SANTA, AND...umm... I'M SORRY, BUT IT SEEMS HE HIT A PATCH OF NASTY WEATHER. HE'S NOT GONNA MAKE IT TODAY.
HAVE A GREAT DAY!
?
AAAAAAAHH!

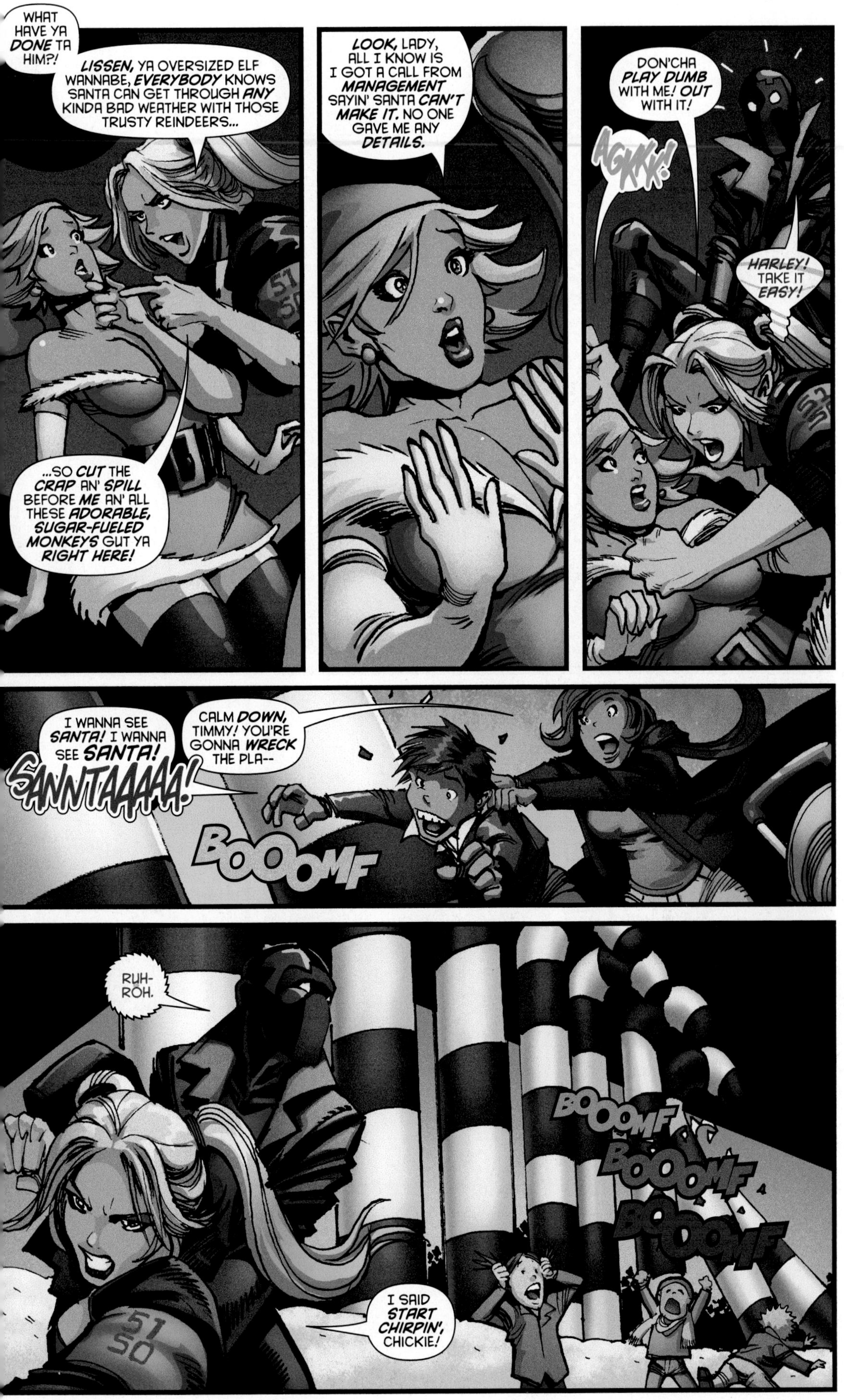
WHAT HAVE YA DONE TA HIM?!
LISSEN, YA OVERSIZED ELF WANNABE, EVERYBODY KNOWS SANTA CAN GET THROUGH ANY KINDA BAD WEATHER WITH THOSE TRUSTY REINDEERS...
...SO CUT THE CRAP AN' SPILL BEFORE ME AN' ALL THESE ADORABLE, SUGAR-FUELED MONKEYS GUT YA RIGHT HERE!
LOOK, LADY, ALL I KNOW IS I GOT A CALL FROM MANAGEMENT SAYIN' SANTA CAN'T MAKE IT. NO ONE GAVE ME ANY DETAILS.
DON'CHA PLAY DUMB WITH ME! OUT WITH IT!
AGKKK!
HARLEY! TAKE IT EASY!
I WANNA SEE SANTA! I WANNA SEE SANTA!
SANNTAAAAA!
CALM DOWN, TIMMY! YOU'RE GONNA WRECK THE PLA--
BOOOMF
RUH-ROH.
BOOOMF
BOOOMF
BOOOMF
I SAID START CHIRPIN', CHICKIE!

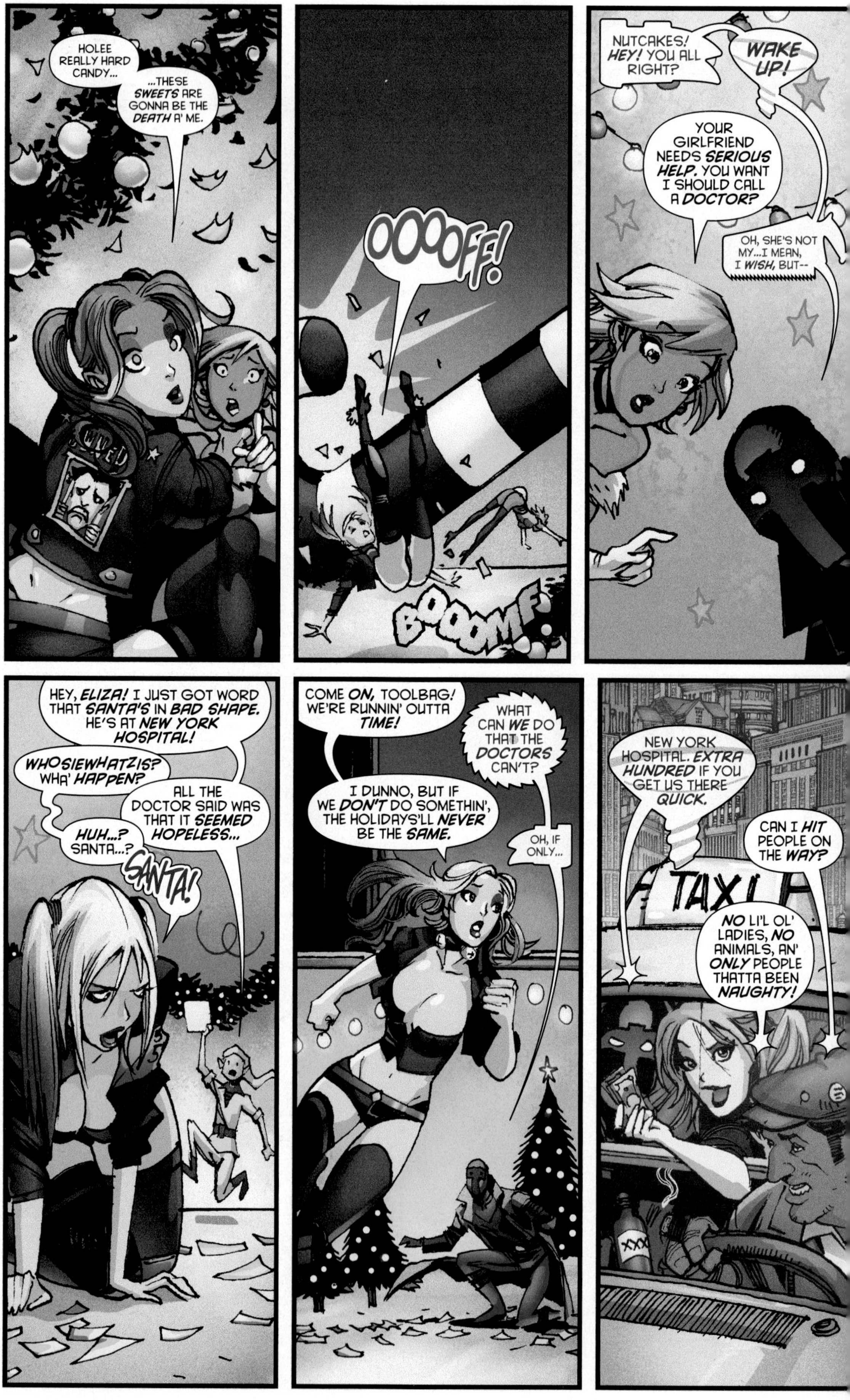
HOLEE REALLY HARD CANDY...
...THESE SWEETS ARE GONNA BE THE DEATH A' ME.
OOOOFF!
BOOOMF
NUTCAKES! HEY! YOU ALL RIGHT?
WAKE UP!
YOUR GIRLFRIEND NEEDS SERIOUS HELP. YOU WANT I SHOULD CALL A DOCTOR?
OH, SHE'S NOT MY...I MEAN, I WISH, BUT--
HEY, ELIZA! I JUST GOT WORD THAT SANTA'S IN BAD SHAPE. HE'S AT NEW YORK HOSPITAL!
WHOSIEWHATZIS? WHA' HAPPEN?
ALL THE DOCTOR SAID WAS THAT IT SEEMED HOPELESS...
HUH...? SANTA...?
SANTA!
COME ON, TOOLBAG! WE'RE RUNNIN' OUTTA TIME!
WHAT CAN WE DO THAT THE DOCTORS CAN'T?
I DUNNO, BUT IF WE DON'T DO SOMETHIN', THE HOLIDAYS'LL NEVER BE THE SAME.
OH, IF ONLY...
NEW YORK HOSPITAL. EXTRA HUNDRED IF YOU GET US THERE QUICK.
CAN I HIT PEOPLE ON THE WAY?
TAXI
NO LI'L OL' LADIES, NO ANIMALS, AN' ONLY PEOPLE THATTA BEEN NAUGHTY!
XXX

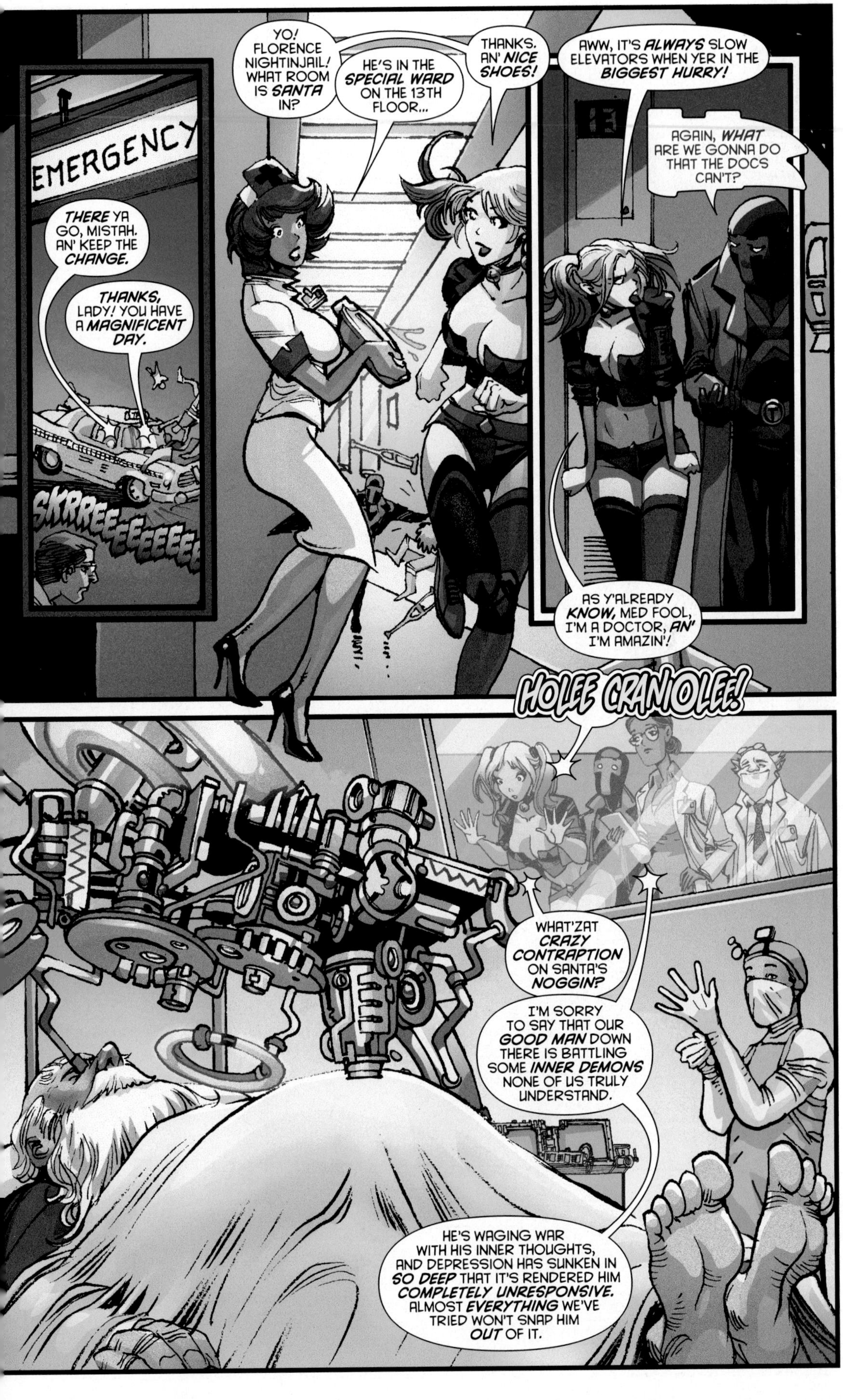
EMERGENCY
THERE YA GO, MISTAH. AN' KEEP THE CHANGE.
THANKS, LADY! YOU HAVE A MAGNIFICENT DAY.
SKRREEEEEEEEEE
YO! FLORENCE NIGHTINJAIL! WHAT ROOM IS SANTA IN?
HE'S IN THE SPECIAL WARD ON THE 13TH FLOOR...
THANKS. AN' NICE SHOES!
AWW, IT'S ALWAYS SLOW ELEVATORS WHEN YER IN THE BIGGEST HURRY!
AGAIN, WHAT ARE WE GONNA DO THAT THE DOCS CAN'T?
AS Y'ALREADY KNOW, MED FOOL, I'M A DOCTOR, AN' I'M AMAZIN'!
HOLEE CRANIOLEE!
WHAT'ZAT CRAZY CONTRAPTION ON SANTA'S NOGGIN?
I'M SORRY TO SAY THAT OUR GOOD MAN DOWN THERE IS BATTLING SOME INNER DEMONS NONE OF US TRULY UNDERSTAND.
HE'S WAGING WAR WITH HIS INNER THOUGHTS, AND DEPRESSION HAS SUNKEN IN SO DEEP THAT IT'S RENDERED HIM COMPLETELY UNRESPONSIVE. ALMOST EVERYTHING WE'VE TRIED WON'T SNAP HIM OUT OF IT.

YOU SAID *ALMOST*...

CORRECT. THERE *IS* ONE THING WE *HAVEN'T TRIED*, BUT IT'S A LONG SHOT... AND IT MEANS *CERTAIN DEATH* FOR THE PERSON UNDERTAKING IT.

I'M *ALL EARS*, AN' I GOT A *LIST* A' THINGS I'M *AFRAID* OF...

...LIKE, PAPER CUTS, JELLYFISH, TICKS, FLYIN' ROACHES...

...BUT *DEATH* AIN'T ONE OF 'EM!

OUR MERRY FRIEND'S BRAIN IS *QUITE DIFFERENT* FROM OURS, AS YOU CAN SEE.

HE HAS, OVER THE YEARS, FILED ANY *GRIEVOUS LIFE EXPERIENCES* AWAY TO A SUBCONSCIOUS PART OF HIS BRAIN. THIS ALLOWS HIM TO *ALWAYS* BE *HAPPY*.

UNFORTUNATELY, THESE FEELINGS HAVE MANIFESTED THEMSELVES INTO A HORRIBLE *"CREATURE OF THE ID"* IF YOU WILL. IT HAS BROKEN OUT OF ITS "CAGE" AND IS MAKING ITS WAY AROUND HIS MIND AND DESTROYING *EVERYTHING* HE STANDS FOR.

TO PUT IT BLUNTLY, IT'S *KILLING SANTA CLAUS!*

SANTA'S BRA

SO... WHAT'ZIS LONG-SHOT CURE?

WE SEND A VOLUNTEER *INTO* HIS *BRAIN* TO *BATTLE* THIS EVIL. SADLY, FOR THIS PERSON, IT IS A *ONE-WAY TRIP*.

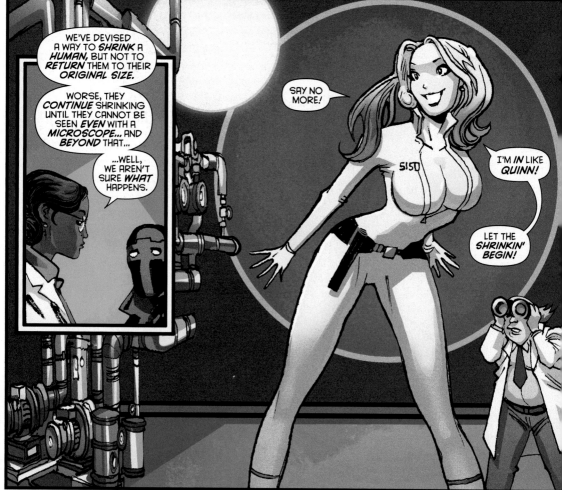

WE'VE DEVISED A WAY TO *SHRINK* A *HUMAN*, BUT NOT TO *RETURN* THEM TO THEIR *ORIGINAL SIZE*.

WORSE, THEY *CONTINUE* SHRINKING UNTIL THEY CANNOT BE SEEN *EVEN* WITH A *MICROSCOPE*... AND BEYOND THAT...

...WELL, WE AREN'T SURE *WHAT* HAPPENS.

SAY NO MORE!

5150

I'M *IN* LIKE *QUINN!*

LET THE *SHRINKIN'* BEGIN!

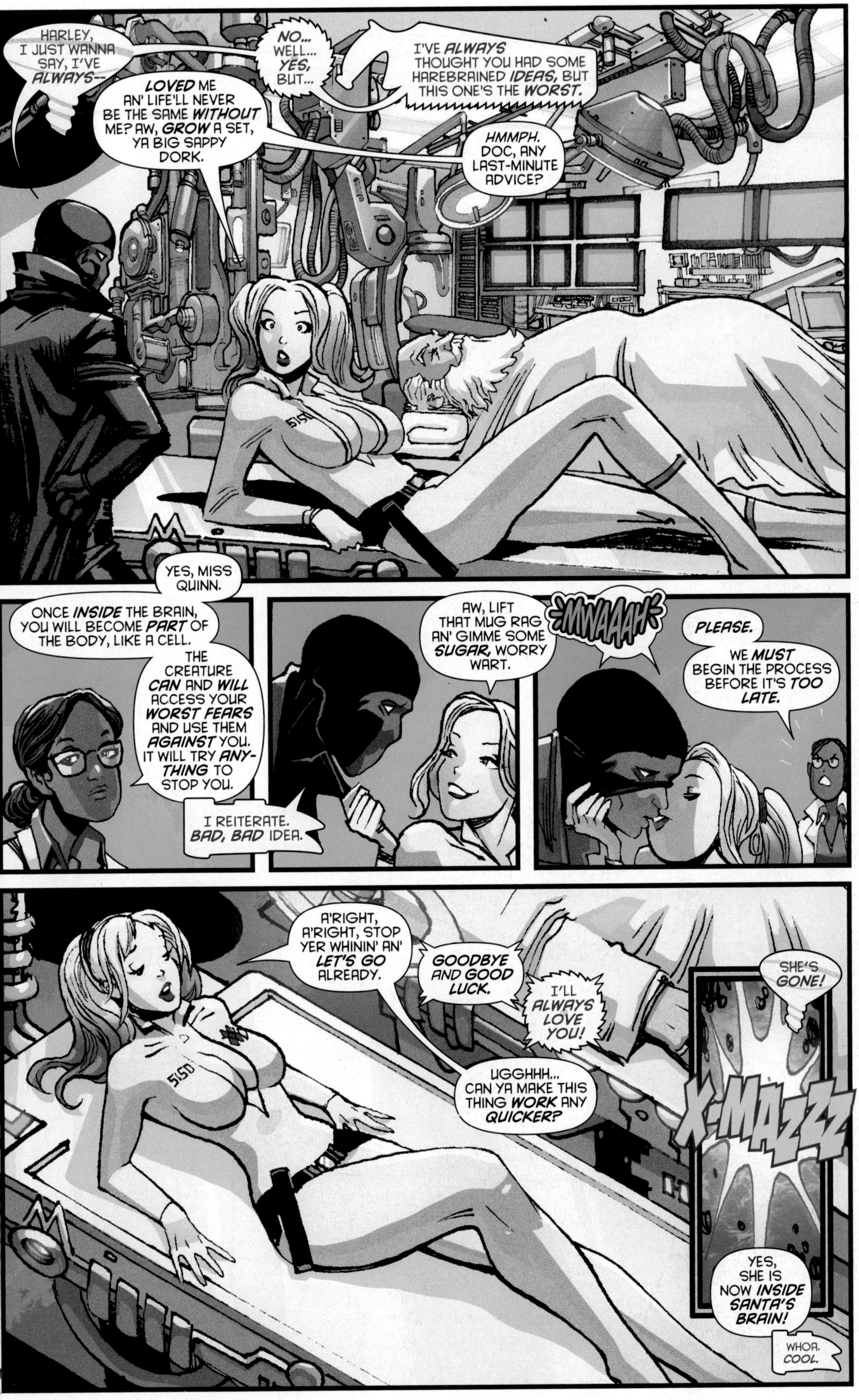
HARLEY, I JUST WANNA SAY, I'VE ALWAYS--
LOVED ME AN' LIFE'LL NEVER BE THE SAME WITHOUT ME? AW, GROW A SET, YA BIG SAPPY DORK.
NO... WELL... YES, BUT...
I'VE ALWAYS THOUGHT YOU HAD SOME HAREBRAINED IDEAS, BUT THIS ONE'S THE WORST.
HMMPH. DOC, ANY LAST-MINUTE ADVICE?
YES, MISS QUINN.
ONCE INSIDE THE BRAIN, YOU WILL BECOME PART OF THE BODY, LIKE A CELL.
THE CREATURE CAN AND WILL ACCESS YOUR WORST FEARS AND USE THEM AGAINST YOU. IT WILL TRY ANY-THING TO STOP YOU.
I REITERATE. BAD, BAD IDEA.
AW, LIFT THAT MUG RAG AN' GIMME SOME SUGAR, WORRY WART.
MWAAAH
PLEASE.
WE MUST BEGIN THE PROCESS BEFORE IT'S TOO LATE.
A'RIGHT, A'RIGHT, STOP YER WHININ' AN' LET'S GO ALREADY.
GOODBYE AND GOOD LUCK.
I'LL ALWAYS LOVE YOU!
UGGHHH... CAN YA MAKE THIS THING WORK ANY QUICKER?
X-MAZZZ
SHE'S GONE!
YES, SHE IS NOW INSIDE SANTA'S BRAIN!
WHOA. COOL.

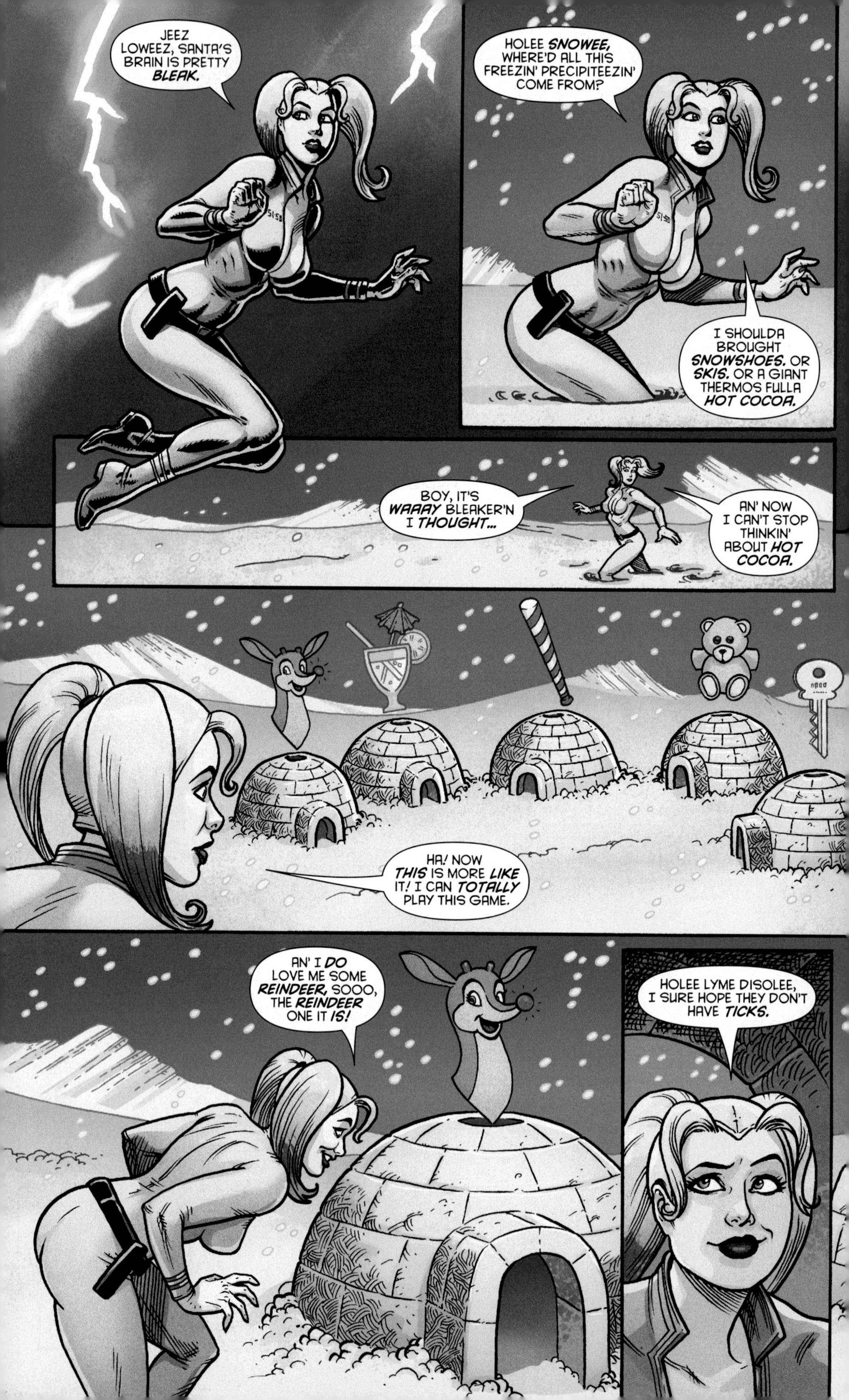
JEEZ LOWEEZ, SANTA'S BRAIN IS PRETTY BLEAK.
HOLEE SNOWEE, WHERE'D ALL THIS FREEZIN' PRECIPITEEZIN' COME FROM?
I SHOULDA BROUGHT SNOWSHOES. OR SKIS. OR A GIANT THERMOS FULLA HOT COCOA.
BOY, IT'S WAAAY BLEAKER'N I THOUGHT...
AN' NOW I CAN'T STOP THINKIN' ABOUT HOT COCOA.
HA! NOW THIS IS MORE LIKE IT! I CAN TOTALLY PLAY THIS GAME.
AN' I DO LOVE ME SOME REINDEER, SOOO, THE REINDEER ONE IT IS!
HOLEE LYME DISOLEE, I SURE HOPE THEY DON'T HAVE TICKS.

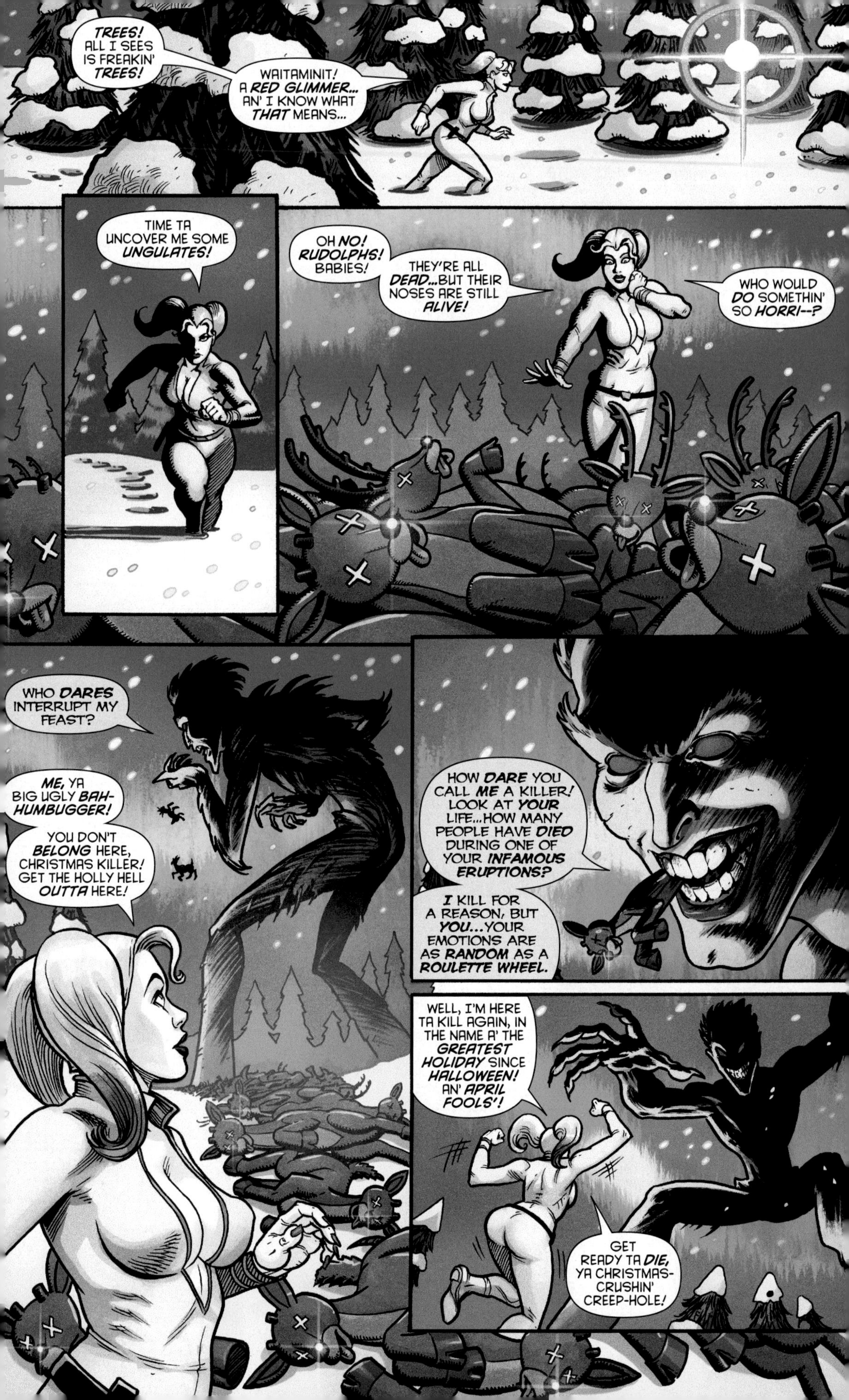
TREES! ALL I SEES IS FREAKIN' TREES!
WAITAMINIT! A RED GLIMMER... AN' I KNOW WHAT THAT MEANS...
TIME TA UNCOVER ME SOME UNGULATES!
OH NO! RUDOLPHS! BABIES!
THEY'RE ALL DEAD...BUT THEIR NOSES ARE STILL ALIVE!
WHO WOULD DO SOMETHIN' SO HORRI--?
WHO DARES INTERRUPT MY FEAST?
ME, YA BIG UGLY BAH-HUMBUGGER!
YOU DON'T BELONG HERE, CHRISTMAS KILLER! GET THE HOLLY HELL OUTTA HERE!
HOW DARE YOU CALL ME A KILLER! LOOK AT YOUR LIFE...HOW MANY PEOPLE HAVE DIED DURING ONE OF YOUR INFAMOUS ERUPTIONS?
I KILL FOR A REASON, BUT YOU...YOUR EMOTIONS ARE AS RANDOM AS A ROULETTE WHEEL.
WELL, I'M HERE TA KILL AGAIN, IN THE NAME A' THE GREATEST HOLIDAY SINCE HALLOWEEN! AN' APRIL FOOLS'!
GET READY TA DIE, YA CHRISTMAS-CRUSHIN' CREEP-HOLE!

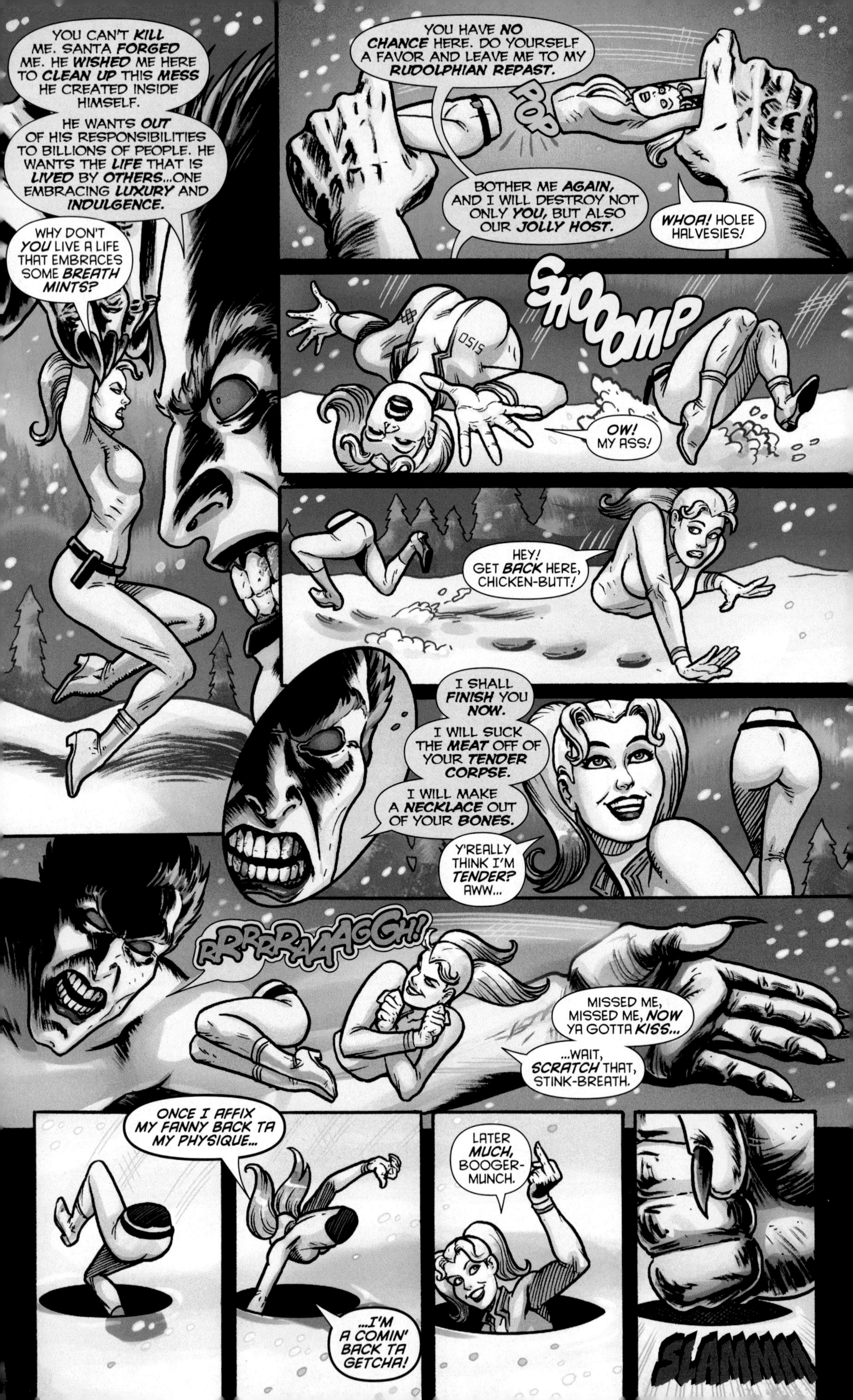
YOU CAN'T KILL ME. SANTA FORGED ME. HE WISHED ME HERE TO CLEAN UP THIS MESS HE CREATED INSIDE HIMSELF.
HE WANTS OUT OF HIS RESPONSIBILITIES TO BILLIONS OF PEOPLE. HE WANTS THE LIFE THAT IS LIVED BY OTHERS...ONE EMBRACING LUXURY AND INDULGENCE.
WHY DON'T YOU LIVE A LIFE THAT EMBRACES SOME BREATH MINTS?
YOU HAVE NO CHANCE HERE. DO YOURSELF A FAVOR AND LEAVE ME TO MY RUDOLPHIAN REPAST.
POP
BOTHER ME AGAIN, AND I WILL DESTROY NOT ONLY YOU, BUT ALSO OUR JOLLY HOST.
WHOA! HOLEE HALVESIES!
SHOOOOMP
OW! MY ASS!
HEY! GET BACK HERE, CHICKEN-BUTT!
I SHALL FINISH YOU NOW.
I WILL SUCK THE MEAT OFF OF YOUR TENDER CORPSE.
I WILL MAKE A NECKLACE OUT OF YOUR BONES.
Y'REALLY THINK I'M TENDER? AWW...
RRRRRAAAGGH!
MISSED ME, MISSED ME, NOW YA GOTTA KISS...
...WAIT, SCRATCH THAT, STINK-BREATH.
ONCE I AFFIX MY FANNY BACK TA MY PHYSIQUE...
...I'M A COMIN' BACK TA GETCHA!
LATER MUCH, BOOGER-MUNCH.
SLAMMM

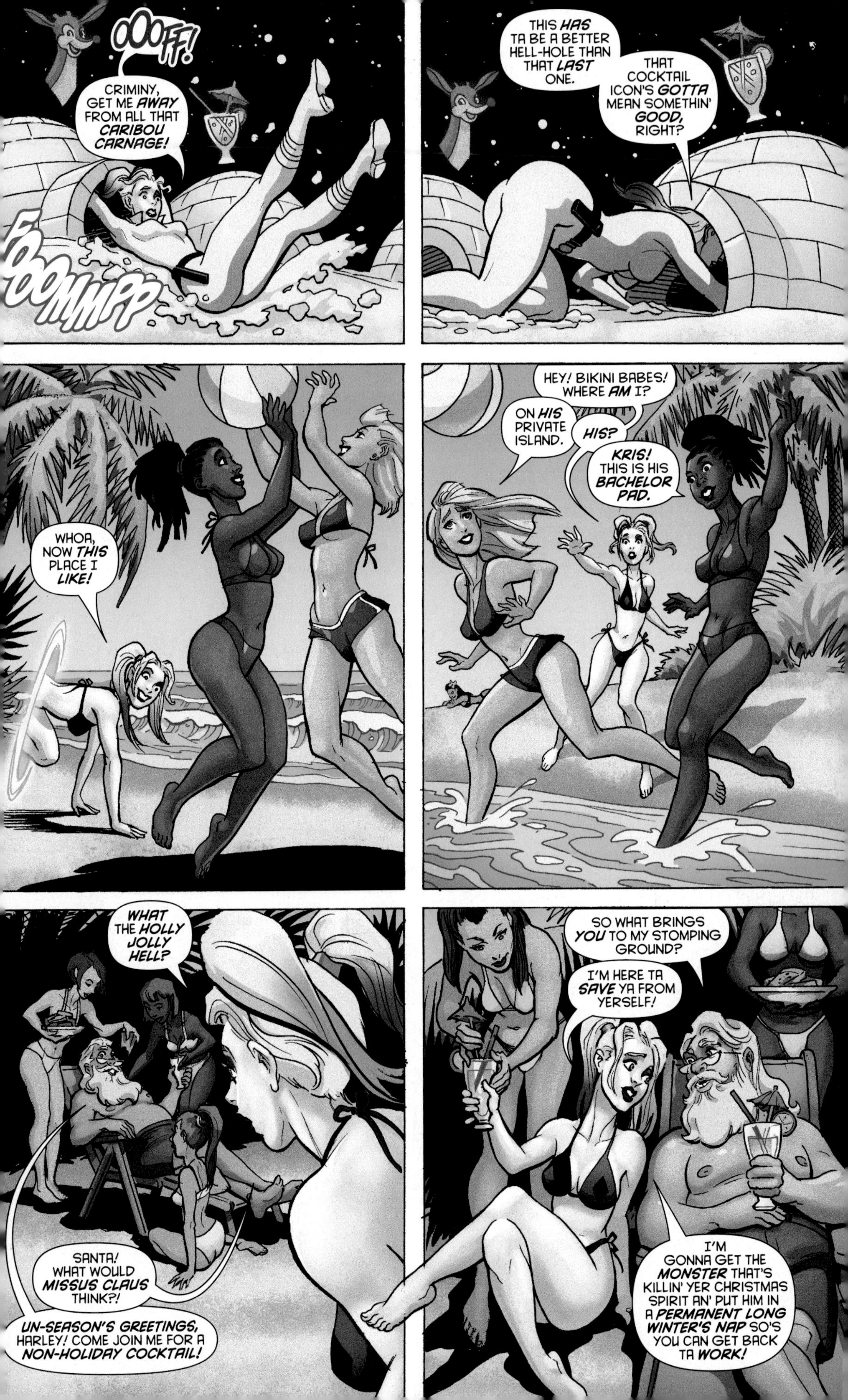
OOOFF!
CRIMINY, GET ME AWAY FROM ALL THAT CARIBOU CARNAGE!
FOOOOMMPP
THIS HAS TA BE A BETTER HELL-HOLE THAN THAT LAST ONE.
THAT COCKTAIL ICON'S GOTTA MEAN SOMETHIN' GOOD, RIGHT?
WHOA, NOW THIS PLACE I LIKE!
HEY! BIKINI BABES! WHERE AM I?
ON HIS PRIVATE ISLAND.
HIS?
KRIS! THIS IS HIS BACHELOR PAD.
WHAT THE HOLLY JOLLY HELL?
SANTA! WHAT WOULD MISSUS CLAUS THINK?!
UN-SEASON'S GREETINGS, HARLEY! COME JOIN ME FOR A NON-HOLIDAY COCKTAIL!
SO WHAT BRINGS YOU TO MY STOMPING GROUND?
I'M HERE TA SAVE YA FROM YERSELF!
I'M GONNA GET THE MONSTER THAT'S KILLIN' YER CHRISTMAS SPIRIT AN' PUT HIM IN A PERMANENT LONG WINTER'S NAP SO'S YOU CAN GET BACK TA WORK!

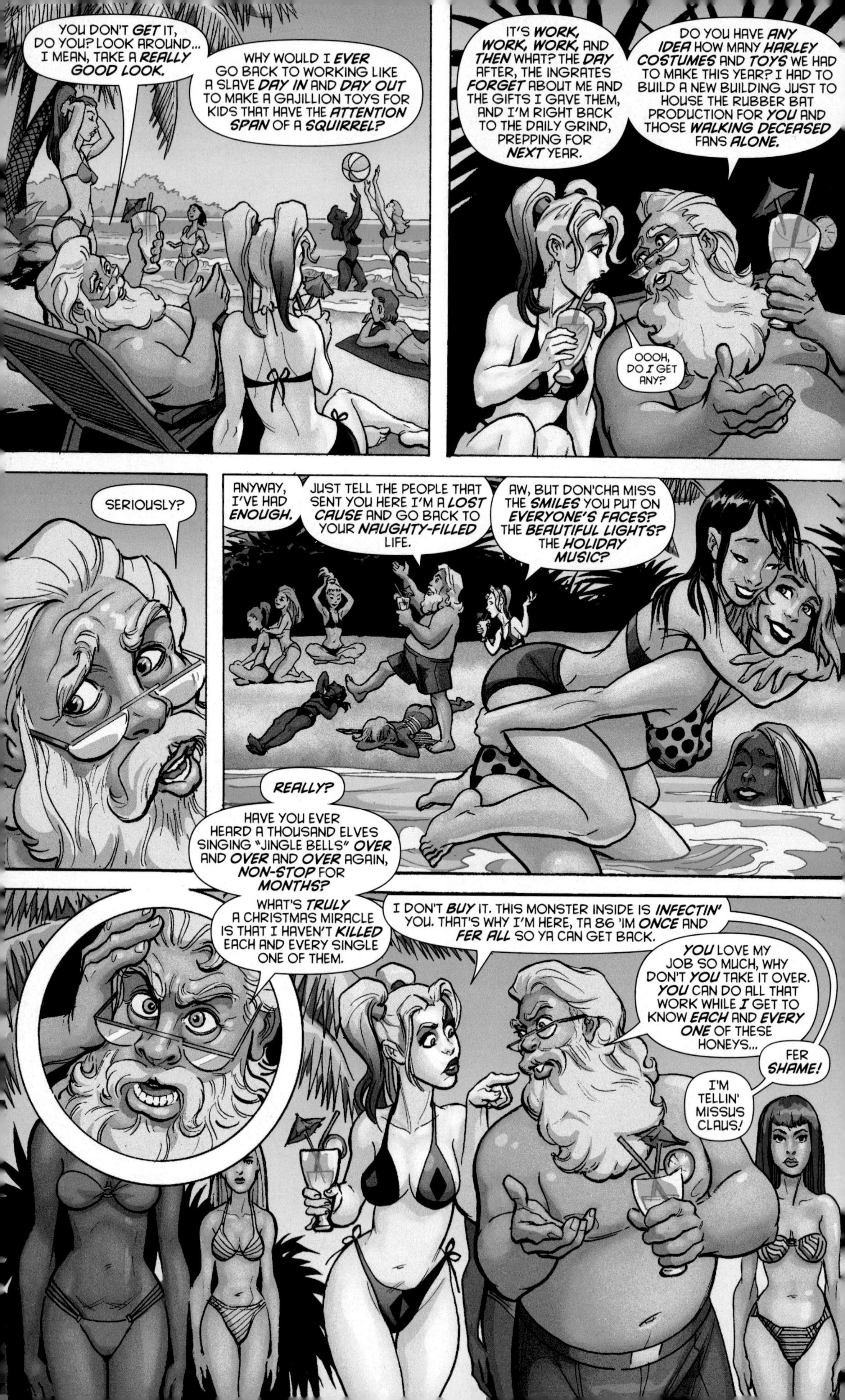
YOU DON'T GET IT, DO YOU? LOOK AROUND... I MEAN, TAKE A REALLY GOOD LOOK.
WHY WOULD I EVER GO BACK TO WORKING LIKE A SLAVE DAY IN AND DAY OUT TO MAKE A GAJILLION TOYS FOR KIDS THAT HAVE THE ATTENTION SPAN OF A SQUIRREL?
IT'S WORK, WORK, WORK, AND THEN WHAT? THE DAY AFTER, THE INGRATES FORGET ABOUT ME AND THE GIFTS I GAVE THEM, AND I'M RIGHT BACK TO THE DAILY GRIND, PREPPING FOR NEXT YEAR.
DO YOU HAVE ANY IDEA HOW MANY HARLEY COSTUMES AND TOYS WE HAD TO MAKE THIS YEAR? I HAD TO BUILD A NEW BUILDING JUST TO HOUSE THE RUBBER BAT PRODUCTION FOR YOU AND THOSE WALKING DECEASED FANS ALONE.
OOOH, DO I GET ANY?
SERIOUSLY?
ANYWAY, I'VE HAD ENOUGH.
JUST TELL THE PEOPLE THAT SENT YOU HERE I'M A LOST CAUSE AND GO BACK TO YOUR NAUGHTY-FILLED LIFE.
AW, BUT DON'CHA MISS THE SMILES YOU PUT ON EVERYONE'S FACES? THE BEAUTIFUL LIGHTS? THE HOLIDAY MUSIC?
REALLY?
HAVE YOU EVER HEARD A THOUSAND ELVES SINGING "JINGLE BELLS" OVER AND OVER AND OVER AGAIN, NON-STOP FOR MONTHS?
WHAT'S TRULY A CHRISTMAS MIRACLE IS THAT I HAVEN'T KILLED EACH AND EVERY SINGLE ONE OF THEM.
I DON'T BUY IT. THIS MONSTER INSIDE IS INFECTIN' YOU. THAT'S WHY I'M HERE, TA 86 'IM ONCE AND FER ALL SO YA CAN GET BACK.
YOU LOVE MY JOB SO MUCH, WHY DON'T YOU TAKE IT OVER. YOU CAN DO ALL THAT WORK WHILE I GET TO KNOW EACH AND EVERY ONE OF THESE HONEYS...
FER SHAME!
I'M TELLIN' MISSUS CLAUS!

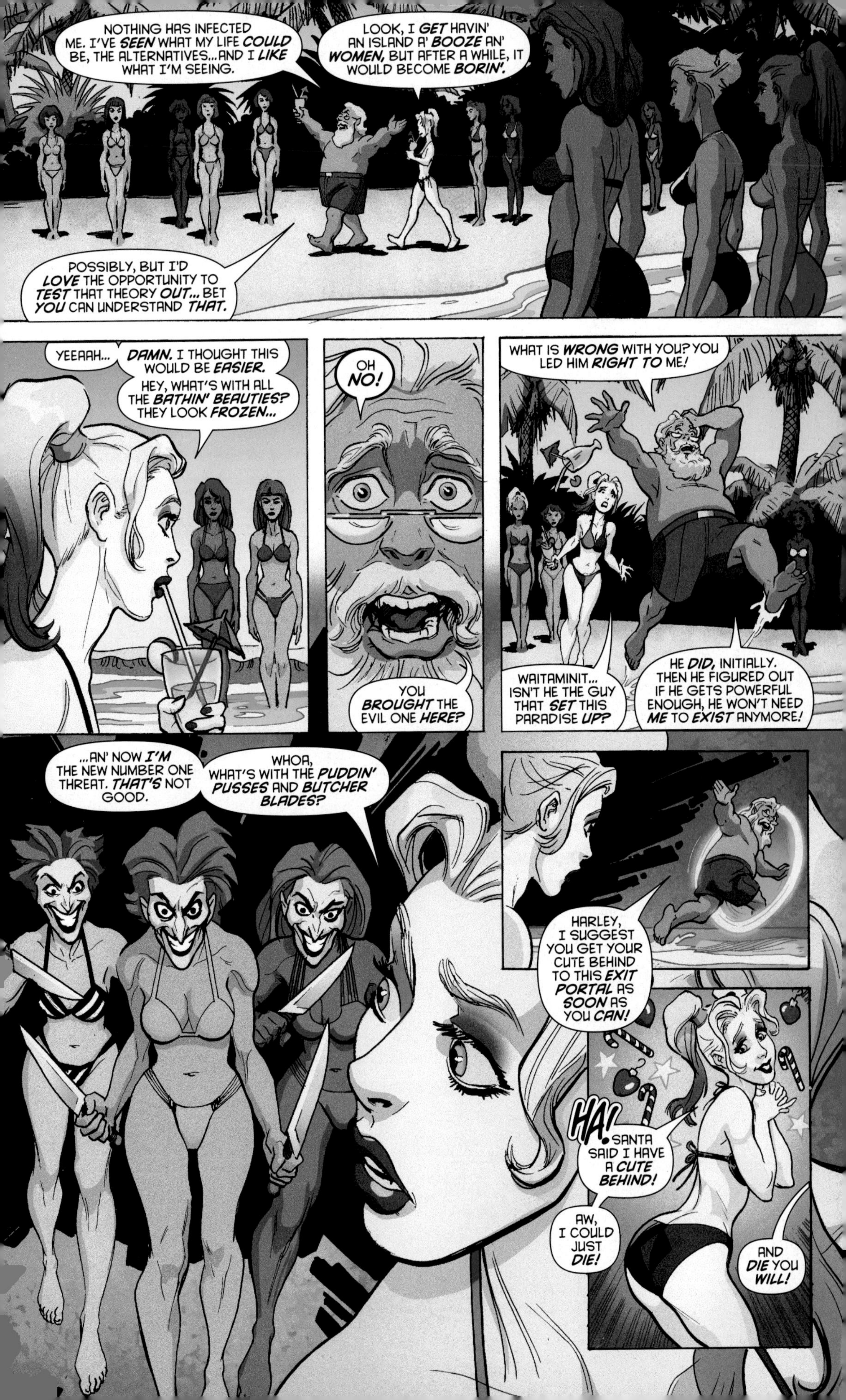
NOTHING HAS INFECTED ME. I'VE SEEN WHAT MY LIFE COULD BE, THE ALTERNATIVES...AND I LIKE WHAT I'M SEEING.
LOOK, I GET HAVIN' AN ISLAND A' BOOZE AN' WOMEN, BUT AFTER A WHILE, IT WOULD BECOME BORIN'.
POSSIBLY, BUT I'D LOVE THE OPPORTUNITY TO TEST THAT THEORY OUT... BET YOU CAN UNDERSTAND THAT.
YEEAAH...
DAMN. I THOUGHT THIS WOULD BE EASIER.
HEY, WHAT'S WITH ALL THE BATHIN' BEAUTIES? THEY LOOK FROZEN...
OH NO!
YOU BROUGHT THE EVIL ONE HERE?
WHAT IS WRONG WITH YOU? YOU LED HIM RIGHT TO ME!
WAITAMINIT... ISN'T HE THE GUY THAT SET THIS PARADISE UP?
HE DID, INITIALLY. THEN HE FIGURED OUT IF HE GETS POWERFUL ENOUGH, HE WON'T NEED ME TO EXIST ANYMORE!
...AN' NOW I'M THE NEW NUMBER ONE THREAT. THAT'S NOT GOOD.
WHOA, WHAT'S WITH THE PUDDIN' PUSSES AND BUTCHER BLADES?
HARLEY, I SUGGEST YOU GET YOUR CUTE BEHIND TO THIS EXIT PORTAL AS SOON AS YOU CAN!
HA! SANTA SAID I HAVE A CUTE BEHIND!
AW, I COULD JUST DIE!
AND DIE YOU WILL!

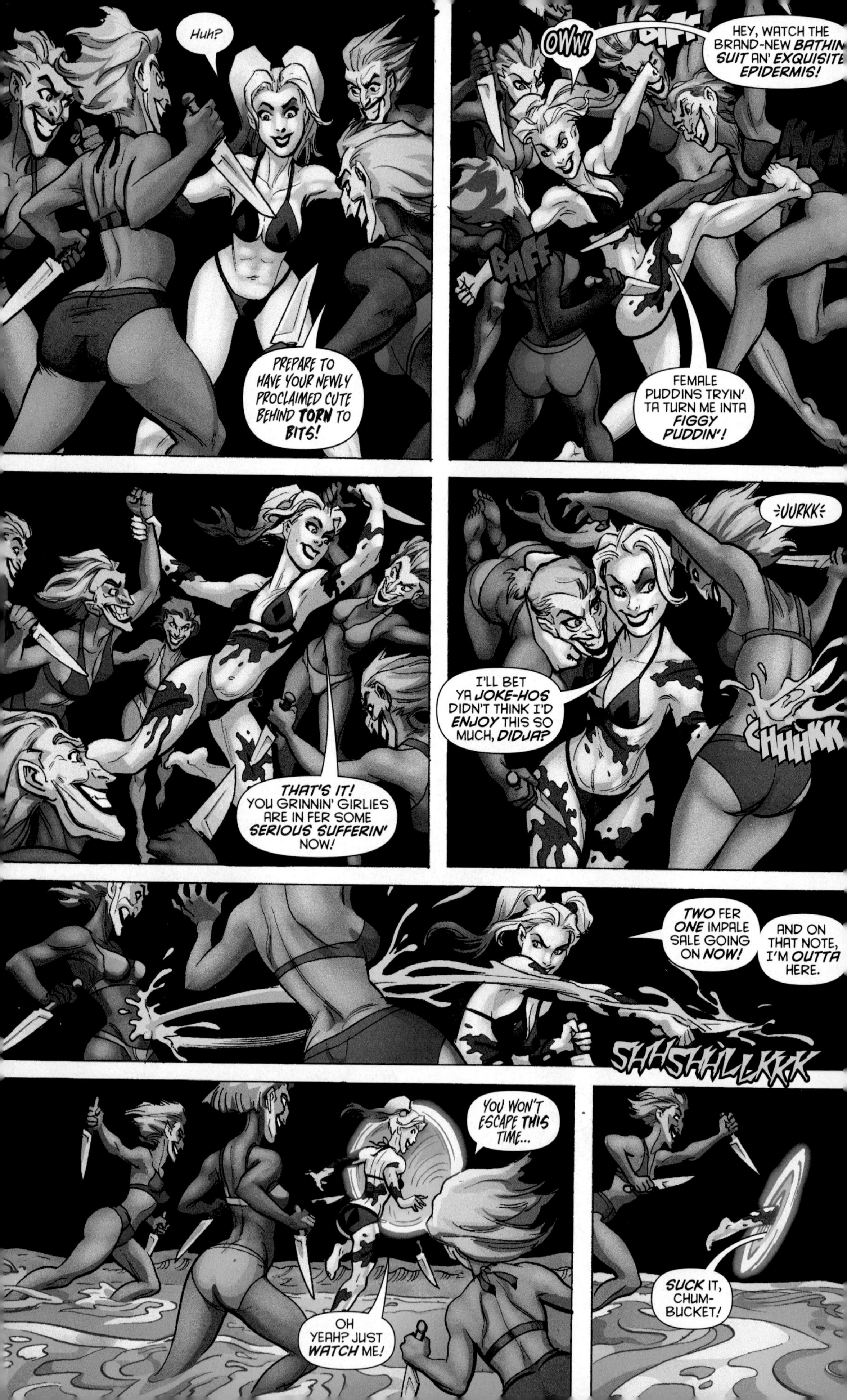
Huh?
PREPARE TO HAVE YOUR NEWLY PROCLAIMED CUTE BEHIND TORN TO BITS!
OWW!
HEY, WATCH THE BRAND-NEW BATHIN' SUIT AN' EXQUISITE EPIDERMIS!
BAFF
FEMALE PUDDINS TRYIN' TA TURN ME INTA FIGGY PUDDIN'!
THAT'S IT! YOU GRINNIN' GIRLIES ARE IN FER SOME SERIOUS SUFFERIN' NOW!
UURKK
I'LL BET YA JOKE-HOS DIDN'T THINK I'D ENJOY THIS SO MUCH, DIDJA?
CHHHKK
TWO FER ONE IMPALE SALE GOING ON NOW!
AND ON THAT NOTE, I'M OUTTA HERE.
SHHSHHLLKKK
YOU WON'T ESCAPE THIS TIME...
OH YEAH? JUST WATCH ME!
SUCK IT, CHUM-BUCKET!

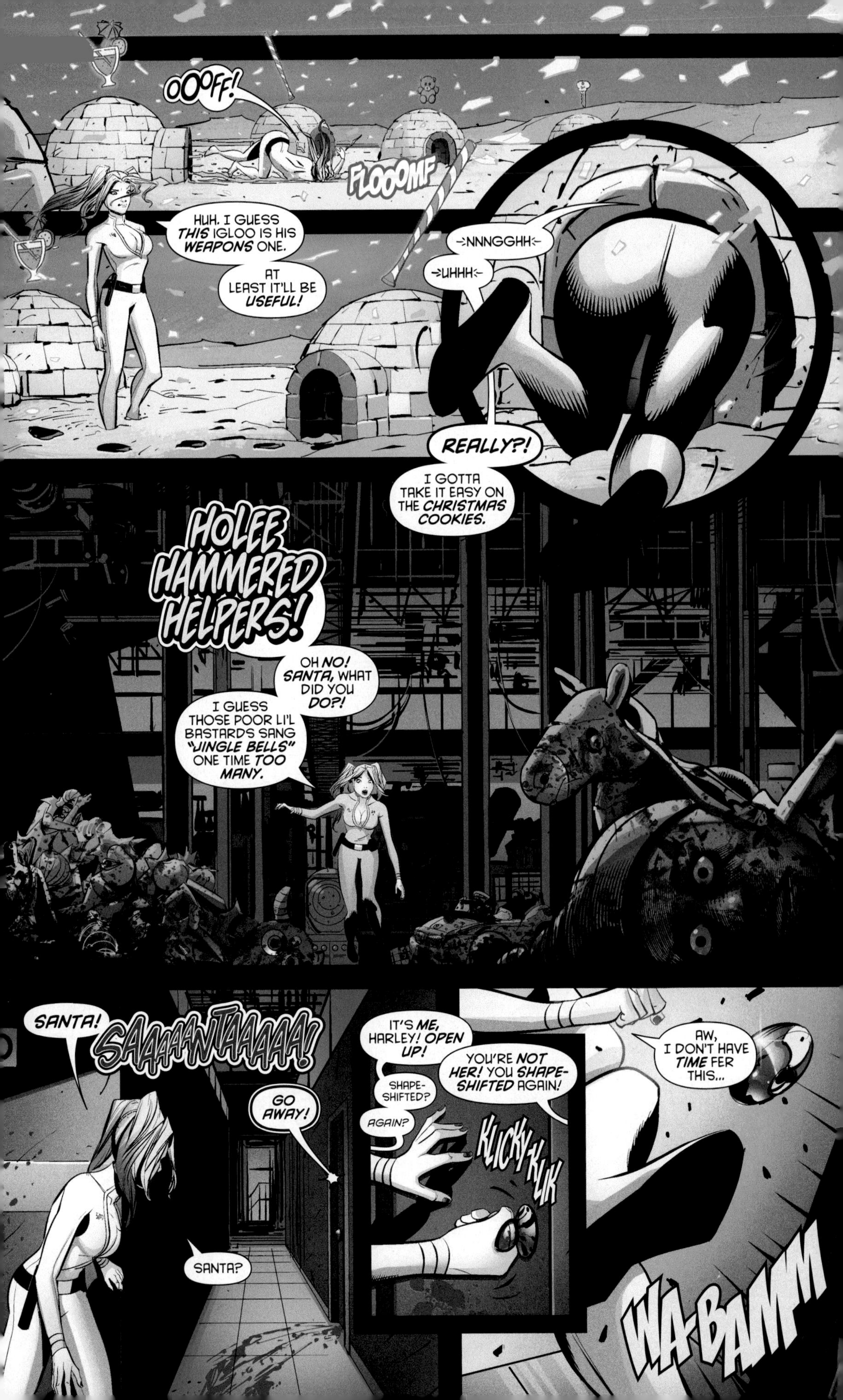
OOOFF!
FLOOOMF
HUH. I GUESS THIS IGLOO IS HIS WEAPONS ONE.
AT LEAST IT'LL BE USEFUL!
NNNGGHH
UHHH
REALLY?!
I GOTTA TAKE IT EASY ON THE CHRISTMAS COOKIES.
HOLEE HAMMERED HELPERS!
OH NO! SANTA, WHAT DID YOU DO?!
I GUESS THOSE POOR LI'L BASTARDS SANG "JINGLE BELLS" ONE TIME TOO MANY.
SANTA!
SAAAAANTAAAAA!
GO AWAY!
SANTA?
IT'S ME, HARLEY! OPEN UP!
YOU'RE NOT HER! YOU SHAPE-SHIFTED AGAIN!
SHAPE-SHIFTED?
AGAIN?
KLICKY-KLIK
AW, I DON'T HAVE TIME FER THIS...
WA-BAMM

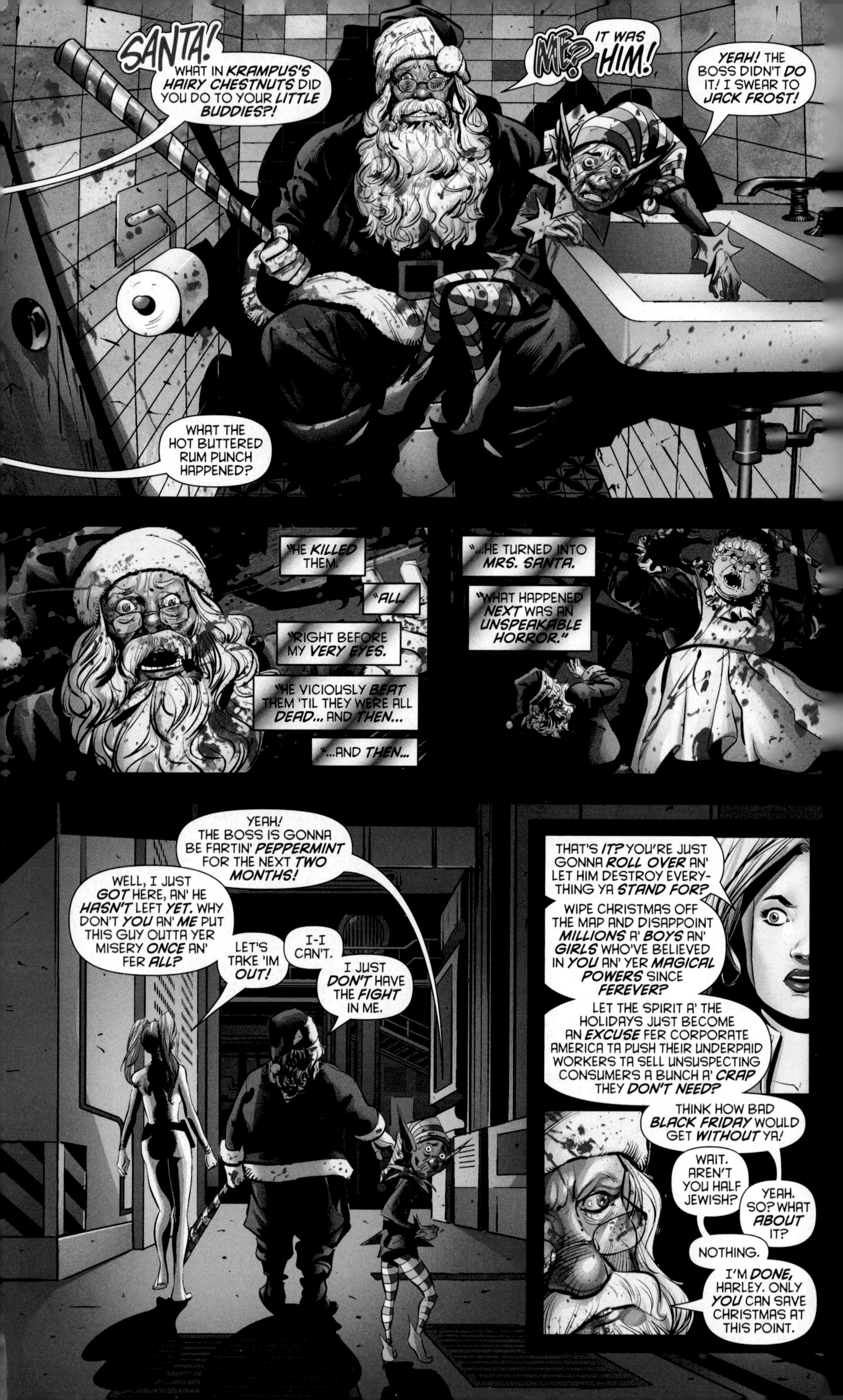

SANTA! WHAT IN KRAMPUS'S HAIRY CHESTNUTS DID YOU DO TO YOUR LITTLE BUDDIES?!
WHAT THE HOT BUTTERED RUM PUNCH HAPPENED?
ME?! IT WAS HIM!
YEAH! THE BOSS DIDN'T DO IT! I SWEAR TO JACK FROST!
"HE KILLED THEM.
"ALL.
"RIGHT BEFORE MY VERY EYES.
"HE VICIOUSLY BEAT THEM 'TIL THEY WERE ALL DEAD... AND THEN...
"...AND THEN...
"...HE TURNED INTO MRS. SANTA.
"WHAT HAPPENED NEXT WAS AN UNSPEAKABLE HORROR."
WELL, I JUST GOT HERE, AN' HE HASN'T LEFT YET. WHY DON'T YOU AN' ME PUT THIS GUY OUTTA YER MISERY ONCE AN' FER ALL?
YEAH! THE BOSS IS GONNA BE FARTIN' PEPPERMINT FOR THE NEXT TWO MONTHS!
LET'S TAKE 'IM OUT!
I-I CAN'T.
I JUST DON'T HAVE THE FIGHT IN ME.
THAT'S IT? YOU'RE JUST GONNA ROLL OVER AN' LET HIM DESTROY EVERYTHING YA STAND FOR?
WIPE CHRISTMAS OFF THE MAP AND DISAPPOINT MILLIONS A' BOYS AN' GIRLS WHO'VE BELIEVED IN YOU AN' YER MAGICAL POWERS SINCE FOREVER?
LET THE SPIRIT A' THE HOLIDAYS JUST BECOME AN EXCUSE FER CORPORATE AMERICA TA PUSH THEIR UNDERPAID WORKERS TA SELL UNSUSPECTING CONSUMERS A BUNCH A' CRAP THEY DON'T NEED?
THINK HOW BAD BLACK FRIDAY WOULD GET WITHOUT YA!
WAIT. AREN'T YOU HALF JEWISH?
YEAH. SO? WHAT ABOUT IT?
NOTHING.
I'M DONE, HARLEY. ONLY YOU CAN SAVE CHRISTMAS AT THIS POINT.

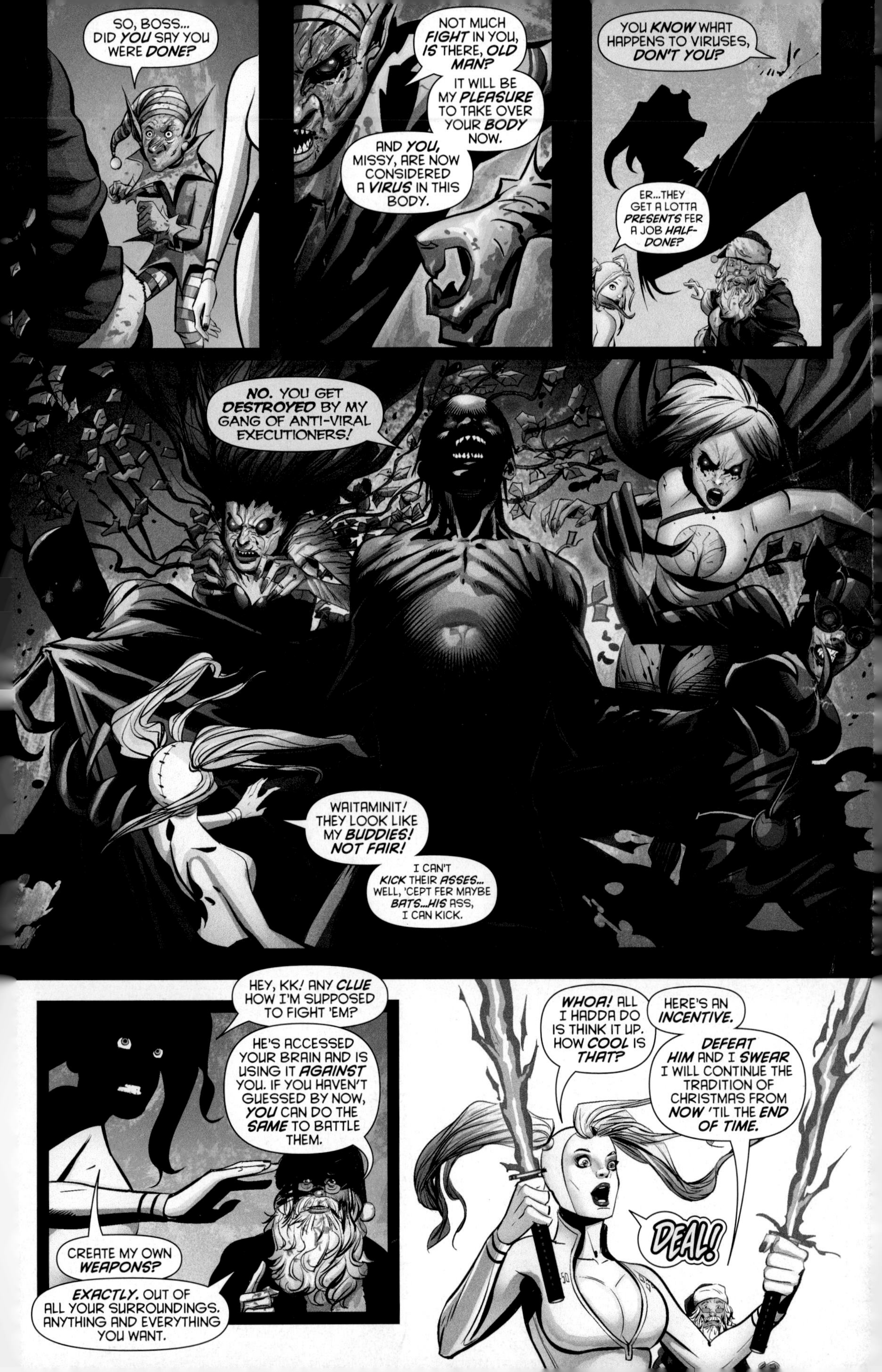

SO, BOSS... DID YOU SAY YOU WERE DONE?
NOT MUCH FIGHT IN YOU, IS THERE, OLD MAN?
IT WILL BE MY PLEASURE TO TAKE OVER YOUR BODY NOW.
AND YOU, MISSY, ARE NOW CONSIDERED A VIRUS IN THIS BODY.
YOU KNOW WHAT HAPPENS TO VIRUSES, DON'T YOU?
ER...THEY GET A LOTTA PRESENTS FER A JOB HALF-DONE?
NO. YOU GET DESTROYED BY MY GANG OF ANTI-VIRAL EXECUTIONERS!
WAITAMINIT! THEY LOOK LIKE MY BUDDIES! NOT FAIR!
I CAN'T KICK THEIR ASSES... WELL, 'CEPT FER MAYBE BATS...HIS ASS, I CAN KICK.
HEY, KK! ANY CLUE HOW I'M SUPPOSED TO FIGHT 'EM?
HE'S ACCESSED YOUR BRAIN AND IS USING IT AGAINST YOU. IF YOU HAVEN'T GUESSED BY NOW, YOU CAN DO THE SAME TO BATTLE THEM.
CREATE MY OWN WEAPONS?
EXACTLY. OUT OF ALL YOUR SURROUNDINGS. ANYTHING AND EVERYTHING YOU WANT.
WHOA! ALL I HADDA DO IS THINK IT UP. HOW COOL IS THAT?
HERE'S AN INCENTIVE.
DEFEAT HIM AND I SWEAR I WILL CONTINUE THE TRADITION OF CHRISTMAS FROM NOW 'TIL THE END OF TIME.
DEAL!

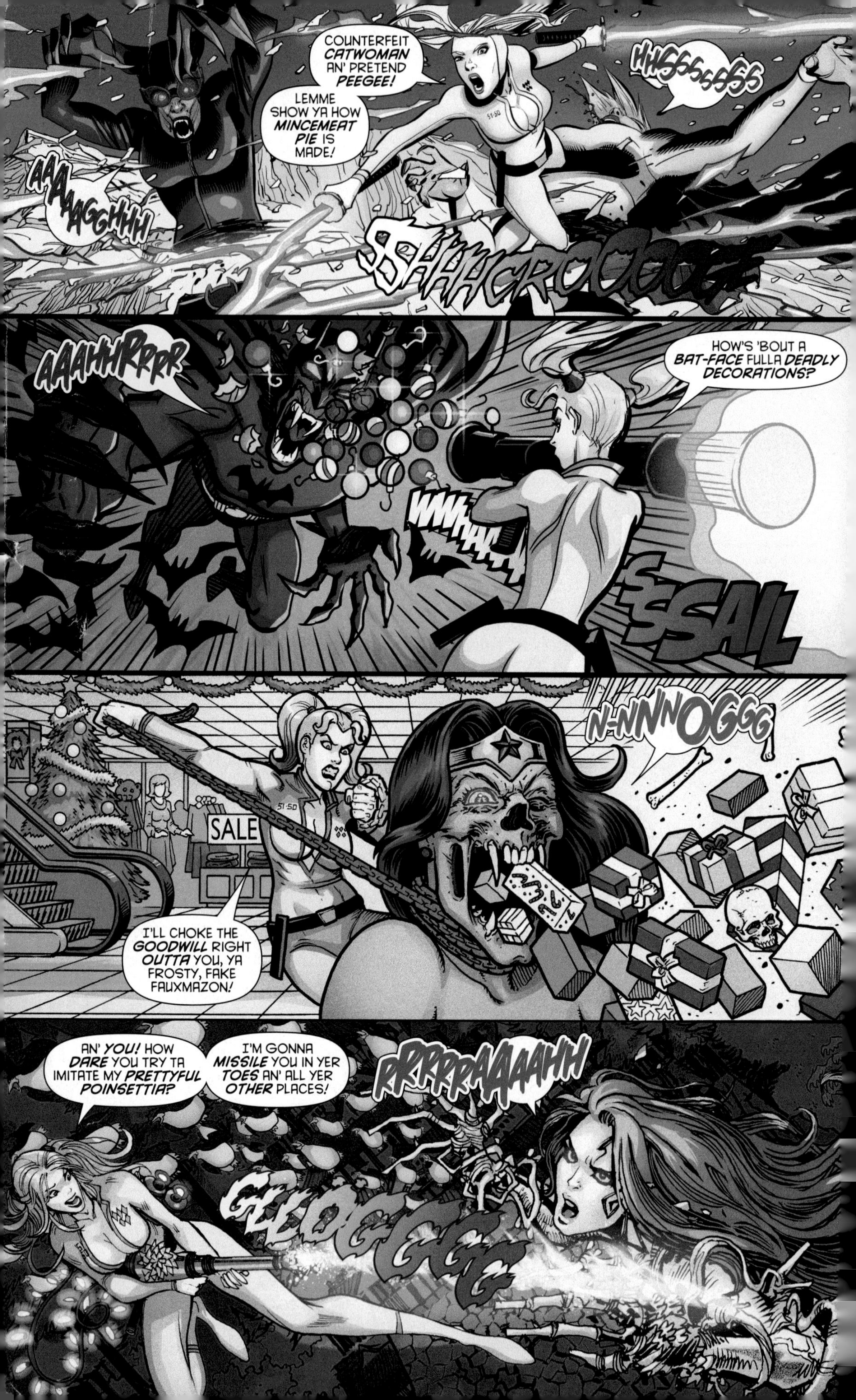
COUNTERFEIT CATWOMAN AN' PRETEND PEEGEE!
LEMME SHOW YA HOW MINCEMEAT PIE IS MADE!
HHSSSSSSSS
AAAAAGGHHHH
SSHHACROOOOGE
AAAAHHRRRR
HOW'S 'BOUT A BAT-FACE FULLA DEADLY DECORATIONS?
SSSAIL
N-NNNOGGGG
SALE
I'LL CHOKE THE GOODWILL RIGHT OUTTA YOU, YA FROSTY, FAKE FAUXMAZON!
AN' YOU! HOW DARE YOU TRY TA IMITATE MY PRETTYFUL POINSETTIA?
I'M GONNA MISSILE YOU IN YER TOES AN' ALL YER OTHER PLACES!
RRRRRAAAAHH
GLOGGGG

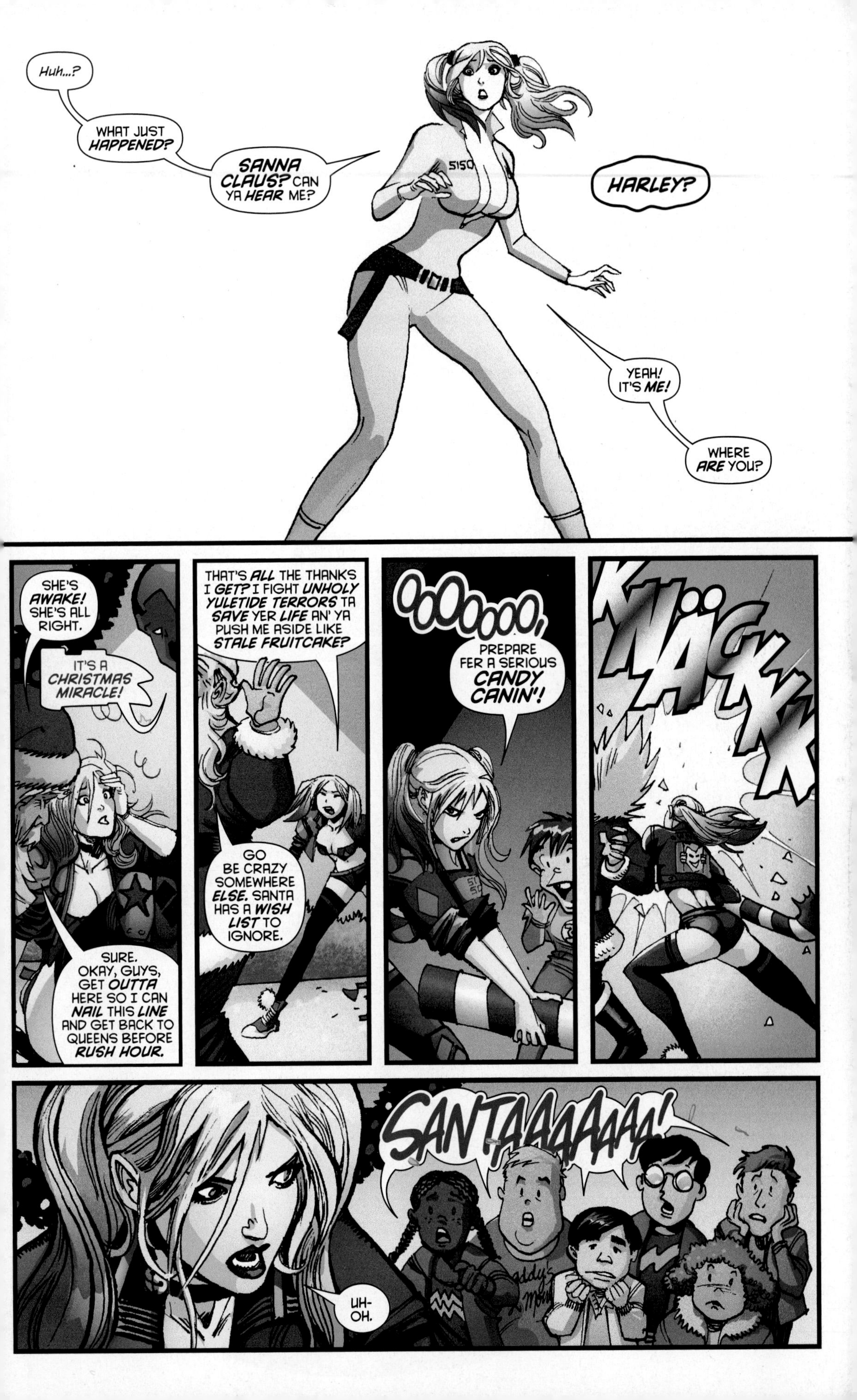
Huh...?
WHAT JUST HAPPENED?
SANNA CLAUS? CAN YA HEAR ME?
HARLEY?
YEAH! IT'S ME!
WHERE ARE YOU?
SHE'S AWAKE! SHE'S ALL RIGHT.
IT'S A CHRISTMAS MIRACLE!
SURE. OKAY, GUYS, GET OUTTA HERE SO I CAN NAIL THIS LINE AND GET BACK TO QUEENS BEFORE RUSH HOUR.
THAT'S ALL THE THANKS I GET? I FIGHT UNHOLY YULETIDE TERRORS TA SAVE YER LIFE AN' YA PUSH ME ASIDE LIKE STALE FRUITCAKE?
GO BE CRAZY SOMEWHERE ELSE. SANTA HAS A WISH LIST TO IGNORE.
OOOOOOOO,
PREPARE FER A SERIOUS CANDY CANIN'!
KNÄCKK
SANTAAAAAAA!
UH-OH.

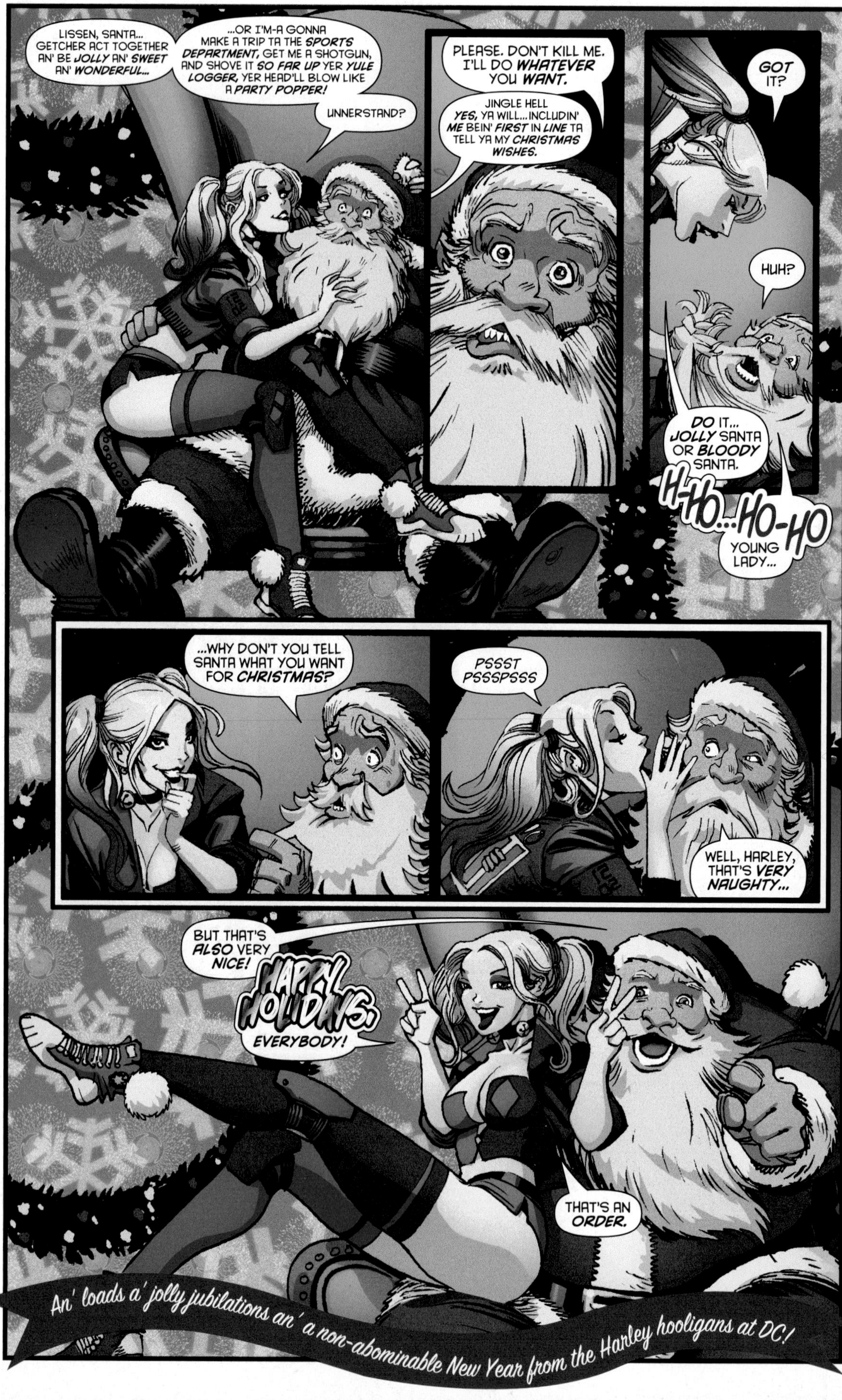
LISSEN, SANTA... GETCHER ACT TOGETHER AN' BE JOLLY AN' SWEET AN' WONDERFUL...
...OR I'M-A GONNA MAKE A TRIP TA THE SPORTS DEPARTMENT, GET ME A SHOTGUN, AND SHOVE IT SO FAR UP YER YULE LOGGER, YER HEAD'LL BLOW LIKE A PARTY POPPER!
UNNERSTAND?
PLEASE. DON'T KILL ME. I'LL DO WHATEVER YOU WANT.
JINGLE HELL YES, YA WILL...INCLUDIN' ME BEIN' FIRST IN LINE TA TELL YA MY CHRISTMAS WISHES.
GOT IT?
HUH?
DO IT... JOLLY SANTA OR BLOODY SANTA.
H-HO...HO-HO
YOUNG LADY...
...WHY DON'T YOU TELL SANTA WHAT YOU WANT FOR CHRISTMAS?
PSSST PSSSPSSS
WELL, HARLEY, THAT'S VERY NAUGHTY...
BUT THAT'S ALSO VERY NICE!
HAPPY HOLIDAYS,
EVERYBODY!
THAT'S AN ORDER.
An' loads a' jolly jubilations an' a non-abominable New Year from the Harley hooligans at DC!

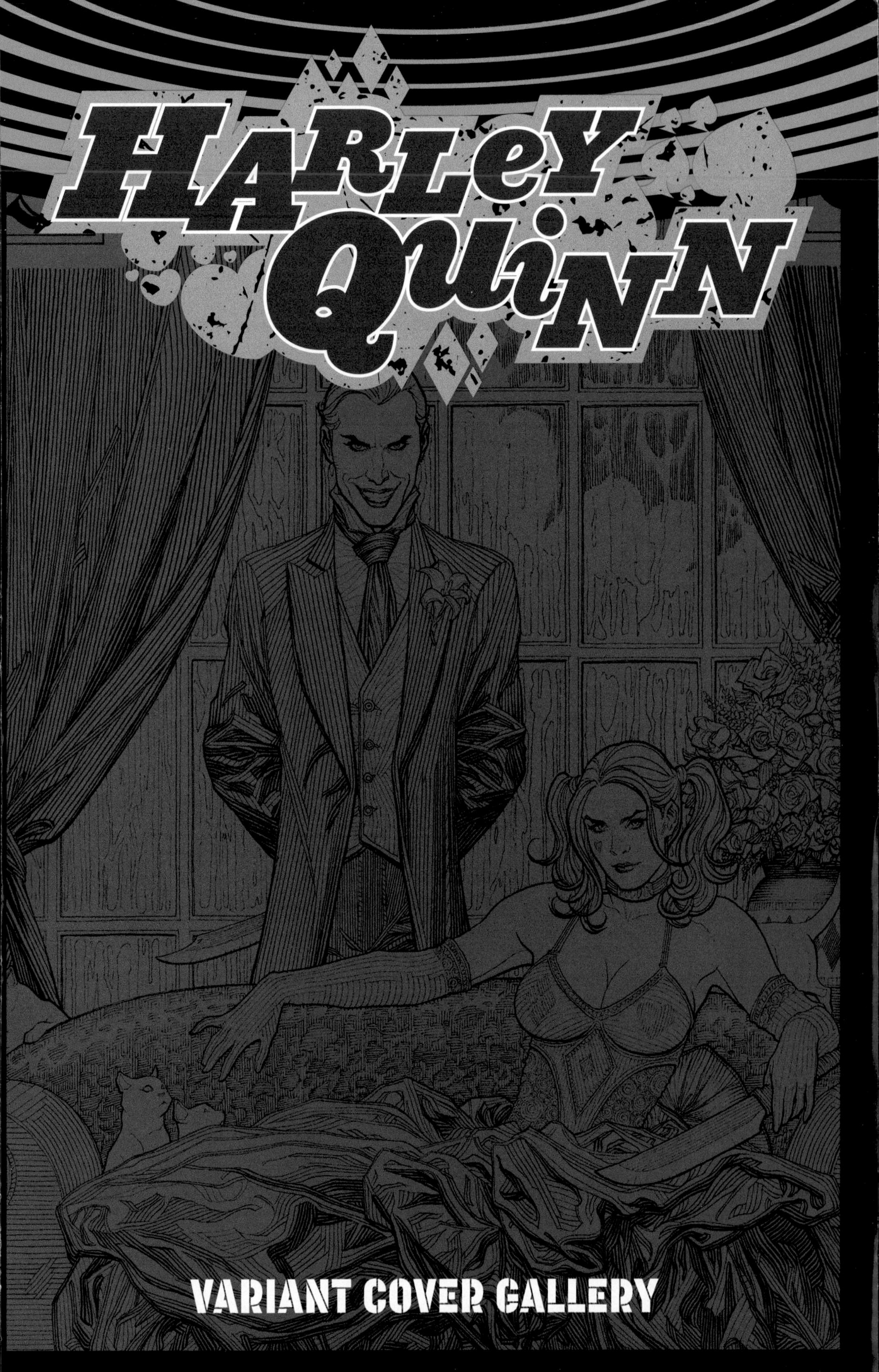
HARLEY QUINN
VARIANT COVER GALLERY

HARLEY QUINN #8 variant cover by FRANK CHO & LAURA MARTIN

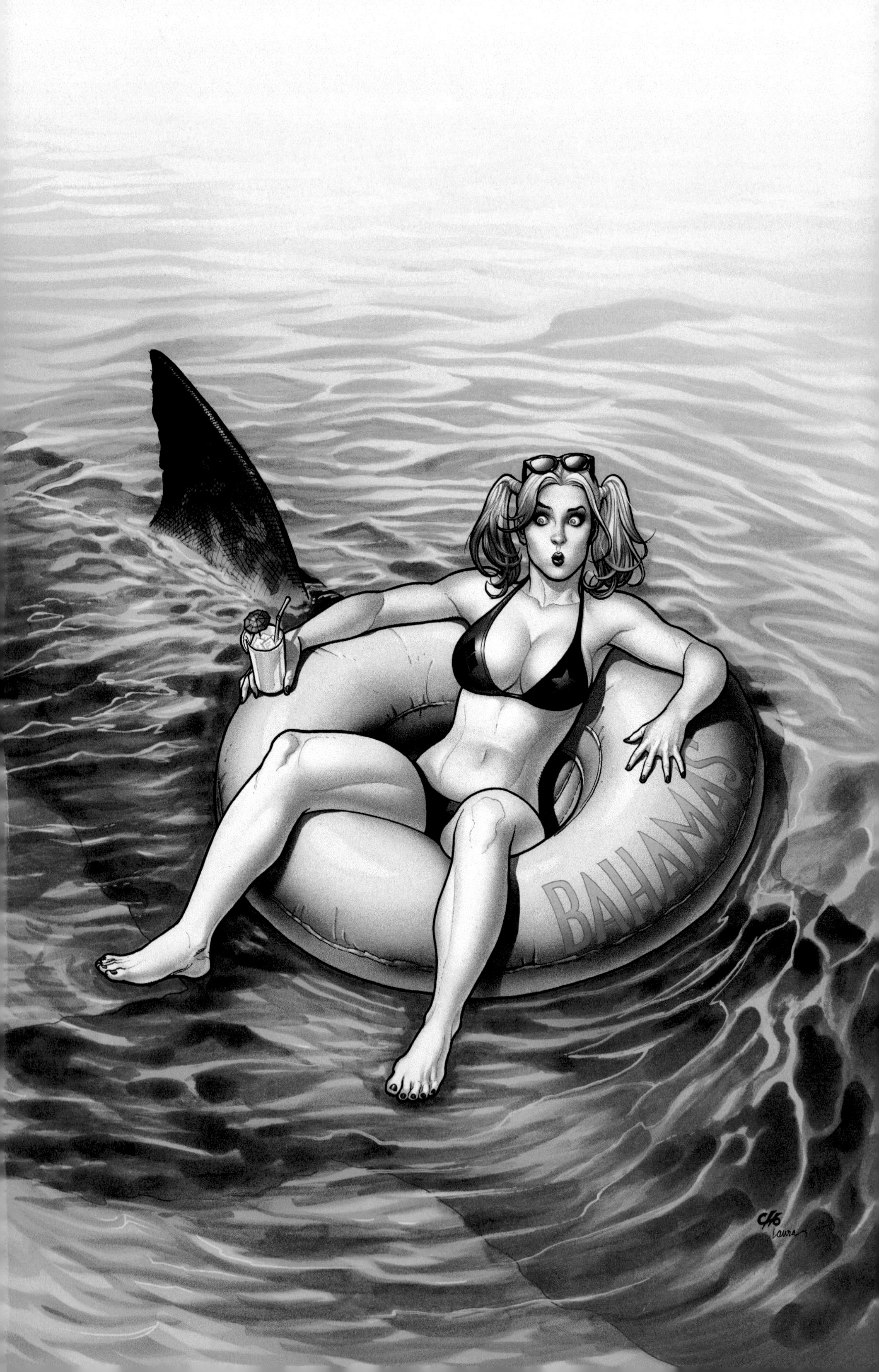

HARLEY QUINN #9 variant cover by FRANK CHO & LAURA MARTIN

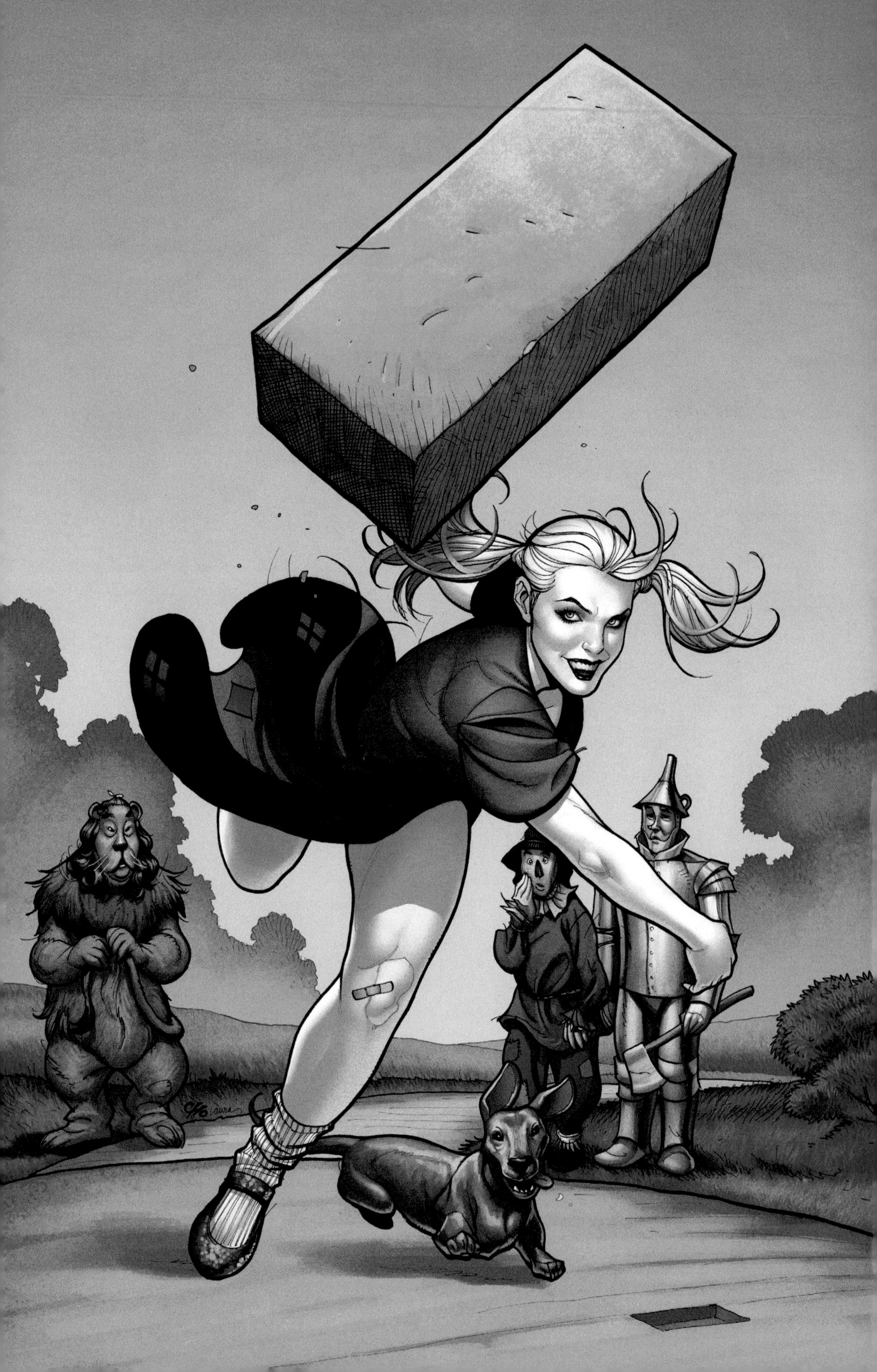

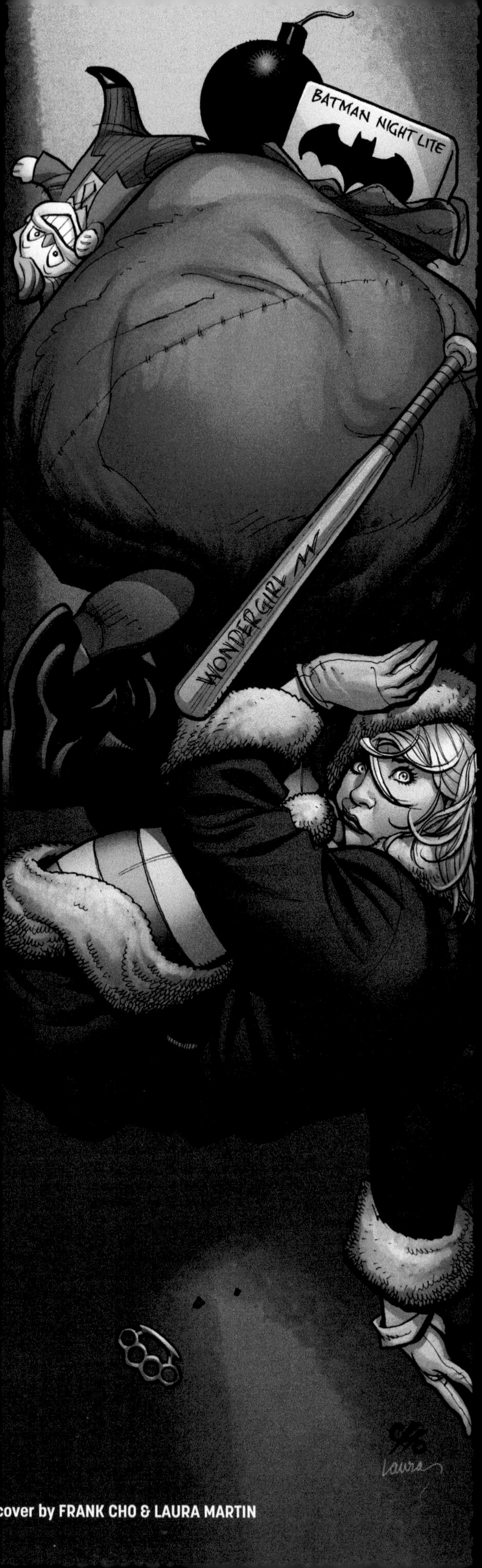
BATMAN NIGHT LITE
WONDERGIRL

HARLEY QUINN #10 variant cover by FRANK CHO & LAURA MARTIN

HARLEY QUINN #11 variant cover by FRANK CHO

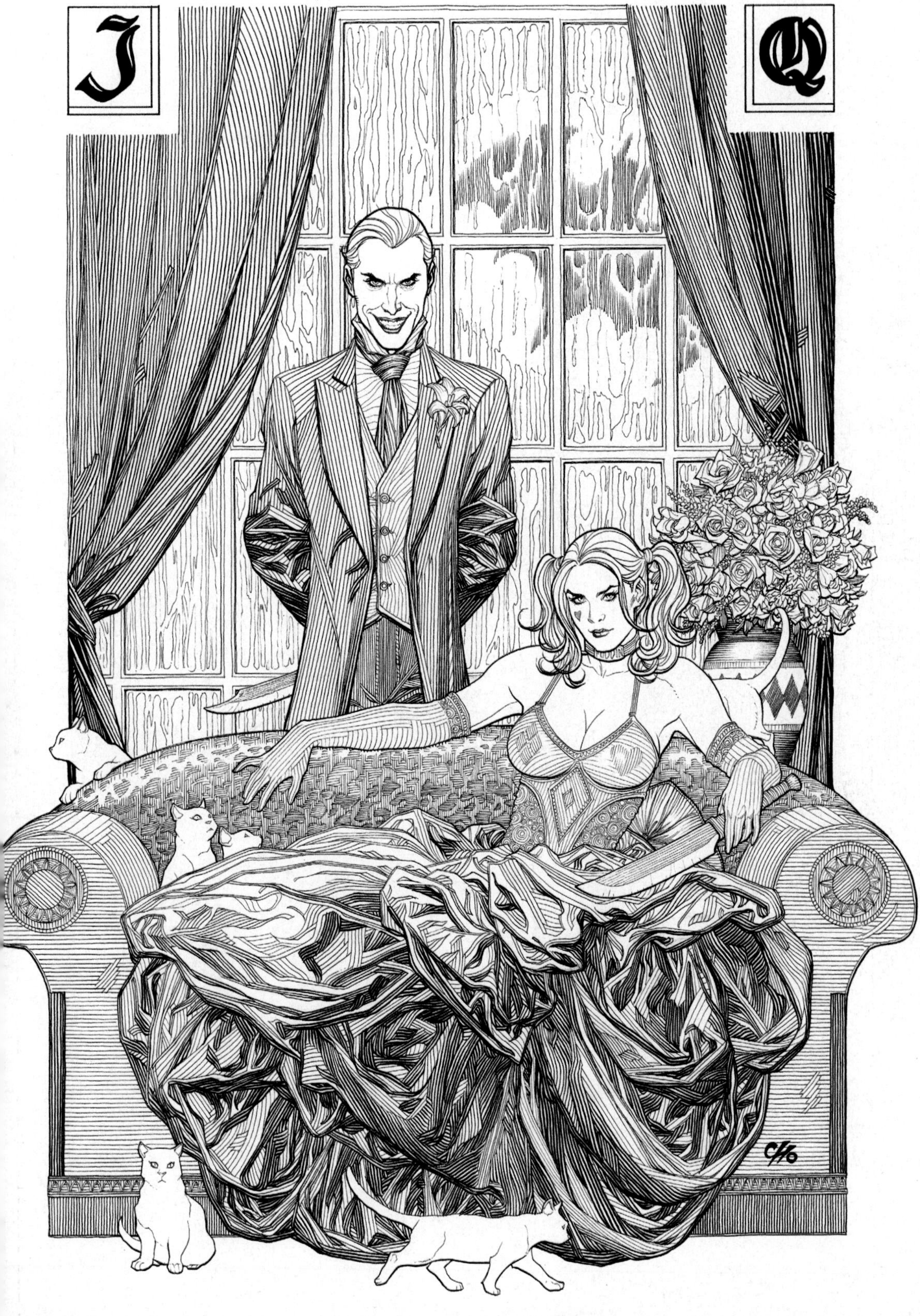
J
Q
CHO

HARLEY QUINN #12 variant cover by FRANK CHO & LAURA MARTIN

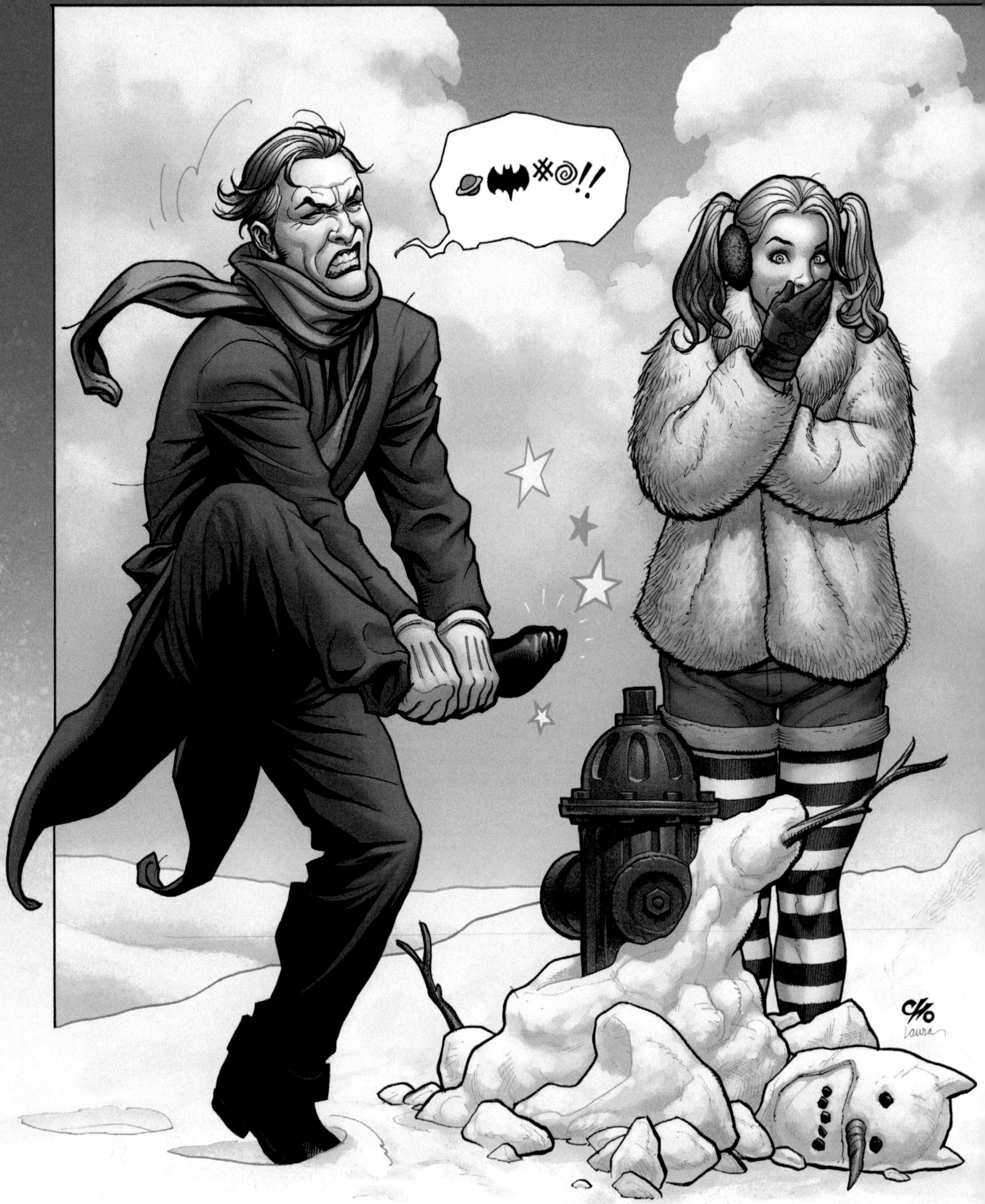

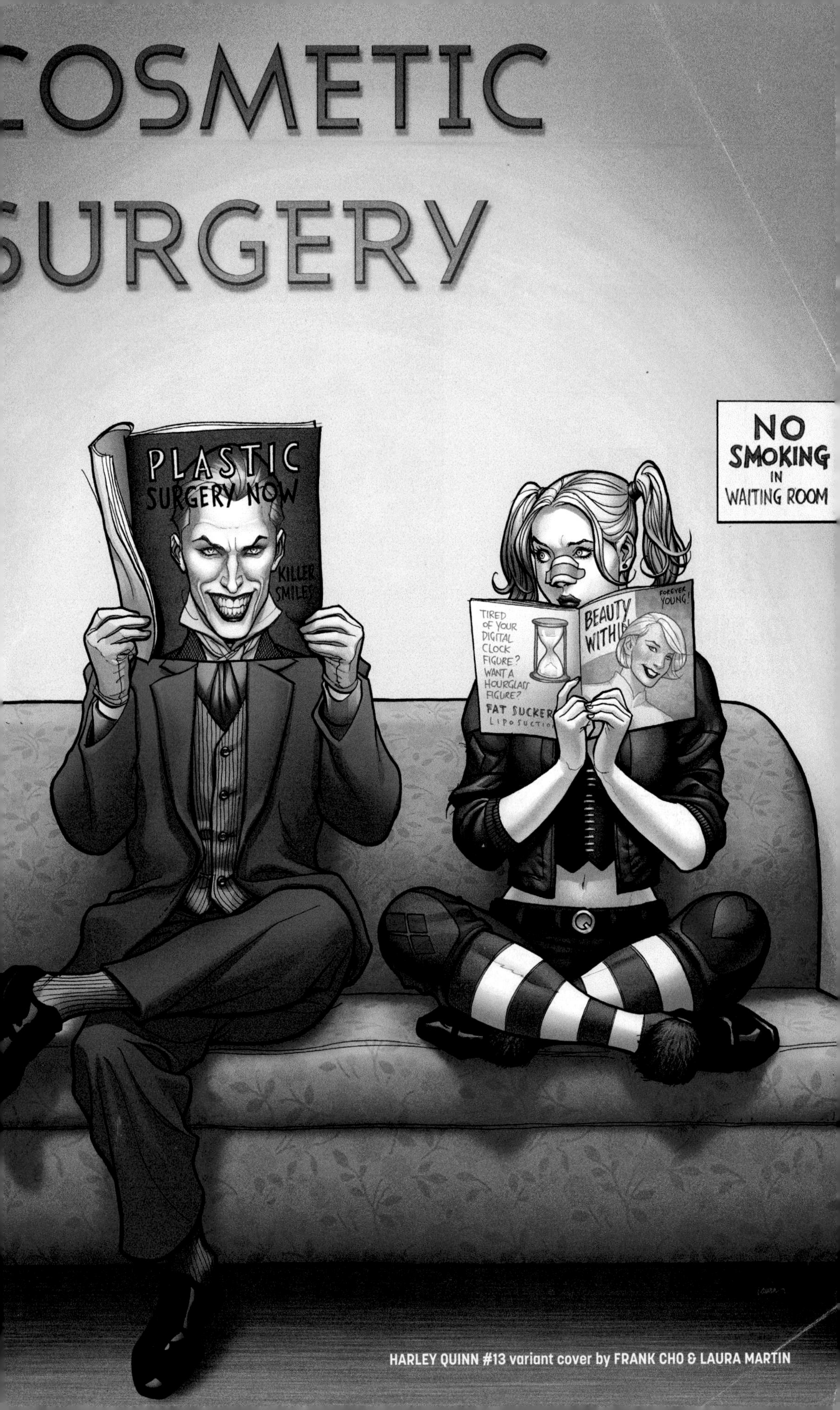
COSMETIC
SURGERY
PLASTIC
SURGERY NOW
KILLER SMILES
NO SMOKING IN WAITING ROOM
TIRED OF YOUR DIGITAL CLOCK FIGURE? WANT A HOURGLASS FIGURE?
FAT SUCKER
BEAUTY
FOREVER YOUNG!

HARLEY QUINN #13 variant cover by FRANK CHO & LAURA MARTIN

"Chaotic and unabashedly fun."
– IGN

HARLEY QUINN

VOL. 1: HOT IN THE CITY
AMANDA CONNER
with JIMMY PALMIOTTI
& CHAD HARDIN

AMANDA **CONNER** Jimmy **PALMIOTTI** Chad **HARDIN**
Stephane **ROUX** Alex **SINCLAIR** Paul **MOUNTS**

HARLEY QUINN
VOL. 2: POWER OUTAGE

HARLEY QUINN
VOL. 3: KISS KISS BANG STAB

READ THE ENTIRE EPI

HARLEY QUINN VOL
A CALL TO AR

HARLEY QUINN VOL
THE JOKER'S LAST LAU

"I'm enjoying this a great deal;
it's silly, it's funny, it's irreverent."
– COMIC BOOK RESOURCES